INTO
THE
CRATER

INTO THE CRATER

THE MINE ATTACK AT PETERSBURG

EARL J. HESS

The University of South Carolina Press

© 2010 University of South Carolina

Published by the University of South Carolina Press
Columbia, South Carolina 29208

3 9547 00348 2242

www.sc.edu/uscpress

Manufactured in the United States of America

19 18 17 16 15 14 13 12 11 10   10 9 8 7 6 5 4 3 2 1

Library of Congress Cataloging-in-Publication Data

Hess, Earl J.
    Into the Crater : the mine attack at Petersburg / Earl J. Hess.
        p. cm.
    Includes bibliographical references and index.
    ISBN 978-1-57003-922-5 (cloth : alk. paper)
    1. Petersburg Crater, Battle of, Va., 1864. I. Title.
    E476.93.H473 2010
    973.7'37—dc22

                                         2010005639

This book was printed on Glatfelter Natures, a recycled
paper with 30 percent postconsumer waste content.

For Pratibha and Julie

There *is* a peculiar uniqueness, however, about the Battle
of the Crater, that had no parallel in our civil war.

G. N. Saussy,
1st Georgia and Jeff Davis Legion

But I should like first to go again and see the place.
I have always wished to. To many living men the Mine
at Petersburg is the most vivid memory of their lives.

Lt. James W. Steele,
Company B, 43rd United States Colored Troops

Forty seven years ago today I was in front of Petersburg Va,
and witnessed the explosion of that mine that Burnsides planted.
It was a never to be forgotten sight of death and devestation.

William Hannibal Thomas,
5th United States Colored Troops

Then Ambrose, "the faithful," bethought him 'twould be fine
Just to surprise the rebels with a small powder mine
And blow up their batteries higher than a kite
And charge upon their rifle pits & put them all to flight

This mine it was exploded just along about daylight
Up went the rebels, cannons, Oh! It was a horrid sight
The niggers they pitched boldly in, but quickly they pitched out
And instead of "Johnny Reb" *our* troops were put to rout.

Sung by 3rd Battalion, 19th U.S. Infantry

CONTENTS

ILLUSTRATIONS

PREFACE

On the clear, still morning of July 30, 1864, the personal fate of many men hung insecurely on whether eight thousand pounds of gunpowder would explode as planned. Two soldiers worked more than an hour to locate and repair a fault in the fuse. For sixteen thousand Federals waiting to follow up the explosion with a sudden attack, the minutes seemed never to end; but for fifteen hundred Confederate soldiers holding a shallow angle in their line called Pegram's Salient, it was just another morning in the lengthening campaign around Petersburg, Virginia. They had no idea of the drama taking place twenty-five feet under the bare earth. Finally, at 4:44 A.M., the earth began to rumble and split open, and fire engulfed the salient in flame, debris, and death.

That moment was a potential watershed in the campaign at Petersburg, and one of the most dramatic moments of the Civil War. The Federals might have shattered Gen. Robert E. Lee's defensive line guarding the city that morning if things had worked as planned following the mine explosion. How much such an event would have shortened the life of the Confederacy is difficult to predict, but the Northerners had reason to hope for the ultimate triumph as the dust and bodies began to descend after the mine explosion created an awesome fountain of debris that rose as much as two hundred feet into the air.

The Crater Battle, or as contemporaries often called it, the Mine Attack, was the centerpiece of Lt. Gen. Ulysses S. Grant's Third Offensive at Petersburg. In preparation since June 25, the mine attack was the most complex operation of the entire campaign. The construction of a 510-foot-long underground gallery, packed at the end with four tons of black powder to be touched off by an improvised fuse, was the most difficult aspect of the preparation. In addition Grant maneuvered troops so as to draw most of Lee's army to the north side of the James River, rendering the lines south of the Appomattox vulnerable by July 30. As Grant later put it, "So fair an opportunity will probably never occur again for carrying fortifications."[1]

Yet the Union effort collapsed soon after the dust settled over what was left of Pegram's Salient, resulting in a confused, and confusing, battle. The Federals got stuck in the five-hundred-yard breach of the Confederate line. Resistance by survivors of the blast held the Federals within the captured works for four hours as Lee's last reserves made their way to the scene of action. Still it took three separate counterattacks and much hand-to-hand fighting before the Southerners restored their line.

Most of the fighting in the Crater Battle took place on a severely constricted battleground, cut up by the jagged hole left by the mine explosion and a jumbled maze of Confederate bombproofs and traverses. Racial hatred reared its head when the Confederates realized that a division of black Union troops participated in the attack. Enraged Southerners killed many blacks in cold blood after they surrendered. In the end, July 30 seemed a day of miraculous deliverance for the Confederates, a day of depressing failure for the North, and a day of immense suffering for hundreds of soldiers who were blown up, shot, or captured on that sun-baked battlefield.

Because of its unique features, the Crater Battle has become widely known among Civil War enthusiasts, but it has not yet been thoroughly studied by historians. The best previously published book is Michael A. Cavanaugh and William Marvel's *The Battle of the Crater: "The Horrid Pit," June 25–August 6, 1864* (1989). Based on sound research and combining analysis and narrative, Cavanaugh and Marvel provide the best short description of the battle, limited only by the constricted parameters of the H. E. Howard series of books on Virginia battles. John Cannan's *The Crater: Burnside's Assault on th Confederate Trenches, July 30, 1864* (2002) contains another telling of the story with a discussion of what one can see on the battlefield today. It was published as part of the Battleground America Guides. Alan Axelrod's *The Horrid Pit: The Battle of the Crater, the Civil War's Cruelest Mission* (2007) provides a short narration of the event that is based on a handful of published sources, mostly of a secondary nature. The latest book about the Crater Battle, John F. Schmutz's *The Battle of the Crater: A Complete History* (2008), is based on much wider research than Axelrod's book. Schmutz discusses the many facets of the subject more fully than any other author, but his interpretation of many points is open to question.

No previous author has yet conducted definitive research with all the sources that are available on the Crater Battle, or mined those sources for a deeper understanding of the tactical experiences and personal stories of units and men involved in it, or questioned key assumptions about the engagement. The battle deserves such an approach, for it was a unique operation, filled with an unusual degree of human drama. Several old ideas regarding the Union failure need to be reevaluated. Were the Federals so paralyzed by the awesome sight of the crater that they simply stayed in the hole instead of moving out to continue the attack as planned? Was Brig. Gen. James H. Ledlie's penchant for staying in the rear, instead of leading his division forward, the real cause of the failure? Should we trust Lt. Col. Henry Pleasants's version of affairs, wherein he portrayed the West Point–trained engineers of the army as trying to hamper his mine-digging effort? Does Brig. Gen. William Mahone's division truly deserve all the credit for saving Petersburg on July 30 through their counterattacks against the Union soldiers who held the breach? To what extent did racially motivated killings take place during Mahone's counterattacks? The answers certainly would enrich our understanding of the battle on July 30.

This book contains a thorough discussion, description, and analysis of the Mine Attack at Petersburg, set within the context of Grant's Third Offensive. It is based on exhaustive (and sometimes exhausting) research that started in 1999. Special attention has been paid to the details of Pleasants's mining operation and Confederate countermining efforts because these were the most unusual elements in the story. The role of blacks and Native Americans serving in the Union ranks, command decisions on all levels, and the personal stories of many individuals are included. The book ends with a look at what happened to the crater from battle's end until today. Throughout, I have attempted not just to describe but also to make reasoned judgments based on the evidence and to explain why things took place as they did on July 30.

Several people offered much needed help in gathering material for this book. Michael A. Cavanaugh generously offered copies of important sources he had accumulated while doing research for *The Battle of the Crater,* and his coauthor, William Marvel, also generously shared with me many archival sources he had found on the battle. A. M. Gambone played a key role in helping me to access the papers of John F. Hartranft, which are privately owned by Helen L. Shireman. I also owe a debt of gratitude to Mrs. Shireman for allowing me to see and use documents from those papers. De Witt Boyd Stone, Jr., also was generous in sharing sources relating to Elliott's South Carolina brigade, and Mark H. Dunkelman helped me in researching sources as well. Richard A. Sauers passed on previously unknown material on Henry Pleasants and encouraged me in working on this book. Michael F. Knight alerted me to rare sources from the holdings of the National Archives. Bruce Baker and Kevin Levin worked hard to find sources at many archival repositories, and Art Bergeron and Clifton Hyatt were very helpful in locating and making available relevant images from the photograph collection at the U.S. Army Military History Institute. Christopher M. Calkins offered much encouragement and allowed access to rare archival sources and photographs at Petersburg National Battlefield. A. Wilson Greene read the manuscript carefully and offered many insights as to how it could be improved.

Most of all, I give my thanks to my wife, Pratibha, for all her love and support.

INTO THE CRATER

1

I THINK WE MIGHT DO SOMETHING

As early as June 21, three days after the first Union effort to take Petersburg ended in bloody failure, Lt. Col. Henry Pleasants of the 48th Pennsylvania believed that he could dig a mine under the Confederate position and blow it up. The thought came to him when Lt. Robert F. McKibbin, a member of Brig. Gen. James Ledlie's 1st Division staff, gave Pleasants a tour of the Union line opposite Pegram's Salient, which also was known as Elliott's Salient. Only 125 yards of bare, sandy soil separated the armies at this point, the narrowest width of no-man's-land along the lines outside Petersburg.[1]

Pleasants "hinted" his idea to Capt. George W. Gowen of Company C, and to Capt. Francis U. Farquhar, chief engineer of the 18th Corps. Both men were prewar acquaintances, and they encouraged Pleasants to take his suggestion up the chain of command. Before he did that, Pleasants asked his regimental officers to compile a list of the "practical miners in each company," which also prompted the rank and file of the 48th Pennsylvania to discuss the prospect of digging their way to the Confederate line.[2]

Pleasants was acting as temporary commander of a brigade in Brig. Gen. Robert B. Potter's 2nd Division of the 9th Corps. Months later Potter contended that he and several others had already thought of mining at Pegram's Salient before Pleasants brought it to his attention. This may well have been true, for Potter had already concluded that it was impractical to attack above ground at the salient. On the bare hillside, the only place to form the troops was in the two covered ways then being constructed. These were sunken roadways leading back from the Union line toward the rear areas, not "a very promising way" of staging an attack.[3]

Pleasants convinced his superiors that an underground approach was better than an attack above ground. On June 24 Potter informed Maj. Gen. Ambrose E. Burnside at 9th Corps headquarters that his brigade leader was "a

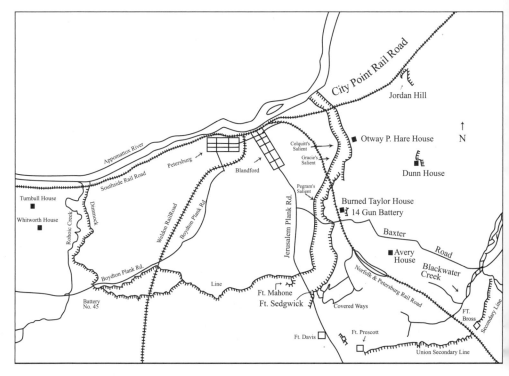

Confederate and Union lines at Petersburg

mining engineer and has charge of some of the principal mining works of
Schuylkill County, Pa." Moreover the 48th Pennsylvania had four officers,
fourteen noncommissioned officers, and eighty-five enlisted men who were
professional miners. Potter relayed Pleasants's proposal in detail, noting that he
planned to dig two tunnels, one to serve as ventilation for the other, and to connect them laterally at short distances. Pleasants thought the elaborate ventilation design was needed because the soil was "full of mephitic vapors." The
brigade leader, however, underestimated the length of the proposed mine at one
hundred yards; he thought his men could dig twenty-five to fifty feet per day.
Pleasants wanted special mining picks; if not available, he was certain they
could be converted from ordinary picks. He also required certain mathemati-
cal instruments as well as wheelbarrows and other equipment. Potter endorsed
the proposal heartily. "The men themselves are quite desirous, seemingly, of
trying it," he assured headquarters. "I think, perhaps, we might do something,
and in no event could we lose more men than we do every time we feel the
enemy."[4]

Burnside was energized by the plan when Potter and Pleasants joined him
for a conference on the night of June 24. He gave immediate approval to start

work and promised to approach Maj. Gen. George G. Meade, commander of the Army of the Potomac, for authorization.[5]

The next day at noon, Pleasants began work on the project that would make his name in Civil War history. At 2:45 that afternoon, Burnside wrote a note to Meade informing him of the plan. "I think we can break the line of the enemy in due time if we can have the necessary facilities," he predicted. Meade did not hesitate to reply. "I am delighted to hear you can do anything against the enemy's line," he wrote at 3 P.M., "and will furnish you everything you want, and earnest wishes for your success besides." Meade later temporized his hasty endorsement after examining the topography around Pegram's Salient, but initially he hoped the mine "would at some time result in forming an important part in our operations."[6]

The man who shouldered the responsibility for digging the mine had been born thirty-one years before in Buenos Aires, Argentina, the son of a Latin American mother and a Philadelphia man visiting the country on business. "His impetuous nature, and quick, fiery temper, but withal generous, good-heartedness, comes of this Americo-Spanish blood," wrote Oliver Christian Bosbyshell, another officer in the 48th Pennsylvania. Pleasants came to Philadelphia at age thirteen and graduated from high school, later earning a bachelor of arts and a master of arts degree. He worked as a civil engineer on Pennsylvania railroads, where he had charge of digging the Sand Patch Tunnel. It was a difficult

Henry Pleasants. Robert Underwood Johnson and Clarence Clough Buel, *Battles and Leaders* (New York: Century Company, 1887–88), 4:546

project, forty-two hundred feet long, but Pleasants dug four shafts two hundred feet deep from the surface to provide ventilation for the slowly progressing tunnelers.[7]

Pleasants left the railroad industry as a protest over the firing of his friend,
the president of the Pittsburgh and Connellsville Railroad, and entered the
anthracite coal business as an engineer at Pottsville, Pennsylvania, in 1857. The
start of the Civil War found him a widower; Pleasants served in a three-months
unit and later accepted a commission in the 48th Pennsylvania. This regiment
was organized in Schuylkill County, a coal-mining district, and many of its
original members were miners. Although most of them were gone by 1864, the
regiment retained its reputation as a coal miner's outfit. The 48th fought at
Second Bull Run, South Mountain, Antietam, and Fredericksburg. With two
divisions of Burnside's 9th Corps, it participated in the occupation of East
Tennessee and the defense of Knoxville. Burnside's men shifted back to Virginia
to take part in the Overland campaign of May 1864, with Pleasants leading the
48th after its colonel, Joshua K. Sigfried, was placed in command of a brigade
in the all-black 4th Division of the 9th Corps. Pleasants was "a soldier of true
grit," commented the admiring Bosbyshell, "possessed of more than ordinary
ability as an engineer."[8]

But Burnside had developed a bad reputation in the Army of the Potomac.
From the Wilderness campaign on, he seemed to not move fast enough or fight
hard enough to satisfy his critics. "Burnside somehow is never up to the mark
when the tug comes," concluded 5th Corps artillery chief Charles S. Wainwright. Oliver Wendell Holmes, Jr., a member of the 6th Corps staff, criticized
Burnside's weak attacks on the Mule Shoe Salient at Spotsylvania by writing,
"he is a d'd humbug."[9]

These criticisms were not justified, for the 9th Corps fought as hard as the
other three corps in Meade's army during the Overland campaign and in the
first round of fighting at Petersburg. It had the losses to prove it. Five of seven
brigades had different commanders by the time the armies settled down at
Petersburg, and captains led some regiments. On June 16–18 Burnside's corps
suffered the second-highest number of casualties in the army while advancing
closer to the Rebel line than any other troops.[10]

The Battlefield to Come

The Union approach to Pegram's Salient, often referred to as the "mined fort,"
was not easy. The modest valley of Poor Creek, also known as Taylor's Creek,
separated the Confederate line from most of the Union position. The forward
Federal line bulged westward across the valley and approached as close as 125
yards from the salient; the Federals often called this section of their trenches
the horseshoe. The house of William Byrd Taylor, burned on June 18, stood

five hundred yards east of Pegram's Salient on the eastern side of Poor Creek, where the main Union position was located.[11]

Unlike most salients, Pegram's did not project forward from the Confederate line. It was a reentrant angle formed by bending the line back as it continued south of Pegram's position. The angle was very shallow, making the salient a poor target because Confederate troops north and south could fire on the flanks of advancing Union troops. Pleasants was mining here only because of the proximity of the opposing lines, not because the terrain suited a Federal attack.[12]

Even from the Confederate perspective, the shallow angle posed problems. Brig. Gen. Edward Porter Alexander, chief of artillery in the 1st Corps, Army of Northern Virginia, assumed responsibility for the guns in this sector. He bluntly termed Pegram's Salient "the weakest part of our whole line, a piece of bad location with a great dead space in front." Alexander referred to the valley of Poor Creek, which the Confederates could not see into because the parapet of the forward Union line blocked their view. This parapet was tall and adorned with loopholes and head logs to protect Federal sharpshooters who "maintained from it a close & accurate fire on all parts of our line near them."

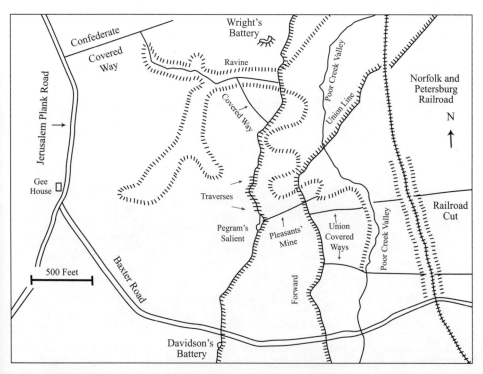

Pegram's Salient

Alexander thought Pegram's Salient was a worse position than the Mule Shoe Salient at Spotsylvania, the scene of a gruesome battle on May 12 that forced the Confederates to evacuate the pronounced bulge and retire to a better line at its base.[13]

Ironically the Confederates never intended to have a salient at this place along the Petersburg line. It was formed because of a mistake by Capt. Richard G. Pegram during the first major battle for possession of Petersburg. The Federals crossed the James River from their trenches at Cold Harbor and struck for the city in mid-June, inaugurating a new phase in Grant's offensive against Lee. Petersburg was protected by a ring of earthworks, designed and built by Charles H. Dimmock in 1862–63, which were thinly held by the over-stretched resources of Gen. P. G. T. Beauregard, commander of the Department of North Carolina and Southern Virginia. Initial Union attacks on June 15 cracked the Dimmock Line east of the city, but the Confederates were able that night to patch together a new position to contain them. Called the Hagood Line, because Brig. Gen. Johnson Hagood had hastily laid it out, the line held against hard but uncoordinated attacks on June 16–17.[14]

At the same time, Beauregard's chief engineer, Col. David B. Harris, and his chief of artillery, Col. Hilary P. Jones, staked out a new line to the rear of Hagood's position. It stretched from the river down to Battery No. 25 on the Dimmock Line. Beauregard evacuated the Hagood Line on the night of June 17, pulling his troops back to this new position, where they were told to dig in before dawn. Harris had laid out the line with white stakes to be more visible in the dark, but Pegram somehow missed them. He chose a place for his Virginia battery and told his men to dig gun emplacements. After they were

Looking toward the Federal position from the crater, ca. 1890. Taken by Bvt. Lieut. Col. George A. Bruce, 13th New Hampshire. RG 6415–MOL-PA 13.36, Civil War Library and Museum, MOLLUS, Philadelphia, Pennsylvania

Modern view from the crater toward the Federal position. Earl J. Hess

well under way, Harris arrived and pointed out the stakes he had placed many
yards to the rear, but Pegram refused to order his tired gunners to abandon
their work and start anew.[15]

Pegram later regretted this decision. His men managed to throw up no more
than "slight earth-works," and several Federal shells went through the traverses
that protected the flank of each gun crew. Moreover the emplacements were not
connected to each other or to the infantry line north and south.[16]

As a result, June 18 was a trying day. The 9th Corps, responsible for this
sector, did some of its best fighting of the campaign. It had to cross a cut of the
Norfolk and Petersburg Railroad that was up to twenty feet deep and which
was enfiladed by Confederate artillery. The troops literally clawed their way up
the bank of this cut to continue the attack. Then they crossed the valley of Poor
Creek, driving out Confederate skirmishers by late afternoon. About one thousand men of Brig. Gen. Orlando B. Willcox's 3rd Division managed to advance
farther and establish the curved horseshoe line on the west slope of the valley.[17]

The first struggle for Petersburg ended that evening as Grant instructed
Meade to rest his exhausted army while he pondered what to do next. The
Confederates all along the Harris Line began to improve their defenses. An
infantry regiment arrived at Pegram's battery and provided the labor to connect its gun emplacements and shore up the traverses and parapets. The line

Stephen Elliott. RG6675, vol. 85, p. 4298,
Massachusetts Commandery, Military Order
of the Loyal Legion and the U.S. Army
Military History Institute

would hold, but it was not properly located. Alexander noted that there was a long, open slope behind Pegram's Salient up to the ridgelike high ground that carried the Jerusalem Plank Road southward out of Blandford, the eastern part of Petersburg. This slope was clearly visible to the Federals, forcing the Rebels to dig a covered way from the road down a ravine that lay just north of Pegram's position in order to connect the line with the rear areas. A spring two hundred yards up slope from the trench fed a small rivulet that flowed in this ravine. Bushes and trees filled the widened, swampy area where the ravine drained into Poor Creek, obstructing Federal view in this sector. Another, smaller ravine lay to the south of Pegram's position, which offered fewer opportunities for men to move back and forth to the line.[18]

The Confederate Defenders

The defense of this ill-placed sector of trenches rested on the infantry and artillerymen that held it. Pegram's battery consisted of four twelve-pounder Napoleons and was part of Maj. James C. Coit's artillery battalion of Beauregard's command. Coit had another unit, Capt. Samuel T. Wright's Virginia battery, posted in the sector, but the rest of his battalion was either on detached duty in South Carolina or positioned north of the Appomattox River. Pegram's battery had been recruited from the 12th Virginia, a regiment raised mostly in the Petersburg area. Lt. W. P. Robinson's men of the Ringgold (Virginia) Battery relieved Pegram's gunners for three weeks while the crews went to the rear for rest. During those three weeks, Robinson directed his gunners in strengthening the works, for they were so meager that his men had to kneel or sit during the day. Any time they raised a hat on a stick above the parapet it was perforated by a Yankee bullet.[19]

The infantry manning this sector of the Confederate line belonged to Maj. Gen. Bushrod R. Johnson's division of Beauregard's command. An Ohio-born West Point graduate, Johnson resigned from the U.S. Army in 1847 and lived in the South. He sided with the Confederacy and fought in the western theater, having been captured at Fort Donelson and wounded at Shiloh. Johnson commanded a hard-fighting brigade of Tennessee regiments at Perryville and Stones River, and a division at Chickamauga. His command was detached to help Lt. Gen. James Longstreet try to capture Knoxville, Tennessee, in late 1863, and went with Longstreet when the latter rejoined Lee's army just before the opening of the Overland campaign. Johnson and all the western troops that came east were given to Beauregard. His division consisted of four brigades, a mixture of eastern and western regiments.[20]

One of Johnson's units, Brig. Gen. Stephen Elliott's South Carolina brigade, held the line on both sides of Pegram's battery. A son of the plantation elite, Elliott had been a successful cotton planter and militia officer before the war and had participated in the defense of the South Carolina coast during the first half of the conflict. He commanded Fort Sumter when its garrison repelled an attempted landing by the U.S. Navy in September 1863. After promotion to brigadier general, Elliott took command of Brig. Gen. Nathan G. Evans's South Carolina brigade, often called the Tramp Brigade for its wanderings from one assignment to another. Evans had been a hero in the early part of the war but had since fallen into disrepute for a drinking problem and an irascible temper. His replacement, Brig. Gen. William Stephen Walker, had been wounded and captured on May 20 at Bermuda Hundred shortly before Elliott assumed command.[21]

Another unit of Johnson's division, Brig. Gen. Henry A. Wise's Virginia brigade, was positioned south of Elliott's men. Wise was put in charge of the 1st Military District of Beauregard's command on June 1, so Col. Thomas Goode of the 34th Virginia took command of the brigade. He had graduated from the Virginia Military Institute and had been an officer in the U.S. Army before the war, with service in Kansas and Utah. Ransom's North Carolina brigade held the line north of Elliott's position. Originally led by Brig. Gen. Robert Ransom, it distinguished itself from the Seven Days to Fredericksburg and then saw service in its native state. Ransom's brother, Brig. Gen. Matt W. Ransom, led the unit to further distinction in the capture of Plymouth on April 20, 1864, and in the May 16 battle of Drewry's Bluff, where Beauregard's outnumbered command saved Richmond by driving back the Army of the James and confining it to the Bermuda Hundred peninsula, the wedge of land at the junction of the James River and the Appomattox River. Col. Lee M. McAfee now commanded this hard-fighting Tar Heel unit.[22]

The Confederates were unaware that their opponents had developed a plan to breach their line at what many considered a weak spot. Likewise, Pleasants and his superiors assumed they were undermining a stronghold in the Rebel works. The narrow no-man's-land that separated Pegram's Salient from the Union horseshoe was wide enough to hide some of the truth from both sides.

2

UNDERGROUND WAR

Although Pleasants masterminded the mine project, he relied on Sgt. Henry Reese of Company F to oversee the enlisted men's work. Born in Wales twenty-seven years earlier, Reese had red hair and stood nearly five feet ten inches tall. He was married to a Welsh woman who had also immigrated to the United States. Reese remained at the mine twenty-four hours a day, sleeping and taking his meals at the entrance.[1]

While there were enough professional miners in the 48th Pennsylvania to do the skilled work, most members of the regiment contributed unskilled labor to the project. Two officers superintended each shift, which normally lasted two and a half hours, with a ration of whiskey at the end. Pleasants relocated the regimental camp so it was only four hundred yards from the entrance of the mine.[2]

Starting the gallery in the bank of Poor Creek, the Pennsylvanians dug fifty feet on June 25. They averaged closer to forty feet per day thereafter, nearly two feet per hour. The men started with no special tools or equipment, using shovels and picks belonging to the pioneer detachment of the brigade. The typical army pick was not well suited for mining because its flukes were too broad for swinging in confined places. The men filed down the flukes to resemble civilian mining picks. Disposing of the dirt became a problem, involving more men than any other aspect of the project. Proper wheelbarrows were not available, so the Pennsylvanians took hardtack boxes and nailed strips of hickory wood to them, reinforced the boxes with bands of iron taken from pork and beef barrels, and dragged out boxes full of dirt from the gallery. They cut brush to cover up the piled dirt. Toward the end of the digging, members of the 23rd United States Colored Troops (USCT), in the 4th Division of the 9th Corps, were employed to carry dirt from the mine in sacks. They also hauled timber to the gallery for framing its sides. Sandbags filled with dirt taken from the gallery often were used to enlarge the parapets of 9th Corps trenches. Pleasants employed 210 men each day; some of them worked shirtless, looking to an observer like "so many brown gophers" as they popped "in and out of the hole."[3]

Framing the gallery was essential for safety. Pleasants used timber framing, constructing each section out of four pieces—two vertical timbers with a cap and a sill, notching the ends together to make a solid joint. This was done outside so as not to make noise underground, then each frame was set in place with the posts 3 to 30 feet apart. Where the walls or ceiling seemed likely to cave in, the men attached boards to the frame to construct "a complete casing." The Pennsylvanians scavenged timber from a bridge of the Norfolk and Petersburg Railroad, and Pleasants found a working sawmill six miles away to cut planks. He assigned as many as two companies of the 48th Pennsylvania to haul the wood. For lighting, the men placed candles or lanterns every 10 to 20 feet along the gallery walls, although bottles also served as candle holders for the men who dug at the head of the excavation.[4]

Pleasants encountered his first problem after a week of fast digging. On July 2 his miners hit "extremely wet ground" about 250 feet into the gallery. It caused the timber framing to sink and nearly collapse altogether, "the roof and floor of the mine nearly meeting," as Pleasants put it. Then the diggers hit a stratum of marl "whose consistency was like putty." Pleasants told his men to incline the floor of the gallery 13½ feet in 100 feet to avoid it.[5]

The mine penetrated ground that had at one time been the bottom of the sea, exposed by the westward movement of the Atlantic Plate. Theodore Lyman of Meade's staff noted that "a good many different shells" could be found in the sandy soil. The marl layer that Pleasants encountered provided his men with a hobby, for it was soft enough to fashion into different shapes while hardening solid when exposed to sun and air. They made pipes, crosses, marbles, and 9th Corps badges. D. S. Way, a staff officer from the 18th Corps, saw the men making these badges by stamping an impression on a ball of marl, cutting the borders in the shape of a shield, and drying them. Pleasants's men sold these souvenirs for a quarter each.[6]

Petersburg was located near the fall line, the most apparent boundary between the Atlantic coastal plain to the east and the foothills to the west. The ridge behind Pegram's Salient, on which Blandford Cemetery and the Jerusalem Plank Road were located, lay 144 feet above sea level. Most sediments of the coastal plain lay in deep layers about 150 feet thick under the surface of the land. Pleasants's miners encountered three shallow layers however; the first two, Bacon's Castle Formation and the Yorktown Formation, only in a marginal way. Formed in the late Pliocene era (roughly three million B.C.), these two layers were exposed when Poor Creek deepened over time, bending

Ground under which the Union troops tunneled, 1889. Vol. 118, 6095,
Massachusetts Commandery, Military Order of the Loyal Legion and the
U.S. Army Military History Institute

Clay badge of the 9th Corps.
Adopted in April 1864, corps
headquarters described it as
a "shield with the figure 9 in
the center, crossed with a foul
anchor and cannon." (General
Orders No. 6, Headquarters,
Ninth Corps, April 10, 1864,
OR, vol. 33, 837). Earl J. Hess

down along the edge of the creek valley in a process geologists describe as
"creep and colluviation." The miners initially tunneled for a few feet through
Bacon's Castle and Yorktown before entering a third formation called East-
over, remaining in it for the rest of the gallery's length. The layer of marl

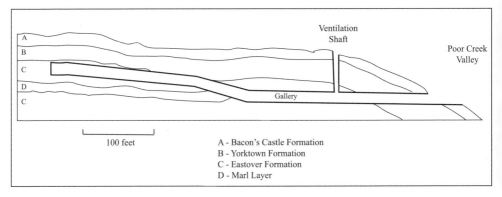

Geological layers

Pleasants encountered lay horizontally just a few feet below the top of the East-
over Formation.[7]

The Federals encountered a fossil while digging about thirty feet below the
surface, usually identified as coming from a mastodon. This huge, elephant-like
creature had become extinct in North America by the end of the Pleistocene
era (ten thousand years ago). Brigade leader John F. Hartranft kept it for a couple of months, describing it as supposedly "a joint of the back bone of a large
animal or fish." He planned to send it to a museum in Pennsylvania, but a veteran of the 48th Pennsylvania recalled that a doctor from Canada acquired it
and the bone eventually wound up in a Toronto museum.[8]

After dealing with marl and mastodons, Pleasants made sure the gallery
was exactly the right length to plant a powder charge under the Confederate
line. He had to measure the distance from the mouth of the mine to Pegram's
battery emplacement by triangulating with an "old-fashioned theodolite," because more sophisticated equipment was not available. His crew laid out short
lines at five different locations within the Union position and created the
other two sides of an imaginary triangle from each end of these lines to
Pegram's Salient. The degrees of the angles at the sides were noted and the
distance to the salient deduced from this and the length of the third, base
line. Pleasants concluded that Pegram's guns were 133 yards away from the
forward Federal position. He accurately measured the distance back from the
forward line to the mouth of the gallery to complete his estimate of how long
to dig the tunnel.[9]

Ventilation was a relatively easy problem to solve. Pleasants had suggested
digging two galleries, side by side, and connecting them with cross passages for
a full draft of air, but that would have taken too much time. Instead he dug a
shaft from the gallery up to the surface, twenty-two feet tall. It emerged just
behind the forward Union line. His men constructed a square wooden tube and

laid it along the length of the gallery, with a furnace at the bottom of the shaft. Here a fire was kept burning day and night, heating the air and creating a draft up the shaft that pulled air out of the gallery through the tube. With this air came the gases and exhalations of the workers. As the gallery lengthened, Pleasants reversed the flow of air. He placed a canvas partition with a door in it across the gallery just outside the shaft, with the wooden tube sticking through the partition. This forced fresh air from the mouth of the gallery into the tube, taking it to the farthest extent of the excavation. Because of the partition, the stale air in the gallery was drawn out by the fire and up the shaft. Of course smoke came out of the upper end of the shaft, easily seen from the Confederate line. The Union soldiers built fires at several locations to convince their opponents that all the smoke was coming from campfires.[10]

Burnside visited the mine on July 7, two weeks after its start, and brought Gov. William Sprague of Rhode Island and Gov. David Tod of Ohio on July 11. Burnside promised the men he would maintain their ration of whiskey as long as it took to complete the gallery.[11]

Ironically the chief engineer of the Army of the Potomac had written the first American manual for military engineers ever published, which included a thorough description of mining and countermining, yet he had no involvement in the project at all. Ninth Corps personnel bypassed Maj. James Chatham Duane in planning the work, and there is no indication that they read his book either. The mine was a 9th Corps project, pure and simple.[12]

Duane's *Manual for Engineer Troops* laid out the plans and nomenclature for military mining. The practice of undermining defensive walls by digging tunnels under them was almost as old as organized warfare. The most important change over time was the introduction of gunpowder in the late fifteenth and early sixteenth centuries. The process was later systematized along scientific lines. Duane's book simply restated for American readers what already was known among European military engineers.

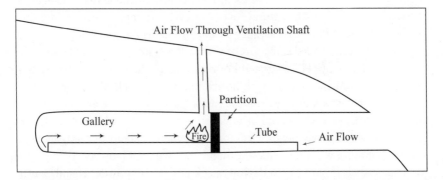

The ventilation scheme

Partially collapsed Union gallery, ca. 1934. Petersburg Museums

A gallery often started with a vertical shaft from which the horizontal excavation began. The tunnel was termed a "gallery" if it was bigger than 3 by 4
feet; Pleasants made his 4½ by 4½ feet. If smaller than 3 by 4 feet, the tunnel
was termed a "branch." Both galleries and branches were termed "ascending"
or "descending" if they were inclined. If the gallery was intended to be only a
few feet below the surface, a vertical shaft could be replaced by a descending
gallery until the miners reached the desired depth, and then they could dig at
an even plane. If a shaft was not used, Duane recommended that a gallery be
started behind a "bank or natural cover," or even a parapet. Pleasants did this,
using the bank of Poor Creek valley to start his gallery at an even plane.[13]

Duane recommended some sort of ventilation system when any gallery was
at least 60 feet long. He suggested boring shafts to the surface or connecting
two or more nearby galleries with horizontal passages. He also offered plans
for mechanical ventilation systems that drew fresh air into the gallery, made of
tubes constructed of wood, tin, or india rubber with a "fan-blower" or black-
smith bellows to move the air. Pleasants's scheme was almost exactly like this
except that a fire was more efficient than hand-operated blowers.[14]

Duane spelled out how to deploy the explosive in a powder chamber usually located at the end of the gallery or branches. Any charge greater than one

hundred pounds should be placed in cube-shaped boxes, and the gallery or branch should be completely filled up with material to contain the blast, otherwise most of it would blow out of the gallery instead of up against the target. This process of stopping up the gallery was known as tamping. Duane noted that any material could be used, but sandbags were the easiest to install.[15]

Thus far, what Duane detailed was common sense to civilian miners, but the military miner devoted a great deal of thought to analyzing the effects of the powder charge so he could gauge how and when to use mines against targets. The crater produced by the springing of the mine was conical in shape, the radius was at the surface, and the line of least resistance was the line from the charge directly to the surface. If the radius of the crater was the same as the line of least resistance, it was termed a "one-lined crater," or a "two-lined crater" if it was doubled. Another term for a two-lined crater was "a common crater," because that was deemed the more natural way for the crater to form. When the hole was less than doubled, the conclusion was that the mine had too little powder; it had too much when the crater was more than doubled. Duane noted that every mine explosion pulverized and compressed the earth near the crater; if the gallery of an enemy countermine was within the "sphere of action," it could collapse as a result. Also, the pulverization around a crater made it difficult to dig another gallery though the affected earth, because it would be very unstable.[16]

Confederate Countermeasures

Pleasants would soon have to deal with his enemy, because the Confederates were aware of the danger at Pegram's. Brigadier General Alexander was the first to draw attention to it. He noticed in late June that sniping was severe only at this point, that it tended to slacken right and left of the salient. "This satisfied me very soon that something was going on there," he later recalled. He initially thought the Federals would begin sapping toward Pegram, digging an approach trench with a sap roller carefully placed to protect the diggers. He ordered a supply of hand grenades for the defenders of the salient, but the weapons were never delivered.[17]

Alexander began to organize defense in depth at the salient, placing fourteen guns along the Jerusalem Plank Road about eight hundred yards to the rear. He placed two other artillery pieces in a detached earthwork down slope from the road to cover a shallow ravine to Pegram's right. This position was commanded by Lt. John Hampden Chamberlayne. Four other guns, commanded by Capt. David Norvell Walker (Company A, 13th Battalion Virginia Light Artillery) and Capt. Crispin Dickenson (Company B, 13th Battalion Virginia Light Artillery), were put in another detached position to fire lengthwise down the Confederate trench line in case it was occupied by the enemy.

This latter position was located farther down slope from the road than Chamberlayne, but also to the right of Pegram's battery.[18]

Alexander also put the four guns of Capt. George S. Davidson's Company C, 13th Battalion Virginia Light Artillery, in a redan on the Confederate line two hundred yards to the right of Pegram's position. Davidson's two left pieces were posted to rake the front of Pegram's Salient, striking the flank of a Union attacker. Alexander told Davidson to build tall, narrow embrasures for his guns; he did not want him to fire anywhere except down no-man's-land, and that as rapidly as possible if the Federal troops advanced.[19]

Alexander was puzzled that he did not see signs of sapping, even though he inspected the ground at Pegram's every day. On June 30 it suddenly dawned on him that the enemy might be digging underground. While making his way to Lee's headquarters, he jumped out of the trench to walk across open ground and was shot in the shoulder. It was not a dangerous wound, but it earned him a furlough. On the morning of July 1, as he was on his way home, Alexander stopped at Lee's headquarters but found the general out. He reported his suspicion to Col. Charles Venable. A correspondent named Lawley, who worked for the *Times* of London, happened to overhear the report and took an interest in it. He claimed that no one could ventilate a gallery five hundred feet long, citing a four-hundred-foot-long tunnel constructed at Delhi during the Indian Mutiny of 1857 as the longest military mine on record. Alexander assured him that there were coal miners in the Union army with civilian experience that allowed them to ventilate five hundred feet easily.[20]

Three days later engineer officer Marshall McDonald, serving on the 1st Corps staff, carefully surveyed the lines and found no signs of approaches. He did see a hole that looked like a mine shaft; if it was, then he was sure the Federals were trying to undermine Pegram's guns. Ironically this was no mine shaft, but McDonald's report added fuel to the suspicion planted by Alexander. The gallery was nearly under Pegram's Salient when the Confederates finally decided to dig a countermine to protect the position. Lt. Hugh Thomas Douglas of Company F, 1st Confederate Engineers, was put in charge of the job. Born in Virginia and a successful civil engineer in Ohio before the war, Douglas began his service as a sergeant in a Virginia battery before he was detailed to engineer duty. Discharged from his battery, he worked for a long while as a civil assistant to engineer officers in the field, obtaining a commission in the newly raised engineer regiment by late 1863. Confederate chief engineer Jeremy F. Gilmer called Douglas "an intelligent active and practical man," seemingly the right attributes for taking on Pleasants and his coal miners.[21]

Douglas's company was tending the pontoon bridge across the James River at Chaffin's Bluff when he received the order to report for duty at Petersburg.

He arrived at Pegram's Salient on July 10 and established his company camp at Blandford. Douglas found that someone had already started to dig a shaft, six feet deep, and learned that another shaft had been started at Colquitt's Salient, several hundred yards north of Pegram's, where the lines also were relatively close together.[22]

With no experience at this sort of work, Douglas learned quickly what was required. He began a second shaft at Pegram's, two hundred fifty feet from the first, one on either flank of the battery position. Shaft No. 1, on the left, was made eighteen feet deep, and No. 2, on the right, was sunk fourteen feet. Douglas guessed the depth of Pleasants's mine incorrectly; it was at least twenty-five feet deep. The plan was to extend galleries out from the bottom of each shaft well forward of the Confederate parapet, connecting the two forward ends with a cross passage.[23]

Douglas submitted requisitions for needed material, including ten pounds of leather to make knee pads for the miners. By July 13, after three days of work, his men had completed both shafts and had dug seven and a half feet of both galleries, and one of them already had been framed. The galleries were six feet high and three feet three inches wide. Douglas's men dug from one to four feet ahead of the timber framers, making up to about five feet of progress each day. More men, five detailed soldiers from Brig. Gen. Thomas L. Clingman's North Carolina brigade, arrived on July 11. On July 14 sixty detailed soldiers from McAfee's North Carolina brigade and Goode's Virginia brigade reported for duty. Few if any of these men had experience as miners, but they could haul dirt and framing material from and to the shafts. Douglas used up to one pound of candles each night and needed three post augers so he could "bore forward from the heading of the galleries" to find the Federals. He also asked that a surgeon be assigned to his growing workforce.[24]

Douglas organized two detachments, both commanded by a noncommissioned officer, for each shaft. Each detachment comprised fifteen men and Douglas organized two additional detachments for work at Colquitt's Salient. Their shifts lasted twelve hours, from 8 A.M. to 8 P.M. Two men carried dirt from the head of the gallery to the bottom of the shaft, two men cranked a windlass to bring the dirt up, two men dumped the dirt out of the container, and two more hauled it away.[25]

Douglas also issued regulations to govern nearly every aspect of the work. He wanted a berm of earth erected around the shafts to prevent rainwater from falling in and ordered a well two feet deep, covered with a grating, at the bottom of each shaft to handle accumulated water. Douglas mandated that the framers keep within two feet of the miners as the gallery lengthened. He planned to make both galleries at Pegram's level for twenty feet and then, given the slope downward toward the Union line, to descend at the rate of one foot for every ten feet. For a time, Douglas used the gallery at Shaft No. 2 as a listening gallery and pushed the other gallery forward to intercept the Union mine. To detect where the Federals were, he wanted his miners to pause every fifteen minutes and listen for them. By July 16, each detachment was digging about four feet, making a total of eight feet per day at each gallery.[26]

The only shaft at Colquitt's Salient was about twelve feet deep, as Douglas reported the gallery was six feet below ground. He pushed it forward at the same rate as those at Pegram's, digging the gallery at a level for ten feet, then descending one foot for every ten feet. For some unexplained reason, Douglas thought the countermine at Colquitt's was "the most important one" along the line.[27]

More detailed infantrymen arrived on July 18, thirty-one from Elliott's brigade and nineteen from Brig. Gen. Archibald Gracie's Alabama brigade. The next day, one hundred engineer troops arrived from Charleston, South Carolina, the whole of Company F, 2nd Confederate Engineers. Douglas also persuaded the authorities to issue whiskey, sugar, and coffee to sustain his men's underground labor.[28]

On July 19 an unusually heavy rain hit the Petersburg area. The diggers made only one and a half feet of progress at Pegram's Gallery No. 1, a bit more than three feet at No. 2, and six feet at Colquitt's. Relatively little water came into the shafts, but the trenches were so soaked with mud that the details assigned to haul the dirt away were bogged down.[29]

Douglas began to sink a shaft at Gracie's Salient, located just across Poor Creek from Colquitt's Salient, on July 22. He went down at least ten feet and began a gallery. It turned out that Gracie had some cause for concern, for Douglas could clearly see a Union sap roller fifty yards from the Confederate line on the morning of July 23. The fortification manuals endorsed the use of a countermine to blow up the head of an aboveground sap. Here was a definite target to aim at, in contrast to the situation at Pegram's, where Douglas still had not verified that the Federals were digging a mine. Nevertheless he ordered a branch dug off to the right from Gallery No. 1 at Pegram's, aiming to join Gallery No. 2 as quickly as possible. The next day, the diggers at No. 2 started a branch to the left to meet their comrades partway.[30]

Heavy rain on the night of July 24 impeded progress at all countermines because the ground was so slippery with mud the men could not keep their footing. By July 26, however, Gallery No. 1 at Pegram's was eighty-two feet long and No. 2 was seventy-two feet. The branches were progressing slowly. Douglas bored directly upward from the head of No. 2, curious to know how deep it was, and broke ground at nine feet seven inches. No. 1 was exactly ten feet deep at a distance of sixty feet from the shaft. A Federal shell wounded a man at No. 2, but three days later another shell exploded harmlessly at the very edge of the shaft.[31]

The flow of equipment and supplies barely kept Douglas's miners at work. He received 3,300 feet of one-inch plank for framing, two circular saws, and another posthole auger on July 28. The saws were damaged, so Douglas made more augers out of them.[32]

Douglas was engaged in a strange contest with Pleasants, not knowing who his opponent was or exactly what, if anything, he was doing. He never detected unmistakable signs of Union mining anywhere along the line. His only real mistake lay in not sinking the shafts deep enough; without knowing that Pleasants began in the valley of Poor Creek, he could not have guessed the depth of the Union gallery. As a result, the Federals literally dug their way under Confederate Gallery No. 1. Douglas was unable to complete the branches designed to connect No. 1 with No. 2, but that would not have stopped the Federals even if they had been finished before the mine was sprung on July 30.[33]

Completing the Union Mine

Pleasants's gallery was 440 feet long and "ascending slightly" for drainage by July 14. Because the surface continued to slope uphill, the gallery would actually deepen as it progressed. Pleasants pushed his men harder as he closed in on the target, lengthening their shift to three hours but encouraging them "on very friendly terms about the tunnel." He was too busy to tend to brigade matters, so Col. Zenas R. Bliss replaced him as commander of the 1st Brigade, 2nd Division on July 25. Potter instructed Bliss to help Pleasants in any way possible, but the new brigade commander had little opportunity to contribute to the project. Once Burnside asked him to escort some visiting French officers into the gallery. They went halfway in before deciding they had seen enough. The Frenchmen gave way to Pleasants's men by stepping off the plank walkway onto the muddy floor. "It was dark and close," recalled Bliss; the air was foul and the dim light given by candles barely illuminated the gallery. "I was in the mine several times," Bliss continued, "and it was a most uncomfortable place to work in. None but men who had been miners all their lives could have withstood the foul air and the heat."[34]

Pleasants reported the gallery complete at 510.8 feet in the early morning hours of July 17. He estimated the head rested sufficiently under Pegram's guns to have the desired effect, but the Federals started to dig branches to the right and left along the Confederate line to extend the area of damage as widely as possible.[35]

Later on the morning of July 17, three deserters from the 49th North Carolina in McAfee's brigade crossed the lines. They informed the Yankees that the Confederates knew of the mine and were taking countermeasures. In fact one member of their company, who was a professional miner, had worked for Douglas. Burnside concluded that the Rebels were digging in the right place to intercept Pleasants, but that they were too shallow. Still the corps leader felt it was important that the mine be sprung as soon as possible, and Meade forwarded the information to Grant immediately.[36]

Pleasants stopped work for a time on the night of July 17 so he could listen for sounds of Rebel digging. While he lay at the head of the gallery, Capt. William Winlack of Company E lay at the right branch, and another man lay at the left branch. They rested quietly for half an hour, listening for any sound in the still earth. Then Pleasants whistled softly as a signal to gather at his location. The three held a hushed conference, with Pleasants whispering into Winlack's ear, "What do you think about any counterboring?" Winlack replied softly, "the rebels know no more of the tunnel being under them than the inhabitants of Africa." Pleasants thought the same, but when he whispered to the third man he received a reply that was too soft to understand. Pleasants lost his temper and shouted, but fortunately the Rebels heard nothing.[37]

Pleasants pushed forward to complete the branches. Only a start had been made on July 17, but the men dug twenty-five feet of the left branch and fifteen feet of the right branch in twelve hours. Meanwhile other workers hammered together wooden hoppers to be used as magazines for the powder. Pleasants encountered some underground springs, which slowed his progress. The problem with the springs was probably worsened by the heavy rain that fell on July 19. Soldiers in the 5th Corps just south of the mine had to drain their trenches of water and repair their parapets. Pleasants was further delayed by the need to stop work and listen for sounds of enemy countermining. During one of these listening sessions, Pleasants heard the Rebels at work in the gun emplacement above and feared they might be digging the countermine everyone dreaded. He decided to curve the right branch a bit toward the Confederate position, assuming they would extend their countermine forward. The branch "did not move out of line much," Pleasants later said.[38]

Everyone who worked in the branches could hear digging, pounding, and the hammering of nails, but the consensus of opinion was that the Rebels were making gun emplacements. Everyone assumed that a countermine was in progress, but they hoped Pleasants had gotten the jump on his opponent and had missed the Confederate gallery.[39]

Pleasants was fortunate that the Confederates had not learned of his mine earlier because word of it had begun to spread among the Federals as early as June 27. George B. Carpenter of the 4th Rhode Island announced that "we are undermining the Rebel forts, running tunnels almost every way." Maj. Charles J. Mills, an officer on Ledlie's division staff, told his father about the mine but

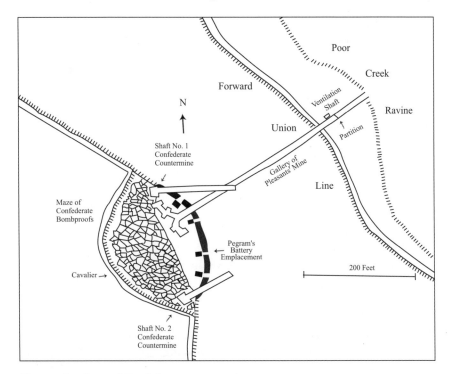

Pleasants's mine and Confederate countermines

warned him it was "a strict secret." Even Henry Heisler of the 48th Pennsylvania announced to his sister that the mine was "a regular Pennsylvania blow up. Harry Reese is the Boss miner and is working it as fast as the boys can carry out the dirt. He says he would willingly work day and night with very little rest, for to have the satisfaction of applying the match to it." Heisler predicted that the 48th Pennsylvania would next take on Fort Darling at Drewry's Bluff to open the road to Richmond. Pleasants also wrote a long letter to his uncle on July 25, giving details about the mine and the difficulties he encountered in digging it. "Be sure not to speak of this matter outside of Uncle James and Aunt Emily, until the thing is done," he warned, "then I will give you a fuller account."[40]

There were plenty of rumors among the Confederates about what their enemy was doing. A man in Maj. Gen. George Pickett's division, stationed on the Howlett Line on Bermuda Hundred, heard talk that "Grant was undermining our position" somewhere, but he also heard "that is false, it is impossible." Col. Walter H. Taylor, Lee's chief of staff, wrote home that "Burnside has some thousands of negroes underground—not dead & buried—mining our works."

He did not put any faith in the rumor, however, and spun a fanciful yarn for his "Bettie" about Grant digging all the way under Petersburg so as to emerge far to the rear of the Confederate line. The inventive Yankees had built a railroad line through the tunnels to facilitate their work. Taylor claimed it must be true, for people reported smoke oozing up between the paving stones and rumbling noises coming from the ground, "to say nothing of an unearthly whistle." More seriously Confederate soldiers often yelled out across the lines to question their opponents if the mining rumors were true.[41]

Above the ground, the sniping and artillery fire continued unabated as Pleasants drove his men forward beneath the surface. Zenas Bliss established his brigade headquarters in a bombproof three feet deep and four hundred yards behind the forward line, yet people still were killed if they did not duck into the entrance quickly enough. Capt. John C. Hackhiser of the 28th USCT reported that "there is a constend firing from morning till night, and from night till morning, and it is not very save for anyone to show him self above our works it is almost sure death." The covered way leading to Poor Creek valley and the mouth of Pleasants's mine was "enfiladed for a considerable distance" and dangerous to use until improvements rendered it safer. Nevertheless the 9th Corps lost more men on a daily basis than any other unit in Meade's army. In late June and early July that amounted to 48 men per day, or 1,440 per month.[42]

Pleasants drove his men toward the completion of their monthlong project with intensity. A problem developed as they neared the end, when Winlack fooled around with a tape measure and suddenly realized that both branches were nine feet too short. Reese agreed to report to the temperamental Pleasants but waited until the lieutenant colonel was in a good mood. "Now, you must not get mad if I tell you what's the matter," he began, but Pleasants lost his temper anyway, and Reese remembered long afterward that "it was a hotter place than the mine for a little while."[43]

After Pleasants corrected the problem, his men finished the left branch at midnight on July 22, with a total length of 37 feet. The right branch was done by 6 P.M. the next day, at 38 feet. The men spent several hours cleaning up the branches and gallery, then drained the excavation and completed the framing. By the time everything was done, about July 27, Pleasants estimated that his men had excavated 585.8 feet of combined gallery and branches and had moved 18,000 cubic feet of earth. Pleasants had won his race against Douglas.[44]

3

THE THIRD OFFENSIVE

As June turned into July, Grant increasingly felt compelled to organize another offensive at Petersburg. He wanted to continue trying to find a way to bypass or pry the Confederates out of their trenches. Lt. Gen. Jubal A. Early's invasion of Maryland played a key role in his anxiety to move operations forward. Detached from Lee's army in mid-June to secure Confederate control of the Shenandoah Valley, Early accomplished that goal and then sought to threaten Washington, D.C., in hopes of drawing Grant away from Petersburg. Also, Maj. Gen. William T. Sherman's Union army group was closing in on Atlanta, and Grant wanted to prevent the dispatch of Confederate troops from Lee's army to Georgia.

The mine itself became an increasingly prominent factor in Grant's mind as it neared completion. Meade and Grant never doubted Pleasants's ability to set off the mine, but neither was convinced that Pegram's Salient was the best place to launch a follow-up attack. Grant had authorized the explosion of two Union mines against the 3rd Louisiana redan at Vicksburg the year before; the first, on June 25, was followed up by an attack, but the second, on July 1, was not. He recognized that it was possible to explode Pleasants's mine just to damage Confederate defenses and kept that option open for some time.[1]

Grand Tactics

Grant wanted Meade's opinion on whether a frontal attack anywhere along the line was feasible, and the army commander relied on his corps leaders to supply the answer. Burnside argued that an attack following the explosion of Pleasants's mine would give him a better than even chance to break the Confederate line. Then Burnside stated that his chances would be even better if he could "say when and how the other two corps shall come in to my support." Meade relayed this opinion to Grant and sent Duane and his artillery chief, Brig. Gen. Henry J. Hunt, to confer with Burnside about the mine, but he also informed Burnside that he retained the right to give orders to his other corps commanders. This evoked a letter of apology from 9th Corps headquarters, as Burnside explained that he only wanted some latitude beyond corps boundaries to ensure the success of his operation.[2]

Meade agreed that any 9th Corps attack should await the completion of the mine, but he also reported that none of his other corps commanders held any hope of attacking in their sectors. The army leader feared that a turning movement around Lee's flank could isolate the advancing columns and lead to defeat in detail. He argued that some type of siege approach, underground or above, was the only feasible course of action.[3]

Meade's thoughts were reinforced by Duane and Hunt. Hunt had already talked with Burnside about the mine on June 26 and had visited the 9th Corps line on several other days to arrange for the placement of artillery. He had also talked with Pleasants on June 29 about his underground progress. In fact, that day Meade had ordered Hunt to requisition twelve thousand pounds of powder and one thousand yards of modern safety fuse for the project. Duane had no previous exposure to the mine, but the two officers worked hard for a couple of days to fulfill Meade's directive, reporting their opinion that a follow-up attack after the mine explosion was "impracticable" because of the shallow angle of Pegram's Salient and the ascending slope behind it. They recommended the construction of "regular approaches" on Maj. Gen. Gouverneur K. Warren's 5th Corps front. A few days later, the two revised their opinion by suggesting that Warren could improve Burnside's chances of success by pushing saps along the Jerusalem Plank Road and drawing Confederate attention from the 9th Corps front. If Burnside could not reach the crest of the ridge in his attack, he should dig in as far as his men could go and then begin sapping the rest of the way to the road. Meade endorsed the plan on July 11, probably believing it was the best way to avoid a potentially disastrous flanking movement west of the Jerusalem Plank Road.[4]

At least for the time being, Grant agreed with Meade. He authorized the army commander to begin "gradual approaches" on the 5th Corps front but remained uncertain about the chance of success. Meanwhile the report by Duane and Hunt had sparked an interest in Pleasants's mine among Grant's staff members. Engineer John G. Barnard passed on a set of questions requesting detailed information about the project. Pleasants responded on July 7 with a written report.[5]

Pleasants also had a personal interview with Barnard that left him seething with anger. According to the lieutenant colonel, Barnard began by asking, "What experience have you ever had, sir, as an engineer?" Referring to

Barnard as an "old fool," Pleasants the next day told Oliver Bosbyshell that he blurted out, "I'm a better engineer than you've got in the whole Regular Army." Barnard responded, with considerable sarcasm, "I'm happy to know you! I'm happy to know you." Pleasants explained his comment by saying that, as a practical engineer, his livelihood relied on daily use of the theodolite, an instrument forgotten by a cadet as soon as he left West Point. The two then had a long talk during which Barnard's attitude softened. He asked Pleasants to recommend other places to mine. Pleasants, however, was still angry and ended the interview by telling Barnard that he would "see him in h-l first!"[6]

This was an unfortunate interchange between two men who should have been cooperating with each other instead of fighting. Most of the blame rests on Pleasants. He was an unknown factor to Barnard, and even though the latter began the interview badly, he had every right to find out how much Pleasants knew about his profession. Pleasants was by nature impulsive, temperamental, and often harsh in his personal dealings. The tone of the interview was guided both by a clash of personalities and by a common distrust between civil and military engineers, with the result that Barnard's olive branch was rejected.

Unfortunately this interview was the wellspring of Pleasants's lifelong bitterness toward Barnard and the other military engineers of Meade's army. Pleasants's cousin, who bore his exact name, authored two books in the 1930s that perpetuated the idea that Pleasants succeeded in the mining project despite hostility and lack of cooperation from the military engineers. Nothing could be further from the truth. Barnard's evaluation of the project was positive. He termed the mine "exceptionable, so unprecedented." Barnard admitted that the "ordinary rules of mining did not apply" to it, but he believed in the project. Ironically one of the haughtiest professional military engineers in the U.S. Army admired the pragmatic character of the Pleasants mine and had nothing but support for it.[7]

The same cannot be said of the Army of the Potomac in general. As rumors sifted along the lines, many of Burnside's colleagues clucked their tongues. John Gibbon, a division commander in the 2nd Corps, later wrote that "Burnside was permitted to have charge of the whole arrangement just as if the mine was some pet scheme of his own in which the rest of the army had no interest." Cyrus B. Comstock, one of Grant's staff officers, recorded that Burnside was "full of his mine" and acted as "his own engineer." Comstock examined the gallery on July 2, but he continued to doubt that the 9th Corps could succeed in a follow-up attack. Charles Wainwright, artillery chief of the 5th Corps, claimed that the mine "causes a good deal of talk and is generally much laughed at."[8]

Ambrose E. Burnside. LC-DIG-
cwpb-05368, Library of Congress

The notion that Burnside was acting as his own engineer was in a sense true, for the corps leader refused to cooperate with engineer officers sent him by army headquarters. He had worked closely with his previous engineer, James St. Clair Morton, but apparently felt incapable of relying on any other engineer after Morton was killed on June 17. Meade sent him Capt. Frederick Harwood, but Burnside rejected him because Harwood had a habit of delegating responsibility for needed work to enlisted men instead of personally supervising it. Lt. William Benyaurd was next, but Burnside refused to allow him to work on the mine. Duane was willing to offer his help, but, given Burnside's attitude, Meade told him not to interfere.[9]

The military engineers associated with the Army of the Potomac were quite interested in what Pleasants was doing. Benyaurd gave a tour of the mine to Lt. Col. Ira Spaulding, commander of the 50th New York Engineers, and topographer Nathaniel Michler. They were fascinated with what they saw and admired Pleasants's handiwork. Yet Pleasants continued to spread the word that his efforts were derided by the "regular army wiseacres," who claimed his mine could never be completed owing to ventilation problems. "Old Burnside stood by me," he wrote his family on July 25, and "told me to go ahead and I have succeeded." This is worse than hyperbole; it is a deliberate twisting of the facts and an unfair denigration of the professional military engineers serving at Petersburg.[10]

Siege

Grant had given Meade tentative approval to start siege approaches, but he did not feel completely comfortable with the slow operations of sapping. The lieutenant general much preferred an attack or a flanking movement. The 19th Corps was being shipped from Louisiana to Virginia, and Grant hoped to use it in an offensive at Petersburg. He also made it clear to Meade that any above-ground siege approaches had to serve as the springboard for attacking the Confederate lines at short range. On his part, Meade was convinced by the Duane-Hunt report that sapping was not only feasible but necessary on the 5th Corps front; Rebel artillery placed in a salient near the ruins of the Gregory House east of the Jerusalem Plank Road had to be reduced before Burnside could launch his follow-up attack, because the guns could deliver cross fire on the ridge slope behind Pegram's position. Meade admitted that sapping would be slow and tedious, but he thought it the best policy to follow.[11]

Meade issued orders on July 9 to begin siege approaches, putting Duane in charge of construction and Hunt in charge of the artillery support. The two officers wrote a proposal for how to proceed, which conformed with Meade's views. There already was a siege train, consisting of heavy mortars and artillery pieces, created in April at Hunt's suggestion. It was the first time since the Peninsula campaign of 1862 that the Army of the Potomac had created such a train.[12]

Yet no sap was started; nothing in fact was done day after day on the 5th Corps front. On July 14 the planning continued when Meade asked Duane's opinion on what should be done if the Confederate lines were broken by the explosion of Pleasants's mine. Duane had no confidence that Burnside could take the crest of the ridge unless the Rebel guns at the Gregory House were put out of action, and he even admitted for the first time that sapping might not accomplish the latter goal. Duane told Meade that he might have to launch a flank movement west of the Jerusalem Plank Road to turn Lee's right and clear the Confederates out of the salient at the Gregory House. On July 16 Meade admitted to Grant that preparations for besieging Petersburg were moving along slowly. He needed more than a week yet to finish gun and mortar emplacements to support the sapping. Meanwhile Pleasants was reportedly nearing the end of his digging, but Meade wanted to postpone springing the mine until his sapping operation against the Gregory House came close to having an effect on the Rebels.[13]

The delay in commencing siege approaches on Warren's front drained Grant of all patience with the plan. He preferred more active operations in the field as promising quicker, more decisive results. Sapping made sense, as it did at Vicksburg, if the enemy were cut off from the outside world and there was no opportunity to outflank his defenses. At Petersburg there were several such opportunities, but Grant could not easily tell which were the best. Engineer Nathaniel Michler well understood that, despite the popular tendency to refer to Petersburg as a siege, "no regular siege was intended, as it would be impossible."[14]

Grant had a good excuse for ignoring siege approaches in developments far away in Maryland, where Early conducted an unexpected advance on Washington. Grant ordered Meade to send a division of the 6th Corps, which arrived at Baltimore on July 8. Later he was forced to dispatch the rest of the 6th Corps and the newly arriving 19th Corps. When rumors reached him on July 12 that Lee was sending A. P. Hill's 3rd Corps to help Early, Grant's first thought was to take the offensive at Petersburg and capitalize on reduced Confederate strength. That rumor proved false, and Grant continued to delay offensive action. But Confederate deserters came into Federal lines on July 17 (perhaps the same men who brought word of Confederate countermining efforts at Pegram's Salient), claiming that Lee intended to attack Meade as a way to divert Grant's attention from a contemplated shift of Rebel troops to Georgia. No attack or shift of troops occurred, of course, but Grant later claimed that this incident was the last straw. "I concluded, then, a few days later, to do something in the way of offensive movement myself." He could thereby pin Lee's men in the trenches at Petersburg. Moreover word arrived from Burnside just then that the mine was nearing completion. Grant wanted it timed to coincide with his projected offensive so that he could convert it from a limited move to keep Rebel troops at Petersburg into a decisive stroke to take the city.[15]

For the first time, nearly a month after Pleasants had begun to dig, the Union high command made a firm decision to use the mine in an offensive move. But Grant still wanted options at every phase of what would become the Third Offensive at Petersburg. Therefore he devised a complex plan that combined a flanking movement around the Confederate left, north of the James River, with a possible frontal attack following the mine explosion. If the flanking movement worked, there would be no need for the 9th Corps advance, and the mine could be exploded merely for effect. If the flanking movement failed, then Pleasants and Burnside might be able to deliver Petersburg into Grant's hands. All of this jelled in Grant's mind between July 17 and 24, but he waited until the night of the 24th before making a final decision to go ahead.[16]

Deep Bottom

Grant's plan for flanking Lee involved use of a bridgehead that had been established on the north side of the James at Deep Bottom, on a sharp curve in the river several miles from the Outer Line of the Richmond defenses. Chaffin's

Bluff, heavily fortified since 1862, was the anchor of the Outer Line. Two thousand men of the Army of the James, under Brig. Gen. Robert S. Foster, established the bridgehead on the night of June 20, digging a defensive line to protect the approach to a pontoon bridge that linked Foster with the south side. Lee wanted to eliminate Foster's bridgehead, but his local commanders realized the Federals were too heavily fortified for a direct attack, so they resorted to countermeasures to contain them. They constructed a new defensive position, called the New Market Line, from the Chaffin's Bluff works eastward toward New Market Heights, a tableland north of Deep Bottom, and to a point just west of Bailey's Creek, a stream that flowed southward toward the river's curve at Deep Bottom. The new line then turned northward and ran west of the creek toward a series of roads that connected Richmond with many points along the north shore of the James. Lee had few troops to man this New Market Line, but he could rapidly shift men into it as needed.[17]

The Confederates began to harass Foster's command and Union shipping on the James. Lt. Col. Thomas H. Carter positioned the four twenty-pounder Parrott rifles of Capt. Archibald Graham's Rockbridge Battery behind works at the foot of New Market Heights on the night of June 28, supported by Brig. Gen. Martin Gary's cavalry brigade. Graham opened fire on Union ships near Deep Bottom the next morning at the comparatively long range of two thousand yards. The artillery duel that followed led Carter to shift Graham half a mile to another position closer to his targets, at Tilghman's Gate. Graham also maintained a scattering fire on Foster's position. He again shifted his post on the night of June 30.[18]

This tactic only annoyed the Yankees; what was needed, if Lee's desire to get rid of Foster could be effected, was infantry. Lane's North Carolina brigade, under Brig. Gen. James Conner, and Brig. Gen. Samuel McGowan's South Carolina brigade left the lines at Petersburg on the evening of June 30 to move into the nearly vacant Outer Line north of Chaffin's Bluff. They reinforced the gunners in the forts and batteries, some cavalry, the Richmond City battalion, and some reserve regiments as the only Confederate troops north of the tidal stream.[19]

"I do not like the continuance of the enemy on the north side of the James River," Lee informed Lt. Gen. Richard S. Ewell, the commander in that area. But he could spare no more troops, and even warned Ewell that Conner and McGowan had to be ready to return to Petersburg if needed. He also could not spare heavy artillery to reach Deep Bottom more effectively from the New Market Line. Ewell stepped up Graham's activities, but it had no better effect than his earlier efforts. By July 20 Lee made a concerted effort to find more resources.[20]

Foster also engaged in some aggressive action of his own. He sent the 11th Maine to level the earthworks Graham had initially used. Located near the spot where the New Market Road crossed Bailey's Creek, the Maine troops quickly shoveled it in but were driven away when Confederate cavalry attacked on July 21. Knowing that it would interfere with Rebel communications along the north side of the river and protect his own position, Foster sent the 11th Maine back to retake the place the next day and dig in to hold it. Grant also was able to shift Col. Leonard D. H. Currie's brigade of the 19th Corps to the north side on July 23. Currie established positions at and near Tilghman's Gate to prevent the Rebels from using the place to fire on shipping.[21]

Lee felt compelled to counter these moves by shifting all of Kershaw's division, forty-two hundred men, to the north side on July 23. He told Kershaw to drive the Federals away. "We cannot afford to sit down in front of the enemy and allow him to intrench himself wherever he pleases," Lee instructed Ewell, adding that he could "ill spare" Kershaw's men from Petersburg. With Ewell's blessing, Kershaw took charge of the operation. First, a portion of his available troops attacked the 11th Maine in its position on the New Market Road just before midnight on July 24 and drove it back to the Deep Bottom defenses. On the 26th Kershaw sent Col. John W. Henagan's South Carolina brigade across Bailey Creek to drive in Currie's picket line at Tilghman's Gate. The 19th Corps troops fell back to a redoubt at nearby Curle's Neck.[22]

Grant Makes a Decision

These preliminary moves might have developed into a full-scale attack on Deep Bottom and Curle's Neck if Grant had not launched his Third Offensive. Events compelled him to make a move soon, because word arrived from Georgia on July 24 that Sherman had been fighting outside Atlanta for the past two days. Grant consulted with staff member Comstock about the best course to follow. Comstock talked with Meade and found out that Duane was sure the Confederates had established a second line behind Pegram's Salient. This led Comstock to urge Grant to strike west of the Jerusalem Plank Road, but the general in chief suggested a cavalry raid to tear up the Weldon and Petersburg Railroad, a major supply line for Lee from the south. When Comstock pointed out that Lee could be supplied by other railroads as well, Grant suggested operating north of the James and either hitting the railroads there or striking directly for the Confederate capital.[23]

Meade continued to believe that an attack at Pegram's Salient was inadvisable, yet he was willing to try it. He recommended that the 2nd and 9th Corps constitute the attacking force. Warren would have to hold down the Union left, for Meade feared the Confederates would try to outflank him if the attack failed. He also had to admit that conducting siege approaches was now a moot point. Meade still had not been able to bring up the necessary materials; even if they were readily available, sapping would not prevent Lee from dispatching troops to Georgia. The Federals would have to attack at Pegram's before the engineers reduced the Rebel guns at the Gregory House. Meade suggested they wait until the 6th Corps returned from Maryland so he could use it to outflank Lee and take the guns from the west. But that was not feasible because no one could predict when that corps might return.[24]

With the qualified willingness of his chief subordinate at Petersburg, Grant virtually ordered the preparations for a 9th Corps attack by spelling out his specifications for it. Burnside should mass his troops and those of the supporting corps for maximum punching power and push on through the breach created by the mine as far as possible. If he encountered too much resistance, he could retire to minimize losses. As much artillery as possible should be concentrated to support him, and corps commanders all along the line should prepare to exploit any success. The 18th Corps could be brought up to support Burnside, plus a division of the 10th Corps from Bermuda Hundred. Grant wanted the attack to take place in two days, on July 26; otherwise, he preferred to raid the Weldon and Petersburg Railroad as far south as the North Carolina line. "Whether we send an expedition on the road or assault at Petersburg Burnside's mine will be blown up," he concluded. Grant told Meade he would sleep on it and issue orders the next morning.[25]

A heavy rain fell on the night of July 24 as Grant pondered his decision, causing a great deal of discomfort for the troops along the line. Three regiments of the 9th Corps occupied low-lying trenches and "had to stand up . . . all night" because they were flooded. The miserable weather moderated at dawn, and Grant wasted no time in issuing directives that set the Third Offensive into motion. He opted for a major, complex movement rather than a simple frontal attack or an even simpler raid on the railroad. Maj. Gen. Winfield Hancock's 2nd Corps would use the bridgehead at Deep Bottom to threaten the anchor of Richmond's Outer Line at Chaffin's Bluff. While Hancock kept the Rebels occupied, Maj. Gen. Philip Sheridan would lead two cavalry divisions in a sweep around their left and tear up the Virginia Central Railroad, one of three rail lines linking Lee with supplies from the rest of the Confederacy. If Sheridan could make a dash through the Richmond defenses at a weak spot and capture the city, Hancock could push through to hold it. Otherwise, Sheridan would return to Deep Bottom. Burnside was also to ready the mine and prepare for a follow-through attack if either became necessary.[26]

Meade relayed instructions to Hancock and Sheridan. The 2nd Corps was due to start on the afternoon of the 26th and cross the Appomattox River on a pontoon bridge at Point of Rocks after dusk. Then Hancock had to march across Bermuda Hundred during the night and cross a newly laid pontoon bridge upstream from the mouth of Bailey's Creek at Deep Bottom. This would allow him to strike directly for Chaffin's Bluff instead of attacking the New Market Line. Meade ordered yet another pontoon bridge thrown across the Appomattox River at Broadway Landing to accommodate Sheridan's crossing, but the troopers would also utilize the older pontoon bridge at Deep Bottom. A bit of good news filtered in that day and on July 26. Confederate deserters claimed that there was no second line of works behind Pegram's Salient. Observations from a newly constructed signal tower led the high command to partially confirm this, although it appeared that there were detached works rather than a continuous line. The mood at Meade's and Grant's headquarters brightened with stronger hopes for Burnside's success.[27]

Confederate Preparations

As high level plans developed, Burnside reminded army headquarters on July 24 that the Rebels were actively countermining at Pegram's Salient. "We hope they will miss us, but we may be discovered," he warned. Moreover the Confederates had been busy planting ordnance behind the salient during the past month. Alexander acquired several twelve-pounder mortars and gave them to Capt. James N. Lamkin's Nelson Light Artillery, a Virginia battery. They were mostly planted along the Jerusalem Plank Road. It was general knowledge among the Rebels that the Yankees were digging under Pegram's guns. One day Beauregard and David B. Harris visited Lt. Col. Fitz William McMaster of the 17th South Carolina, in Elliott's brigade. McMaster's bombproof was only twenty yards from Pegram's emplacement, so he became alarmed when the two told him, "In a week's time they will blow us up here." Fortunately for him, McMaster's unit was moved, and he found new quarters seventy-five yards farther from the salient, thereby surviving the blast.[28]

No one worried about the security of this sector more than Bushrod Johnson. Suspicious that an attack was planned on Pegram's position, he required brigade leaders to report regularly on the condition of their earthworks and to recommend improvements. His division suffered losses of up to fifteen men a day from Union shelling and sniping. Elliott's men constructed sharpshooter loopholes with two-bushel sacks filled with dirt. They had to replace the sacks regularly because Federal sharpshooters tore them to shreds. Elliott's companies stood to from 1 A.M. to dawn every night in case of an attack.[29]

Johnson stretched his division to its limit and was able to take only one regiment out as a reserve. He devised a better plan to have each brigade hold one-fourth of its manpower in reserve and wanted to construct an earthwork well to the rear that was big enough for a battery and one regiment of each brigade to find shelter. This would constitute a line of detached reserve posts, not a continuous second line for the men to fall back to in case of attack. This worthy idea was not acted on before the Third Offensive, but Johnson lectured his subordinates that the line had to "be held at all hazards."[30]

The Confederates constructed a parapet a short distance behind Pegram's guns that would play a role in the battle. Beauregard later took credit for ordering the construction of the cavalier at Pegram's and for similar constructions at Gracie's and Colquitt's salients. Whether he deserved that credit is unknown, but Johnson thought it should have been extended all along the line instead of ending at the flanks of the battery positions. Large work details of up to a hundred men from Elliott's and Goode's brigades worked on it from at least June 29 on. The cavalier was about one hundred feet behind the exterior slope of the frontline parapet, at the farthest. Lt. Col. William H. Stewart of the 61st Virginia described it as an "irregular and ungraded embankment;" at ten feet in height, it overlooked the frontline parapet. By July 9 the cavalier was tall enough to be manned by two companies of Elliott's brigade on a regular basis. A Federal observer judged it to be "quite high and . . . rather formidable."[31]

Between the cavalier and the front line the ground was honeycombed with bombproofs and dugouts to shelter the men. Unlike the Federals, who normally constructed large shelters well behind the line, the Confederates tended to allow individuals to dig anywhere. Alexander described these excavations as "little caves and cellars in which all sorts of individual ingenuity was displayed in the arrangement of these sleeping & dodging places." They were a feature of every salient along the Confederate line. Between Pegram's guns and the cavalier, the Confederates cut up the ground into a maze of holes, providing an unintended obstacle to an attacker.[32]

4

DEEP BOTTOM

Hancock prepared thoroughly for the start of the Third Offensive. He kept his 2nd Corps troops in their camps all day July 26 so there would be no delays in starting them toward Deep Bottom late that afternoon. Brig. Gen. Francis C. Barlow's 1st Division led the way, followed by Brig. Gen. Gershom Mott's 3rd Division and John Gibbon's 2nd Division. Three batteries of artillery accompanied Barlow; the other two division commanders took only two. The rest of the artillery trailed behind the corps column, guarded by a detached brigade. The men were told that if they fell into Confederate hands, they were "to give only their names and regiments, and no information which will disclose the strength of the command."[1]

Maj. Gen. Benjamin F. Butler, whose Army of the James controlled this area, provided guides to direct Hancock's men to Deep Bottom, and Duane supplied maps of the route. Barlow left promptly at 4 P.M., and Mott departed an hour later after his men were issued four days' rations and sixty rounds of ammunition. The troops crossed the Appomattox on a pontoon bridge at Point of Rocks and then marched across Bermuda Hundred in the dark, their way lighted by fires Butler's troops built along the road. They took ten-minute rest breaks every hour.[2]

Hancock rode ahead to meet Sheridan at Foster's headquarters at about midnight. Here he learned some disturbing news. Foster informed him that Lee had by now massed seven brigades in the area, and they were well entrenched from Chaffin's Bluff to New Market Heights. The Confederate defenses were formidable, according to Foster. "They will take time to take," Hancock informed Meade, "and the operation will lose the character of a surprise." Instead of attacking Chaffin's Bluff directly, Hancock suggested he capture New Market Heights and hold the line of Bailey's Creek while Sheridan rode off to his mission. Then Hancock could try to advance to Chaffin's if possible. This meant that the infantry as well as the cavalry needed to cross the lower pontoon bridge, because the upper bridge gave access only to the front of the New Market Line, which Hancock hoped to outflank. Meade wired his approval of this plan at 2:15 A.M., July 27. The lower pontoon bridge, laid only a few hours before by Butler's engineers, now had to bear the entire traffic of the Deep Bottom offensive. Barlow began to cross at 2:45 A.M., soon followed by Mott. Sheridan's troopers, now reinforced by Butler's lone cavalry division under Brig. Gen. August V. Kautz, had to wait for the infantrymen. Foster's men had spread hay and reeds on the bridge so the sound of tramping feet and hooves would not carry across the waters of the James to anxious ears in the New Market Line.[3]

Foster also helped Hancock, Sheridan, and Kautz by trying to reoccupy Tilghman's Gate. The 11th Maine and 10th Connecticut advanced toward the objective but were unable to attain Currie's former position. They planted themselves seventy-five yards from New Market Road and fifty yards from Graham's former artillery emplacement, where the men could fire on troop movements along the road.[4]

The series of small, obscure movements near Deep Bottom changed into a pitched battle early on the morning of July 27 as the 2nd Corps and Sheridan's and Kautz's cavalry deployed for action. The New Market Line, facing south from Chaffin's Bluff to New Market Heights, was complete. But the extension of it northward along the west side of Bailey's Creek was barely started. The Confederates had cleared a deep field of fire in front of it, about one thousand yards between the base of the heights and the stream, but there was only a crude, shallow trench west of the cleared area. The projected line ran northward far enough to intersect the Darbytown and Charles City roads. If Hancock could move swiftly enough to cross the James and advance northwest across Bailey's Creek, he could gain New Market Heights and have a clear way to Chaffin's Bluff.[5]

High-Level Plans

As the three infantry and three cavalry divisions prepared to move north of the river, Meade worried that the Confederates might intercept Pleasants's gallery. If so, he anticipated exploding it without a follow-up attack as early as 4 P.M. on July 27 but hoped Burnside could preserve it for future use. Burnside did not think the Rebels were about to break into the gallery, but he worried that the left branch might cave in because of the shock of Pegram's gunfire overhead. Pleasants directed that additional shoring be added to counteract this effect. Meade soon felt confident enough to recommend that Pleasants save his mine for a follow-up attack. He also instructed Burnside to submit a plan detailing how the mine would be exploded and how his corps would conduct the advance.[6]

Burnside soon put his plan into the hands of Capt. Francis M. Bache for delivery to Meade's headquarters. He detailed Pleasants's idea for eight magazines and from 9,600 to 11,200 pounds of powder, intending to park the powder wagons in woods one mile away to lessen the chance of a Confederate artillery round setting them afire. Burnside wanted to use the two brigades of his black division to spearhead the attack, placing them in "double column closed in mass." The head of each brigade would rest in the forward line at the horseshoe. After passing through the gap blown in the Rebel line, the lead regiment of each brigade was to wheel right or left and sweep along the rear of the adjoining Confederate trench to widen the gap, while the rest of each brigade advanced to the crest of the ridge behind Pegram's Salient, gaining the Jerusalem Plank Road. The white divisions of the 9th Corps were to follow. If successful, Burnside hoped to send his black troops into the town itself, so they could garner the credit for its capture. He rated their chances of success as "more than even."[7]

Meade's signal officers detected signs of Rebel troop movements to the north side of the James River, and reports in the *Richmond Examiner* also seemed to confirm that Lee was shifting manpower. Grant was encouraged. He thought that either Hancock could break through at Deep Bottom or Lee would weaken the Petersburg line so much that the 9th Corps could succeed. By midafternoon on July 26, Grant instructed Meade to have Burnside prepare to spring the mine and attack, but he would give final authorization after further developments.[8]

Meade was willing, but he felt uncomfortable unless the 2nd Corps could support Burnside. "It is not the numbers of the enemy which oppose our taking Petersburg," he wrote Grant, "it is their artillery and their works which can be held by reduced numbers against direct assault." Meade needed more troops to protect the 9th Corps artillery because Burnside would have to use all his available manpower in the assault. He wanted to keep Warren's 5th Corps in place to Burnside's left to anchor the army's left flank and suppress Rebel batteries that could enfilade the attacking units. The 18th Corps was needed to cover the rest of the Union line. By the night of July 26, Grant admitted that there appeared to be so many Confederate troops streaming to Chaffin's Bluff that Hancock likely would not be able to break through. If so, the 2nd Corps could be withdrawn during the night of the 27th and brought back in time to support the mine attack.[9]

In the middle of all this planning, Grant received his first indication that Abraham Lincoln wanted to confer with him about the situation in Maryland, where Union authorities were trying to coordinate disparate units to deal with Jubal Early. Grant understood the necessity for such a conference, but begged to postpone it at least until after July 29. "I am commencing movements tonight from which I hope favorable results," he informed Secretary of War Edwin M. Stanton. "They may have the effect of drawing the enemy back from Maryland." He informed Stanton of his plan to send the entire 19th Corps to the area as well.[10]

July 27

Even before Barlow's division stepped off the pontoon bridge at Deep Bottom, the Union high command had come to hold limited hope that Hancock could achieve anything north of the James. The 2nd Corps deployed in an area called Strawberry Plains, owing to its flat, cleared nature, soon after reaching the north bank. Barlow held the left, his left flank touching the swampy bottomland of Bailey's Creek near its junction with the river. Mott was positioned to his right, and Gibbon stood in reserve to the rear. With the cavalry deploying to Hancock's right and rear, Barlow's and Mott's skirmishers moved forward.[11]

The Confederates had already established a new position to oppose Hancock, consisting of three brigades that had moved across Bailey's Creek and aligned themselves along the southern side of the New Market Road. Brig. Gen. Benjamin G. Humphreys commanded all the troops in the area during Kershaw's temporary absence. Humphreys placed his own Mississippi brigade east of the creek facing south. Henagan's South Carolina brigade aligned to its left, but there was space allowed for Graham's Rockbridge Battery between them. These two infantry brigades fielded twenty-four hundred men in all, but they were supported by Gary's North Carolina cavalry brigade. Hancock marshaled more than thirteen thousand infantry to oppose Humphreys.[12]

The Union soldiers pushed the Confederates back quickly, and mostly by their skirmish line. Col. James C. Lynch led Barlow's skirmishers, consisting of the 183rd Pennsylvania, 28th Massachusetts, and 26th Michigan. They stalled partway in their advance toward the Rebels. Just then, the left wing of Mott's skirmish line redirected its advance to aim more pointedly at Graham's guns, and this compelled Henagan to adjust his right wing to more properly face it. This maneuver created a gap of about fifty yards in the center of the Rebel position, and Lynch's skirmishers exploited it. They captured Graham's four twenty-pounder Parrotts, along with his caissons and ammunition chests. Humphreys pulled back both brigades, recrossing Bailey's Creek and taking position in the partially constructed extension of the New Market Line northward.[13]

Graham blamed the loss of his artillery on Henagan, claiming the infantry "gave way without making an effort to save the guns." He suffered only one

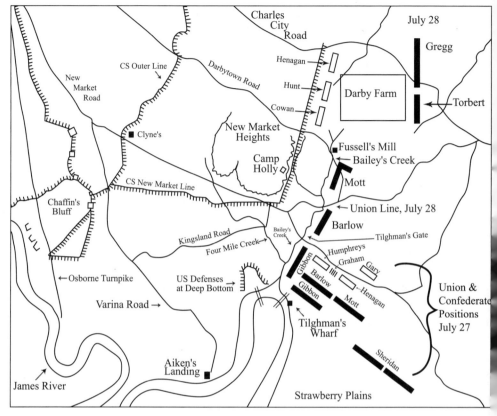

First Deep Bottom

casualty, but the supporting units lost fifty-five men. Ironically all four of the Confederate guns had once belonged to the Union. One of them had been taken when Stonewall Jackson captured Harpers Ferry in September 1862, and the other three when Ewell captured Winchester in June 1863.[14]

Some of Foster's men played a small role in the capture of Graham's battery. The 10th Connecticut continued to hold the advanced position gained the previous day, close to the New Market Road but out of the way of Hancock's advance. The men fired at Graham's position enough to prevent the Rebels from using their horses to evacuate the guns. The 11th Maine rested at Strawberry Plains on the morning of July 27, where its men had a close view of both Hancock and Sheridan. Everyone from this vantage point could see, off in the distance, the action of Lynch's skirmishers as they advanced, but the Maine soldiers were more interested in gaping at these two famous generals. "Both sat their horses as only perfect horsemen and hard riders can," recalled the historian of the 11th Maine, "and both puffed away at their cigars, and both seemed as flattered as amused by the admiring glances and the not always low-spoken remarks of our men."[15]

Hancock followed up his success with a slow left wheel to bring the corps to the east side of Bailey's Creek, a process that took nearly all morning. When completed, the corps faced west with Gibbon anchoring the left, Barlow in the center, and Mott holding the right. Mott had the longest route to wheel, and he also had to refuse his right flank to protect against any Confederates lurking to the north. Gibbon established a picket line to link his left with the James River at Deep Bottom. Sheridan's cavalry also moved forward, but not to ride for the railroads. The troopers rode north until hitting the Darbytown Road, and then they advanced along it toward Richmond while protecting Hancock's right. They found Confederate troops behind crude earthworks on the west side of Bailey's Creek but did not push against them. After a morning of careful positioning, Hancock announced that he was almost ready to move against the Confederate line west of Bailey's Creek by noon.[16]

But Hancock had little confidence in his chances of success. As early as 7:30 A.M., he had concluded that the Rebels had not been surprised by his arrival north of the James and doubted if he could cross Bailey's Creek, much less drive on to Chaffin's Bluff. Hancock possessed little information about the strength and position of the enemy, and artillery fire coming from the north indicted that the Rebel line extended some distance farther than his own line, which was about a mile long. Hancock suggested that Sheridan might set out immediately and try his best, even though the infantry was not in a good position to support him. Meanwhile he laid plans to extend the Union line northward to find the Confederate flank and turn it. Hancock estimated that one-third of his manpower was not yet available because of heavy straggling the previous night. Meade was unwilling to authorize Sheridan's advance and deferred that decision to Grant, who was already on his way to Deep Bottom. Meade sagely advised Hancock that, if he could not cross Bailey's Creek that morning, he certainly would not be able to do it later.[17]

Hancock and Sheridan preferred to have direct instructions from Grant before launching a major attack across Bailey's Creek. Cyrus Comstock, Grant's aide-de-camp, had arrived at 7 A.M., a bit after the capture of Graham's guns. He later reported to Grant, "It is thought the chance of surprise is over." Another one of the lieutenant general's staff officers, Horace Porter, visited Hancock that morning and found him resting as his corps slowly advanced to the creek. Porter assured Hancock that Grant was on his way.[18]

Grant reached the vicinity of Deep Bottom by about 1 P.M. but rode around for two hours without finding Hancock. He wrote instructions for him and then returned to City Point. Grant fully accepted the fact that it was impossible to advance to Chaffin's Bluff, but he still hoped the 2nd Corps might find and turn the Confederate left. This would allow Sheridan to set off on his raid. If it was not possible to turn the flank, then Hancock was to remain until further orders. Grant also requested the corps leader to send him duplicate copies of his dispatches to Meade so he could keep in touch with developments. Hancock assured Grant that he was trying to extend northward and turn the Rebel flank, but his men were exhausted from their night march.[19]

The Confederates had barely enough men north of the James to meet the Federal challenge. Ewell commanded about six thousand miscellaneous and largely second-class troops in the area, but he cooperated with the one and a half divisions Lee had already sent to help him. Ewell was responsible for holding the New Market Line from Chaffin's Bluff to a point nearly to New Market Heights. Conner, temporarily commanding Lane's and McGowan's brigades of Wilcox's division, and Kershaw's four brigades held the line from there and up the northward extension west of Bailey's Creek. Kershaw's troops moved to Conner's left to further extend the line northward. Ewell tried to call out the Local Defense Troops, but Secretary of War James A. Seddon warned him that this would greatly disrupt government work because so many of them were employees.[20]

By the latter part of the afternoon, Sheridan reported that the Rebel left ended at Fussell's Mill, just north of the Darbytown Road. The Confederates had cavalry on the Charles City Road as well. Hancock could not position his infantry for a turning movement before the end of the day, but he tested the Rebel line opposite his left wing and found it too strong for an assault. Sheridan believed he could head for the railroad if he went by way of yet another thoroughfare, the Long Bridge Road, and crossed the Chickahominy River at Bottom's Bridge. Hancock began preparations to support this move but canceled them when word arrived from City Point that night. Grant did not feel comfortable sending off Sheridan, because Hancock would not be able to support his return to the army from his present location. He wanted the infantry to wait and to try to turn the Confederate flank the next day. Brig. Gen. Henry W. Birge's brigade of the 19th Corps received orders to cross the lower pontoon bridge at dawn on July 28 to support Hancock, and Foster planned to demonstrate from his bridgehead upstream from the mouth of Bailey's Creek to draw some Confederate attention away from the 2nd Corps.[21]

Thus ended the first day of operations at Deep Bottom. Hancock lost ninety-five men that day and did little except to define the Confederate position that barred his way. Meade informed Burnside that he should not hurry with the tamping and priming of the mine, because it would not be exploded until after July 28, and Grant informed Washington that the limited gains of the day were mostly owing to the exhaustion of Hancock's infantrymen.[22]

The only promising development for the Federals was that Lee further stripped his line south of the river by dispatching Maj. Gen. Henry Heth's division and ordering his 1st Corps commander, Lt. Gen. Richard H. Anderson, to take charge of all troops north of the James. He also sent two cavalry divisions led by Maj. Gen. Fitzhugh Lee and Maj. Gen. William H. F. Lee. Anderson arrived at Chaffin's Bluff a little after dusk on July 27. Lee had instructed him to attack, if possible, and he immediately began to make preparations. While Heth covered the New Market Line from Chaffin's to New Market Heights, Kershaw moved four brigades farther to the left along Bailey's Creek. In this way they could extend farther north than Hancock's line and perhaps envelope the Union right. Far from pushing on to Chaffin's Bluff, Hancock would be forced into a defensive battle the next day.[23]

July 28

Hancock was not certain what to do on July 28, even though Birge's brigade, twenty-six hundred strong, had reached Deep Bottom at 6 A.M. He discovered that the Rebel line stretched two and a half miles northward, longer than his own. This meant that Hancock would have to pull most of his left wing out of position to advance around it, uncovering Tilghman's Wharf and endangering his connection with the south side of the James. Birge's brigade would have to compensate. Hancock displayed little enthusiasm for his prospects, asking Meade, "Is the turning movement an absolute one, or am I to make the movement at my discretion?" Meade refused to answer directly, referring Hancock to Grant's orders, but he also allowed the corps leader to be guided by his own judgment. For his part, Grant informed Meade that if Hancock could not achieve anything decisive that morning, he should pull back to Petersburg that night to help Burnside. The cavalry, Foster, and Birge could continue to hold Rebel attention at Deep Bottom.[24]

The Federals had worried Lee into ordering offensive action at Deep Bottom. The Confederates finished their preparations for an attack early on the morning of July 28, initially planning to use four brigades from Kershaw's and Wilcox's divisions. For unknown reasons, one of Kershaw's brigades failed to take part. Lane's North Carolina brigade of Wilcox's division (commanded by Col. Robert Cowan), McGowan's South Carolina brigade of Wilcox's division (commanded by Lt. Col. J. F. Hunt), and Henagan's South Carolina brigade of Kershaw's division moved northward past the Confederate left flank at Fussell's Mill onto ground previously held by the cavalry. They aligned with Cowan on the right, Hunt to his left, and Henagan on the far left. Conner commanded the attack force, which was poised to advance between the Darbytown and Charles City roads against Sheridan's cavalry.[25]

Cowan sent a reinforced skirmish line ahead to pave the way at midmorning. It pushed back the startled Union pickets nearly to the main Federal line, and then Conner gave the order for his three brigades to advance at about 10 A.M. They encountered terrain that utterly disrupted their formations, plodding through a dense woods for two hundred yards before encountering a crossroad that veered sharply to the left. Hunt's Carolinians veered left, too, crowding together into a dense column. Then they encountered a marsh along a branch that drained northeast toward White Oak Swamp, which further dislocated their alignment. A serious gap developed between Hunt and Cowan, because the latter also had to negotiate the marsh. Despite all this, the veterans of Hunt's brigade entered the cornfield of the Darby Farm and pushed across to threaten the main Federal line.[26]

Here Conner achieved some degree of success, confronting mostly Brig. Gen. Alfred T. A. Torbert's 1st Division of Sheridan's Cavalry Corps. The Federals had been alerted to danger by their skirmishers and were "massed and standing to horse" along the low ground of another branch that flowed northeast toward White Oak Swamp. The higher ground of the Darby Farm, with its cornfield, house, and outbuildings, lay between the branches. They received small-arms fire from Conner's men and fell back a short distance to the higher ground east of the branch valley. Here the troopers took shelter behind the shallow crest and prepared to receive their unwelcome visitors. All of the Federals got out of Conner's immediate grasp, but one gun, belonging to Lt. W. N. Dennison's Battery A, 2nd U.S. Light Artillery, was left behind when its horses were shot. Dennison ordered his men to pull it by hand, calling on the 10th New York Cavalry to help, but there was not enough time. The battery and the 10th New York Cavalry belonged to Brig. Gen. Henry E. Davies's brigade of Brig. Gen. David McM. Gregg's 2nd Division.[27]

Hunt's South Carolina brigade was ahead of its comrades to right and left, emerging onto the Darby Farm before anyone else. The beginning of rifle fire from the main Union line caused it to halt in the open expanse of the farmstead, but not before the 12th and 13th South Carolina took possession of Dennison's abandoned gun. The brigade was in desperate need of time to realign so it could navigate the open expanse and hit the Federal position with controlled discipline, but time was not available. Conner and Hunt wanted the men to continue forward immediately, but the increasingly heavy Union fire caused more confusion as it ripped into Hunt's exposed right flank. This caused his two rightmost regiments, the 1st and 14th South Carolina, to lose cohesion. They were "so mixed that you could scarcely distinguish them apart. Companies completely assimilated." Only the timely arrival of Cowan, advancing to Hunt's right, diverted Union fire and allowed Hunt to continue his movement forward. But the Carolinians of both brigades were advancing into a heavy fire on open ground. Hunt again kept ahead of Cowan and managed to reach a point about one hundred yards short of Darby's house and outbuildings before his men decided they could go no farther. Cowan's men halted well back of that point.[28]

A gap of some two hundred yards existed between the two brigades, and Torbert's men took advantage of it. The 6th and 9th New York Cavalry and the 17th Pennsylvania Cavalry of Col. Thomas C. Devin's 2nd Brigade dismounted and counterattacked into that gap, turning Hunt's right flank and compelling the Rebels to retreat after pouring in fire at close range with revolvers. "It was a pleasant sight to see those great, tall Carolinians go across that field on a hen canter," recalled the historian of the 9th New York Cavalry. Trooper Wesley W. Darling wrote home that "they . . . soon showed us the bottoms of their feet." Cowan was hit by fire on his right flank as well, and his men also fell back. Conner was mortified; he fired at the Yankees with his pistol and lost two horses shot under him in the retreat.[29]

The Confederates pulled back in considerable disorder. Augustin E. Shore of the 33rd North Carolina put it bluntly when he informed his brother and sister that "we had our asses whip off us if the truth was knone." Although Hunt's left wing stopped now and then to cover the retreat, it was with difficulty that officers rallied their troops in the vicinity of Fussell's Mill. J. F. J. Caldwell of the 1st South Carolina complained that the "general carelessness of officers, and the excitement and stubbornness of the men, had lost us what should have been a brilliant success." Exactly what role Henagan played in this attack is unclear, for there are no accounts of his brigade's action. Apparently he advanced through wooded terrain north of the Darby Farm and encountered the rest of Davies's brigade of Gregg's division, making little headway before his men were forced to retreat. By noon Conner's promising attack had ended in failure. Hunt alone lost 239 men, and Cowan suffered 138 casualties. Henagan's losses were never reported, but overall Confederate casualties amounted to at least 377 men and three Rebel flags. Sheridan lost about 200 troopers.[30]

The only benefit of Conner's attack was that it diverted Hancock from his tentative plan to assume the offensive. Indications of a Rebel move began to filter into 2nd Corps headquarters at 8 A.M., but confirmation of the attack did not reach Hancock until a staff officer arrived from Sheridan with the news at 10:50. Hancock ordered Gibbon to support the cavalry, but Gibbon also was told to send staff officers to scout the roads he would have to take. Half an hour later, Hancock confronted Gibbon about wasting time, and the division leader blamed it on contradictory orders. One of Hancock's staff officers confirmed Gibbon's story. The incident embarrassed and frustrated Hancock and was the beginning of a series of misunderstandings between him and Gibbon that resulted in the latter's request to be transferred from the 2nd Corps in the early fall. Gibbon brought his division to the battlefield just after the attack ended and relieved Torbert's cavalry between the Darbytown and Charles City roads.[31]

The steam had burned out of the Union offensive at Deep Bottom. Hancock moved Barlow's division to the Charles City Road, where he fully expected another Rebel onslaught and planned to fall back to Strawberry Plains and protect the pontoon crossing at Tilghman's Wharf if needed. He had asked Foster to push forward his planned demonstration west of Bailey's Creek when news of Conner's attack reached 2nd Corps headquarters. Foster skirmished up to the New Market Line in several places, but he did nothing more because he received word from one of Butler's staff officers that Hancock probably would not attack anyway. There was more shifting of infantry and cavalry units that afternoon to strengthen the Federal posture.[32]

On July 28 Grant devoted most of his attention to projected operations south of the river. He asked Meade if it was possible to finish preparations so that Burnside could attack the next morning. The army commander still wanted Hancock to support the move and suggested that the 2nd Corps rest on July 29 before moving south of the river that night, and then the attack could go in on the 30th. Hunt also needed more time to place guns and mortars. Grant was willing to wait, but he decided that one of Hancock's divisions should withdraw from Deep Bottom that night while the rest, plus Sheridan's cavalry, remained one more day to hold the Confederate troops in place. Grant, Meade, and some of their staff members set out for Deep Bottom by boat on the afternoon of July 28 to gauge the situation and tell Hancock of their plans. They reached his headquarters at 5 P.M. for a brief visit, then returned to the south side.[33]

On the Confederate line west of Bailey's Creek, Anderson waited for more troops before attempting another attack. Fitz Lee's cavalry sent out reconnoitering parties to find the Union right flank as Maj. Gen. Charles W. Field's division began to arrive that afternoon. Anderson planned a larger attack by Field to take place on the morning of July 30.[34]

While preparing to move Mott's division from Deep Bottom on the night of July 28, Hancock asked that fires be built along the road crossing Bermuda Hundred. Butler took offense to a hastily worded message from Comstock that Hancock's men had suffered while marching along that road on the night of July 26. Butler's engineer, Brig. Gen. Godfrey Weitzel, nevertheless promised to survey the route and map the location of every stump. "I doubt if there are ten on the whole six miles of road," he informed Comstock. "I will have it carefully cleaned up if anything is found."[35]

Mott moved out at 7:30 P.M. and began to march across the pontoon bridge at Tilghman's Wharf an hour and a half later. After a weary night, his men reached the Petersburg line by dawn of July 29. They relieved a good portion of the 18th Corps, with Mott's left flank touching the far right of Burnside's corps. Foster was afraid that the Confederates might discover how weakly the Federals held the two bridgeheads after the rest of Hancock's and all of Sheridan's men left. Tenth Corps commander Maj. Gen. David B. Birney assured him that his own brigade and that of Birge could hold both bridgeheads with the help of the Federal gunboats.[36]

"We have failed in what I had hoped to accomplish," Grant informed Halleck, "that is, to surprise the enemy, and get on to their roads with the cavalry near to Richmond and destroy them out to South Anna." But he expressed hope that he could turn "this diversion to account, so as to yield greater results than if the first object had been accomplished." Meanwhile Grant and Lincoln agreed to discuss the Maryland situation at Fortress Monroe on the morning of July 31.[37]

July 29

Hancock acted on the defensive all day on July 29. The Federals knew that Heth and Field had been shifted to the north side of the James and there was every reason to expect an attack. Hancock had been cautioned to position his men in a compact formation so the gunboats could fire along his front. Nevertheless the grand tactical situation greatly favored the Unionists. Grant reported to Meade that Lee was "piling everything, except a very thin line in your front, to the north side of the river." Francis Walker, one of Hancock's staff officers, later estimated that five-eighths of Lee's army had been shifted to the north side by July 29, leaving only three divisions to hold the Petersburg line.[38]

That boded well for Burnside, but it also meant that Hancock had to endure a tense day at Deep Bottom as bait. He had only two divisions of his own corps, plus Sheridan's cavalry and Birge's brigade of the 19th Corps. Foster could offer only marginal support from his bridgehead west of Bailey's Creek. The 2nd Corps commander ordered Sheridan (who had been placed under Hancock's direct command the day before) to move large numbers of troopers across open ground to fool the enemy into thinking there was a Federal attack in the making. For the rest of his command, Hancock concentrated on digging fieldworks. Another wedge was driven between Hancock and Gibbon when Hancock lost his temper over a slight error in the placement of one section of the 2nd Division line. Hancock insulted Gibbon, who had personally laid out the fortification, in front of many other generals. Although

Gibbon was able to explain why the error was not serious, and Hancock later apologized to the other officers, the formerly cordial relations between the two men were never reconstructed.[39]

All efforts now at Grant's and Meade's headquarters were geared toward Burnside's attack the next day. Grant fully informed Butler of the general outline on July 29, because some degree of participation by the 18th Corps was necessary. Grant also suggested that Foster level the Confederate works Hancock had captured on July 27 and concentrate his small force inside the bridgehead covering the upper pontoon bridge. The lower pontoon bridge at Tilghman's Wharf was to be dismantled, indicating Grant's plan to send Birge's brigade to Maryland with the rest of the 19th Corps.[40]

Butler's staff and engineer officers had managed to clear Hancock's road of stumps, so they reported, and had arranged for guides as well as for fires to be lit along the way. The 2nd Corps began to cross at Tilghman's Wharf at 8:30 P.M., with Gibbon in the lead, and was fully over by 11:15 P.M. The march across Bermuda Hundred was difficult. The night was unusually dark and several men were hurt when they tripped over stumps. The road was dusty and there was no opportunity to wander off and find water. Hancock's men straggled a great deal despite rumors that ran along the marching column regarding the mine to be blown up at dawn.[41]

Gibbon reached a point to the rear of Mott's division by 3:45 A.M. of July 30, with the rest of Hancock's men trailing in by dawn. Mott had already gathered enough information about this sector of the line to tell Hancock that the Confederate line opposite was very strong.[42]

The Confederates had been fooled into believing that Grant meant to make a single, major effort at Deep Bottom. On the morning of July 30, when the mine exploded and thousands of Federal troops tried to rush through the hole in Johnson's line, Field moved out north of Fussell's Mill only to find that the Yankees had gone. Edward Porter Alexander wrote that Grant's unexpected move left nearly six Confederate divisions "at Deep Bottom with their thumbs to suck." Ewell admitted to his wife that he was baffled. "The movements of the Yankees are incomprehensible on any grounds I can give," he told her. He half seriously predicted that "they are about to try some previously unheard of plan of taking Richmond, by balloons or underwater, or . . . they may suddenly appear in some quarter impossible under every rule that usually governs troops."[43]

Lee began to shift most of the units back to the south side of the James; Heth went to Petersburg, Kershaw to Bermuda Hundred, and the two cavalry divisions also rode southward. Only Field was left to hold the area along with Ewell's men. Before this took place, the Petersburg line was held by only three divisions, Johnson's and Hoke's of Beauregard's command and Mahone's of the Army of Northern Virginia. Opposing them were three corps of the Army of the Potomac and one of the Army of the James.[44]

The operations at Deep Bottom involved a total of 28,303 Federal troops, with losses of 488 men over three days. Only 192 of those casualties belonged to the 2nd Corps; most of the rest were suffered by Sheridan's cavalrymen while dealing with the Rebel attack on July 28. The Confederates employed a total of 16,984 men, losing at least 635 of them. The operation started with the promise of a breakthrough for Grant, but it became merely a side show to the main event, the explosion of Pleasants's mine and the attack by Burnside's 9th Corps.[45]

5

PREPARING, JULY 27–29

Grant operated on two tracks while managing the Third Offensive. First he wanted to see if Hancock and Sheridan could make something of their strike north of the James River. If not, Burnside's mine could pave the way for a frontal attack on the Petersburg lines. Even if the Hancock-Sheridan offensive proved successful, Grant wanted Burnside to spring the mine with no follow-up attack.

Charging the Mine

Until he could tell whether operations north of the James were working, Grant instructed Meade to prepare for anything. The materials for charging the mine were not readily available. As early as July 15 Lt. Morris Schaff of Meade's staff had control of 12,000 pounds of powder at Grant's headquarters at City Point, but the fuse was still on its way from the engineer depot at New York. Burnside believed he could ready the mine quickly as soon as the powder and fuse reached the site.[1]

Burnside also suggested leaving both branches free of tamping and filling up only the first one hundred feet of the gallery with material. From 1,200 to 1,400 pounds of powder would fill each magazine, using up to 11,200 pounds of the available material at City Point. Burnside suggested using a wooden trough of powder to connect the magazines and up to six strands of fuse and two wires (the latter for electrical detonation) running through the main gallery. He requested eight thousand sandbags for the tamping, wanting to fill them immediately and stockpile the lot while waiting for the powder. He further requested four lengths of fuse, each six hundred feet long, enough to make four separate fuses running the entire length of the main gallery.[2]

Burnside wanted to create a big crater without steep sides, thereby opening a wider breach in Confederate lines, and he thought he could use 12,000 pounds of powder without endangering Federal troops near the mine. John Gibbon had accompanied Meade while visiting Burnside one day before the onset of the Third Offensive, and the 9th Corps commander spoke enthusiastically about the huge amount of powder, which would make it a "sure thing." Gibbon knew that too much powder could react negatively in its effect, but Burnside persisted. When leaving, Gibbon remarked to Meade that Burnside had a tendency "to be carried away," mixed with another tendency "to trust too many things *to chance,* exemplified by a favorite expression of his, "Trust to luck."[3]

The powder request was the first thing army headquarters turned down. Duane knew that Burnside was asking for too much, but he wanted to see if there was a precedent to justify it. He obtained "the mining records before Sebastopol," as Theodore Lyman put it. "Finding nothing there, he said the book was a humbug, and determined on 8000 lbs." Meade supported Duane's decision, and his chief of staff informed Burnside on the evening of July 26 that the powder and eight thousand sandbags were on their way. Meade also arranged for three thousand feet of fuse to be shipped to Burnside.[4]

The last flurry of activity on the mine began with the installation of the "hopper like boxes," which served as magazines. They were carried into the mine on July 27 in two parts, a square box to be placed on the floor and a hopper to fit on top of it. The troughs of powder connecting the magazines met at the forward end of the main gallery.[5]

The powder arrived on July 27 in 320 kegs, 25 pounds in each keg. The wagon train carrying it parked a mile to the rear of 9th Corps headquarters. Burnside wanted to wait until dusk before carrying it into the mine so the men would not draw enemy fire. Meade thought this was unnecessary, but Pleasants compromised and waited until 4 P.M. to begin the process. Capt. Charles E. Mallam, a volunteer aide on Burnside's staff, was put in charge of 180 men who were detailed from regiments in Potter's division to carry the "large, coarse blasting powder" into the gallery. Potter intended to find sticks stout enough for them to carry the kegs, or muskets if sticks were not available, but Pleasants devised a better method. His men emptied the powder from the kegs into bags to be slung over the shoulder. This enabled them to walk faster and stoop to be less visible. The detailed men carried bags of powder to the mouth of the gallery where members of the 48th Pennsylvania moved them to the branches. They charged the right branch by 9 P.M., and the left an hour later, after six hours of hard work.[6]

Pleasants supervised the tamping, using 150 men of the 48th Pennsylvania. Although Burnside had suggested it stretch one hundred feet back from the forward end of the gallery, Pleasants emplaced only thirty-four feet of sandbags in the gallery and ten feet in the beginning of each branch. He left the air space

Charging the mine. LC-USZ62–14653, Library of Congress

between the magazines unobstructed to ensure a supply of oxygen for proper detonation. The fifty-four feet of tamping consisted of eight thousand sandbags filled with dirt, with logs interspersed among them. The air in the gallery was "becoming very bad, so much so as to make it difficult for the men to work." After eight hours, Pleasants finished the tamping at 6 P.M., July 28.[7]

The final touch was the placement of the fuse. Duane had described several different types of fuses in his engineering manual. A powder hose (often called a Gomez fuse) was a linen tube filled with powder and protected by a wooden case. It could be run along the floor or along the wall of the gallery under the tamping and was ignited by lighting a piece of port fire stuck into the end. Duane recommended smearing some clay or dirt on the port fire so sparks would not ignite stray powder. A more advanced form of fuse was known as the Bickford fuse. It consisted of gunpowder "enveloped in the strands of a rope" and soaked in "a peculiar composition." Bickford's invention burned slowly and safely, even under water. But the most advanced form of detonation involved electricity generated by a voltaic battery. It was so new that the bugs were not yet worked out; the main problem involved transmitting the electrical charge evenly to different accumulations of powder.[8]

Burnside received the simplest, most standard kind of fuse. Pleasants later admitted that he knew little of fuses, but he found it was usable as long as it was not spliced. The fuse arrived in segments only ten to fifteen feet long, however, necessitating many splices. Because he had asked for something better than "common blasting fuze," Pleasants assumed there was nothing else available at City Point or Fortress Monroe, as no one in the eastern theater had yet exploded a mine.[9]

Pleasants "half filled" the wooden troughs connecting the magazines and constructed two additional wooden troughs out of pine lumber, making them six inches square, which cradled the fuses along the length of the gallery. The troughs were half filled with powder too. These two troughs continued under the tamping part way down the gallery until they emerged from under the sandbags. From there, Pleasants ran three fuse lines with no powder for ninety-eight feet. Each fuse line was segmented into ten-foot lengths, requiring at least thirty-six splices. By 9 P.M. on July 28, Burnside was able to report that the mine was ready.[10]

Planning the Attack

Just as Pleasants began to charge the mine, Burnside submitted a plan of attack to army headquarters. He wanted to spring the mine "just before daylight," or alternatively at 5 P.M., and spearhead the attack with his black division formed in two brigade columns. The leading regiments of each brigade were to conduct a somewhat complicated maneuver as soon as they passed through the gap in the enemy works. The regiment heading the right brigade would sharply turn right and form a battle line perpendicular to the Rebel line. This had to be done by wheeling the companies to the right, with each successive wave of companies extending the line to the left so the entire regiment could deploy into line. It was then to sweep northward and widen the breach as much as possible. The leading regiment of the left brigade was to do the same toward the south. The rest of the 4th Division would move straight forward and gain the crest of the ridge as fast as possible, to be followed by the white divisions of the corps. All of Burnside's troops would have to be relieved of their place in line well before the attack, and Burnside wanted help from other corps to hold the ridge after it was taken. He intended to use his own men to exploit success, sending the black regiments directly into Petersburg.[11]

Burnside's plan had germinated for at least three weeks. Ferrero had developed the details for his part in it soon after Burnside told him he wanted his black troops to lead. Burnside showed Ferrero the ground, and the two mapped

out staging areas for the entire corps. Staff officers also inspected the black regiments and recommended the best ones to lead each brigade.[12]

Ferrero commanded the only black troops ever to serve with the Army of
the Potomac. Most of the regiments had finished their organization in the
Northern states by April 1864 and then were shifted to the field with little
training and no experience. Two of the regiments still had fewer than the
required number of companies. The 1st Brigade, commanded by Lt. Col.
Joshua K. Sigfried, consisted of units raised primarily in Ohio, Pennsylvania,
and Maryland; Col. Henry G. Thomas's 2nd Brigade consisted of men recruited from Indiana, Illinois, and Maryland. By late July, Sigfried had two
thousand men and Thomas twenty-three hundred.[13]

Burnside told Ferrero to train his two regiments to execute the wheeling
maneuver, but there is conflicting evidence as to whether the division leader did
so. Several white officers indicated that no unusual training took place, and a
modern historian has noted that there was little opportunity for the division to
drill given its heavy work on the entrenchments and periodic tours of duty in
them. Capt. Robert Beecham of the 23rd USCT remembered that Thomas's
brigade conducted only one drill from June 22 through July 29. It lasted three

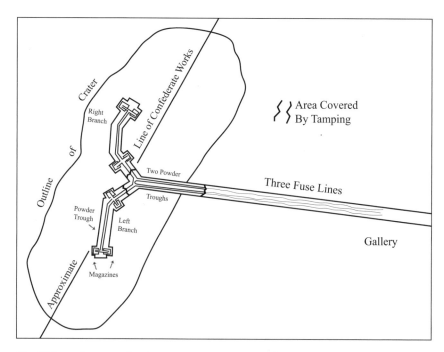

The Union mine completed

or four hours and "consisted of the most common and simple of brigade movements."[14]

Other white officers, however, contended that quite a bit of specialized training took place. Sigfried argued that his troops drilled "until every officer and soldier could have gone into that assault." The 19th USCT of Thomas's brigade practiced forming double columns. Col. Delevan Bates of the 30th USCT put his men through several days of drilling. "Time after time did my regiment go through the imaginary advance," he wrote, "until every man knew what they were supposed to do."[15]

Ferrero told Willcox that "his colored troops had not only been highly trained, particularly for the assault, but that they were religiously and fanatically wrought up to a fever heat of zeal for the work, believing that God himself had now given them a chance to prove the courage of their race and their gratitude for freedom." Thomas recalled that his men held an impromptu songfest one night as they contemplated what was to come. Singing "We-e looks li-like me-en a-a-marchin' on, We looks li-like men-er-war," they joined their voices to steel their nerves for the fight. The blacks prepared emotionally while their white officers examined the lay of the land at the horseshoe. Armed with "a rough outline map of the ground," Sigfried and Thomas tried to observe what they could of the Confederate position. Thomas raised an old hat on a ramrod to draw Rebel fire and took "a hasty observation" immediately after.[16]

Grant finally authorized Burnside's attack on the afternoon of July 28. Meade told him that dawn of July 30 would be the earliest it could happen because Hunt needed to place more guns and the infantry commanders had to mass their men under cover of darkness. Grant arranged for the 2nd Corps to relieve the 18th Corps so the latter could provide ready support for Burnside. He also instructed Meade to send Sheridan's cavalry to Warren's left, both to cover the Federal flank and possibly to attempt to turn the Confederate right. Otherwise he left all details of the attack to Meade.[17]

Eighteenth Corps leader Edward O. C. Ord was one of Grant's trusted subordinates from the West. He had assumed command only on July 20. Someone, probably Butler, suggested that Brig. Gen. John W. Turner's 2nd Division of the 10th Corps also support Burnside. In the end Ord was authorized to use Turner's as well as Brig. Gen. Adelbert Ames's 2nd Division of his own corps to help the 9th.[18]

So far, Grant and Meade had fully supported Burnside's plan of attack, but then Meade began to doubt a key component of the proposal. When Burnside visited army headquarters on the morning of July 28, Meade told him he could not allow Ferrero's division to spearhead the assault. Burnside argued that his white troops were exhausted and reluctant to attack fortifications. Meade relented and promised to consult Grant; he was to speak with him at City Point that afternoon anyway. When Burnside heard nothing from Meade that evening, he assumed the general in chief had supported his original plan.[19]

Initially, when testifying to a military court of inquiry soon after the battle, Meade claimed he objected to Ferrero's division because the troops were too green to lead the attack. When testifying to a joint congressional committee four months later, the army commander said he did not want to be accused of sacrificing black soldiers needlessly. If the attack had failed, as Grant put it in his own testimony to the committee, "it would then be said, and very properly, that we were shoving those people ahead to get killed because we did not care anything about them." Only a successful attack "would have justified" using the black regiments as a spearhead, and Meade did not have enough confidence in their ability. Although racial considerations were at work, there is no reason to assume that Meade was racially prejudiced. The target of repeated, politically motivated attacks since he took command of the Army of the Potomac one year before, Meade wanted to dodge another condemnation of his generalship. For his part, Burnside displayed a commendable lack of concern for prevailing Northern sensitivity about the use of black troops in combat.[20]

Meade delayed in telling Burnside that Grant agreed with him about not using Ferrero's division to lead the attack. His chief of staff wrote a message to Burnside at 10:15 A.M. on July 29, but apparently the corps commander did not receive it before Meade and Ord showed up at his headquarters at 11 that morning. Burnside was surprised and once again argued with Meade that Ferrero's division should spearhead the attack. The army commander put a stop to the discussion by declaring, "'No, general, it cannot; it is final, and you must put in your white troops.'" Meade forced another change in the attack plan, thinking it was more important to pile up troops on the crest of the ridge than to widen the breach. As Meade later testified to the court of inquiry, the question "was one purely of time." There was no need to hold the breach; the Federals had to withdraw quickly if they could not secure the ridge. Meade had a valid point. Losing thousands of men only to push the Rebels back a short distance was not an attractive scenario.[21]

After this conference, Meade and Ord rode away to a 9th Corps signal station so Ord could examine the ground. They returned to Burnside's headquarters about one or two in the afternoon, and Ord promised to send a staff officer to coordinate plans for replacing 9th Corps troops that night. Instead of a staffer, Ord's division commanders arrived later that afternoon for this important task. Burnside was busy for some time showing them around.[22]

Meanwhile Meade planned a conference with Grant and Burnside to take place at army headquarters at 4 P.M. for final approval of all arrangements. An hour passed by and Burnside unaccountably failed to arrive. Meade finally wrote him at 5 P.M., "Are you not coming over? General Grant is here." The general in chief readily approved Meade's attack plan, but he could not wait for the corps commander.[23]

Burnside missed the conference for reasons that remain obscure. It is possible he was busy adjusting his arrangements to suit Meade's new ideas and forgot about the appointment. As soon as Ord's division commanders left, he huddled with his white division leaders to determine who should replace Ferrero at the head of the attack. Willcox's 3rd Division was well situated to lead, but his men were the most tired. Potter's 2nd Division was less fatigued and the second-best situated, but Ledlie's 1st Division seemed the most rested of the three. Still, Burnside could not decide who to saddle with the responsibility, so he said, "It will be fair to cast lots." Ledlie won the draw and, according to Burnside, left corps headquarters "in a very cheerful mood" at about 3 P.M.[24]

Long after the war, Potter claimed that all division commanders were anxious to lead the attack and regretted that they were not chosen. "My division expected and was anxious to have the advance," he wrote, "because they knew the ground, had an interest in the work, were in the best condition, and known to be the best division in the corps." As a personal friend of Potter's, Burnside felt uncomfortable giving the honor to him and opted for drawing lots out of a sense of fairness to everyone. When word spread among Ferrero's troops, "we were terribly disappointed," recalled Capt. James H. Rickard of the 19th USCT.[25]

Meade issued attack orders late on July 29 for all troops involved in the operation, reminding Burnside to cut passages through the abatis fronting his forward line and to prepare a way for his men to cross the Union works. He instructed Warren to mass as many men as he could on his right flank to support the 9th Corps if Ord's two divisions were not enough to ensure victory, and he told Mott to relieve Ord. The rest of Hancock's men would be ready to go in after they returned from Deep Bottom; Sheridan received vague instructions to operate around the army's left flank. Meade wanted Duane to ready the pontoon train in case the Federals broke through and had to bridge the Appomattox River. After the mine explosion at 3:30 A.M. on July 30, Burnside was to push his men as quickly as possible to the ridge crest and stop there. Ord would follow and lodge on the crest to his right, and Warren to his left. Heavy artillery fire, directed by Hunt, was to cover all forward movements. Meade announced that he would occupy Burnside's headquarters site after the 9th Corps commander moved his own headquarters to a newly constructed fort on the main line. "Promptitude, rapidity of execution, and cordial co-operation are essential to success," Meade concluded.[26]

Burnside issued directions to his division commanders at 8 P.M. He instructed Ledlie to go through the breach "and if possible crown the crest at the point known as Cemetery Hill, occupying, if possible, the cemetery." Willcox was to advance to Ledlie's left while Potter advanced to his right to occupy a ridge that seemed to run from Cemetery Hill down toward the Union line. Ferrero received orders to wait until the three white divisions had gone well ahead before he advanced. If possible, Ferrero was to move farther to the right and north to occupy Blandford, near the cemetery.[27]

Burnside spent many hours dealing with the problem of massing his corps of some fifteen thousand men for the attack. Potter and Willcox knew the ground well but Ledlie apparently did not. Burnside sent his inspector general, Col. Charles G. Loring, Jr., to show Ledlie the ground behind the forward line and west of Poor Creek. He assigned one of his staff officers to accompany each of the three white divisions.[28]

Burnside's written order for the attack was clear enough, but there was still some degree of confusion among the division leaders as to what they were to do. Ledlie met his two brigade commanders and staff officers at Battery No. 14 a bit after dusk on July 29. Burnside intended to use the battery, later renamed Fort Morton, as his command post during the attack. Ledlie explained the plan to Brig. Gen. William Francis Bartlett and Col. Elisha G. Marshall. Each brigade was to form "in column of battalion front." That "made three lines of about four hundred men each" for Marshall's command, according to staff officer Col. Thomas W. Clarke. Ledlie then told the two brigade leaders that they were to occupy the Confederate line, Marshall to the right and Bartlett to the left of the crater. The division engineer regiment, the 35th Massachusetts, would dig a covered way to connect the captured position with the forward Union line, according to Ledlie. Potter would extend to Ledlie's right and Willcox to his left, while Ferrero advanced through the crater to the crest of the ridge. "Marshall's distinct instructions were that the security of the lodgment was the prime duty of the 1st Division and the hill was a subordinate object," Clarke recalled. Ledlie detailed two of his aides-de-camp to accompany the brigades in their advance.[29]

These directions contradicted Burnside's plan. In his official report, Ledlie stated that he gave instructions to his brigade leaders to "move through the breach to be made by the mine and then to press forward and occupy the hill beyond," and his aide-de-camp, Maj. William H. Powell, claimed Ledlie received the correct instructions to "go to Cemetery Hill." For some reason, it appears that Ledlie failed to relay those directions to his subordinates. He was not the only one to take away a muddled perception of the plan from Burnside's conference. Although Potter understood everything clearly, Willcox was a bit confused. He believed his division was to sweep down the

Confederate line to the left before heading for the crest of the ridge, to widen the breach and capture the Jerusalem Plank Road, but this was not reflected in Burnside's written order that he was to head straight for the crest. Long after the war, Willcox still felt a bit confused. "Whether right or wrong," he wrote, "my own impression of the vague orders given to me were that I was to follow *through the crater,* whereas, as we see it now, nothing could have been [more] absurd."[30]

Willcox's confusion mitigates the blame one tends to assign to Ledlie for getting his instructions wrong. It is possible that Burnside rambled in the conference, complaining to his subordinates about Meade's interference with his original plan, confusing them as to the exact course of action they were to take the next morning. If that is so, Potter sorted through the verbiage and kept his mind focused on what was important, but Ledlie utterly failed to comprehend Burnside's intention. Willcox left the conference with an understanding that combined both Burnside's and Meade's plans, but Ledlie came away only with Burnside's old plan in mind.

With their erroneous marching orders, Ledlie's brigade leaders spread the word to their men. Bartlett conferred with his seven regimental leaders that evening at his headquarters. He instructed them to hold the breach in Confederate lines, not to go on to the crest behind Pegram's Salient. "Very little was said at this meeting of regimental commanders with regard to minor details," recalled Lt. Col. Joseph H. Barnes of the 29th Massachusetts. "All present saw exactly what was to be done. There was no misunderstanding."[31]

Marshall and Clarke inspected the ground after Ledlie's conference broke up, and Clarke wrote orders for the brigade. Marshall called a conference of his regimental leaders at his headquarters at 8 P.M., explaining everything to them as Ledlie had expressed it. A lower-ranked regimental officer later argued that little information filtered down the ranks as to the details of the plan, and most men knew little of what to expect.[32]

Potter also called a conference of his brigade leaders that night and explained to them the attack plan as Burnside had expressed it in his written order. But Potter believed his men might not be relieved by the 18th Corps soon enough, and he also worried there was not enough room in the covered way to allow him to move forward at a quick pace, so he took the liberty of altering his part of the program a bit. Brig. Gen. Simon G. Griffin was to advance a skirmish line immediately after the mine exploded, pushing it across no-man's-land to protect Ledlie's right flank. When the 1st Division advanced beyond the crater, the skirmishers would advance with it and Griffin could push the rest of his brigade forward to keep pace with Ledlie. Although Potter gave these instructions to Griffin at midnight, he did not think it was necessary to inform Burnside. Griffin issued instructions to each of his regimental commanders and assigned his senior colonel, Daniel White of the 31st Maine, to command the advance of his brigade. White was to direct his own and the 9th New Hampshire and 17th Vermont and form three lines in front of the Union earthworks at 3 A.M., with pioneers ready to cut through the abatis. Griffin told him to advance straight ahead, protecting Ledlie's right flank. Potter informed his other brigade commander, Zenas R. Bliss, that his role was to help Griffin if he could, and otherwise to act as a reserve.[33]

There is no evidence to suggest how Willcox disseminated instructions to his brigade leaders, Brig. Gen. John F. Hartranft and Col. William Humphrey. In Ferrero's command, word filtered down to regimental and company officers to have full canteens and sixty rounds per man ready. There would be "no baggage or extra traps of any kind or description."[34]

The 9th Corps Leaders

Unfortunately Burnside gave the important task of leading the 9th Corps attack to one of the worst division commanders in the war. The 1st Division had started the Overland campaign with a bright star at its head, Brig. Gen. Thomas G. Stevenson, who was soon after killed at Spotsylvania. Maj. Gen. Thomas L. Crittenden, a leftover from corps reorganization in the Army of the Cumberland following the battle of Chickamauga, replaced Stevenson. He "took no pains with the Division, and let everything slide in a way very painful to my mind," as one of his staff members put it. Crittenden asked to be relieved on June 8. John Hartranft was slated to take over the 1st Division, but Maj. Gen. Julius White, who had led a division in the 23rd Corps under Burnside in East Tennessee, became available. Although Burnside contemplated putting White in command, he eventually decided to elevate Ledlie to that position.[35]

Born in Utica, New York, and a civil engineer in the railroad industry, Ledlie entered the war as major of the 3rd New York Artillery and was promoted to brigadier general by the end of 1862. He performed occupation duty in North Carolina and held district commands. Ledlie contracted malaria while serving near New Bern, which severely impaired his health, yet he eventually took command of the 1st Brigade, 1st Division on May 18, 1864. Six days later, while the 9th Corps was crossing the North Anna River, he launched an unauthorized attack by his lone brigade on a heavily fortified position, losing one hundred men and failing to accomplish anything. Many observers saw that he was drunk and overly excited, yet no one reported this to Crittenden or Burnside. On June 17, while his brigade launched an attack on the Confederate works, Ledlie took shelter in a ravine to the rear of the Union position and reportedly was drunk. His staff members again shielded his reputation out of a misguided sense of loyalty to their commander, even though they apparently held him in contempt. As Simon Griffin later wrote, it was "shameful and outrageous" that Ledlie was allowed to command troops. To give Ledlie his due, his drinking was linked to his severe problem with malaria. Whiskey was one of the few palliatives for the tremors and chills that resulted.[36]

Ledlie had good brigade leaders in the 1st Division. William F. Bartlett had lost a leg as captain of the 20th Massachusetts at Yorktown and later took part in the siege of Port Hudson as colonel of the 49th Massachusetts, where he was wounded twice. Bartlett then organized the 57th Massachusetts and was wounded in the Wilderness. At age twenty-four, and with more wounds than most men twice his age, Bartlett returned to duty in July amid hopes that he would replace Ledlie, but he was instead given command of Ledlie's brigade. His mental and moral strength was unimpaired, but Bartlett had difficulty scrambling through the trenches on his wooden leg. Elisha G. Marshall was a West Pointer who had been severely wounded in the attack on Marye's Heights during the Chancellorsville campaign, and he had led the 14th New York Heavy Artillery before taking command of Ledlie's 2nd Brigade a few days before the planned attack.[37]

Potter was one of the best division commanders in the Army of the Potomac. A New York City lawyer before the war, he had ample combat experience in North Carolina, Maryland, and Virginia and had commanded the 9th Corps in East Tennessee. Although Potter had been wounded at least three times, his health was still strong. In addition Simon G. Griffin was a superb brigade leader. A schoolteacher, state legislator, and lawyer before the war, Griffin had served in North Carolina and Maryland and at the battles of Second Bull Run, Antietam, and Fredericksburg and in the West. Zenas R. Bliss, a West Point graduate who later won a Medal of Honor for his role as commander of the 7th Rhode Island at Fredericksburg, held his brigade as the division reserve.[38]

Orlando B. Willcox was also a West Point graduate and had a lot of battle experience in the East and West. His two brigade leaders were reliable as well. John F. Hartranft, a civil engineer and lawyer before the war, had seen service with the 9th Corps throughout its long history, mostly as colonel of the 51st Pennsylvania. Col. William Humphrey, who commanded Willcox's 2nd Brigade, had performed very well during the Knoxville campaign the previous fall.[39]

Ferrero had a solid if unremarkable record of service during the war. Born of Italian parents in Grenada, Spain, he immigrated to New York City with his family as a child. Ferrero took over his parents' dance studio years later and catered to the elite families of the city, even teaching dance to the cadets at West Point. He wrote a book called *The Art of Dancing*, which not only guided the reader through the steps but also discussed the history and social aspects of dancing. He served as colonel of the 51st New York and had held brigade and division commands. Grant praised Ferrero's ability to mold and train the black division while guarding trains and digging earthworks during the Overland campaign. Joshua K. Sigfried, who led Ferrero's 1st Brigade, had formerly commanded the 48th Pennsylvania. Henry G. Thomas had traded his volunteer officer's commission for one in the 11th U.S. Infantry, but most of his time was spent organizing black regiments rather than campaigning.[40]

Burnside's reliable chief of staff, Brig. Gen. John G. Parke, had been suffering from malarial chills for some time and needed rest. Parke had been with Burnside in various subordinate commands since the latter's campaign along the North Carolina coast in 1862. Julius White replaced him late on July 29, new to the task and a relative stranger to Burnside's division leaders. He would fail to keep Meade or Grant apprised of corps progress during the mine attack, which heightened the anxiety felt by both superiors.[41]

Although Burnside had gallantly embraced the mine project and played a key role in its success, he failed to deal with important issues related to the follow-up attack. Meade had a legitimate argument for changing both the lead unit and the mode of approach in the attack plan, but Burnside abdicated his responsibility as corps commander in drawing straws to see who would replace the black division in the vanguard. Burnside ultimately bears the responsibility for allowing a palpably incompetent general to command one of his divisions. Another of Burnside's faults lay in holding a conference from which one of his division leaders came away confused as to what he was supposed to do and another came away with a completely wrong impression about his role in the coming attack. After more than a month of careful preparation, the success of the mine attack rested on a few hours of hasty, frustrated changes of plan, and the man chiefly responsible for dealing with those changes failed to manage them effectively.

6

NIGHT OF JULY 29

The Federals made haste to settle all preparations for the attack on the night of July 29. They barely had time to place the large number of guns needed to support the advance. Henry Hunt had been working ever since June 30 to position artillery near Pegram's Salient, but he, Duane, and Charles Wainwright began to locate new emplacements along the 5th Corps line on July 23. When Hunt received orders to finish preparations five days later, he planted sixteen mortars of 8- and 10-inch caliber, as well as more 4.5-inch siege guns. Hunt visited all batteries within range of the impending attack and gave verbal instructions to their commanders. In addition he issued a circular on the morning of July 29 to make sure everyone knew what was expected of them.[1]

Hunt marshaled a total of 110 guns and 54 mortars to support Burnside's attack, 48 of them along the 5th Corps front. He wanted his subordinates to open fire immediately after the mine explosion and concentrate on Confederate gun emplacements. He cautioned them not to fire on Burnside's advancing troops and to be alert to the movement of Confederate units.[2]

Wainwright busied himself on July 29 to ready 5th Corps artillery, and Hunt helped him a great deal. "He is a host at such a time," Wainwright admitted. Many 5th Corps guns were rolled into their positions after dusk. With a breeze blowing from the Confederate line toward the Federals, and little moonlight, Wainwright's men were able to do this without causing alarm. Everything was in place by midnight. Wainwright also visited each battery location, "instructed, questioned, and cross-questioned all my commanders; each one of whom I had taken to his position during the day and pointed out to him exactly what he was to do." Wainwright issued his own written instructions along with Hunt's circular, then allowed his subordinates to issue whiskey to their tired men. He managed to sleep ninety minutes before forcing himself awake in time for the scheduled explosion of the mine at 3:30 A.M.[3]

On the 9th Corps front, the newly built Fourteen Gun Battery had been armed on the night of July 25. It was located 450 yards behind the horseshoe line, but a grove of pine trees obstructed the view toward Wright's Confederate battery. Henry L. Abbot, who was responsible for the guns in the fort, asked Burnside to cut down the trees, but a detail was driven off by Rebel fire on the night of July 27. Hunt telegraphed another request to Burnside the next night, which produced nothing. Abbot's subordinate at the fort sent some of his artillerymen to partly cut down the grove on the night of July 28. Pressed further on the subject, Burnside refused to do any more before the attack, fearing it might alert the Confederates to Union plans. He agreed to form a detail of men from Ferrero's division to cut the grove as soon as the mine exploded. Burnside gave eighty men to his chief of artillery, Col. J. A. Monroe, but the work party failed to cut more than a handful of trees, losing some men in the process. As a result, Abbot's gunners could not see all their targets. In post-battle testimony, artillery officers tended to overemphasize the significance of Burnside's failure to clear the Fourteen Gun Battery's field of fire, for there is no reason to believe it neutralized artillery support for the attack.[4]

The cavalry also had an assignment. Sheridan had been busy since the afternoon of July 28 trying to deceive the Confederates at Deep Bottom. He sent one of his divisions across the James River after dusk, muffling the sound of horses' hooves by spreading hay, moss, and grass on the pontoon bridge, and then marched the troopers back on foot the next morning to simulate infantry. Grant met Sheridan at Deep Bottom on the evening of July 28, as this division conducted its show, and told him to move to the army's left and try to turn the Confederate right flank when the mine exploded. Grant admitted to Sheridan that he probably would not succeed in doing anything other than diverting Rebel attention.[5]

Within the 9th Corps sector, Burnside instructed Ledlie to prepare at least two hundred yards of the forward Union line so the troops could cross. This was wide enough to allow a regiment to advance in battle line. The only way to accomplish this goal was to fill the trench with sandbags and remove the abatis in front of the parapet, but only eight to ten feet of the trench was filled and nothing was done to the abatis. This would force the attacking units to advance by the flank—in essence, in a narrow column—across the Union entrenchment. It is unclear why more was not done. Meade severely criticized Burnside for failing to do this properly, arguing that the entire 9th Corps should have been able to cross the forward Union line at once and advance to the crest of the ridge in half an hour. Potter testified that no written instructions, except for a brief and general reference in Burnside's attack order, were issued for preparing the Union works. Burnside told Potter to have his engineer regiment ready to open the entrenchments to pass batteries through after the infantry succeeded in gaining the crest. But he also warned Potter not to do anything of the kind before the explosion for fear of alerting the enemy.[6]

Burnside later claimed that he left it up to his division leaders to modify the works and cut the abatis without endangering their men or alarming the Confederates. He correctly noted that the abatis had already been shot up so that it offered no obstacle to his advance. More attention was paid to the failure to cut through the abatis in postbattle inquiries than was justified. The only explanation for the failure to prepare a longer stretch of trench can be that Burnside's men ran out of sandbags. They had received eight thousand empty bags for the tamping operation and had used nearly all of them. What was left probably was used to fill a short section of the trench, and there was no time to obtain more.[7]

Repositioning Federal Units

Burnside spent almost the entire night of July 29 repositioning his units. He preferred that his division leaders form their commands in columns of regiments, but he left the final decision to them. The ground was severely constricted by the Union earthworks and the need to cross the ravine of Poor Creek to approach Pegram's Salient. Two covered ways led from the main Union line toward the creek valley and continued up the opposite bank through ravines to the forward Federal line. Mostly straight, the covered ways had a few zigzags to take advantage of the terrain. Both were about one thousand yards long and wide enough for men to march at least two abreast, perhaps four in places. The forward extensions of the covered ways from Poor Creek to the horseshoe were about one hundred yards long. Theodore Lyman recalled that some sections of the covered way system were a bit exposed to Confederate fire; at only four feet wide, the bank of earth lining the side came up to his shoulder. "Probably it was dug by a small officer who was spiteful against men of great inches," Lyman wrote. According to other witnesses, the covered ways were six feet and ten feet wide in places. Many men were assigned to work on improving these passages on July 28, but they could not take care of all the problems.[8]

Ledlie began to move his division from its position on the left of the 10th Corps at about 9 P.M. on the night of July 29, taking it to the rear to rest. The men set out toward the horseshoe at 1 A.M. on the morning of July 30. They marched through the system of covered ways with extra ammunition beyond the regulation forty rounds, plus three days' cooked rations. Told to hold their tin cups and bayonets, they "marched with the stillness of death; not a word was said above a whisper."[9]

Ledlie replaced Potter's division, Marshall's brigade forming three lines of battle on the open ground behind the forward Union line. The 2nd

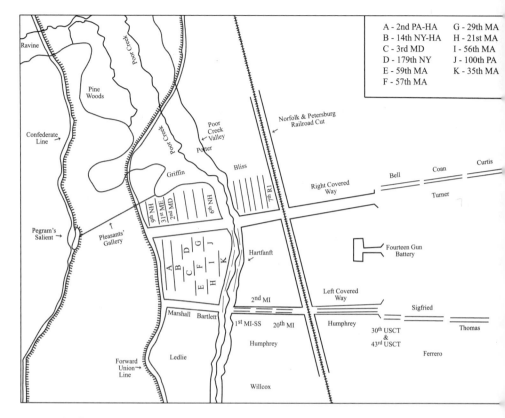

The first Federal wave

Pennsylvania Provisional Heavy Artillery formed the first line, with the 14th
New York Heavy Artillery in the second. The 3rd Maryland Battalion and the
179th New York constituted the third line. The lines were separated by only 5
yards and were about 150 yards long, with four hundred men in each line to
accommodate twelve hundred men in the brigade.[10]

Bartlett's brigade of eighteen hundred men formed behind Marshall in
three lines of battle. His 59th, 57th, and 29th Massachusetts formed the first
line, commanded by Col. Jacob P. Gould. The 21st and 56th Massachusetts,
plus the 100th Pennsylvania, formed the second line, led by Lt. Col. Stephen
M. Weld. The 35th Massachusetts constituted the third line, deployed to act as
engineers. Burnside wanted the engineer units to take tools along to entrench
a position on top of the captured ridge crest.[11]

Ledlie's division barely managed to squeeze into the constricted ground
behind the Federal horseshoe. By 2 or 3 A.M., the men lay quietly in the darkness only a few dozen yards from Pegram's guns.[12]

Potter, who had moved his division out of Ledlie's way, had a difficult time deciding where and how to re-form. He had carefully examined the ground on July 29 and decided that he could not use Poor Creek valley to assemble his men, or as an avenue of approach toward the Confederate line, because it was too exposed to plunging Rebel fire. He could have formed in open ground to the east of Poor Creek, but that area was too rough and too far away from his target. "We will have to hold ourselves in readiness to make our formation as soon as we see what ground General Ledlie leaves to us," Potter wrote, "and adapt ourselves accordingly." At about 1 A.M., Potter pulled his 2nd Brigade under Griffin out of the works and moved it through the right covered way across Poor Creek valley. Griffin formed in column of regiments on the open ground behind the forward Union line, to the right of Ledlie's division. The head of Griffin's column rested two rods behind the Union trench. His column must have been scattered, for Griffin recalled that the men "formed wherever we could find standing room—in the traverses and covered ways in the ravine, and one or two [regiments] close up under our breastworks." Darkness protected Griffin's men from Rebel observation.[13]

Potter's other brigade was late in taking position because 18th Corps troops did not relieve it on time. Brig. Gen. Joseph B. Carr's 3rd Division, a black unit, took the wrong road and failed to show up at 9 P.M. as scheduled. One regiment of Col. Samuel A. Duncan's 2nd Brigade arrived at midnight and relieved two of Bliss's regiments, but the rest had to wait indefinitely. Bliss busied himself by inspecting his position, stumbling over objects in the dark and falling into holes, and he was exhausted when he returned to headquarters. Potter developed a plan to have Bliss leave a picket line in the works and pull out by 3 A.M., whether relief arrived or not. Carr came on the scene just as Bliss began pulling out and promised his troops would be up in half an hour. Several of Bliss's regiments implemented Potter's plan anyway. The 45th Pennsylvania, for example, left 100 of its 221 men behind as a picket. The entire 36th Massachusetts remained in line, apparently never having received instructions to comply with Potter's plan. The regiment's commander tried to talk Carr's black troops into extending their line to replace the regiment, but to no effect.[14]

Bliss barely took his brigade out of line, issued food and extra ammunition, and formed it to support the attack before the scheduled explosion of the mine. He formed in column of regiments to Griffin's rear and on the east of Poor Creek valley, for there was no room on the other side of the stream. The 51st New York, at least, formed in the right covered way. Pleasants's 48th Pennsylvania did not stand with the rest of the brigade. The regiment was detailed to serve as provost guard behind 9th Corps lines, and Pleasants was detached as an aide to Potter so he could observe the operation. The 7th Rhode Island took entrenching tools and placed itself behind Bliss.[15]

In Willcox's division, Humphrey's 2nd Brigade rested in camp well to the rear until the evening of July 29, when it moved forward to bivouac for a few hours. Lt. Col. Byron M. Cutcheon of the 20th Michigan recalled that the "night was warm, the sky was clear," as cooks prepared rations and coffee. After they brought the refreshments forward at 3 A.M., the men fell into line, deposited their knapsacks, and moved forward through the left covered way.[16]

Willcox did not share Potter's concern about using Poor Creek valley as a staging area, because he positioned Hartranft's brigade in the ravine to Ledlie's left and rear. Exactly how Hartranft placed his seven regiments is unknown, except that the 13th Ohio Cavalry (dismounted) filed up a depression that ran west from the creek. Humphrey strung his seven regiments out in a battle line that moved by the flank through the covered way, with the 1st Michigan Sharpshooters in the lead, stopping at Poor Creek valley. Behind the sharpshooters, the 2nd Michigan and Cutcheon's 20th Michigan followed. The rear of the column extended back to the entrance of the covered way, making the roadbed "densely gorged with troops." They would wait here a relatively short time before the scheduled detonation of the mine. When the first hint of dawn arrived, William H. Randall of the 1st Michigan Sharpshooters could dimly see Hartranft's brigade crowded in the narrow valley of Poor Creek and realized how far up the opposite slope he would have to go to reach the forward Union line. What lay beyond, he could only guess.[17]

Although Ferrero would no longer lead the 9th Corps attack, Sigfried's brigade still led his division. The brigade was positioned on the far left of Burnside's line, connecting with the 5th Corps, when Warren relieved it at 2 A.M. of July 30. Sigfried marched his men to the entrance of the left covered way, near the Fourteen Gun Battery, where they deposited their knapsacks. The brigade formed a battle line as Sigfried informed Lt. Col. H. Seymour Hall what was expected of his 43rd USCT, positioned second in the brigade column of regiments. When given the order, the brigade would move by the flank through the covered way. He told Hall to have his men fix bayonets and load their muskets, but not to cap them, because he wanted no temptation to halt and fire before reaching the objective. The 43rd was to cross the Union works, advance through the breach, then redirect the formation so the battle line faced toward the enemy, and head for the ridge crest.[18]

Thomas learned of the change in attack plan only at 11 P.M. July 29. He walked back to his brigade, "dejected and with an instinct of disaster for the morrow. As I summoned and told my regimental commanders, their faces expressed the same feeling." Thomas allowed his men to rest in their bivouac among the trees to the rear of the main Union line. Lt. Col. John A. Bross of the 29th USCT paced about, "seeming somewhat anxious and agitated," but later composed himself and engaged in conversation with his officers. No later than 3 A.M., the men were called to eat breakfast and move forward behind Sigfried's brigade near the entrance to the covered way.[19]

Although some 18th Corps troops were scheduled to relieve 9th Corps units in the trenches, Ames's division readied to go in after Burnside if needed. With the addition of Turner's division, the only 10th Corps unit involved in the operation, Ord would have a substantial force to throw into the attack. He and Meade spent the morning of July 29 going over the ground and consulting with Burnside. Meade offered engineer officer Nathaniel Michler to 18th Corps headquarters, but Ord declined, believing he and his staff had so thoroughly examined the ground that Michler's assistance was not needed. Butler, however, allowed his only engineer troops, a battalion of the 1st New York Engineers, to be ready to reverse the captured Confederate works if needed.[20]

Ord used not only Carr's 3rd Division but also Brig. Gen. Hiram Burnham's 1st Division to relieve 9th Corps troops that evening. Burnham, like Carr, had assumed his new command only on the evening of July 29. Carr also visited Burnside's position to see the lay of the land. Turner did the same thing, having a brief talk with Burnside about his division's role in the attack, and then walking around to see the landscape accompanied by a 9th Corps staff member.[21]

The 2nd Corps had a supporting role to play in the attack as well. After resting his men from their excursion to Deep Bottom, Mott moved forward to relieve the 18th Corps on the evening of July 29. With only forty-five hundred troops against Ord's six thousand, Mott relied on Carr to fill in the empty spaces on the corps line and at Turner's position.[22]

Burnham's 1st Division and Duncan's black brigade followed guides in a roundabout march to the rear so they could more easily approach 9th Corps positions and relieve Burnside's troops. Ord got a little nervous, believing that Mott was late in relieving his men and anticipating it would take three hours to reposition his troops. Meade calmed him by noting that Burnside did not have to wait until relief actually arrived before evacuating his position. The night would conceal empty Union trenches from Confederate observation until relief troops filled them again. As we have seen, however, this advice was not relayed to Potter, who fretted in his own way about delays in relieving Bliss's brigade.[23]

Carr managed to complete the relief of Burnside's men in time. Two brigades of Burnham's division replaced Willcox's troops on Burnside's left, while Duncan relieved Potter's men and some of Ledlie's division. A white brigade of the 3rd Division rested to Duncan's rear as a reserve to fill in the empty trenches after the 9th Corps launched its attack. Ames's division and Turner's division followed Nathaniel Michler to their assigned positions close to the rear of Burnside's assembly area. Ames had prepared his 2nd Division for action by requiring the men to carry sixty rounds of ammunition, shelter tents, and blankets rolled over their shoulders, plus two days' cooked rations.

Any spare entrenching tools were also taken along. Ames positioned his men by
1 A.M.[24]

After marching all the way from near the Hare House, Turner took his division to the woods in rear of the 9th Corps lines by midnight and waited until Ledlie had passed this point on his way to the horseshoe. Then Turner moved up until the head of his column of regiments was near the entrance of the right covered way. Here he waited for the attack to begin.[25]

The rest of the 2nd Corps completed the repositioning of the Federal troops. Gibbon's 2nd Division left Deep Bottom at 8 P.M. on July 29 and endured a tough night march with lots of straggling. Gibbon reached the Friend House at 3:45 A.M., roughly the scheduled time for the mine explosion and too late to act as additional reserve for the attack. But the rest of Hancock's corps made it to the vicinity of the battlefield before the fighting ended.[26]

Warren assembled a number of 5th Corps troops for Burnside to use if needed. Meade had alerted him as early as July 26 to prepare to help the 9th Corps, but he was not, on any account, to endanger the army's left flank by doing so. In fact, Meade wanted Warren to hold his corps line with minimal troops, massing the rest for offensive action either in support of Burnside or to counterattack a Rebel column trying to turn the army's flank. Warren put together a sensible plan on July 27 to accomplish these aims. Brig. Gen. Lysander Cutler's 4th Division of 1,959 men held a narrow front and thus had two battle lines; Cutler could spare the second line to support Burnside. Brig. Gen. Romeyn B. Ayres's 2nd Division of 4,758 men could be devoted entirely to the operation, and Brig. Gen. Charles Griffin's 1st Division of 4,979 men could hold its own sector and at least part of Ayres's trenches. Brig. Gen. Samuel E. Crawford's 3rd Division of 4,336 men anchored the flank along the Jerusalem Plank Road. Two days later, on the eve of the attack, Warren thought he could spare two of Crawford's brigades if army headquarters allowed him to temporarily abandon a redoubt located on the road south of the army's left flank. Because this work supported rather than anchored the flank, Meade agreed.[27]

When final orders for the mine explosion and follow-up attack were issued, Warren positioned Ayres's division behind Cutler and intended to use it and Cutler's reserve brigade as a ready support for Burnside. Cutler's frontline brigade and Griffin's division to its left (now temporarily commanded by Brig. Gen. Joseph J. Bartlett) were to open artillery and musketry fire immediately after the mine explosion, and Bartlett was to be ready to attack straight ahead from his position if needed. Crawford would retain all his force to secure the left flank. Warren made a trip to Burnside's headquarters on the evening of July 29 to make sure he understood all that was required of his corps.[28]

Burnside moved his headquarters to the Fourteen Gun Battery, where he had a good view of the horseshoe and Pegram's Salient. The battery was about six hundred yards from the Confederate position, on the other side of Poor Creek, and about fifty yards behind the main Union line, which ran near the Taylor House. His staff got very little sleep the night of July 29 before establishing headquarters at the battery by 3:30 A.M. Ord and his staff had arrived at the Fourteen Gun Battery half an hour earlier and got their bearings. After a brief consultation with Burnside, Ord and his staff members waited in a covered way that led directly to the emplacement, avoiding the main covered way, which was jammed with Humphrey's brigade. Burnside and his staff members joined them, all waiting for the expected explosion.[29]

Meade moved his headquarters three-quarters of a mile to Burnside's old headquarters site, a "knoll behind the Dunn house, near Harrison's Creek." He could not see Pegram's Salient from there, but a telegraph line linked him with the rest of the army. Grant joined Meade as Meade's staff settled in just after Burnside's people left the site.[30]

The Confederates

Under cover of night, the Confederates bedded down with no indication of what was to come. Just north of Pegram's Salient, they had dug four or five traverses extending about twenty yards to the rear from the main trench line. This was to protect the infantry from enfilade fire from the left. They dug more short ditches to the rear of this collection of traverses, with sleeping holes carved into the sides of the ditches. Farther north of the salient, a wide ravine drained toward the main trench line from near the Jerusalem Plank Road. The stream ran under the Confederate parapet through a culvert located four hundred yards north of Pegram's guns. Three hundred yards from the guns, a covered way started to the rear from the main line, making its way through the ravine up to the Jerusalem Plank Road. The covered way passed a spring two hundred yards behind the main line, which also was located at the mouth of a branch that drained into the main ravine. This branch ravine stretched southward to a point almost directly behind Pegram's battery position. The covered way, which zigzagged now and then to better protect men who used it, terminated at the Jerusalem Plank Road seven hundred yards behind the main line, and about one thousand yards from Pegram's guns.[31]

By the night of July 29, Lee had only three divisions south of the Appomattox River. Two of them, Johnson's and Hoke's, belonged to Beauregard's Department of Southern Virginia and North Carolina; Mahone's belonged to Hill's 3rd Corps of the Army of Northern Virginia. Hoke held the left, Johnson the center, and Mahone the right.[32]

Landscape behind Pegram's Salient, looking northwest, ca. 1890. Taken by Bvt.
Lieut. Col. George A. Bruce, 13th New Hampshire. RG 6415–MOL-PA 13.38,
Civil War Library and Museum, MOLLUS, Philadelphia, Pennsylvania

Elliott's South Carolina brigade held the threatened salient, positioned to
either side of Pegram's artillery. Col. Alexander D. Smith's 26th South Carolina
joined McAfee's North Carolina brigade on Elliott's far left, and Col. Fitz
William McMaster's 17th South Carolina covered the sector nearly to Pegram's
guns. Capt. R. H. Glenn's 18th South Carolina occupied nearly half of the cavalier, and Col. David G. Fleming's 22nd South Carolina held the rest. Fleming
placed two companies of his regiment into the main line for about seventy
yards south of Pegram's position. Capt. E. R. White's 23rd South Carolina held
Elliott's right flank, joining Goode's Virginia brigade. Elliott placed his headquarters at the spring, where the branch ravine joined the main ravine near the
covered way. He had fewer than fifteen hundred men to hold about 500 yards
of trench.[33]

The left flank of Goode's Virginia brigade rested about 200 yards south of
Pegram's position, with a sharp dip in the landscape between, and about 275
yards north of the Baxter Road. Goode had his 26th Virginia on the left, then
the 46th Virginia was next in line, with the 34th Virginia and the 59th Virginia
holding his right. The right flank of McAfee's North Carolina brigade rested
about 250 yards north of Pegram's position.[34]

Fortunately for the Confederates, they assembled artillery in key positions
to defend the sector. Capt. Samuel T. Wright's Company of Virginia Heavy
Artillery, also called the Halifax Artillery, had formerly been designated
Company C, 12th Battalion Louisiana Heavy Artillery. It had been redesig-
nated and was now part of Maj. James C. Coit's battalion of Beauregard's

View from Wright's battery position toward the crater, 1892. Taken by C. R. Rees of Petersburg, August 17, 1892. George S. Bernard, ed., *War Talks of Confederate Veterans* (Petersburg, Va.: Fenn and Owen, 1892)

command. Positioned in a hollow on the ridge slope 100 yards behind McAfee's brigade, and 555 yards northwest of Pegram's position, Wright's guns were in the proper place to enfilade Union troops as they advanced to the crest of the ridge. They were also shielded from view of Federal artillerymen in the Fourteen Gun Battery by the grove of pine trees that Burnside failed to cut. Wright's position was further strengthened by heavy earthworks. E. Porter Alexander thought the placing of Wright's guns was the "most important work done on our side during the month of July, in preparation for the defense of this position."[35]

Next in importance to Wright's emplacement was the positioning of two Napoleons of Capt. George S. Davidson's Virginia battery 373 yards south of Pegram's guns, just on the south side of the Baxter Road. Lt. James C. Otey led the battery, which was designated Battery C, 13th Virginia Light Artillery; it was part of Maj. Wade Hampton Gibbs's battalion of Hill's 3rd Corps, Army of Northern Virginia. Otey's guns were positioned on a rise of ground along the ridge slope, exposed except for the thickness of the parapets and traverses of the gun emplacement. The left gun, located 100 feet from the road, had a superb opportunity to fire on Union troops holding the salient. The other two Napoleons belonging to the battery were in a less advantageous position north of the Baxter Road.[36]

Several other artillery and mortar emplacements covered Pegram's Salient. Capt. George G. Otey's Battery A, 13th Virginia Light Artillery, had two

Napoleons located 100 yards south of Davidson's battery position. It was led by Capt. David Norvell Walker and belonged to Gibbs's battalion. The Ringgold Battery, designated as Battery B, 13th Virginia Light Artillery, was commanded by Capt. Crispin Dickenson. Located 100 yards south of Walker's position and 573 yards from Pegram's Salient, two of its Napoleons under Lt. W. P. Robinson could cover the salient with their fire, but the other two could not. The Ringgold Battery also was part of Gibbs's battalion. The only other artillery that could play a role in countering Burnside's attack was Capt. Henry G. Flanner's battery, designated Company F, 13th Battalion North Carolina Artillery. With six Napoleons, Flanner was located at the junction of the Jerusalem Plank and Baxter roads, more than 500 yards from the salient. His unit belonged to Maj. John C. Haskell's battalion of Anderson's 1st Corps, Army of Northern Virginia.[37]

The Confederates had an array of mortars behind Pegram's Salient, most belonging to Haskell's battalion, which deployed sixteen mortars. Six were placed in a line between the Baxter Road and Blandford Cemetery, and the rest were secreted in ravines and sunken emplacements between the salient and the Jerusalem Plank Road. Many of the mortars were manned by Capt. James N. Lamkin's Nelson Virginia Battery, which had served in South Carolina for a time before leaving its guns behind and rushing to Virginia just before the opening of the Overland campaign. Lamkin's men served as infantry for a while until the mortars arrived, and then they were trained to operate the weapons.

View from Davidson's battery position toward the crater, 1892. Taken by C. R. Rees of Petersburg, August 17, 1892. George S. Bernard, ed., *War Talks of Confederate Veterans* (Petersburg, Va.: Fenn and Owen, 1892)

The rest of the mortars were used by ten men detailed from George Otey's Battery A and ten from the Ringgold Battery, under Capt. John B. Langhorne of the former unit. They had three twelve-pounder mortars located 100 to 150 yards behind Walker's position and roughly 400 yards from the salient. Langhorne later acquired control of two six-pounder and two larger mortars in other positions that were capable of firing on the salient.[38]

Countermining to the End

Hugh Thomas Douglas continued to countermine, unaware that he was beaten by Pleasants. Pushing forward at the rate of 4 or 5 feet per night in both galleries, he bored up to the surface and discovered that the forward end of the right gallery was 9 feet 7 inches below ground. By July 29 the two galleries at Pegram's were about 25 feet long. Douglas reported that the total amount of countermining accomplished by his hard-pressed workers at three locations along the line amounted to 368 feet 9 inches.[39]

Alexander concluded that Douglas's work was "badly planned" and "slowly executed," but Pleasants had a head start of two weeks and worked more men than Douglas, some 400 compared to 220. Douglas's left gallery intercepted the direction of approach by Pleasants, but it was too shallow to cut into the Union gallery.[40]

A few days before, on July 26, a New York newspaper reprinted a piece culled from the Richmond *Whig* about rumors of Yankee plans to undermine the entire city of Petersburg. Charles I. Browne, a resident of the place, reported seeing sketches of plans to dig several galleries under Petersburg. To counter charges that this was preposterous, the editor of the *Whig* asked Southerners if they could name any "feat ever attempted with the pick and spade [that] the Yankees have failed to execute?"[41]

The Night before the Battle

William Francis Bartlett was about to lead a brigade into battle for the first time and was worried about his limited mobility. "I hardly dare hope to live through it. . . . If I could only ride, or had two legs, so I could *lead* my brigade, I believe they would follow me anywhere. I will try as it is."[42]

Capt. John B. Cooper warned company officers in the 9th New Hampshire that, "when you gather here to-morrow night, some of us will not be present; probably we shall never all meet here again." Lt. J. J. Chase of the 32nd Maine saw the surgeons accumulating bandages, setting up operating tables, and parking ambulances nearby. Tools for burying the dead were piled up at the brigade quartermaster's tent. Members of the 1st Michigan Sharpshooters pushed messages to friends and family into the hand of William H. Randall to be delivered "in case they fall."[43]

Henry Goddard Thomas gulped down a breakfast of one slice of "raw, fat salt pork" between two pieces of hardtack. He then opened a jar of cucumber pickles received from home and shared it and black coffee with his officers. Most officers in Ferrero's division reminded their companies of what had happened at Fort Pillow in Tennessee the previous April, when Confederate Maj. Gen. Nathan Bedford Forrest's command killed many black Union soldiers in cold blood after they had surrendered. The white officers warned their black men not to expect kind treatment if captured. Some of the black noncommissioned officers gave inspirational speeches to their men. Delevan Bates admitted that talks like these, coming "from men of their own color were perhaps of more practical value to the common soldier than all that was said by the officers." Black chaplains among the regiments of Ferrero's division held short prayer meetings or agreed to write to the kinfolk of those who would fall the next day.[44]

At Grant's headquarters, the mood was hopeful. "Everything looks very favorable for the success of an assault tomorrow," wrote Cyrus Comstock in his diary. Pleasants also had confidence. "I have worked harder of late with body and brain than I ever did in my life before," he wrote to his uncle. "I have projected, undertaken and completed a gigantic work; and have accomplished one of the greatest things in this war." Pleasants expected to "blow fort, cannon and rebels to the clouds," but he also gave a thought to the human consequences of his actions. "It is terrible, however, to hurl several men with my own hand at one blow into eternity, but I believe I am doing right."[45]

On the Confederate side of no-man's-land, James Coit visited Pegram's battery on the night of July 29, staying until midnight. He found the gunners in "remarkably good spirits, singing songs." Then he returned to his headquarters near the spring, next to Elliott's headquarters, and went to sleep.[46]

SPRINGING THE MINE

Henry Pleasants had received instructions to fire the mine at 3:30 A.M. on July 30. He initially intended to light the fuse at 3:35 and expected the powder to detonate between five and ten minutes later. But Pleasants had a change of mind and walked into the gallery to light the fuse at 3:15 instead, probably in an attempt to meet Burnside's prescribed time for the explosion. Having applied the match, he walked out of the gallery and climbed onto the forward Union line, watch in hand, to witness his handiwork.[1]

While Pleasants waited, some of Meade's staff members noted how dark it was and suggested the attack be postponed, so the general sent a note to 9th Corps headquarters at the Fourteen Gun Battery. Burnside replied at 3:20 A.M. that the mine would be sprung on schedule.[2]

Despite all Burnside's expectations, the mine did not go up at 3:30. Experience with coal mining had taught Pleasants to wait some time before investigating the delay. Henry Reese also knew that the primitive fuse was likely the cause. He approached Pleasants, who was "standing on an earthwork, watch in hand, anxiously looking toward the fort," and volunteered to enter the gallery. Lt. Jacob Douty of Company K volunteered to go with him. Reese recalled that Pleasants "wouldn't permit us to make the venture until he felt sure the fire was out, and not slumbering." After an hour had elapsed, Pleasants finally allowed the two men to go in.[3]

Grant joined Meade a little after 4 A.M. and immediately asked, "What is the matter with the mine?" Meade answered, "I don't know—guess the fuse has gone out." Signal officers had by now strung a telegraph wire connecting Meade with Burnside at the Fourteen Gun Battery, but the army commander sent two staff members instead of a telegram. Still no word arrived, so Meade's chief of staff, Maj. Gen. Andrew A. Humphreys wired a message to Burnside at 4:15, to which he received no reply. Humphreys sent another wire at 4:20, and still no reply. Finally Meade sent a dispatch by Captain Sanders at 4:35, telling Burnside that Grant wanted the attack to take place even if the mine did not work, and he received no reply to this as well. Humphreys also informed Mott and Warren that a short artillery bombardment would precede the infantry attack if Burnside could not spring the mine. Finally one of the two officers initially sent to the Fourteen Gun Battery reported that Pleasants was working on the problem.[4]

Burnside presented a nonchalant attitude toward the delay in detonating the mine. An 18th Corps staff officer, Thomas L. Livermore, observed him and Ord waiting in the covered way behind the Fourteen Gun Battery. The 9th Corps leader alternately stood or sat "without any apparent desire to forward affairs and said languidly to an aid, 'Pell, won't you go up and see what's the matter.'" Maj. James L. Van Buren hurried forward. When Captain Sanders arrived from Meade's headquarters, Burnside confessed that he did not know what was happening but promised to inform army headquarters when he found out.[5]

The delay caused anxiety among the troops as well, for rumors and common sense had indicated that the mine would be sprung at dawn. Now it was possible for Byron Cutcheon to see Pegram's Salient. The minutes ticked by, leading to "the most intense and anxious waiting" of his life. It soon became light enough for the Federals to see Rebel soldiers waking up and moving about their works. The gunners of Capt. Jacob Roemer's 34th New York Battery had been ready since 3 A.M. with "pieces loaded and lanyards in hand ready for immediate service." On the 5th Corps sector, artillerymen and infantrymen alike had stood upon their works before the light became too revealing, hoping to get the best view of the explosion. Awakening Confederates saw this unusual activity and began to gather in clusters to figure out what it meant. Union troops at the rear of Burnside's deep formation could see Ledlie's division, exposed on the open ground behind the advanced Federal line. Ledlie's men were already fatigued; most of them had not slept during the night; and all were "in a feverish state of expectancy," which deepened into intense nervousness as the daylight increased. Ledlie sent Maj. William H. Powell back to the Fourteen Gun Battery to find out what was wrong.[6]

Meanwhile sporadic sniping began as soon as it was light enough to pick out targets. Several observers thought this indicated the Confederates had no clue what was in store. Stephen Weld's men in Bartlett's brigade ducked when balls fell close by. "Steady, men, that bullet has gone by you by the time you hear it," Weld told them. Just then another bullet whizzed very close to him, and he flinched. "Every one laughed and I did not blame them, but a more mortified man than I was never lived." Some men in Hartranft's brigade were hit by stray bullets. Weld reported that his troops were "disappointed and discouraged at having to lead, as we had heard all along that the negroes were to do this." Moreover they had "no confidence in Ledlie. He had failed us on several occasions."[7]

Among Potter's waiting troops, Capt. Ervin T. Case of the 9th New Hampshire noticed one of his lieutenants off to the side shedding tears. Case tried to console him, and the lieutenant admitted that he was not afraid to die, but worried about his wife and four children.[8]

Pleasants assumed the mine was salvageable, or else he would not have allowed Reese and Douty to enter the gallery at 4:15. After going part way in, Reese suddenly realized he would need a knife, so he raced back to find one. All three fuses had burned at least forty feet, according to Pleasants, but had gone out, probably because of the dampness. Reese gave more than one interview about the event, but never clearly explained what had happened, other than to report that the fuses had stopped burning at a splice. Conflicting evidence places the fault both in the fuse and in the powder train, because Pleasants later testified that Reese and Douty had to tear away some tamping before finding the trouble spot. Reese thought he could more easily repair the break with some twine, so more time was consumed in going back to find a supply. He broke the fuse beyond a wet spot and repaired it. Applying the final match, Reese and Douty hurried into the broad daylight.[9]

Thirty years later Reese had a long conversation with James Guthrie about this moment. "Feel?" he responded to Guthrie's question about his emotions. "I didn't stop to feel. I had been in tight places in coal mines before the war and didn't mind this affair; but when I got outside, and stood a few minutes looking toward the fort that was doomed, and at the ranks of brave men soon to go charging perhaps to destruction or capture, I felt something trickling near my eyes, but . . . I guess it was only sweat.'"[10]

Burnside agreed with Grant and Meade that he ought to attack even if the mine did not work, and he was on the verge of issuing an order to that effect. But when Reese and Douty appeared, Pleasants assured Van Buren that the mine would go up in eleven minutes and asked the staff officer to pass that information to Burnside. Van Buren also made certain that the officers from Meade's staff were informed as well. Burnside was relieved not to have to send his divisions into an uncertain assault without the mine to prepare the way.[11]

Finally, at 4:44 A.M. according to Pleasants's watch, the ground began to rumble and crack open a hundred twenty-five yards away, slowly pushing up columns of earth. Reese later described it as "a heavy jar, a dull thud, a big volcano-puff of smoke and dust, and up went the earth under and around that fort for a distance in the air of a hundred feet or more, carrying with it cannons, caissons, muskets and—men." Pleasants later took satisfaction in the apparent fact that the explosion "so completely paralyzed" the Confederates.[12]

In the ranks of Marshall's brigade, the Federals closest to the explosion, the men were lying down. Resting his head on one hand while lying on his side, Charles Houghton looked forward when he heard the sound. "I shall never forget the terrible and magnificent sight," Houghton recalled. "The earth around us trembled and heaved—so violently that I was lifted to my feet. Then the earth along the enemy's line opened, and fire and smoke shot upward seventy-five or one hundred feet."[13]

Thomas W. Clarke, the assistant adjutant general of the brigade, was consulting with Marshall inside the forward trench. The brigade leader was "leaning with his left arm on the parapet" while telling Clarke that the explosion was delayed. Clarke partially faced Marshall, resting his right arm on the parapet, and was just starting to rise and walk away when the explosion occurred. He quickly looked toward Pegram's and saw "a lily-shaped fountain of dark red and yellow fire, with brown spots and streaks in it, in shape like an old ring jet of water, called the 'lily,' in the Boston Frog Pond fountain." Momentarily forgetting the purpose of the explosion, Clarke asked Marshall, "Colonel, was anything ever so beautiful as that?"[14]

Among the 2nd Pennsylvania Provisional Heavy Artillery, Marshall's lead regiment, the men had grown so tired of waiting that most assumed the mine was a bust. Many of them stood up and leaned on their muskets before the earth suddenly exploded. Clarence Wilson recalled that the mixture of "fire and flames" went up and "parted like a great plume—a magnificent but awful spectacle." Then the ground "trembled, rocked and bulged like a great earthquake, throwing some of my regimental boys flat on the ground."[15]

Bartlett's brigade was only slightly farther away than the 2nd Pennsylvania. For Stephen Weld, it seemed as if the mass ascended at least fifty or sixty feet into the clear sky, "almost slowly and majestically, as if a volcano had just opened, followed by an immense volume of smoke rolling out in every direction." Weld thought the noise was "very slight indeed," a "rumbling, muffled sound." The air around the plume of dirt and smoke was filled with "timbers, sticks, and debris of all kinds." The shaking of the earth literally lifted some of Bartlett's men off the ground as they lay waiting for orders. Those who had the presence of mind to watch the plume noticed that it "seemed to stand still when it reached its height and fell as a shower from a fountain."[16]

Maj. William H. Powell had just reached the rear of Bartlett's formation, on his way back to Ledlie with a message from Burnside to wait for the explosion, when the mine went up. He noticed that as the plume reached its peak, the debris spread out and began to fall in a wide pattern across no-man's-land, even onto the forward Union line and many troops of Marshall's brigade. Clarence Wilson expressed it well when he wrote that the "sensation we experienced was that we were about to be swallowed up by the earth's crevasses.

The mine explosion. Robert Underwood Johnson and Clarence Clough Buel, *Battles and Leaders* (New York: Century Company, 1887–88) 4:561

The black smoke rolled down upon us and it seemed as though the earth and timber would fall upon us." By instinct, many of Ledlie's men rose up and tried to back away to avoid being pelted. It is also possible, as George Kilmer of the 14th New York Heavy Artillery asserted, that many of Ledlie's troops were temporarily panicked, especially when it became clear that bodies were part of the debris rising up in the plume. Quite a few men broke ranks and recoiled some distance toward Poor Creek, causing a delay of at least ten minutes in launching the attack. It took about that amount of time for the plume to mostly descend anyway, clearing the way for the infantry advance.[17]

To Ledlie's right, the explosion also took many men in Griffin's brigade by surprise. Ervin L. Case looked at his watch and muttered to himself, "I guess the game's up for to-day," just before the mine roared into life. The ground trembled as Griffin saw the plume ascend at least eighty feet, he thought, to be followed by "a dull, heavy thud." Lyman Jackman noted that the explosion resembled pictures of a volcano he had seen "in the school geographies." The morning sun shone on the column of debris as it reached its highest altitude and "lighted it up, presenting a grand appearance." Well to the rear of Potter's division, the men of the 4th Rhode Island were frozen by the sight as the plume spread out "like a great fan" at its height, "balanced a moment in space, and fell back with a sound of thunder to the earth."[18]

In the ranks of Hartranft's brigade, Sgt. Howard Aston of the 13th Ohio Cavalry (dismounted) also saw fire, smoke, bodies, timber, and artillery equipment in the column rising from the explosion. "I felt very weak and pale," he recalled, "and the faces of my comrades never looked more blanched." Byron Cutcheon estimated he was 225 yards from Pegram's Salient, waiting in the covered way, when the mine exploded, yet he could plainly see "a monstrous tongue of flame . . . followed by a vast volume of white smoke" that seemed to spout 200 feet into the air. All manner of material and humanity was visible in the column. Shaken by the sight, Cutcheon continued to watch as the debris, dust, and smoke settled and seemed to hide what was left of the ruined fort from Federal view.[19]

Behind Willcox, members of the 43rd USCT could see the explosion clearly. Lt. M. L. Warson of Company F recalled that the earth shook a bit, emitting "a dull rumbling sound" before a large area of earth rose "like an island which seemed suspended in the air and held as by invisible hands, supported as it were by gigantic columns of smoke and flame." Soon after, the island broke up in the air as the force of the explosion shot upward. "Great blocks of clay were flying upward," recalled Freeman Bowley. Even from this distance, 300 to 400 yards from the Rebel fort, Sigfried's men thought they could see bodies mingled in the uplifting column of debris. Chaplain Garland H. White of the 28th USCT, an escaped slave and Methodist minister, described the explosion as sending "both soil and souls to inhabit the air for a while, and then return to be commingled forever with each other."[20]

Eighteenth Corps troops remained near the entrance to the covered way on the right when the explosion took place, about as far from it as Ferrero's troops. The men in Ames's division had been told to "stand on tiptoe, with teeth apart, to prevent anticipated injuries from the concussion." It was unnecessary, but some of them "made an awkward appearance in their efforts to carry out instructions and with open jaws, raised heels and an anxious countenance, awaited the great event."[21]

The view and sound of the explosion softened with distance. Ellis Spear in the 5th Corps had anxiously waited for the spectacle since dawn, but everyone had grown tired of the delay. Spear turned to Capt. Joseph Fitch and said, "Adjourned," but then saw Fitch's face "light up." Spear quickly turned back in time to see the explosion rise with "great rolling domes of white smoke, dense & low, with black objects shooting up through the mass." He did not recall hearing any sound, because "my eyes absorbed all my available senses." Corp. William R. Ray of the 7th Wisconsin lay on the ground and dozed off when it seemed the explosion was postponed. He was awakened by a rumbling of the earth and initially "looked at the ground to see the crack that might engulph me the next minute." Fifth Corps soldiers much farther away than

Spear and Ray claimed views of the explosion. Even men in Crawford's division at Fort Davis, the extreme left of Meade's line, reported hearing the dull rumble of the mine two miles away as if it were thunder.[22]

Some 2nd Corps units arrived at their supporting position only a short time before the explosion, after a hard, all-night march from Deep Bottom. Gibbon established his division headquarters at the Friend House by 3:45 A.M., an hour before the mine went up. He could see the "immense mushroom-shaped column of dense smoke" rising above the trees that intervened between his location and Pegram's Salient.[23]

Meade's headquarters personnel, one mile from the explosion, heard the dull sound and described the spectacle as "a mass of earth about 50 feet wide and 120 long" ascending at least 130 feet into the air. Theodore Lyman, with his back turned at the time, did not see it, but he relayed other men's impressions of it as "looking like the picture of the Iceland geysers."[24]

The Confederates

Although the mine explosion was a matter of awe and curiosity for most Federals, it was a matter of life or death for the Confederates who occupied Pegram's Salient. Many others were far enough away to recall the moment with some detachment. William Russell of the 26th Virginia in Goode's brigade had just stepped up to the parapet when he heard "a tremendous dull report and at the same time felt the earth shake beneath me." Glancing left, he saw the "awful scene" as the column of dirt and debris rose. Goode was preparing for the day when the explosion occurred, his aide pouring water into his hands from a canteen so he could wash his face. The shaking earth reminded Goode of a bowl of jelly; it woke up all his sleeping men. Younger Longest thought it was "a greate sight to see men flying in the air at such a rate." The ground trembled also to the north of Pegram's Salient, where Calvin T. Dewese of the 56th North Carolina thought it resembled a "mighty earthquake." He looked to his right to see rising above the treetops a great mass of earth, "like a mountain."[25]

Nearly six hundred yards south of the targeted fort, the blast of Pleasants's mine caused everything to "heave and stagger." Lt. W. P. Robinson of the Ringgold Battery "jumped up and looked down the line to the left and saw my conception of a volcano. I saw what appeared to be arms and legs and cannon all going up in the air."[26]

Much farther to the right, Brig. Gen. William Mahone's division held the Confederate flank west of the Jerusalem Plank Road. Many of his men had chatted the evening before "about mines and explosions of every kind, but no one knew much about the subject, as we had no previous experience." But the next morning several of them saw the column of earth rise above the trees. To the left of the crater, a member of Gracie's brigade was jolted awake by the mine explosion. He heard a comrade yell at the top of his voice, "Whoop! The earth is rising up!—a whole acre of ground is going up into the air over yonder!"[27]

Pegram's Battery and Elliott's Brigade

All the Confederates previously mentioned served in units far enough away from the mine explosion to avoid its effects. Those men serving in Pegram's Virginia battery and Elliott's South Carolina brigade, on the other hand, were the bull's-eye. Sgt. Thomas J. La Motte of the 17th South Carolina had just returned at 4 A.M. from leave in Richmond and was kneeling on a blanket in the dugout of his captain, William Dunnovant, when the mine went up only forty yards away. First there was "a muffled rumble," then immediately the ground shook. Dunnovant and La Motte stood up as the earth "heaved and opened a stream of mingled fire, smoke and dust pouring forth and rising in a column." La Motte yelled, "There goes the mine!," and ran out into a chaos of dust and panicked men who were rushing through the maze of bombproofs.[28]

Pleasants's mine "overwhelmed" Pegram's battery and the entire 18th South Carolina. Three companies of the 22nd South Carolina and part of Company A, 17th South Carolina, also were consumed by the explosion. According to Capt. John Floyd, the right wing of the 18th regiment was "enveloped, covered up with timbers, earth and debris," because the right flank rested at Pegram's gun emplacement.[29]

Lt. H. Hill of Company C and Sgt. T. J. Greer of Company A, 18th South Carolina, were buried in the explosion, but they managed to dig out before the Federals attacked. Greer used a bayonet while Hill moved dirt out of the way with his hands. Hill later told Hugh Toland how he desperately craved to "see one ray of light, or breathe the fresh air once again" while digging. When he emerged from the shattered ground, Hill fainted and was taken to a Confederate field hospital. When he arrived at the hospital, Toland claimed, the thirty-year-old lieutenant's black hair had turned white.[30]

The physical damage to Pegram's Salient was immense. More than half of the forward parapet and the right end of the cavalier were obliterated, and the two left guns of the battery were thrown up and out of the damaged fort. One landed twenty yards and the other forty yards in front of the main Confederate line, but about thirty yards of the forward parapet remained intact on the right. Burnside was surprised that the damage was not more extensive. He noted that the Confederates had stuck fence rails into their parapet and sharpened the ends to form an inclined palisade. Pleasants's mine did not shake the ground enough to loosen them.[31]

Douglas's counterminers were affected by the explosion. No one was working in the gallery of Shaft No. 1, but eight men under Sgt. A. H. Smyth were inside the gallery of Shaft No. 2. The explosion knocked Smyth to the floor, but the gallery remained intact. He took three of his men out and saw the devastation aboveground; approximately 150 yards of the Confederate line was destroyed. All except one man of the countermining detachment returned to the engineer camp at Blandford that morning. Smyth reported the last progress made in trying to intercept Pleasants—two feet three inches at Gallery No. 1, where work had ceased at 1:30 A.M., and three feet five inches at No. 2.[32]

Pegram's battery, at the epicenter of this great blast, suffered fewer casualties than expected because Pegram had undertaken a policy of withdrawing half his personnel every night in anticipation of the mine explosion. Twenty enlisted men and two officers manned the guns that morning, while the remainder rested to the rear. Nineteen of them died in the explosion. Pegram himself happened to be off duty that morning, relieved by Lt. William B. Hamlin and Lt. Christopher S. Chandler, who perished in the explosion.[33]

Losses in the supporting infantry units were very high. The 18th South Carolina, holding the left half of the cavalier with 350 men, lost 163 troops, almost half of its strength. Reports indicated that essentially all of Company A and C were lost. In Company B, only one man survived the mine blast. Sixty-two of the total casualties remained missing long after the war ended. The figure of 163 lost comes from a postwar report of regimental losses written by surgeon Hugh Toland of the 18th South Carolina and therefore seems more reliable than other reports that place the total at 86.[34]

The 22nd South Carolina held the right half of the cavalier with 300 men. The explosion killed or wounded 170, more than half of them. Colonel Fleming was sleeping in a bombproof that was completely buried by the falling debris. His men searched for three days but never found him. Company B lost 27 of 32 men, and Company G lost 31 out of 34. The clerk who wrote the record of events for Company K reported that 23 men of the unit were "blown up and supposed to have been killed."[35]

Bushrod Johnson later reported that 278 of his men were lost in the mine explosion, but that was based on a low estimate for the 18th South Carolina. Surgeon Toland's report, probably more accurate, places total losses at 352.[36]

Pleasants's mine created immense human destruction with a single blow, and it also created a weird physical landscape. Pleasants, who entered the crater during the battle, reported that the crater was 200 feet long, 50 feet wide, and 25 feet deep. Confederate engineer E. N. Wise carefully measured it after the battle. He found the hole to be 126 feet long at the surface, 69 feet long at the bottom, 87 feet wide at the top, and 38 feet wide at the bottom. Wise agreed with Pleasants that the hole was 25 feet deep. Another Confederate officer estimated that the blast took 100,000 cubic feet of earth into the air.[37]

The dimensions and technical information failed to do justice to the bizarre impressions men felt when they viewed the crater at close range. Lt. Col. Charles G. Loring of Burnside's staff recalled the "jagged masses of clay" that stuck out of the crater's sides, which consisted of loose sand. The hole was "an obstacle of fearful magnitude" to any unit that tried to pass through it. Shaped like, in one man's words, "a vast wash basin," it seemed more like "a long Irish potato" to Lt. Col. William H. Stewart of the 61st Virginia. "This great fresh earthen cavity was like the mouth of a volcano with a rim around about twelve feet above the natural land." Many people recalled the lumps of clay, pulverized and broken into numerous sizes by the blast. Most of them were small, no bigger than a man's fist, but one in particular was so large that observers remembered it for the rest of their lives. It was the size of "a small house," according to E. P. Alexander. Charles Houghton of the 14th New York Heavy Artillery likened its size to that of "a hay-stack or small cottage." It rolled out and lodged either on the lip of the crater or just a bit forward toward the Union line. The clod "remained a feature of the locality for many months," according to Alexander.[38]

8

THE FIRST UNION WAVE

Charles Wainwright, the 5th Corp artillery chief, believed the guns of Warren's corps opened fire sixty seconds after the mine began to lift Pegram's artillery out of the ground. A total of 164 guns and mortars bombarded the Confederate positions, making this one of the largest concentrations of artillery ever assembled on a Civil War battlefield. The gunners pummeled more than two miles of Rebel trenches, while at least a dozen pieces trained their sights on the immediate area of the crater. The Union bombardment continued intensely for at least an hour before slackening.[1]

For the infantrymen of the 118th New York, awaiting orders in Ames's division, the concussion of the bombardment dwarfed the impact of the mine. Smyth's brigade of the 2nd Corps had just arrived at the scene, and the men plopped down for rest. Ten minutes later, they felt the ground tremble with the bombardment, although they had not felt or seen the mine explosion three-quarters of a mile away. William Henry Lewin of the 58th Massachusetts, assigned to cooking duty well behind the line, reported that "such a racket of canon I never heard[;] you would thought that thay was a goin to taire the world up." Wainwright believed the noise was as great as that made by the artillery at Gettysburg, although with different timbres owing to the greater variety of ordnance opposing the crater.[2]

With such a heavy concentration of artillery fire, it took only about five minutes for the smoke to accumulate and obscure targets. Shell explosions within this shrouded landscape took on "a lurid appearance, very difficult to describe." The powder smoke accumulated in the still air and tended to hang "but a short distance above the earth." Wainwright could observe only the nearest mortar crew, working to reload their pieces, and then a black object rushed out of the smoke cloud into the clear air above. On another part of the line, engineer Farquhar could not see anything for at least a half hour after the explosion.[3]

Infantry units to right and left of Burnside also opened small-arms fire immediately after the mine explosion. Hiram Burnham's troops poured in volumes of fire for some time after the blowup. William R. Ray in the 5th Corps fired as quickly as he could, with the aid of three or four comrades who reloaded muskets for him. Everyone in the front rank of his regiment did the same. In this way they were able to deliver an incredible amount of fire for a few minutes. The Confederates were so well protected by their earthworks that it is doubtful they were injured by it. After a bit the firing slackened considerably. "But the greater part of the Boys thought it was fun to fight the rebs behind our own brestworks. At least when they didnt fire any." Officers sent word to stop shooting entirely, except when a good target presented itself.[4]

Ledlie Goes In

The responsibility of leading the way rested upon the men of Ledlie's division. Frightened by the falling debris, many troops had recoiled to escape the hail of dirt and timbers. It took at least ten minutes to re-form the ranks. When that was done, brigade leader Marshall shouted to his officers, "Gentlemen, take command of your lines. Second Pennsylvania rise up. Forward, march! By the right flank; march. Over the parapet, and swing up your left."[5] Marching by the flank meant that the men turned either right or left in place and marched forward, forming a narrow column of two men abreast, which could move ahead or turn right or left as needed. Marshall moved both lines of his brigade by the right flank, the right of the first line moving across the sandbag bridge first. These men entered the breach well before the left flank of his second line crossed the sandbags.[5]

Marshall personally led the right flank of the 2nd Pennsylvania Provisional Heavy Artillery, a large regiment that constituted his first line, through the narrow opening of the Federal trench. Lt. Col. Gilbert P. Robinson of the 3rd Maryland Battalion led the second line. The sight impressed members of Ledlie's engineer regiment, the 35th Massachusetts, which was posted in rear of the division. They could see the narrow column crossing the Union parapet, and it reminded them of "the assaults into the deadly breach so famous in history." An observer in Humphrey's brigade to the rear noticed some degree of disorder as Marshall's men moved across no-man's-land, "but no more than often happens in such a charge." Apparently the 14th New York Heavy Artillery in the second line did not wait its turn to move by the flank, but advanced straight ahead and tried to cross the Union trench. They stuck bayonets into the wooden revetting that held up the scarp of the trench and the interior slope of the parapet, using them as steps to climb up. Men had to hold the end of the bayonet at their hips or shoulders for this to be effective. Those who got out first helped to pull others out of the ditch. There was no time to re-form ranks once in no-man's-land, so the regiment moved forward in driblets. The first Federals to reach the Confederate line realized that falling dirt and debris had covered the Rebel obstructions in front of Pegram's Salient; the explosion had neutralized the abatis.[6]

Bartlett's brigade moved toward the advanced Union line as soon as Marshall cleared the way and duplicated Marshall's method of crossing it. While some units moved by the flank across the sandbag bridge, Stephen Weld's left wing of the brigade tried to move ahead and clambered over the works. Many of Weld's men could not climb out of the eight-foot-deep trench and had to wait for an opportunity to use the sandbags. Weld himself waited until two-thirds of his command was across no-man's-land before he went across himself, under a scattering of Confederate musket fire. Weld recalled that his feet kicked up clouds of dust, most of it recently deposited by the mine explosion, as he ran with his men.[7]

The 35th Massachusetts advanced in line behind Bartlett, but only the right-center of the line found the sandbag bridge and crossed easily. The regimental left wing tried to cross the open trench, but Capt. Clifton A. Blanchard, who commanded the regiment this day, ordered it to move to the right and wait its turn to cross over the sandbags. Ledlie stood nearby and watched; he approached Blanchard and gave him a word of instruction, and then the regiment moved across no-man's-land. Ahead they could see a "cloud of dust and smoke, now orange red in the first rays of the rising sun," where Pegram's Salient used to be.[8]

Some time before the tail of Ledlie's division left the Union position, the forward end of it entered the breach. Marshall's men paused when they reached the uplifted edge of ground that constituted the crater's lip. They climbed up and over it, "jumping, sliding, and tumbling into the hole, over the debris of material, and dead and dying men, and huge blocks of solid clay." They entered the confused horror of the crater. "The whole scene at the explosion struck every one dumb with astonishment," recalled William H. Powell. Marshall's men tumbled in without order and began to round up dazed Confederate survivors. Fifty men belonging to Companies A, B, and F, 17th South Carolina, fell into Union hands, as did thirty-five men of Company C, 22nd South Carolina.[9]

The Federals also discovered that quite a few Confederate survivors were partially buried by the explosion. As Powell put it, some were covered "up to their necks, others to their waists, and some with only their feet and legs protruding from the earth." J. D. Lynch of the 2nd Pennsylvania Provisional Heavy Artillery felt the ground move beneath him as he sat down a few minutes after

entering the crater. Other men joined him in digging on the spot, and they discovered two Confederates, both of them unhurt. One of the Rebels told his res-
cuers that he had been asleep when the mine went up and fought his way
through the loose earth that covered him, desperately seeking air. Lynch and
his comrades fed the two with breakfast from their haversacks.[10]

Wilson Henry Moore of the 22nd South Carolina had just been relieved
from guard duty before the blowup. He slept behind the trench because there
was no room in it. Moore was one of only five men in his company who survived; his comrades sleeping in the trench were buried, but he was only covered
with a light layer of dirt and debris. Moore put his hands up, which enabled
the Federals to locate and dig him out. Capt. George B. Lake of the 22nd South
Carolina found himself buried alongside a relative, W. J. Lake, whose thigh had
been broken by falling debris. Both men assumed they would die, but members
of the 14th New York Heavy Artillery dug them out. It is quite possible, as
Andrew Humphreys concluded, that those Confederates who survived the
blowup "were on the edge of the explosion; those over it never woke."[11]

The shock of the explosion created confusion and submission among those
Confederates who mingled with their captors inside the crater. A story later circulated among Lee's men that an Irishman, stunned by the blast, recovered to
see Yankees and Rebels mixed up in the hole and asked, "I say, Byes! Have we
tuk them or have they tuk us?"[12]

The Federals took more than just prisoners. Two of Pegram's guns on the
right wing of the emplacement remained intact. Members of the 14th New
York Heavy Artillery dug them out of the debris, and Sgt. Wesley Stanley of
Company D assembled gun crews from among his comrades to put them into
operation. Some members of the 2nd Pennsylvania Provisional Heavy Artillery
offered their help as well. Charles Houghton of the 14th New York Heavy
Artillery was certain there had to be a magazine filled with ordnance somewhere, and Stanley succeeded in uncovering it to provide ammunition. Stanley
sighted the southernmost gun to fire at Davidson's Confederate battery and
repositioned the other piece to fire west in case the Confederates tried to counterattack.[13]

Marshall made some effort to expand his hold outside the crater. The 2nd
Pennsylvania Provisional Heavy Artillery advanced beyond the hole for a distance. Gilbert Robinson thought it went as far as 150 yards, although how any
organized body of men could have advanced into the maze of bombproofs and
sleeping quarters behind the crater is difficult to understand. That maze still
contained many Confederate soldiers, who took potshots at the Pennsylvania
soldiers, often at their backs, and the Federals quickly retired to the relative
safety of the crater. The 3rd Maryland and 179th New York moved north out
of the crater a bit.[14]

Very soon after most of Marshall's men entered the breach, Bartlett's brigade came in as well. Despite his cork leg, Bartlett reported that he "got up to the enemy's works about as soon as any one" else in the brigade. Thomas W. Clarke saw Bartlett "hopping along very cheerily, aiding himself by a stout Malacca cane with an ivory cross handle." The crater seemed more like a prison to Stephen Weld than a military position. Trapped Confederates still wriggled here and there, "some with their legs kicking in the air, some with the arms only exposed, and some with every bone in their bodies apparently broken." Marshall and Bartlett tried to form a line inside the crater, but the western slope was too steep for the men to stand in compact ranks. They had to lie on their backs and dig in their heels to get a footing, or squat as best they could. They needed entrenching tools to form a fire step, but none were available. The engineer regiment, the 35th Massachusetts, came into the breach right after Bartlett's brigade, but by then the crater was so jammed with the majority of two brigades and numerous captured Confederates that no one placed the regiment in a position where the men could work or could pass their few tools to the crowded men who needed them.[15]

The Federals already were in trouble, because they assumed their mission was to consolidate and hold the breach and because their efforts to expand a bit out of the hole had so easily evaporated. They did not know what else to do. Marshall sent Maj. William H. Powell back to Ledlie to ask for instructions. Powell found, as he crossed the rim of the crater, that Wright's battery to the north was already sweeping no-man's-land with canister. He survived the run and found Ledlie and other staff members "in a protected angle of the works." Ledlie gave instructions for Marshall and Bartlett to advance forward out of the breach. Powell found the Confederate fire sweeping no-man's-land to have already increased in the few minutes it took for him to consult with Ledlie.[16]

Meanwhile Marshall had advised Bartlett where to position his men in the crowded space held by the Federals. He was supposed to place three regiments in the main Confederate line north of the crater with Marshall's 3rd Maryland Battalion and the 179th New York. Two regiments were to occupy the southern portion of the crater, and the rest were to strengthen the ragged line in the center, precariously posted on the western slope of the hole. But Bartlett apparently misunderstood these directions and jammed all or most of his men in the right portion of the crater and in the main Confederate line north of it. Lt. John W. Morrison reported that the 100th Pennsylvania moved up the Confederate line northward for about 150 yards until it discovered Rebels only 20 yards away. The Pennsylvanians took sandbags from the works and made sharpshooter loopholes with them on top of a convenient traverse, forming the right flank of Ledlie's position. Most of Weld's men crowded into the Rebel trench north of the crater. Weld tried to clear Confederates from the traverses and bombproofs behind the line as well.[17]

Marshall's troops also tried to consolidate their position. Robinson positioned the 3rd Maryland Battalion in traverses behind the Confederate line. Armed with Spencer repeaters, the Maryland men, who numbered only fifty-six, did effective work in sniping at short range whenever they saw a target.[18]

Griffin Goes In

Potter advanced his lead brigade simultaneously with Marshall at about 5 A.M., and to Marshall's right. Col. Daniel White led the 9th New Hampshire, 31st Maine, and 2nd Maryland of Griffin's brigade. The 9th New Hampshire rested only ten yards behind the forward line until White gave the order to advance. The men of all three regiments moved across no-man's-land without ceremony. "It was a *helter-skelter* charge," reported Sgt. Newell Dutton, "each one for himself to see who co'd get over the ground quickest and escape a murderous cross fire that was raking us."[19]

Regimental members claimed that the 9th New Hampshire was the first Federal unit to raise a flag inside the crater, but it is difficult to verify that honor. The New Hampshire men entered the breach while the air was still misty with fine dust dropped by the explosion.[20]

Griffin led the other wing of his brigade forward right after White departed. Ironically no survivors of the battle in Griffin's brigade described how the men crossed the forward Union trench, but they apparently did so as a battle line and re-formed quickly on the other side. Traversing no-man's-land, they encountered pretty strong Confederate fire.[21]

Just before starting the advance, Lt. James J. Chase of the 32nd Maine noticed the face of his sergeant, Charley Cole, a brave young soldier with a good record. Cole had begged to be relieved of duty the night before because of a premonition of death. He was the sole support of a widowed mother. "I never shall forget the forlorn, despairing look he gave me from those large dark eyes," Chase recalled. "Courage, Charley!," he shouted at Cole, but the noise of battle drowned out Cole's reply. While crossing the forward Union line, Chase's sword strap caught on something and he fell flat on his face. A nearby officer assumed he was malingering and demanded, "Why in h-l don't you go forward?" Chase lost his temper as he rose and retorted, "Go yourself!" A shell burst nearby, breaking up any further confrontation. No more than twenty-five yards from the Union line, volleys of musket fire swept across no-man's-land. Chase recalled that "the effect of this volley was horrible, men appeared to be falling in every direction and the shrieks and groans of the wounded were heartrending." The regimental commander shouted for the Maine men to lie down just in time to avoid the worst of another volley. While prone, Chase glanced back and saw Charley Cole lying close by. A second later, a bullet smashed into Cole's forehead and killed him instantly. An order came to rise and run for the breach, and Chase's comrades got into the crater as best they could. "Some jumped in, some tumbled in, others rolled in."[22]

Griffin's men were appalled when they saw what lay before them. Don E. Scott of the 11th New Hampshire told his mother that the scene "beggars description." The hole was a mad house of poorly organized manpower, studded with "huge lumps of dirt" and "half buried guns, carriages, wheels, swab sticks & countless artillery appurtenances." Scott thought "the greatest sight was to see men half buried alive—some with their heads downwards & their feet & legs protruding—others with their feet down & buried to their waists & even shoulders with one arm out, and some with neither."[23]

Potter had wanted Griffin to advance to the right of Ledlie's division into unoccupied space, but the men of his brigade had veered to the left in the dusty fallout of the explosion. It is possible that Confederate small-arms fire coming from the survivors of Elliott's brigade to the north compelled the advance to veer left as well. Griffin entered the hole, wormed his way to the top of the

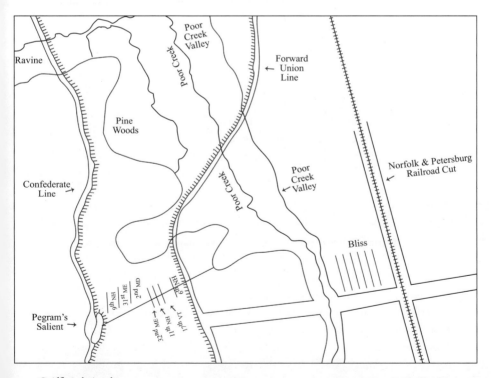

Griffin's brigade

western slope, and did his "best to rally the troops out of the crater and form a line up there, but Ledlie's men would not come up." His officers tried to work their troops into any available space they could find. "The first half hour having been lost," Griffin sardonically reported, "all was lost."[24]

White cooperated with Robinson and Weld in occupying several yards of the main Confederate line to the north. But this was only an incremental success; it did not produce a breakthrough for the Federals. Other men of Griffin's brigade remained inside the crater and helped to dig out Confederate prisoners.[25]

One of Griffin's regiments did not come into the breach. The 6th New Hampshire, at the tail end of the brigade column, stopped to hold the forward Union line as a reserve. Confederate artillery fire raked the trench, so Lyman Jackman and other regimental members found four empty barrels and set them up as flank protection. Zenas Bliss came forward from his waiting brigade east of Poor Creek to see what was going on, and he joined Jackman in taking shelter behind these barrels. When a Confederate shell skipped by, throwing dirt onto them, Bliss remarked that he was ready to leave, and Jackman decided to go too. Their places were quickly taken by four men of the regiment, two of whom were killed and the other two wounded when another shell smacked into the barrels only a few minutes later.[26]

After some time the commander of the 6th New Hampshire asked permission to move forward, and Griffin sent back word from the crater to do so. He did not want the regiment to enter the breach, because it was too crowded already, but allowed it to lie prone in no-man's-land. The Hampshire men found after a few minutes that no-man's-land was no improvement on the forward Union line. The patch of pine trees lay between their position and Wright's battery, and shells slammed into the trees, sending showers of splinters onto the regiment. Jackman often felt the air pressure of rounds that sailed only a foot from his body. The men used their tin cups and bayonets to scrape up enough dirt to cover their heads, and waited for an order to advance.[27]

But that order never arrived. The breach was already too small for the troops in it, and the Federals never managed to organize an effective effort to move them forward toward the crest near the Jerusalem Plank Road. What should have been an open door became a stumbling block to a Union advance. The physical dimensions and obstructions of the crater robbed Ledlie's division and Griffin's brigade of mobility, as did the maze of Confederate bombproofs behind it and the complex nature of the main line to the north. The Confederates offered enough resistance to complicate an already bad situation. From this point on, every new unit thrown into the breach depressed Union fortunes even more. William Powell accurately described the problem: "Every organization melted away, as soon as it entered this hole in the ground, into a mass of human beings clinging by toes and heels to the almost perpendicular sides."[28]

Hartranft Goes In

Very soon after Ledlie's men cleared the way, Hartranft brought his brigade out of the bottomland of Poor Creek and followed them. While awaiting his turn, Hartranft formed a column of regiments, putting two small regiments together to form one unit in the column where necessary. Each unit in the column crossed the sandbag bridge by the right flank. Hartranft waited until the fourth regiment had started before he personally crossed the forward Union trench.[29]

But Hartranft's brigade stopped in no-man's-land because of the crowded condition of the breach. The lead units halted just in front of the Confederate line and the eastern rim of the crater, forcing the tail end (at least two regiments) to wait inside the Union position. The rest of the brigade stretched out across the intervening space. All of Hartranft's men who were forced to mark time in no-man's-land lay down as flat as possible to save themselves. The 13th Ohio Cavalry (dismounted) lost several men lying down halfway across no-man's-land. "At every discharge of grape, I could feel the wind from the missiles," Howard Aston remembered, "and I'd flatten myself out and dig my nose deeper in the ground." After about ten minutes' delay, Aston's regiment moved forward.[30]

Hartranft packed his lead units into the left end of the hole, where about ninety feet of the connecting Rebel line south of the crater was empty. Hartranft also came upon Wesley Stanley and his comrades of the 14th New York Heavy Artillery as they were uncovering the two guns of Pegram's battery that had been buried.[31]

It was now at least 6 A.M. Howard Aston thought the crater was packed with two thousand men, probably three hundred of them clinging to the rim firing at the Confederates. The rest "seemed to be bewildered and oblivious to orders." Aston noticed two or three brigade leaders urging them to get out of the hole and continue the attack, to no avail. There were still Confederates buried in the sandy dirt. One Rebel, who was unable to extricate himself completely, pleaded with the Federals, "My good Yanks, help a feller out; you alls ain't going to let me be buried alive." Someone finally gave him a hand. Hartranft was appalled at the conditions in the crater and wrote a note, recalled division commander Willcox, "beseeching me not to put in another soul."[32]

Willcox had wanted to push Hartranft's lead regiment, the 27th Michigan, down the Confederate main line to the south to widen the breach, in conformity with his vague understanding of Burnside's plan. He thought that pushing south with his entire division, its left resting on the Confederate trench and the right brushing the Jerusalem Plank Road, was the best way to secure Ledlie's flank, but that was impossible to do now. The 27th tried to move south, but its commander was shot early in the effort and Goode's Virginia brigade offered too much resistance. Elements of the 13th Ohio Cavalry (dismounted) followed the 27th Michigan at least twenty yards but could not offer much help in the cramped conditions of the trench. Howard Aston, after this failed effort, returned to the crater because the main line did not offer security from Confederate fire.[33]

In response to Hartranft's urgent pleas, Willcox held Humphrey's brigade within the Union position. Humphrey brought his men out of the covered way and formed a line on the ground from which Marshall had started his advance, just behind the forward Union trench, and waited for orders.[34]

By about 6 A.M., all Union regiments participating in the first wave had entered the breach. Besides Humphrey, several other units waiting their turn to participate in the attack adjusted their positions. Turner moved his division into the covered way on the right some time after the start of the advance. Ferrero moved his two black brigades into the left covered way soon after Humphrey pushed out of it. Ames's division remained in place as a reserve.[35]

Marshall, Bartlett, and Griffin tried to organize a push out of the crater on the right while leaving Hartranft to his own devices on the left. Thomas W. Clarke described the effort as a well-considered plan to push Robinson's 3rd Maryland Battalion to the west. Bartlett was to move three of his regiments to the north, in front of the Confederate main line, so as to attack the Confederates who were delivering flank fire on Robinson. The 2nd Pennsylvania Provisional Heavy Artillery, the 21st Massachusetts, and the 100th Pennsylvania were to move out west and align with Robinson, while the 14th New York Heavy Artillery was supposed to form a second line behind the Maryland battalion. It is quite possible that the brigade leaders worked out a logical plan such as this, but executing it was a very different story. Moving units in such orderly fashion proved impossible; apparently some elements of these units moved out as planned, but the effort fell apart when the commander and the color-bearer of the 21st Massachusetts were shot and the Maryland battalion and the 14th New York Heavy Artillery were hit by flank fire.[36]

Clarke may have exaggerated the orderly nature of operations; most other survivors of the battle describe conditions as chaotic. According to William Powell, returning to the hole after delivering a message to Ledlie, "It was as utterly impracticable to re-form a brigade in that crater as it would be to marshal bees into line after upsetting the hive." It was "equally as impracticable to re-form outside of the crater, under the severe fire in front and rear, as it would be to hold a dress parade in front of a charging enemy." Powell blamed it on the absence of an officer of higher authority, referring to Ledlie. If the troops had immediately advanced north or south out of the hole to widen the breach instead of consolidating their position, the crater would have been cleared for the advance of support troops. But there were no division- or corps-level commanders on the spot who could take charge of the situation. Powell, in another apt analogy, deemed the brigade commanders' efforts to push out of the hole as useless as "the dropping of handfuls of sand into a running stream to make a dam."[37]

Other survivors recalled the frustrations of that morning with pain. "It was altogether the most miserable and meanest experience I ever had in my life," said Stephen Weld. "You could not fight, you could not give an order, you could not get anything done." Weld suggested that Bartlett was of little use in the jumbled conditions of the crater because of his wooden leg. But the worst problem was the breakdown of unit cohesion and the impossibility of re-forming battle lines or columns on the constricted, irregular ground of the crater.[38]

Amid all this chaos, the 35th Massachusetts tried to perform engineer duty. The regiment began working on the crater face nearest the Union position, but within fifteen minutes of entering the hole, half of the regiment's officers were shot down. The rest divided the 35th into three battalions to speed the work as an officer went back to ask permission to dig a covered way connecting the crater with the forward Union line. Even though the men of the 35th worked hard, there were too few of them to make much progress and their efforts were hampered by the crowded conditions. More and more wounded men littered the slopes of the crater, getting in the way of shovels and spades, until frustrated officers shouted, "Bury them if they won't move!"[39]

Ironically, whereas the engineers of the 35th Massachusetts strove to do their duty, most infantrymen inside the crater seem to have dropped their responsibilities. If Aston was right, only a small portion endeavored to return Confederate fire along the crater rim. The others apparently milled about. Lt. John Grierson of the 14th New York Heavy Artillery reported that his men were "waiting in the works to rest. Made a break fast of Rebel hoecake."[40]

The Generals

Powell's criticism of Ledlie has resonated through the decades because the commander of the lead division in Burnside's attack never left the Union lines. His absence in the hole was obvious, and his activities and location were equally obvious to those who remained within the Union position. Moreover, unlike the other division leaders, who sincerely tried to figure out what to do about the situation, Ledlie gave up any real opportunity to influence the actions of his command.

Orville P. Chubb, surgeon of the 20th Michigan, set up his field hospital in a bombproof only ten rods behind the forward Union line as soon as

Humphrey's brigade moved out of the covered way and took post where Ledlie's division had assembled. The bombproof had been used as a regimental headquarters, but it would do just fine as a dressing station. Soon after settling in, Ledlie arrived and sat down outside the bombproof for a while. Then he moved inside to rest, and Ferrero came in soon after that. Chubb noticed that a staff officer arrived with orders from Burnside to move the division out of the breach. Ledlie expressed surprise that his men had not moved beyond the crater and sent several messages urging them on. He claimed to be unable to go himself because a spent ball had hit his leg. Ledlie's staff milled about outside the bombproof; at least two of them were hit by stray bullets, and one of them died. Lt. Col. Charles G. Loring of Burnside's staff had accompanied Ledlie's troops when they entered the crater. Ten minutes later he came back to report to Ledlie of conditions there and then went on to tell Burnside, so there could be no reason for Ledlie to be surprised that something was wrong.[41]

It is true that neither Potter nor Willcox left the Union lines, but then only half of their divisions had gone up in the first Union wave. Both men remained behind to coordinate the dispatch of reinforcements and remained keenly aware of developments. Henry Pleasants, serving as a volunteer aide for Potter, entered the crater very early in the attack and returned to him with a full report of conditions there. Willcox moved his division headquarters up to the forward Union line, from where he could catch a glimpse of the crater. It looked like a "large ampitheatre," he thought. Willcox's headquarters were "in a warm place during the whole fight," and at least one orderly was hit while standing next to him.[42]

Burnside felt almost a prisoner at his headquarters in the Fourteen Gun Battery. He understood the situation in the crater only through messages brought back by staff officers. Ord was with him and later testified that cannon smoke so obscured the view he could see nothing from the battery for at least an hour after the explosion. Visibility increased only slightly after that, but it did not help, because the Federals inside the breach were huddling inside a hole that was thirty feet deep.[43]

Yet Burnside received enough information to know, in general, what was going on in the crater. Loring brought back the first report by 5:30 A. M., which prompted Burnside to send instructions for Ledlie to push out of the breach and up to the ridge crest. The first of many messages from army headquarters arrived a few minutes later, asking for news. Burnside responded that his men held the enemy line and were preparing to move on. This set up the pattern of the morning, with 9th Corps headquarters the target of two streams of paper flowing from front and rear into the Fourteen Gun Battery, neither of them bringing good news. Burnside became dependent on the stream coming in from the crater, and he felt harassed by the stream that came from Meade.[44]

Very soon after responding to Meade's first inquiry, Burnside got into trouble with his army commander, through no real fault of his own. Loring found that it was nearly impossible to execute the order to move out of the breach. He wrote a note for Burnside that Ledlie's men could not be moved. Unfortunately he gave it to a courier who did not remember that Burnside had shifted his headquarters to the Fourteen Gun Battery and took it to the former 9th Corps headquarters site, which now was occupied by Meade. The army leader received this note at about 5:45 and was angry to discover such important news by accident. He sent a message to 9th Corps headquarters urging Burnside to push on with Ord's troops as well as his own.[45]

By 6 A.M., with no further word from Burnside, Meade dispatched a string of messages relaying intelligence from Confederate prisoners that the Rebels had no second line on top of the ridge crest. Also there were no signs that Lee was shifting reinforcements from north of the James River. "Our chance is now," he urged Burnside. "Push your men forward at all hazards (white and black) and don't lose time in making formations, but rush for the crest." Ten minutes later a return message arrived from the Fourteen Gun Battery that Burnside had issued orders to this effect.[46]

Meade also began to wonder if the 5th Corps should attack as well, but he felt uncomfortable ordering it. Warren's primary responsibility was to anchor the army's left flank, and Meade still worried that the Confederates might advance west of the Jerusalem Plank Road. Humphreys sent a telegram to Burnside at 6 A.M., asking him if he needed support from the 5th Corps. At 6:20, about the time that Warren visited the Fourteen Gun Battery to see what was happening, Burnside responded positively but added, "I will designate to you when it ought to move. There is scarcely room for it now in our immediate front."[47]

Soon after sending this note to army headquarters, Burnside issued another round of instructions to all his division leaders to clear the breach and move on to important objectives. He told them to advance toward the crest regardless of lack of support to either flank and regardless of the plan he had given them the night before and regardless of anything Ledlie's stalled division was doing. A decided note of desperation at the rapid fading of hope is evident in the dispatches.[48]

Eager to see what was happening, Burnside and Warren left the Fourteen Gun Battery and entered the covered way to the rear. They spent several minutes trying to look past the bulky fort toward the breach, with little success. The pair returned to the battery to find another message from Meade, sent at 6:50 A.M., testily informing Burnside that Warren's corps had been ready since 3:20 that morning and that he wanted the 9th Corps commander to offer a professional judgment as to whether there was any practical benefit to moving it forward, "without waiting for your column." Meade went on to vent some of his own frustration. "What is the delay in your column moving? Every minute is most precious, as the enemy undoubtedly are concentrating to meet you on the crest, and if you give them time enough you cannot expect to succeed. There is no object to be gained in occupying the enemy's line; it cannot be held under their artillery fire without much labor in turning it. The great point is to secure the crest at once, and at all hazards."[49]

By 7 A.M., more than two hours after the explosion, Meade and Burnside were well aware that the attack was reaching a crisis point. As both men were stuck at their headquarters, the frustration they felt tended to be vented toward each other. Meade thought it was his duty to remain at Burnside's old headquarters site in case an important telegram or dispatch arrived that demanded immediate attention. To prove the wisdom of this decision, he noted that his headquarters received or sent more than one hundred messages between 5 and 10 A.M. that day, one about every three minutes. It was impossible, he argued, to go forward and conduct a personal inspection of affairs.[50]

Meade also sent a string of messages to Warren, prompted by early news from signal officers that there seemed to be no Confederates west of the Jerusalem Plank Road. This raised the possibility of a 5th Corps attack a good distance south of the crater, rather than directly in support of Burnside's advance, and Humphreys began suggesting the idea to Warren by 5:50 A.M. Warren hesitated, arguing that it was difficult to tell how strongly the Rebels held the line in his front. At 6:15 A.M., just before arriving at Burnside's headquarters, Warren reported the Confederate line was still strongly held.[51]

Warren also reminded army headquarters that most of his command was massed on the corps right as a reserve for Burnside. Only Crawford's division was immediately available for an attack along the Jerusalem Plank Road. After receiving more messages to push forward, Warren sent a request to Crawford asking if he could comply with his available troops. At most, Warren thought Crawford might advance with one and a half brigades, but Ayres could pull his small division from the right to help him if Meade approved. Ayres spent part of the morning with Warren at corps headquarters, located at the Five Gun Battery near the Avery House. Thomas L. Livermore, an 18th Corps staff officer who spoke a bit with Warren at the Fourteen Gun Battery, thought the 5th Corps commander "seemed very anxious to be allowed to assault," but his actions indicated otherwise. Meade shared a bit of Warren's caution regarding the wisdom of attacking along the road. He wanted Crawford to conduct a reconnaissance in force with Baxter's brigade and a portion of Lyle's brigade, to see if the Confederate line was strongly held near the leadworks, located near the Weldon and Petersburg Railroad about two miles west of the Jerusalem Plank Road. Only after the results of this reconnaissance were known would Meade decide whether to transfer Ayres's division from the right to the left of the 5th Corps, but that would take quite some time.[52]

Meade also tried to coordinate the actions of the only cavalry force yet at his disposal, Brig. Gen. James H. Wilson's division. The rest of Sheridan's cavalry corps had not yet returned from Deep Bottom when Humphreys sent a message to Wilson instructing him to cover the left flank of Warren's projected attack along the Jerusalem Plank Road. Wilson had orders to ride west and gain the Weldon and Petersburg Railroad, then advance northward along it, keeping pace with the 5th Corps troops.[53]

Meade kept in close touch with Hancock to the right of the area of operations, asking if the Confederate line north of the crater was thinly held and vulnerable to an attack by Mott's division. Hancock's initial response, a little after 6 A.M., was similar to Warren's. It was difficult to tell anything, given the fact that most troops on both sides of no-man's-land kept well down in their trenches. Ord, whose troops had held this part of the line before the attack, left word for Mott that there was no possibility of attacking in this area if the enemy line was held with any force. Brigade commanders reported to Mott that Union artillery fire elicited some return skirmish fire.[54]

To find out if the main line was held, Hancock ordered Mott to send forward some troops at 6:30 A.M. A skirmish line went forward from Mott's left brigade, the one nearest Burnside's attack; several men were shot down while crossing the parapet, and their comrades took shelter wherever possible.[55]

Grant chose not to be tied to the telegraph or to dispatches. He had a restless desire to see what was happening from a close perspective and waited for the mine explosion at a point to the rear of the 9th Corps position. Staff officer Horace Porter wrote a popular book after the war, playing rather loose with facts in order to tell a dramatic story. To the degree that he is a faithful historian, one gets a picture of Grant waiting for the blowup, leaning against a tree: "His lips were compressed and his features wore an expression of profound anxiety, but he uttered few words. There was little to do but wait." Nervously looking at his watch, Grant had just put it into his pocket when Pleasants's mine went up. According to Porter, Grant had a clear view of the debris and dirt plume; he then waited forty-five minutes to give Burnside's men a chance to do something.[56]

Leaving the tree, Grant, with Porter and an orderly, rode forward and encountered Thomas's brigade of Ferrero's division still waiting outside the left-side covered way. Thomas first became aware of Grant's presence when he heard "a quiet voice behind me" ask, "Who commands this brigade?" When Thomas turned around, he saw the stocky general in chief on his horse wearing "a broad-brimmed felt hat and the ordinary coat of a private. He wore no sword." Grant asked him why his men were not engaged, and Thomas explained that his orders were to follow Sigfried, and that both brigades had to wait until Ledlie and Willcox cleared the way in front. "'Will you give me the order to go in now?" Thomas presumptuously asked him. Grant hesitated and said slowly, "'No, you may keep the orders you have.'" Then he turned his horse and left with Porter and the orderly in tow.[57]

Grant headed for Meade's headquarters, passing by Turner's division still waiting outside the right-side covered way. He raised his hat to the commander of a Pennsylvania regiment (either the 76th or 97th, in Lt. Col. William B. Coan's brigade) when that officer saluted him. The Pennsylvanian was greatly impressed by this, as he told Porter long after the war's end. The men recognized Grant, too, and began to cheer him until the regimental commander put a stop to it as a violation of orders to remain quiet. Grant also visited the 2nd Pennsylvania Heavy Artillery in Ames's division (not to be confused with the 2nd Pennsylvania Provisional Heavy Artillery, a different regiment in Marshall's brigade of Ledlie's division) as it waited in reserve. Capt. Nicholas Baggs recalled seeing Grant ride up to the regiment alone. "He was in a fatigue suit and smoking a cigar." Henry Pippitt saw the general in chief "walking around thier in crowd just [as] if thier was nothing going on."[58]

Another of Grant's staff members, Cyrus Comstock, went from Burnside's headquarters to Warren's headquarters during the early hours of the attack, gathering news that he relayed to Grant by dispatches. Comstock confirmed what Grant picked up from his own observation, that 9th Corps troops were stuck in the breach. Grant informed Benjamin Butler of affairs as early as 6:30 A.M. He hoped Burnside might yet succeed, but if Lee began to shift troops from the north side of the James, Butler should be ready to attack wherever the enemy was weak. Butler was on the alert, informing 10th Corps commander David B. Birney and keeping abreast of reports from the picket line. He also suggested to Grant that Federal guns try to fire on the bridges across the Appomattox River if signal officers detected signs of troop movement across them.[59]

HOLDING THE LINE

Few commands were as stunned by the opening of a battle as was Stephen Elliott's that morning. Nearly one-fourth of its manpower was killed, wounded, or captured within minutes of the mine explosion, and the other three-fourths of the men were shaken and vulnerable for a while. Elliott could count on fewer than twelve hundred troops to hold the breach against four Union brigades that probably outnumbered his remnant four to one.[1]

Sgt. Thomas J. LaMotte of the 17th South Carolina had been on leave in Richmond for several days before July 30, returning to his regiment at about 4 A.M. He was kneeling on a blanket in Capt. William Dunnovant's bomb-proof, telling him the news from the capital, when Pleasants's mine exploded forty yards away. There was "a muffled rumble like the sound of a very distant thunder," LaMotte recalled, and "then almost simultaneously, a tremor of the ground beneath us." Both men stood up as the earth "heaved and opened a stream of mingled fire, smoke and dust pouring forth and rising in a column for about fifty feet, spreading out like a tree top, then slowly settling down like a cloud in the still atmosphere of that early summer morning."[2]

LaMotte yelled, "There goes the mine!," and rushed out to find lots of Elliott's men running north in panic and into the maze of ditches to the rear of Pegram's battery. Other Confederates, "paralyzed with fear," were too confused to run. An observer noted that some men "vaguely scratched at the counter-scarp as if trying to escape."[3]

Col. Fitz William McMaster of the 17th South Carolina emerged from his bombproof seventy-five yards from the explosion to witness a mad scramble away from the expanding hole. Lt. J. R. Moss of the 17th ran out of his quarters without shoes or coat and did not recover his wits until after he had reached McAfee's brigade to the north. The panic that gripped Elliott's survivors lasted about fifteen minutes; the arrival of Ledlie's division galvanized their energies toward holding what was left of the line. Sgt. Smith Lipscomb of the 18th South Carolina survived the explosion although his thigh bones felt as if they were "almost Shivered." Lipscomb lay down for a few minutes to rub his legs until the Federals appeared on the scene. They called on him to give up, but Lipscomb found new strength and scrambled away to join what was left of his regiment north of the crater.[4]

The Yankee challenge brought a cheer from at least some of Elliott's men, and the immediate opening of fire. Some South Carolinians joined in the firing as soon as they dug themselves out. For the most part, the Federals "could be dimly seen through the dust and smoke, crowding near our works. The space between the lines seemed packed with them." LaMotte caught glimpses of the Yankees leaving their own line on a narrow front and entering the breach in groups. Only eight to ten men out of twenty-nine in LaMotte's company were available for duty. Pvt. Starling Hutto of Company H, only sixteen years old, stood atop the parapet to get a better fire. McMaster pulled him down and sternly told him to take cover.[5]

As Ledlie's men moved into the Confederate line north of the crater, they came closer to Elliott's left wing. Some of LaMotte's men were trying to build a traverse with sandbags and noticed Yankees only thirty yards away. LaMotte told them to walk close to the sides of the trench to lessen their exposure, but Lt. Samuel C. Lowry of Company F was hit in the forehead by a bullet and died instantly at LaMotte's feet. Company D, 17th South Carolina, held at the first traverse north of the crater, and Company C held the second traverse.[6]

Stephen Elliott and two of his staff members were in their headquarters bombproof when the explosion occurred. As various officers scurried off to stop stragglers, re-form the troops, or take orders to regimental leaders, Elliott desperately sought a way to seal the breach. He wanted all available men to move into the cavalier, but the confusion was too great for immediate action. The brigade commander and Maj. James C. Coit made their way to the left wing north of the crater soon after the men opened fire on Ledlie. Coit discovered that Pegram's battery was gone, so he began to make his way to Wright's battery. Maj. John C. Haskell arrived on the scene looking for infantry support. He told Elliott that his guns and mortars would be helpless against a Union advance. Elliott agreed but admitted that his men were "very much demoralized" and he doubted if he could do much to help. Soon after, Elliott managed to bring up the head of Col. Alexander D. Smith's 26th South Carolina and arranged for united action between that regiment and McMaster's 17th South Carolina. According to McMaster, Elliott wanted to form a battle line in the open, perhaps seventy-five yards from the hole, and "drive the enemy out of the crater."[7]

Elliott and Smith planned to lead the men of the 26th, to be followed by McMaster's regiment. At about twenty minutes after the explosion, Elliott jumped out of the trench into the open, with Smith and a handful of Carolinians right behind. Elliott was shot after taking only a few steps, a bullet penetrating the upper part of his lungs. Smith was lightly wounded in the shoulder. "Colonel, you must take charge of the brigade," Elliott told McMaster as he was carried into the trench. The new commander realized it was impossible to continue the counterattack and told the men to take cover in the trench north of the crater. Coit, who witnessed the aborted advance from his position at Wright's battery, called it "the only mistaken movement" he witnessed on the Confederate side that day. Thomas LaMotte went further than that. He was convinced that Elliott's wounding saved the battle and the brigade, because the two regiments would have been shredded, leaving the works north of the crater empty. The Federals "would have found an unobstructed entrance into Petersburg that morning," he concluded.[8]

Taking stock of the situation, McMaster could count up to sixteen Union flags inside the crater. There was not much firing because both sides were taking cover, but it was obvious that the Federals might try to leave the hole, enter the ravine, and make their way onto the crest and into Petersburg. McMaster hit on an effective plan. He told Smith to take his 26th South Carolina, with three of the biggest companies of the 17th South Carolina under charge of Capt. E. A. Crawford of Company K, and go to the small ravine that lay 350 yards west of the crater. It drained into the main ravine through which the Confederates had run their covered way. McMaster hoped that his men could prevent the enemy from advancing northward out of the hole directly into the main ravine, but he also wanted to deliver fire on the area west of the hole and near the head of the branch ravine. Smith and Crawford would have to block that line of Yankee advance with about three hundred men. They moved through the covered way, ascending the main ravine until reaching the mouth of the branch ravine, keeping under cover the entire way. McMaster also sent word to Johnson calling for more help and sent a message to the right wing of Elliott's brigade south of the crater telling it to hold its ground.[9]

The Confederate trench north of the crater was jammed with Elliott's left wing, which was all that was left of the 17th and 18th South Carolina. McMaster later recalled that "it was tedious to move in it." To the extent possible, he directed the men to build traverses at key locations to protect themselves from enemy fire. McMaster also adjusted his position a bit, moving the command a short distance north to more advantageous ground at a sharper angle in the works. Some members of the 18th South Carolina could not "see any good Genl-Ship in" this and protested the apparent giving way in the face

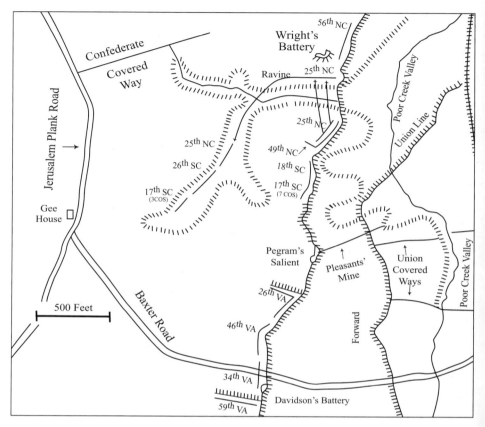

The Confederates hold on

of the enemy. Sgt. Stout Noland of Company B jumped on top of the parapet to exhort his comrades to "not . . . give up our line." Smith Lipscomb grabbed his jacket to pull him down, but not before a bullet hit Noland's mouth, disfiguring but not killing him. After settling in their adjusted position, Lipscomb took cover and fired sixty rounds at the crater, using guns reloaded by his men and exhausting the ammunition supply readily available, to little purpose.[10]

McAfee and Goode

The 25th North Carolina, the right flank of McAfee's brigade, lay only 250 yards north of the crater and on the south side of the main ravine that drained through the Confederate line. The 49th North Carolina, the next regiment, lay 400 yards north of the hole and on the north side of the ravine. W. A. Day of the 49th went to sleep just before dawn on July 30, having finished a tour of picket duty, and was jarred awake by the explosion. He was "almost buried in the dirt" that fell from the roof of his bombproof because the logs were loosened by the explosion. Day found his comrades falling into line when he emerged from the bombproof.[11]

Regimental commanders reacted quickly. The 25th North Carolina pulled out of the trench and formed line in the open, on the north side of the main ravine and facing south. The regiment formed, in short, a refused right flank to protect McAfee's position; its own left flank rested behind the right rear of the 49th North Carolina. The 25th apparently assumed the whole salient was gone and prepared to stem the expected Union attack northward from the breach.[12]

Soon after McMaster sent away Smith's 26th South Carolina and three companies of the 17th South Carolina under Crawford, McAfee dispatched the 25th North Carolina to help. The regiment moved into the covered way by the right flank and followed the South Carolinians into the branch ravine. The troops took position in the small ravine with Crawford's men on the right, where it was quite shallow, with Smith's 26th South Carolina in the center and the 25th North Carolina on the left.[13]

The 49th North Carolina then extended its line along the trench, crossing the main ravine, to close up on McMaster's left wing. The Tar Heels of the 49th thought they were saving the day. Rushing along the trench as fast as possible, they saw the South Carolinians moving northward away from the crater as part of McMaster's effort to consolidate his position. Shouting, "Hold on; we are coming!," the regiment closed the gap between the two units. A portion of the 49th moved into a covered way extending back from the main trench to form a short, refused line. Whether it was the entire right wing of the regiment that did this, or only two companies, is difficult to determine.[14]

McAfee had to adjust the rest of his units to cover the brigade sector. The 56th North Carolina followed up the 49th, and was in turn followed by the 35th and 24th North Carolina. All these regiments deployed in a single line from the main ravine to the left end of McAfee's section of the line.[15]

South of the 49th North Carolina, McMaster had seven companies of the 17th South Carolina and what was left of the 18th South Carolina in position. For a time there was a lull in the fighting. Some Federals wandered into the maze of bombproofs, and others found their way into a section of the abandoned cavalier. With the opposing lines only tens of yards apart, the men yelled out to "guy each other" or to throw bayonets at their opponents. "It seemed to me about this time the *laziest* fight I ever saw," McMaster wrote. He lit his pipe for a quick smoke as his men "longed for hand-grenades." McMaster accidentally knocked the stem from his pipe and a nearby soldier playfully yelled, "Hold on, men! The colonel can't fight without his pipe." He then picked up the stem and handed it to McMaster.[16]

Smith, Crawford, and the 25th North Carolina kept up a continuous fire
at the crater from their cover in the shallow ravine. The Carolinians also managed to scratch out a crude line of trench inside the ravine, especially at the
more shallow end where Crawford's men were stationed. Later that morning,
McMaster made his way through the covered way to visit Smith and see how
the men were faring in the ravine.[17]

McMaster's visit to Smith was part of his effort to maintain contact with
the three widely separated segments of his brigade. What was left of the right
wing remained south of the crater, cooperating with Goode's Virginia brigade
to contain the Yankees on the right of the breach. Goode's left flank was about
200 yards from the crater, with the 26th Virginia on the left, then the 46th,
34th, and 59th Virginia to their right. Soon after the explosion, Goode moved
the 59th into "a covered way, or ditch, running perpendicular to the line of
works." The one hundred men on duty in the 59th could then fire on the
Federals if they tried to advance through the hole. Goode also advanced the
26th Virginia a bit northward to a traverse only 30 yards from the crater. Here
the regiment could face at least some of its manpower northward toward the
Union flank if the enemy advanced.[18]

McMaster sent couriers with messages to his Carolinians south of the
crater. What was left of the 22nd and 23rd, now led by Capt. J. N. Shedd of
Company E, 22nd South Carolina, gathered near Goode's 26th Virginia and
constructed new traverses where needed. Goode instructed the rest of his
brigade to fire in an oblique direction to the left to harass the Federals crossing from their own forward line to the captured works. Because Goode had
moved his left flank about 170 yards northward, his command also was
stretched pretty thin. In the center the men stood 10 feet apart; on the left they
were massed in the narrow trench and passages to the rear of the main line.
Although the Virginians reportedly lay down a heavy fire as their contribution
to the defense of the breach, at least one witness in the 23rd South Carolina
claimed that some of them refused to expose themselves and instead just
pointed their muskets down the length of the Confederate trench. This, of
course, would have tended to worry those Carolinians and Virginians alike
who were packed in that section of the line only 30 yards from the enemy. The
Carolinians sent back word, threatening to return fire if the Virginians did not
behave, and they stopped immediately.[19]

McMaster's left wing and the supporting Tar Heels north of the crater were
pressed by Federals who tried to push up the Confederate trench and widen the
breach. Thomas LaMotte and about ten survivors of his company held behind
the second traverse north of Pegram's Salient, taking potshots at the Yankees.
At one point LaMotte saw other members of McMaster's brigade begin to
move toward the Federals in the cavalier and assumed a counterattack was

under way. He set out as well but soon noticed that his comrades were surrendering to the enemy. Fortunately LaMotte had time to return to the second traverse before it was too late. Soon after, he noticed that his men were picked off by a stealthy Federal. Only by careful watching could he see that the Yankee was hiding behind a group of canteens hanging from a forked stick where the cavalier joined the main line.[20]

Before much time passed, the Federals made significant efforts to push northward out of the crater. Pvt. W. A. Hoke of the 17th South Carolina knocked down four Yankees before he was bayoneted. The enemy continued up the line, capturing twenty-eight men of Company D, 17th South Carolina, but LaMotte and his men held them off at the second traverse. In the lull that followed this sharp fight, LaMotte suggested the defenders pile sandbags across the trench. At about the same time, McMaster saw Lt. Henry Pratt shot in the head and recalled that the evening before Pratt had talked excitedly about his plans to plant clover on his South Carolina farm after the war to copy the Virginia farmers. McMaster had reminded him that one out of three Confederates would likely die in the conflict, and Pratt had confidently replied, "I do not expect to be that one."[21]

Fortunately for the Confederates, the remnants of McMaster's left wing stopped the Federals. In the process the 49th North Carolina lost its trusted commander, Lt. Col. John A. Fleming. Although no one recalled exactly when it happened, many members of both McMaster's and McAfee's brigades remembered the incident. According to one account, Fleming grabbed the regimental colors, planted them on top of the parapet, and called for his men to clear out the trench recently taken by the Federals. A ball smashed into his face and out the back of his head. But according to McMaster, Fleming had just pointed out a good place to build a barricade across the trench and was about to start the work when he was hit in the neck. All agreed that the bullet badly disfigured Fleming and that he died almost instantly.[22]

Nevertheless the Confederate position north of the crater was at least temporarily secure. Although not designed for defense against an enemy inside the trench, the Confederates modified their works with sandbag traverses. Also a significant bend of the trench was located on top of the southern slope of the ravine, north of the crater, and it was securely held by men of the 49th North Carolina. Unless the Federals found a way to attack McMaster's and McAfee's troops from a different direction, the Confederates could hold here for some time.[23]

Johnson and Hoke

Bushrod Johnson sent word to his subordinate commanders to move toward the breach right after the explosion of Pleasants's mine woke him up. He also sent staff members to ask help from division commanders to his right and left. The messenger sent to William Mahone soon reported that he already was on the move. At some point early in the battle, Capt. W. Gordon McCabe arrived at Johnson's headquarters to find out how he could get a couple of batteries into action to help contain the Yankees. "General Johnson knew nothing of the extent of the disaster," McCabe later recalled. "He had not even been to the front."[24]

Maj. Gen. Robert F. Hoke told Johnson's messenger that he had no troops to spare because he was responsible for holding two salients that might also be targets of Federal attacks. Some time after Johnson's staff officer left, Beauregard arrived at Hoke's headquarters and voiced the opinion that Pegram's Salient was the only target. Beauregard probably based this view on the dimensions of the Union effort under way at that location. He ordered Hoke to send a regiment from Brig. Gen. Thomas L. Clingman's brigade to help Johnson, and the 61st North Carolina was soon on its way.[25]

Some time after dispatching the 61st, Hoke received another directive from Beauregard to send more help. He started a regiment from Brig. Gen. Johnson Hagood's South Carolina brigade, and later a third regiment from Brig. Gen. Alfred H. Colquitt's Georgia brigade. The three regiments were "quite a reduction" in his available manpower. Of the three regiments sent, however, only the 61st North Carolina participated in the battle.[26]

Confederate Artillery

James C. Coit had arrived at Wright's battery about twenty-five minutes after the explosion. No Confederate artillery had yet opened fire, even though the Federal guns had been booming ever since the explosion. Coit gave the order to open fire, and Wright's gunners responded. They sighted their pieces on the hole itself and targeted the Federals when they spilled out into no-man's-land to take shelter behind the lip of the crater. Wright's battery was at a slightly higher elevation up the ridge slope than Pegram's Salient, and the gunners had an edge in their attempt to land shells almost anywhere they chose.[27]

Richard G. Pegram and one of his lieutenants had taken a break in Petersburg for a few days to rest and work on his battery's muster rolls. Rolled out of bed by the explosion, Pegram went up to the line and encountered Coit at Wright's battery. Coit told him the bad news, that the salient was a shambles and his gunners either killed or scattered. He then ordered Pegram back to battalion headquarters to gather information about survivors and to ready a section of guns belonging to the battalion that was not yet in line. Pegram spent the entire day at battalion headquarters within the main ravine as thousands of Union and Confederate soldiers struggled for possession of his battery site.[28]

The collection of mortars near Pegram's Salient opened fire soon after the explosion. Richard W. Flournoy recalled that the mortar he served had already obtained the range to Poor Creek valley, where everyone assumed the shaft of the Union mine was located. His comrades opened fire on that area for a while until a message arrived that Pegram's battery had been replaced by a hole filled with Union soldiers, and the mortar men shifted their sights to that location as a target.[29]

Lt. W. P. Robinson's Ringgold Battery opened fire with two guns 573 yards south of the crater. Before long, Robinson estimated that fifty Union guns and mortars were trying to knock his men out, but they suffered little because of their well-constructed earthworks. Haskell had begun to keep two reserve batteries of his battalion harnessed every night since July 27. Thus, when the mine exploded, he was ready to move them into action. Haskell placed the pieces near the top of the ridge along the Jerusalem Plank Road in "some half-completed gunpits," as well as in "a shallow sink in the road." He then went forward to ask Elliott for infantry support; he returned to the guns when Elliott could not help. Haskell told some of his spare gunners to pick up muskets from the battlefield and be ready to repel a Federal attack.[30]

When W. Gordon McCabe went to Johnson's headquarters to get information about how to deploy two of his batteries (Brander's and Purcell's), he obtained no information from the harried division leader and was on his own. His commander, Col. William Pegram, found a way to place the guns fifty yards behind and to the right of the Gee House. Here, west of the Jerusalem Plank Road, the artillery was about five hundred yards from the crater. It was nearly 9 A.M. before the guns were in place and ready for action, only because the Jerusalem Plank Road, the nearest link between Johnson's headquarters and the Gee House, was swept by enemy fire.[31]

Another artillery unit had been planted near the Gee House many days before the battle. Capt. Henry G. Flanner's North Carolina battery occupied a detached artillery emplacement without infantry support. The six guns opened at a distance of five hundred yards when the Yankees attempted to move out of the crater and played an important role in persuading them to return.[32]

Because the Federals were locked in a static position within close range, more than a dozen Confederate mortars began to pound them. Joseph William Eggleston, commanding a mortar emplacement, had seen panic on the faces of his men after the mine exploded, but he jumped onto the magazine to demonstrate a calm attitude. Eggleston could not see Pegram's Salient because of the dust and cannon smoke. Unwilling to fire on that area for fear of hitting Confederate troops, he opened on Union gun emplacements. His men had earlier recorded the range and direction of at least ten Federal artillery positions.

To further inspire them, Eggleston "deliberately filled and lighted my pipe and saw the effect on the men immediately."[33]

Because the noise of the battle was nearly deafening, Eggleston relayed the range and direction by speaking close to the ear of each responsible gunner. Keeping a close eye on his watch, he changed the target every five minutes. The sun already was burning hot and no water was readily available. "Three times our parapet was shot through and each time I had to seize a shovel and be the first up to mend the break," Eggleston recalled. "The men always took my shovel away from me but it was imperative that I lead the way." He and his crew continued in this way for hours that morning.[34]

Sgt. A. Whit Smith was in charge of three six-inch mortars near the Baxter Road, south of the crater. He fired until only ten rounds were left for each piece; standing orders compelled him to retain at least this number to repel an infantry attack. His mortars fell silent long before the battle was decided, and Smith refused entreaties sent by infantry commanders to resume firing.[35]

Davidson's battery, located 373 yards south of the crater, suffered enormously that morning. All the guns were on a rise of ground on the ridge slope, comparatively exposed to Union fire, and Lt. James C. Otey could not stand the Federal cannon. He lost his nerve and deserted his battery early in the engagement, followed by some of the gunners. When battalion commander Wade Hampton Gibbs found out about this, he took personal charge of the battery. Three members of Alexander's staff, plus Pvt. L. T. Covington of Pegram's battery, helped him. They started firing the left gun about 6 A.M., but Gibbs was severely wounded by a bullet when he looked across the parapet to see the effect of his rounds. The ball broke his collar bone and cut an artery; the surgeons feared for his life, but he survived.[36]

Fortunately Gibbs had spoken to Capt. David N. Walker of George Otey's Battery A before going to Davidson's position and instructed him to round up an officer and some artillerymen to work the guns. Walker sent for his reserve gunners, who were stationed at his battery camp a mile to the rear. Not long after, Walker saw Gibbs as the wounded artillery officer was transported to the rear, and he assumed command of the battalion. Walker rushed to Davidson's position to find the battery silent and only two or three men at their post. Because this was "the point of most importance" in Gibbs's command, Walker devoted his attention to getting Davidson's guns back into action. Enemy rounds had caused the embrasure of the leftmost piece to cave in. Walker asked Goode for help, and the infantry commander brought Capt. Samuel D. Preston's Company C, 34th Virginia. This company and another in the regiment had previously trained as artillerists. Goode also left his aide, Capt. Alexander F. Bagby, at the artillery position to report to him if trouble developed and then rushed back to his brigade. Walker also relieved Alexander's staff members, because they had little or no skill working the guns. Preston directed the clearing of the embrasure; he and one of his men were shot in the process.[37]

Bagby tried to keep the battery operating. He saw Samuel P. Ryland, an orderly on Goode's staff, passing the artillery position and called out to him. Bagby talked Ryland into helping to fire the leftmost gun, but a bullet struck Bagby in the head and killed him instantly. At about 9 A.M., Ryland reported the bad news to Goode, who again rushed to Davidson's battery to see for himself. The place was a scene of confusion because there were no officers available to take charge. Goode dispatched Company K, 34th Virginia, the other company with artillery training. Some time later Walker and his reserve gunners from George Otey's Battery A arrived on the scene. With help from Goode's infantry, the Confederate gunners maintained fire from at least two pieces in Davidson's battery for the remainder of the battle.[38]

Although Davidson's battery failed to capitalize on its position to punish the Federals more severely, the Yankees were highly aware of it and considered launching the 5th Corps in a frontal attack. Alexander thought that the reduced participation of Davidson's battery in the engagement might have been a blessing in disguise. "Had Davidson fired vigorously, it might have precipitated Warren's assault, & it would, at least, have been better made than that of the 9th Corps. All's well that ends well."[39]

The artillerymen considered themselves unsung heroes of the battle, along with the engineer officers who planned and built the earthworks that protected their guns. David Walker, who survived the bloody exposure at Davidson's battery, argued that the Crater engagement was mainly an artillery battle; the guns and mortars not only contained the Federals in the breach but also punished them psychologically for hours before fresh Confederate troops could launch a counterattack.[40]

Shelling Petersburg

The city of Petersburg itself became a target of Union artillery. Whether intended or not, some sections were hard hit on the morning of July 30. For two hours after the mine explosion, it "fairly rained upon our streets," as the *Petersburg Express* put it. The only reported injury was sustained by Robert Green, the chief engineer of the town's fire department, who lost a finger to a shell fragment.[41]

The shelling tried the patience and stamina of residents. Anne A. Banister endured the trial with an older brother who was dying of illness; she had also lost her father earlier in the year. The artillery bombardment rattled her composure: "It seemed as if the very earth would open and swallow us up," she remembered. "Window panes were shattered and the whole air was filled with rumbling noises which terrified and deafened one. We could not hear each other when we spoke." Shells ploughed up the family garden and hit nearby buildings. Within range of Union guns at Fort Stedman and Battery No. 5, Banister and her family took refuge in the basement while the shelling continued.[42]

Beauregard and Lee

Beauregard was sleeping in a bed at his headquarters at Dunn's Hill, near the bridge that crossed the Appomattox River on the north side of Petersburg, when "a dull, heavy sound which shook the atmosphere" tumbled him out of bed. He quickly dressed and ordered his staff members to get ready, shortly after which Col. Samuel B. Paul rushed in to report what had happened. Years later, Beauregard remembered that Paul was highly excited. He stopped him in midsentence, forced him to sit down, and offered him some water. Paul then proceeded calmly, telling his commander what he knew of the mine.[43]

Beauregard sent Paul to inform Lee, whose headquarters was only three hundred yards away, that he hoped to meet him at Johnson's headquarters. Paul arrived as Lee was eating breakfast "in front of his tent" and gave his report. Lee dispatched one of his staff members, Charles Venable, to William Mahone's division to get two brigades to the crater as quickly as possible. The emergency did not allow him to filter this directive through A. P. Hill's corps headquarters.[44]

But Hill already knew of the explosion. It had awakened him at his headquarters on the edge of town near Halifax Street. He prepared to ride to Mahone and tell him personally to shift troops to the threatened sector. Just before he left, a hurriedly scribbled note, "on a small piece of paper that we could hardly decipher," arrived by messenger from Beauregard, giving the news that Pegram's battery had gone up in the explosion. Hill and most of his staff then dashed off, leaving only William H. Palmer with a courier to man the headquarters post. Fifteen minutes later Lee rode up "unattended." Palmer told him of Hill's intentions, and the two set out for Mahone's division as well. Palmer led Lee through ravines and around hills, avoiding the Jerusalem Plank Road and other high ground exposed to Union artillery. Hill reached Mahone's headquarters before Venable and rode along the division line with Mahone while discussing which brigades to send.[45]

By the time Lee and Palmer neared Mahone's position, two brigades were already on the move to the left. There was no longer any need to ride that far, so the pair stopped where they were and Lee tried to catch a glimpse of the battlefield. Palmer counted eleven Union flags flying inside the breach before word arrived from Hill sending him to report to Mahone about any Union moves toward the Confederate flank. Lee left Palmer and arrived at Bushrod Johnson's headquarters, a house near Blandford Cemetery, a bit after 7 A.M. Beauregard had already been there before Lee's arrival, had consulted with Johnson, and had concluded his division commander was doing all he could. Then Beauregard rode to the Gee House, near the junction of the Baxter and Jerusalem Plank roads, where he had a superb view of the battlefield. Beauregard's staff members joined him, and when word arrived that Lee had made it to Johnson's headquarters, Beauregard rode there to meet him.[46]

There was relatively little else the commanders could do at this point but wait. Beauregard told Lee about the Gee House and suggested they wait there. The pair rode in a roundabout way to avoid exposing themselves along the Jerusalem Plank Road, seeing the vanguard of Mahone's column passing by on its way. The Gee House provided a ringside seat for the engagement. A one-story structure with a basement, it was located on the ridge crest only 530 yards from the crater. A. P. Hill had stopped at the Gee House on his ride to Mahone's division to catch a brief view of the battle. Beauregard and Lee took shelter in the basement, viewing events through a window as Venable took notes for Lee regarding orders and dispatches. The house was "riddled by shot and shell," but the basement offered protection for the group.[47]

The commanders remained at the Gee House for nearly the remainder of the battle. As he waited, Lee began to fret and find fault. He was "very severe during the morning upon certain officers high in rank," according to W. Gordon McCabe, who personally overheard the comments but refused to name the officers in question. At one point, Lee noticed some reserve guns nearby and told Capt. James N. Lamkin to find men to put them into action. Lamkin detailed some gunners from other pieces and soon the artillery opened fire.[48]

In contrast to the department commanders, Bushrod Johnson stayed at his headquarters throughout the first half of the battle. His biographer believes he displayed "amazing lack of dash and decision," which was uncharacteristic of his actions in previous battles. Johnson kept in touch with developments through dispatches, and he did not hesitate to send orders to subordinates, but he did not budge from his house near Blandford Cemetery until late morning. He became the target of much criticism from officers who saw him there. Yet there is no reason to be too severe on Johnson. Beauregard, his immediate superior, thought he was doing everything one could expect, and Lee never criticized him either. Johnson urged his own troops to hold the breach, and he obtained some reinforcements from Hoke. Other than perhaps bolstering morale among his brigade commanders, there was little to be gained by traveling from one part of his line to another, and Johnson undoubtedly wanted to stay at headquarters to receive reports as soon as they arrived.[49]

Johnson's division never received the credit it deserved for holding the mined salient virtually without assistance before Mahone's fresh troops arrived four hours after the explosion. Elliott's brigade, particularly, deserved more attention from contemporaries and historians alike. It was traumatized by the explosion, losing as many men within a few minutes as if it had fought for hours in a heavy engagement. Yet the survivors managed to recover their nerves within about a quarter of an hour and offer enough resistance to hold the breach against four times their number. Admittedly the brigade maintained a passive, defensive posture most of the morning; but that was all the South Carolinians needed to do. McMaster's contribution to ultimate victory that day lay in his ability to calm the men, assume secure positions within the maze of earthworks, and post an adequate force in the branch ravine to block an attempt to advance westward from the crater. The South Carolinians had a tentative hold on their line, but it was enough to keep the timid Union efforts to expand out of the breach in check.

10

THE SECOND UNION WAVE

By 7 A.M. the pressure to break the human logjam inside the captured works forced the Federals to send in their second wave of units. Bliss's brigade of Potter's division, Humphrey's brigade of Willcox's division, and all of Ferrero's and Turner's divisions were ready for orders to advance.

Bliss's Brigade

Not long after the explosion, Bliss had moved his regiments toward the entrance of the right covered way to avoid advancing across open ground. To his surprise, he found the roadway crowded with men of Turner's division. Col. Louis Bell's brigade had stopped partway along the covered way for a few minutes before Bliss's men showed up. Bliss moved his men by the left flank into the crowded road anyway so he could face right, or north, upon emerging from the Union position. The roadway was so packed that he sent a staff officer to inform Potter of the problem and asked if the brigade could advance in the open after all. Potter sent word to drive through the covered way, fixing bayonets if necessary to clear the path. Bliss took Potter's advice; the bayonets forced Turner's men to press closely to the side walls, and the 9th Corps troops moved forward.[1]

When Bliss's vanguard reached the eastern edge of Poor Creek, it began to take a fork to the right that led northwestward across the valley. A staff officer told Bliss to go due west instead, and some of the troops had to backtrack to do so. When the van reached the forward Union line in the horseshoe, Ledlie told Bliss he was going the wrong way. The brigade once again reversed its direction and took the right fork after all. The men jogged across the valley of Poor Creek by the mouth of the mine gallery as a Confederate shell exploded in front of a member of the 48th Pennsylvania, who was standing at the gallery. It tore his body apart and sent his hat flying fifty feet into the air. With all the

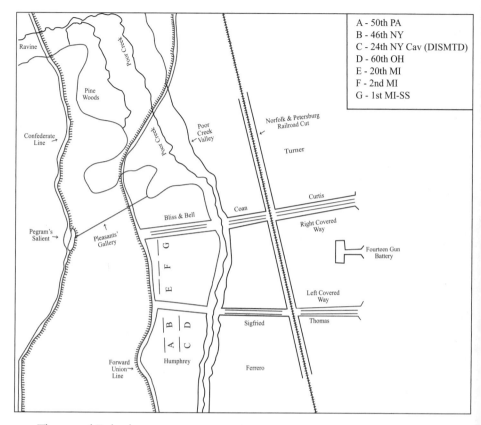

The second Federal wave

difficulties he encountered, Bliss spent an hour in moving his brigade through the covered way and up to the forward Union line. There he found Simon Griffin, who had returned briefly to the Union position, and Griffin told him he should wait before pushing any more troops into the breach.[2]

Soon after, Griffin went back into the Confederate line and sent a message for Bliss to put three of his regiments in the captured works, but Potter sent an order that ran counter to Griffin's directive. Potter thought there were already too many men in the breach, and he wanted to direct further advances to the right. He told Bliss to move his right wing directly to the mouth of the ravine north of the crater, while his left wing advanced north between Poor Creek and the Confederate line. Bliss decided to implement a little of both Griffin's and Potter's suggestions. He chose the 58th Massachusetts, 4th Rhode Island, and 45th Pennsylvania to go into the breach and arrayed the 51st New York and 2nd

New York Mounted Rifles (dismounted) behind the forward Union line. He directed the two New York units to advance directly toward the mouth of the ravine. Bliss told the commander of the 7th Rhode Island, Potter's designated engineer regiment, to keep his men in reserve. He did not have the services of the 36th Massachusetts. That regiment was not relieved in time to participate in the attack, and it remained in the trenches all day.[3]

Bliss's first three regiments advanced at the double-quick over no-man's-land after scrambling across the Union trench. The men stopped and lay on the ground just outside the eastern rim of the crater because the hole was already so crowded. A bit of room opened up soon after, and the 4th Rhode Island filed through the mass and entered a covered way that aimed toward Cemetery Hill, to the northwest. The 45th Pennsylvania had arrived behind the Rhode Islanders when they were still lying down in no-man's-land but did not follow them when the 4th moved forward. Instead the 45th moved by the flank around the hole and entered a Confederate covered way. The 58th Massachusetts followed the 4th Rhode Island but split into two wings because of the cluster of men that got in the regiment's way.[4]

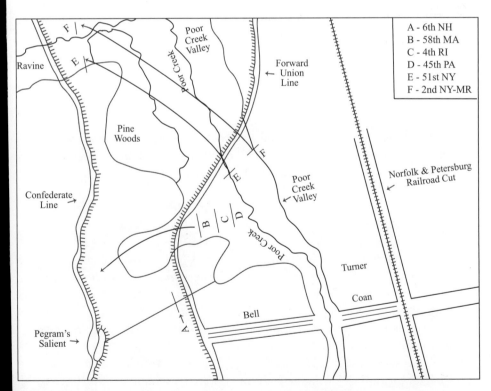

Bliss's brigade

Even though he remained within the Union position, Bliss tried to coordinate the movement of his three regiments by sending messages into the Confederate works. He wanted the 4th Rhode Island, 45th Pennsylvania, and 58th Massachusetts to advance due northward, behind the Confederate line, as he sent the rest of his brigade toward the ravine mouth. According to Bliss, Griffin intercepted and countermanded two of his messages because he did not understand their purpose. Only the third message got through to his regiments, but by then they had obeyed orders from other officers to attack in different directions.[5]

Capt. Theodore Gregg's 45th Pennsylvania moved relatively intact into the Confederate covered way. Described as four feet wide and three feet deep, it had dirt piled on both sides to add more protection. The covered way was about one hundred feet long with two shorter traverses on the side, one about twenty feet from the western end and heading south, the other about forty feet from the western end and heading north. The Pennsylvanians did not have much opportunity to settle in because a staff officer brought Bliss's instructions to advance due north; the movement of the 45th Pennsylvania flag would be the signal for the 2nd New York Mounted Rifles and the 51st New York to attack the mouth of the ravine. At almost the same time, William F. Bartlett ordered Gregg to advance against Wright's battery as soon as possible. As Gregg tried to form his command, Simon Griffin told him to attack south of the crater to divert attention from his own men. "I received so many orders from so many different commanders at that time that I did not know which to obey," Gregg complained. He finally decided to execute Bartlett's order and managed to bring close to one hundred men of his regiment out of the traverse. They were repulsed by infantry and artillery fire and fell back to the traverse, but it had meanwhile been occupied by members of the 58th Massachusetts. These men had gotten out of the crater and had filled whatever hole they could find.[6]

The 58th Massachusetts could not fully extricate itself from the confusion in the crater, or from orders to advance north, which were later countermanded in favor of orders to advance west. The best that can be said is that some members of the 58th advanced "some rods" to the west before retiring to the relative safety of the captured Confederate works. The 4th Rhode Island also advanced to the west after struggling through the packed crater. About sixty of its men moved as much as one hundred yards west of the hole, if some survivor accounts can be taken for granted, before the regimental fragment retreated.[7]

Bliss ordered the 51st New York and the 2nd New York Mounted Rifles to cross the forward Union line and advance toward the mouth of the ravine. The two regiments were separated from each other, the 51st on the south side of the ravine and the 2nd to the north. Capt. George Washington Whitman, brother of the poet Walt Whitman, commanded the left wing of the 51st New York. He jumped atop the Federal parapet and "sung out for the men to follow me, and the way they tumbled over them breastworks wasent Slow." The two New York regiments lodged in the fortified Confederate skirmish line soon after the North Carolina skirmishers fell back to their main line. Here the New Yorkers stayed; not only was there a large gap between the two regiments, but there was a gap between the 51st and the Union units in the crater area as well.[8]

The 7th Rhode Island remained in reserve near the mouth of the mine gallery. As the head of Turner's division followed the tail of Bliss's brigade, Capt. Percy Daniels lost contact with Potter's division. He went into the captured works to see if anyone besides Bliss could tell him what to do, but he returned without success. Daniels ordered his men to drop their entrenching tools and deploy in the forward Union line.[9]

Turner's Division

Turner's men had waited in column near the entrance to the right covered way when the mine exploded. The men of Louis Bell's brigade endured "ricocheting shot from the enemy's batteries and rifle pits" as they lay on the ground,

The second Federal wave. Robert Underwood Johnson and Clarence Clough Buel, *Battles and Leaders* (New York: Century Company, 1887–88) 4:552

suffering several wounded. Turner moved Bell and the rest of his command into the covered way as soon as possible, as much to secure cover from this fire as to be in a position to attack. Then Bliss's brigade wanted to move forward, and Turner's troops were forced to squeeze to the side. Ord told Turner to move up behind Bliss and support Potter's troops. Bell's column reduced to two files, and then only one, owing to the flow of wounded going to the rear. When Bell reached the forward Union line, Turner realized Bliss was hesitating, so he also stopped and awaited developments.[10]

The covered way was wide enough for four men abreast, as one member of the 4th New Hampshire recalled, and it provided eight feet of vertical protection for Turner's men. One of the wounded Federals who passed by had the lower part of his jaw torn away, his tongue dangled out, and his head was "a shapeless mass," which sickened everyone who glanced his way. A wounded officer came by shouting, "Go quick boys! Go quick! It's your only salvation." Col. N. Martin Curtis's brigade, bringing up the rear of Turner's column, entered the covered way in single file because of the volume of stragglers and wounded that came through. Many of the wounded men were carried on blankets by four to ten men each.[11]

Turner's four thousand troops were stuck in the narrow roadway for some time, the head of Bell's brigade at least four hundred yards down the covered way. Turner had understood during his conference with Burnside that the 9th Corps was to sweep the Confederate line, enabling his men to advance across open ground to the north, but that had obviously not been done.[12]

Curious to see what was happening, Turner stood on the parapet of the forward Union line. He caught a glimpse of the numerous troops inside the crater and noted the heavy cross fire over no-man's-land. The Confederates seemed to be holding steadily in the main Rebel line north of the crater. Surprised and worried, Turner darted into the hole, claiming the distinction of being the only division commander to enter the breach, and returned a few minutes later unharmed.[13]

As early as 6 A.M., army headquarters had begun urging Ord to attack regardless of Burnside's actions, but the 18th Corps commander could not see how to use Ames or Turner effectively. Yet the orders from Meade compelled action, and Burnside also encouraged Ord by telling him, "Now you can move your troops forward." Another order arrived from army headquarters about 6:30 A.M. urging a forward advance. Ord relayed it to Turner and Ames, but both commanders responded that it was next to impossible until the way was cleared.[14]

Ord was surprised; he had assumed Burnside had opened several avenues of advance up to and across the Union line. "Old General Ord chafed and paced up and down, impatient at the bad state of affairs," recalled a staff officer at the

Fourteen Gun Battery. Ord impulsively left the fort and started for the breach, and staff officer Thomas Livermore volunteered to go with him. Livermore was glad when the pair met Turner near the forward Union line as the division commander was returning from his own inspection of the crater. "General, unless a movement is made out of the crater towards Cemetery Hill, it is murder to send more men in there," Turner said to Ord. He added that it might be possible if Burnside's troops could get out of the breach; "there is a furor there, and perhaps they may move off sufficiently for me to pass my division out." Ord agreed. "Well, do so if they move," he told Turner.[15]

The 18th Corps commander gave Turner instructions to move out toward the right, finding any way he could to cross the Union line. Upon returning to the Fourteen Gun Battery, Ord dispatched a message to Meade announcing that the captured works were "already full of men who cannot develop." His own troops "must go in by head of column and develop to the right."[16]

Ferrero's Division

Bliss was out of the way, Ord was determined to push on, and Turner was ready to advance by about the time Ferrero's division began to cross no-man's-land out of the left covered way about 7:30 A.M. Like Turner, Ferrero had waited for more than two hours before getting word to go in. Sigfried had led his brigade into the left-side covered way immediately after Humphrey's brigade left it, about 6 A.M., and stopped at Poor Creek valley while Humphrey deployed his regiments on the open ground west of the creek and east of the forward Union line. Sigfried's men gawked at the stream of prisoners and wounded Federals that flowed backward through the sunken roadway. The Confederates became frightened at the sight of black men with guns in their hands and pleaded with the white Yankees "not to let the niggers bayonet them." They were reassured when a black corporal offered water to a wounded Rebel.[17]

While waiting, Sgt. John H. Offer of the 30th USCT, the regiment leading Sigfried's column, tried to encourage his men. "Now, . . . this am gwine to be a gret fight, de gretest we seen yet. . . . If we take Petersburg, most likely we take Richmond, and 'stroy Lee's army, an' close de wah. Eb'ry man orter liff up his soul in pra'r for a strong heart. Oh! Member de poor color'd man ober dere in bondage. Oh! Member Gineral Grant and Gineral Burnside, and general Meade, an' all the gret Ginerals is right ober yonder watching ye, and any skulker is gwine to get a prod of dis bayonet. You heah me!"[18]

As Offer exhorted the men at the head of the division column, Thomas's command fretted at the tail. "We sat down at first, resting against the walls of the covered way," recalled one, but then they stood to make room for the injured men going to the rear. Some of the more lightly wounded called out,

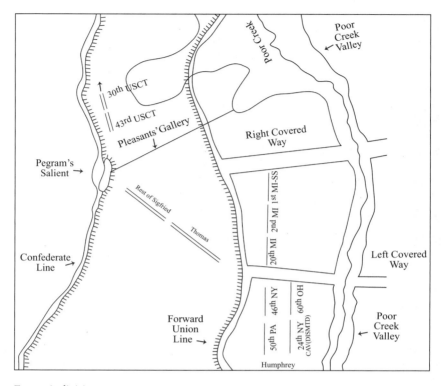

Ferrero's division

"I'm all right, boys! This is good for a thirty days 'sick-leave.'" The more seriously injured were not so jocular. Some were "plucky and silent, their pinched faces telling the effort they were making to suppress their groans; others, with the ashy hue of death already gathering on their faces, were largely past pain. Many, out of their senses through agony, were moaning or bellowing like wild beasts." The inexperienced black troops saw and heard the worst for more than an hour. "There could be no greater strain on the nerves," Thomas admitted. "Every moment changed the condition from that of a forlorn hope to one of forlorn hopelessness. Unable to strike a blow, we were sickened with the contemplation of revolting forms of death and mutilation."[19]

Ferrero already had taken abode with Ledlie in and around Surgeon Chubb's dressing station when an order to advance arrived. Ferrero told the messenger that he would do so "as soon as those troops were out of the way." This happened two or three times, Chubb recalled, before a peremptory order to attack arrived. Ferrero had no choice; he left the bombproof, followed by Ledlie.[20]

Burnside had hesitated to employ the black division because "those new troops could not be used to advantage in the crowded condition" of the captured works, but Meade insisted on a maximum effort before all chance of success had passed. Burnside finally sent the peremptory order close to 7:30 A.M., and Charles G. Loring came upon Ferrero just as he was about to obey the order. Loring thought it an unwise move and took the responsibility to countermand the directive, then made his way to the Fourteen Gun Battery to tell Burnside of conditions in the crater. His superior knew the situation all too well, but his hands were tied. After Loring confirmed the order, Ferrero instructed Sigfried and Thomas to move by the flank. They could decide whether to advance in column or line after they left the covered way, Sigfried to go right and Thomas left.[21]

Col. Delevan Bates roused his 30th USCT at the head of Sigfried's column by yelling, "Attention, battalion!" The men stood up and responded to his order to fix bayonets. Then "Trail arms!—Forward, March!'" rang out. The regiment, moving by the right flank, negotiated the narrow sandbag bridge, the men skipping over the bodies that littered no-man's-land. Lt. Freeman S. Bowley of Company H recalled that he "lost a file of men by one charge of grapeshot." The same charge also smashed the head of the regimental color-bearer and scattered his brains and blood across the flag, as well as took out half the color guard. Bates cried, "Forward, 30th, forward, boys, forward! Forward!," to keep the men going. As the head of his regiment entered the breach, Bates did not have "a definite idea of what we were expected to do."[22]

Bartlett was not happy with the additional manpower and urged Bates to take his men out. The colonel led his regiment as best he could into a traverse that headed northward, but it was already filled with white troops. Bates instructed his men to climb out of the works altogether and advance along the front of the Confederate main line, "just outside the abatis," until he overlapped the section still held by the Rebels. His troops received a lot of Confederate artillery fire, but they obeyed when Bates put his hat on the tip of his sword and made gestures indicating that they should face toward the works, cross through the abatis, and climb the parapet. Freeman Bowley caught glimpses of his men as they turned and started to rush forward. "Their usually black faces were of an ashy color," he recalled, "the eyes were set and glaring; the lips tightly drawn, showing the gleaming white teeth[,] and the expression of every face showed a determination to do or die." Some South Carolinians resisted and were shot or bayoneted in the trench, while others fled or surrendered as a section of the main Rebel line north of the crater fell into Union hands. Bates later claimed that his regiment captured 250 Confederates, two hundred yards of Rebel trench, and a flag.[23]

Bates had the assistance of the next regiment in Sigfried's column, the 43rd USCT. Col. H. Seymour Hall had aroused his officers by telling them, "Gentlemen, we have a little work to do this morning. I hope every man will do his duty." As the regiment approached the forward Union line, Ferrero shouted, "here comes the Forty-third; let's give them three cheers." He waved his hat and led the cheering by assembled staff members as Hall's men clambered across the sandbag bridge. The black troops advanced with enthusiasm, according to observers in Humphrey's brigade, which was assembled in a column of regiments to the side of the covered way. The 43rd became strung out as it traversed the fire-swept ground between the Union and Confederate lines. Some of the troops fell out of the column, but watchful officers gathered them up as a gap developed between the 43rd and the 30th.[24]

Hall could see how hopeless it was to enter the crater and moved the 43rd to the right, continuing to advance by the flank and at a double-quick. He left his adjutant near the hole to make sure the regimental column continued to move as he led the vanguard northward behind the 30th, stopping the men and ordering them to face left. This meant that his rear rank now was in front, but the men had no difficulty obeying Hall's order to cross the Confederate obstructions and parapet in order to take the position.[25]

Many men found that the abatis had been flattened by falling debris, and they scrambled across it. Capt. Albert D. Wright led six of his troops across the abatis, firing his pistol at every musket that appeared across the parapet, and then led his group into the Confederate trench. They moved north to clear the works for comrades who were having difficulty crossing the entanglement. His group captured a Confederate flag and the color guard, even though Wright's pistol was empty. The Confederates begged him not to let the black soldiers kill them. Hand-to-hand fighting erupted elsewhere, with bayonet thrusts and powder burns resulting from short-range firing. One Confederate surrendered by tying a white towel on his bayonet. Hall reported taking one hundred Confederate prisoners, the flag that Wright captured, and a Union flag that the Rebels had earlier taken. He estimated that not more than five minutes had passed from the time his regiment left the covered way until it seized one hundred yards of enemy trench. Hall was hit in the right shoulder as he stood on the parapet, about to give an order to continue the advance, and was taken to the rear. He lost his right arm as a result.[26]

The left wing of the 43rd USCT entered a part of the Confederate trench north of the crater that was already occupied by Federal troops, and some members of the regiment dropped away and took refuge in the relative safety of the crater itself. Wright directed his men to create a sandbag traverse across the trench for shelter, but he was hit in the right arm and headed for the Union position, carrying the captured Rebel flag. The colonel of another regiment in Sigfried's brigade, inside the crater, tried to take it from him, but a few troops of the 43rd shouted at the colonel and he gave up. Wright made it back to the Union position and offered the flag to Ferrero before having his wound treated.

Lt. Robert W. Armstrong of Wright's company was credited with retaking the captured Union flag from its Confederate possessors. Bates and Hall reported capturing a total of 350 prisoners and three hundred yards of Rebel trench; it is impossible to verify the former figure, and the latter estimate was probably exaggerated as well.[27]

The other regiments of Sigfried's brigade followed the 43rd USCT. The 27th was "exposed to the meanest enfilading fire" as it crossed no-man's-land, with "canister, grape and musket balls . . . tearing the ground in our midst." The regiments piled into the breach, many of the men creating hazards as they added weight to the already dense mass of humanity inside and north of the crater. "They came tumbling over each other," recalled Howard Aston, "down upon the troops already there, crushing and wounding many, both by trampling and with their bayonets." Some black troops nervously fired on a group of the 9th New Hampshire, returning from a failed attempt to advance west, until Capt. Andrew J. Hough waved a Union flag to signal his identity.[28]

Soon after Bates completed the capture of one section of Rebel trench, Maj. Van Buren of Burnside's staff approached him and asked, "Well, Colonel, what next?" Bates responded, "This is as far as my orders go." Van Buren then pointed to what he later referred to as a white house on Cemetery Ridge (perhaps the Gee House). "That will be your next objective point; advance at once." But it would take some time for Bates to maneuver his regiment through the crowd and into position before he could expand out of the captured works. Meanwhile the men of the 30th USCT were mixed up with other regiments in Sigfried's brigade. Moreover bullets were sailing into the captured works "through all the little alleyways," and they "found victims in the most unexpected places."[29]

The men of Thomas's brigade had waited more than an hour in the crowded covered way before gaining an opportunity to advance. Col. Charles S. Russell of the 28th USCT said good-bye to his regimental chaplain before the unit set out. "Take care of yourself—for today someone must die, and, if it be me, I hope our people will get the benefit of it." Like the rest of Thomas's command, the 28th advanced through the covered way by the left flank, hindered by the flow of wounded to the rear. The men began to receive Confederate fire while crossing Poor Creek. The 19th USCT brought up the end of the brigade column. As it approached the advance Union line, Ferrero came forward and detached Capt. Samuel Knorr's Company A, sending it to the rear to act as provost guard. He then said to Frank Holsinger of Company I, "Now, Captain, forward. God bless you."[30]

Thomas's men endured severe fire as they crossed the open space between the Union and Confederate positions. The regiments moved at the double-quick, but instead of filing left and facing west with the front rank, the brigade filed right and faced west with the rear rank. This "would have a tendency to confuse anything but the best-drilled troops," thought Capt. Robert Beecham of the 23rd USCT. Thomas actually steered the brigade to the right because he wanted to avoid the crater, jamming most of his men into the area north of the hole. Col. John A. Bross called on his regiment to "Forward, 29th," and pushed through the white crowd filling the entrenchments. At least part of the 19th USCT entered the crater. It was "an awful sight," according to Capt. James H. Rickard, with "soldiers both black & white clambering through the fort over the shrieking wounded."[31]

Many of Ledlie's and Potter's men claimed that Ferrero's attack disrupted their efforts to expand out of the breach. At least a half hour before the black division advanced, Marshall and Van Buren had worked their way into the crowded trench north of the crater to reconnoiter. They found that the Confederate bombproofs posed an almost insurmountable obstacle. Charles G. Loring described the physical environment in clear terms: "There was one uniform front line; then in the rear there were various lines, traverses between, and bomb-proofs. It was more like a honey-comb than anything that can be seen on our lines." Moreover Rebel infantry three hundred yards away were peppering the area with rifle fire. Van Buren urged Marshall to try an advance anyway, regardless of the problems.[32]

As much as possible, Marshall and Bartlett organized their men and prepared to advance west across the jumbled ground. Suddenly Marshall noticed a movement of troops up from the Union line. "Here is Ferrero," he shouted. "Hadn't we better hold on to what we have got, till we see what the Egyptians can do for us?" Bartlett agreed, but the blacks disrupted efforts to proceed with the forward move, while gaining little ground themselves.[33]

Moreover a small number of black soldiers tried to kill or injure unarmed Rebel prisoners. The memory of Fort Pillow was fresh in their minds. That terrible atrocity had seen the massacre of several hundred black troops after their surrender, when the post had fallen to Nathan Bedford Forrest's command less than four months earlier. Lt. Richard M. Gosney of the 28th USCT wrote that Ferrero's black troops went into the attack on July 30 "not expecting any quarter, nor intending to give any." Lt. James W. Steele knew the troops of the 43rd USCT "were thinking of Fort Pillow, and small blame to them," but he was determined to get the captured South Carolinians off safely to the rear despite the protests of his men. "I was met by cries that they would kill us," Steele recalled, "and had killed us wherever they could find us, and we were going to change the game." Steel knocked the barrels of bayoneted rifles away to prevent the blacks from following through with their threats. He "argued and cursed alternately" until he got the Rebels safely away. A member of Bell's brigade later claimed that he saw a black soldier kill a Confederate prisoner "in an agony of frenzy" with a bayonet. Pvt. Wilson Henry Moore of the 22nd South Carolina survived the mine explosion but suffered a fractured leg. He recalled that three white Federals protected him from black soldiers who wanted to club him to death.[34]

Humphrey's Brigade

Humphrey had positioned his regiments where Ledlie had assembled, on the open ground between the forward Union line and Poor Creek. He formed them in two wings, the right consisting of the 1st Michigan Sharpshooters, 2nd Michigan, and 20th Michigan, from right to left, and placed to the right of the left-side covered way. The left wing consisted of the 46th New York and 50th Pennsylvania, with the 60th Ohio and 24th New York Cavalry (dismounted) to the rear as a second line behind the left wing, and to the left of the covered way.[35]

Humphrey's men waited for at least an hour as the turmoil in the breach unfolded. The 27th Michigan lost four men, and Capt. Charles V. De Land of the 1st Michigan Sharpshooters was forced to go to the rear when a shell burst kicked up dirt and rocks into his face. William H. Randall saw a young comrade hit by a bullet and fall as if dead. A few minutes later, however, the man rose and rejoined the Sharpshooters, having been stunned by the impact of the bullet. Worse still, a shell fired from a Union battery position exploded among troops of the 20th Michigan, taking the leg off an unfortunate man. Several others in the 20th were hit by Confederate bullets as well.[36]

The order to advance arrived as soon as the tail of Thomas's column passed by. The men of both wings scrambled across the forward Union parapet in battle lines. "One of our Sergts refused to go," recalled William H. Randall of the 1st Michigan Sharpshooters, "and I was obliged to use force to make him go." Humphrey's men received heavy fire all the way across no-man's-land. Randall remembered that his men "commenced dropping up and down the line" as they neared the Confederate works. Byron Cutcheon had started his 20th Michigan by jumping onto the Federal parapet and calling on the men "to 'forward'" and then climbed down and made his way through the Union abatis. Glancing back, Cutcheon took pride in seeing that the 20th was "coming over the works in good shape," but a canister round from Davidson's battery raked the regimental line "within a rod of me" and killed or wounded several of his men.[37]

In his haste to double-quick across no-man's-land, Cutcheon stubbed his foot on the six-inch-tall stump of an elder tree as he twisted to cheer his onrushing troops. He "fell, full length," and those to the rear assumed he was hit. But Cutcheon rose quickly and continued running, "constantly feeling the wind of bullets which 'fluffed' past my face." He was supposed to guide the

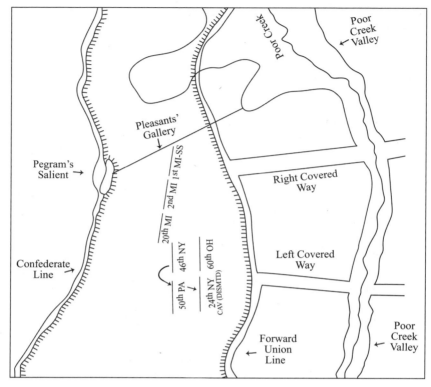

Humphrey's brigade

20th to the right, but soon lost connection with the 2nd Michigan. The 20th continued straight ahead, losing 15 of 115 men in crossing less than two hundred yards of open ground between the lines. Cutcheon's regiment hit the Rebel works about seventy-five yards south of the crater, roughly where the left flank of Goode's brigade was located. The Federals climbed the parapet and took a section of the line. Cutcheon's men captured up to forty prisoners, probably a mixture of Virginians from Goode's brigade and South Carolinians from Elliott's. Two of the prisoners were officers; ironically one of them was mortally wounded by Confederate fire while being led back to the Union position. Cutcheon reported that about half a dozen of his men dropped out of the attack, and he intended to prefer charges against them. Some of the troops also became detached from the 20th Michigan and joined Humphrey's left wing in its advance across no-man's-land.[38]

To Cutcheon's right, the 1st Michigan Sharpshooters and 2nd Michigan moved into the southern portion of the crater and into empty segments of the Confederate line south of the hole. To Cutcheon's left, Humphrey's left wing failed to make an impression on the Rebel defenders. Capt. Alphons Serviere ordered his 46th New York to advance as soon as he saw Cutcheon start to cross the forward Union line, but Cutcheon went too fast for his men. The New Yorkers advanced only about one hundred yards across no-man's-land before they stopped and retired. Serviere blamed it on the lack of support to his right. Worse than this, in retiring, the 46th New York ran into the 50th Pennsylvania and brought most of its men back to the rear as well. The confusion prevented the second line, consisting of the 60th Ohio and 24th New York Cavalry (dismounted) from advancing as well. These regiments reassembled in convenient positions within the Union line and fired at the Rebels, and some were used as provost guards, but the entire left wing of Humphrey's brigade failed to touch the Confederates.[39]

Cutcheon blamed the failure of the left wing on the quality of manpower in the 46th New York. He later commanded Humphrey's brigade and came to know the material in this unit. It was "a German regiment from New York City," he judged, "and composed of *very poor material.* I never knew them to behave decently while I commanded them. Most of the men could speak but little English, and they had been drilled in their native tongue."[40]

By the time Humphrey's brigade finished its advance, half entering the breach and the rest retiring to the Union line, the Federals controlled about 150 yards of Confederate trench south of the crater. The mingled troops of Ledlie, Potter, and Ferrero occupied about 200 yards of Confederate line north of the crater as well, extending up to near the southern edge of the wide ravine. Counting Pegram's former battery position, Burnside's breach in the Rebel line amounted to about 500 yards of entrenchments, north to south. East to west, however, the Union toehold was narrow indeed.[41]

Turner's Division

John Wesley Turner had gone back to the crater just before Ferrero advanced. The black division's entry into the breach appalled him. "The men literally came falling right over into this crater on their hands and knees," he recounted. "They were so thick in there that a man could not walk. Seeing that I was going to be covered up there, and be entirely useless, I thought I would go out."[42]

As soon as he returned to the Union line, Turner told Louis Bell to move his brigade by the right flank across the parapet and angle off to the right so as to hit the Rebel line near the mouth of the ravine. "We ran with our heads down, as if facing a storm," recalled Elias Bryant of the 4th New Hampshire, who was hit in the thigh only a few yards across no-man's-land. Bell's men stopped just outside the Confederate line because of the crowded nature of the captured works and waited for orders. Turner sent word for the brigade to

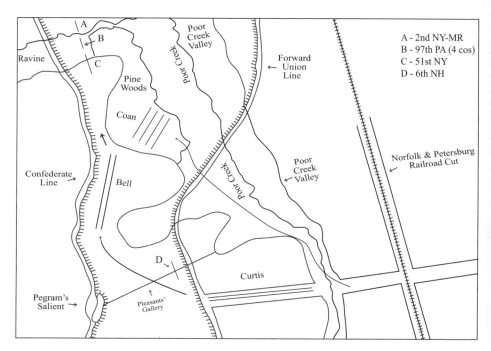

Turner's division

move northward, outside the Rebel line, as William B. Coan's brigade moved forward to directly hit the mouth of the ravine. Bell started to do this but his command increasingly received fire as it moved.[43]

Coan's brigade was pulled in several directions as it tried to advance. First, Joseph Carr saw the 51st New York and the 2nd New York Mounted Rifles in the captured Rebel skirmish line and noticed the gap between the two regiments. He ordered Coan's 47th New York and 97th Pennsylvania to advance and fill that gap. On the way, six companies of the 97th became detached from the rest owing to a contradictory order given by an unidentified staff officer. Maj. Isaiah Price led the remaining four companies forward and occupied a section of the empty trench between the two New York regiments, but there is no evidence that the 47th New York did the same. Coan next sent the 48th New York across the forward Union line and into the pine grove on the Federal side of no-man's-land. The New York regiment was "exposed to a murderous fire" while crossing the parapet and lost many good men, including its commander, Maj. Samuel M. Swartwout. Eventually Coan received word from Turner to assemble his entire brigade in the pine trees in preparation for an advance toward the ravine. Each unit did so by moving along the creek bottom by the right flank and formed battle lines when near the assembly point.

The 47th New York and the six errant companies of the 97th Pennsylvania joined this brigade assembly. Turner himself accompanied Coan when the men began to move across no-man's-land to support Bell's advance along the Confederate line.[44]

Turner wanted Curtis's brigade, the last of his division, to act as a reserve. Curtis moved his men up to the forward Union line, and they received artillery fire as they crossed Poor Creek. "Some of us jumped over the creek, and some jumped into the creek and waded out, but we soon got to the bank on the other side of the swamp," recalled John C. Rowland of the 112th New York. Curtis then began to form a column of regiments.[45]

The advance of Turner's division might have secured the mouth of the ravine, but the Rebels were aware of this movement. McMaster prepared his South Carolinians to resist it, cooperating with the extreme right of McAfee's brigade. Coan's men made it at least halfway across no-man's-land, sheltering as much as possible in the patch of trees that closed to a distance of only seventy-five yards from the Confederate line. Lt. Caswell A. Connor of the 49th North Carolina told his men to spread their cartridges on the floor of the trench to

Landscape near Pegram's Salient, looking northeast, soon after the war. Vol. 6, 289, Massachusetts Commandery, Military Order of the Loyal Legion and the U.S. Army Military History Institute

make it easier to reload. "Hold them back, boys! Hold them back! By everything you hold dear on earth, hold them back!" he shouted.[46]

The Tar Heels braced for their toughest fight of the battle so far, but the expected contest never took place. Just as Bell and Coan were closing on their target, Weisiger's Virginia brigade of Mahone's division launched a dramatic counterattack, altering the course of the battle. It created a panic among the black troops jammed into the breach and resulted in a massed retreat from the captured works. This retreat disrupted all of Turner's plans. He looked to the left and saw that about two-thirds of Bell's men were swept to the rear by the retreating black troops, and about the same proportion of Coan's brigade were caught up in the retrograde movement as well. The rest retired in order, and most men of both brigades reassembled within the forward Union position alongside Curtis's troops.[47]

Ames's 18th Corps division still stood in reserve, but there seemed to be no opportunity to use it. Ames positioned his men in column behind Curtis's brigade and filled up the covered way after Turner vacated the narrow passageway. He could see that there was no room within the forward Union position or in the captured works for his command and consulted Turner. They decided to tell Ord in no uncertain terms that the battlefield was too crowded, and that the covered way was a poor avenue of advance. After an exchange of messages and a personal conference, Ord told Ames not to take his division into the battle. Meade confirmed this with an order to pull Ames back to the rear at 9:45 A.M.[48]

The Federals faced a cycle of diminishing returns as they committed their second wave to battle. They added more confusion than order, more chaos than control, and more potential victims to Confederate fire by pushing forward the men of Bliss, Ferrero, Humphrey, and Turner into a contest of dubious worth.

11

AN END AND A BEGINNING

By 9 A.M. thirty-nine regiments out of fifty in the 9th Corps were inside the captured works. All of Ledlie's eleven units, all but six of Potter's fifteen regiments, and all but five of Willcox's fifteen units were in the breach. All Ferrero's nine regiments lodged in the Confederate works, but none of Turner's thirteen units actually stepped foot inside them, although Bell's brigade was very close to the Rebel line. Ames's division, the 2nd Corps, and the 5th Corps never made a move to cross no-man's-land.[1]

The crowding of about ten thousand Federals in the five-hundred-yard breach destroyed command and control. It was an interracial force as well. "White men and negroes lay indiscriminately together," recalled the historian of the 58th Massachusetts, "piled up three and four deep. It was impossible for any to use their muskets." The historian exaggerated on that last part, claiming the Federals were essentially in a "defenseless condition."[2]

The Yankees endured the artillery and small-arms fire that poured into the breach. James J. Chase was hit near the left temple as he watched Capt. Herbert Sargent, who now commanded the 32nd Maine, climb onto a pile of clay thrown up by the mine explosion to obtain a better view. The ball went through his nose and forced his left eye out of its socket. Initially everyone told Chase he would die, even predicting he had but fifteen minutes left. Chase was frightened and prepared for the worst. Someone loaned him a mirror and he saw how awful his face appeared, with an eye dangling against his cheek. But then Sargent took charge and encouraged the seventeen-year-old lieutenant, telling him he would live, and pouring water over the eye to wash away the dust. Sargent even took a penknife and cut the jagged edges of bone that protruded toward the right side of Chase's face. "I want to save that eye," Sargent said, "for it is a great blessing to have one if you can't have two." With Sargent's encouragement, and a dose of whiskey, Chase felt more confident. Two men carried him into the crater, where others procured a blanket and carried him across no-man's-land, at times dragging him along the way. The men who carried him in the blanket collapsed from exhaustion when they got to the Federal line, and Chase endured another jolting trip farther to the rear to reach a field hospital.[3]

Chase was lucky to have survived the bullet as well as the trip across no-man's-land, for the Confederates were laying down a continuous hail of bullets and shells on that narrow strip of ground. Leander Cogswell, acting inspector general on Griffin's staff, crossed it four times with messages and received several bullet holes in his hat and clothing. The Federals inside the Union line knew that the worst artillery fire in no-man's-land came from Wright's battery to the north and Davidson's battery to the south. They could not respond with counterfire from the Fourteen Gun Battery, so Hunt tried without success to lay down mortar fire on Davidson's gun.[4]

The 35th Massachusetts, Ledlie's designated engineer regiment, continued to dig in the captured works without success. So many wounded men and stragglers gathered on the west side of the crater, protected by the lip, that the men eventually gave up all work except attempts to connect the hole with the forward Union line. The ground was "so hard baked it could with difficulty be broken by the pick-axes." Moreover the Massachusetts men suffered from "nervous prostration" because they had worked very hard in the hot sun and were worn out.[5]

Ledlie continued to make Surgeon Chubb's field hospital his home. Safely ensconced fifty yards behind the forward Union line, he sometimes wandered out to sit down behind the parapet. Ledlie asked Surg. H. E. Smith of the 27th Michigan for a stimulant, claiming he suffered from malaria and from the pain inflicted by a spent ball. Smith offered him some rum. Ledlie also wished to give command of his division to Bartlett, but a staff officer reported he was inside the crater and could not be reached easily. Ferrero mostly stayed with Ledlie in the bombproof that served the 27th Michigan as a field hospital and partook of Smith's rum as well.[6]

Byron Cutcheon braved the trip back across no-man's-land to seek Willcox and help organize a further push. On entering the bombproof hospital, he found Ledlie "bracing up with 'dutch courage' from a flask." Cutcheon rested half an hour with Chubb and Smith before resuming his search for Willcox. William H. Powell also entered the bombproof on one of his return trips from the breach to offer yet more advice about conditions there to Ledlie. The division leader mouthed orders to push forward to the crest without offering to do anything to effect that goal himself. Powell later wrote that these words, "coming from a commander sitting in a bomb-proof inside the Union lines, were disgusting." He returned to the hole and relayed Ledlie's words, "which I knew beforehand could not possibly be obeyed; and I told General Ledlie so before I left him."[7]

Several other 9th Corps officers remained in the Union position. Potter mostly stayed behind the parapet of the forward line, never entering the breach. Willcox also remained behind. Turner entered the captured works twice before his division advanced. Among the brigade leaders, Marshall, Bartlett, Griffin, Hartranft, and Thomas set foot in the captured works. There is no evidence that Sigfried or Humphrey ever did so. Zenas Bliss remained in the forward Union line, where he recalled nearly being killed by more than one Confederate shell, even though all but two of his regiments went into the enemy works.[8]

Burnside and Meade

On the higher level of command, as Cyrus Comstock put it, "Meade & Burnside managed to quarrel again." "I am doing all in my power to push the troops forward," Burnside reported soon after the second Union wave went in, "and, if possible, we will carry the crest. It is hard work, but we hope to accomplish it. I am fully alive to the importance of it." This wording set off Meade's temper. "What do you mean by hard work to take the crest?" he retorted, admitting that he knew from other sources no serious effort had yet been made to expand out of the breach. "Do you mean to say your officers and men will not obey your orders to advance? If not, what is the obstacle? I wish to know the truth, and desire an immediate answer."[9]

Meade sent this demand with Capt. William Jay of Warren's staff, who handed it to Burnside at the Fourteen Gun Battery with the words, "General Meade desires me to say that this is for you personally." Burnside thought this meant it was for his attention, rather than that of a staff member, and he took the tone of the dispatch personally. He hastily replied, explaining that he did not mean to imply his men were insubordinate, only that it was difficult to get them out of the maze of Rebel works. "I have never in any report said anything different from what I conceived to be the truth. Were it not insubordinate I would say that the latter remark of your note was unofficer like and ungentlemanly." Before Meade received this message, he got a report from Capt. W. W. Sanders of 9th Corps headquarters that Griffin's brigade had entered the breach but was stalled. Meade softened his earlier tone by writing that this news "modifies my dispatch; still I should like to know the exact morale of your corps."[10]

Then Burnside's latest note arrived at army headquarters, and Meade was not pleased at the suggestion that he had acted in an "ungentlemanly" way. The army commander requested a copy of the letter that inspired the accusation, as he "did not keep a copy of it, intending it to be confidential. Your reply requires I should have a copy." Burnside now understood that he had gone too far and would have to pay for his error of judgment.[11]

At the top of the Union high command, Grant spent the first half of the morning quietly moving about to observe the day's operations. He left Meade at army headquarters and rode toward the Fourteen Gun Battery. "Grant is very desirous always of seeing, and quite regardless of his own exposure," as Theodore Lyman put it. Sometime before 8 A.M., Ord happened to meet Grant when he was returning from the forward Union line. Whether he met Grant inside the crowded covered way or near its entrance, or at the entrance to the separate covered way leading to the Fourteen Gun Battery, is unclear. The general in chief instructed Ord to tell Burnside not to send more men into the breach, but to bring up tools and entrench his position. Ord relayed the information and then urged Turner to begin his advance against the Confederates north of the crater. Grant thought he had seen and done enough and returned to City Point. He also benefited from a stream of messages Comstock wrote, mostly while at 5th Corps headquarters.[12]

Fifth Corps

Warren waited, with Meade's approval, until division commander Crawford completed a reconnaissance before deciding whether to commit his 5th Corps to action and which target it should attack, Davidson's battery or the Confederate position at the leadworks. Meanwhile he visited Burnside to find out more about the small artillery position in his front that was damaging 9th Corps troops. Burnside suggested he go forward and look at Davidson's battery from the most advantageous angle, and Warren reiterated his opinion that it had to be taken if the Federals hoped to widen the breach. Burnside asked him if 5th Corps troops could do it. Warren thought so, even though they would have to attack across open ground. Returning to his headquarters, Warren informed Meade that the Rebel guns ought to be captured before the 5th Corps attacked.[13]

Ten minutes later, about 8 A.M., the results of Crawford's reconnaissance arrived. Crawford reported that the lead works were more than a mile away from his picket line and Wilson's cavalry division was moving away from his left flank. He would have no support to his right flank either, if he advanced toward the works; moreover Crawford reported having too few troops to make the attack. Warren suggested that Ayres reinforce Crawford, or that his entire corps support Burnside; he did not have enough strength to do both. Forty-five minutes later Meade told Warren to support Burnside and make an effort to capture Davidson's battery.[14]

It would be up to Ayres to take the artillery position, so he and Warren rode to the Fourteen Gun Battery to scout the terrain. Ayres thought he could take the guns if Burnside's men made some room for his division near the crater. He planned to move by the flank across no-man's-land and then turn left to sweep down the Confederate line to Davidson's position. Along the way both men noticed the panicked retreat of Ferrero's black troops out of the breach; the Confederates had counterattacked and altered the tactical situation. "I am, therefore . . . , no more able to take the battery now than I was this time yesterday," Warren announced to army headquarters. "All our advantages are lost." Meade suspended orders for the 5th Corps to advance, greatly disappointing Burnside. Warren later tried to deflect responsibility for failing to utilize his large command on July 30. He claimed that the leadworks were out of his area of responsibility and too much time had been wasted in efforts to determine whether he should have advanced toward them or toward a closer target, like Davidson's battery. This incurred Meade's anger because it sounded as though Warren was critical of army headquarters, adding more controversy to the troubled relationship between the two men.[15]

Second Corps

Hancock began the day's operations with a hopeful inquiry directed at Burnside: "What success this morning? How did your mine work?" Burnside responded with an accurate report of what had transpired thus far, along with an exaggerated claim that his men were "gaining ground." Ord told Hancock and Mott that an attack on Mott's front was impossible. This was ground formerly held by 18th Corps troops, so Ord knew what he was talking about. The Confederate abatis was well built and firmly wired together, yet everyone wondered if the Rebels were still holding the trenches on this sector, so Mott organized demonstrations to find out.[16]

Robert McAllister's brigade held Mott's right, his own right resting on the Appomattox River. Rather than send out skirmishers, he staged a noisy performance. Officers shouted orders to prepare an advance, and then at the command to march, the rear rank of the brigade raised their muskets and cheered three times. Other men, positioned in places to see the enemy trench, reported that many Rebels appeared at the firing step to meet the expected onslaught. The demonstration indicated that the line was fully manned, and the Confederates fired a volley in McAllister's direction before they realized they had been tricked. On another part of Mott's line, Regis de Trobriand advanced his skirmish line to determine Confederate strength and lost sixteen men in the process.[17]

Ferrero's Division

The black troops made more strenuous efforts to expand out of the captured works than any other Federal soldiers that morning. Shouting "no quarters, remember Fort Pillow," as they entered the breach, many had maintained their enthusiasm for battle despite the difficulties of working through a mass of dispirited white troops. In fact it is likely that Ferrero's officers managed to retain a higher degree of command and control than those in other units because of the color of their men; it was difficult for the black troops to hide in the white crowd.[18]

As soon as possible, officers of the 4th Division pushed their men out of the crowded breach. Powell recalled one file closer, a big, powerful sergeant stripped to his waist, who manhandled the troops out of the crater. "None ob yo' d-n skulkin', now," he bellowed while grabbing a man at the waistband with one hand. The sergeant carried him up the slope and threw him over the lip as his regiment moved on.[19]

Henry Thomas made the first move to expand westward from the breach by forcing a number of men from the 31st USCT into the open ground. The South Carolinians that McMaster had positioned in the shallow ravine west of the crater immediately opened fire. Thomas led the group, followed by two staff members, Capt. Marshall L. Dempey and Lt. Christopher Pennell. Four white orderlies carried the brigade guidon. Behind the group, Lt. Col. William E. W. Ross led about fifty members of the 31st USCT who could be pried out of the breach. Confederate fire quickly put a stop to the advance. About half the men who set out were hit, and the loss of officers was great. Ross fell right after leaving the works, and his second in command, Capt. Thomas Wright, was shot "as he stooped over him." Thomas reported that the men of the 31st USCT "were largely without leaders, and their organization was destroyed."[20]

Thomas's brigade staff took heavy casualties as well. Two of the four orderlies were wounded, one of them while he carried the guidon. Pennell took charge of the banner and ran along the captured works to encourage more men, brandishing his sword in the other hand. Soon a bullet found its mark, "whirling him round and round several times before he fell." Thomas recalled that some nearby members of Bartlett's brigade were so fascinated by the spectacle that they too were hit before taking shelter. Thomas and Dempey were the only officers who survived the aborted attack.[21]

Thomas sent word back to the Union line through Major Van Buren that he needed a cooperative advance to the right and that he would attempt another attack soon. Instead of help, Thomas received an order from Ferrero to advance toward the ridge crest immediately. He began to sort the 28th and 29th USCT from the mass of humanity in the breach to act on this directive.[22]

A staff officer took Ferrero's order to advance to Sigfried's brigade as well. Unable to find Sigfried, he told Delevan Bates that "a charge must be made on Cemetery Hill at once." Bates found it impossible to organize a true battle line. Instead he pulled out two hundred men of his regiment and shouted, "Come on! Come on!" The men were met with a hail of rifle fire immediately after leaving the works. Bates was hit in the right cheek, the ball exiting behind his left ear. Half the officers and one-third of the enlisted men who followed him fell, too. Bates's first thought was to return to the captured works for shelter. He staggered back, helped by some of his men, who also poured water over his face to revive him when he fainted. Then a few men carried Bates back to the Union line, although they dropped him halfway across no-man's-land to duck a charge of canister sailing low over the ground.[23]

Only a few minutes after the repulse of Bates's attack, Thomas's troops made another attempt to advance out of the captured works. Officers of the 23rd, 28th, and 29th USCT separated their men from the white troops in order to get a "regimental following." The 31st USCT was in no shape to participate. It "had been so shattered, was so diminished, so largely without officers," reported Thomas, "that I got what was left of them out of the way of the charging column as much as possible." Col. John Bross of the 29th became the inspirational leader of this effort. "He had attired himself in full uniform" and "was conspicuous and magnificent in his gallantry," Thomas recalled. He led from 150 to 400 troops, according to various estimates. The 43rd USCT of Sigfried's brigade prepared to cooperate with Thomas but never got into a position to aid Bross.[24]

Bross made a magnificent show as he worked to inspire the men just before setting out. "He passed along our front," remembered Capt. Robert Beecham of the 23rd USCT, "carrying his regimental colors, notifying the brigade that he would lead the charge in person, and giving the order for us to follow." Bross further told the men, "I want you to follow this flag. I am going to lead you to victory. We'll show the world today that the colored troops are soldiers." Beecham could not help but admire the man for "his lofty courage," and he was determined to help him in the effort. But "the thought—the conviction—was stamped upon my brain: 'It is utter madness. That grand man will throw his life into the breach and death and defeat will be our reward.'"[25]

Beecham recalled that the enlisted men "formed promptly. There was no flinching on their part. They came to the shoulder touch like true soldiers, as ready to face the enemy and meet death on the field as the bravest and best soldiers that ever lived." But the white officers, all of whom had seen much of the war before their appointments to the black regiments, probably understood how difficult it would be to survive the coming ordeal.[26]

The men crowded out of the captured works in preparation for the advance. An artillery round exploded among them, almost detaching the right arm of Sgt. Thomas Hayse of the 28th USCT. Hayse dropped the regimental flag and spun around; he fell into the cavalier and "impaled his leg on an upright bayonet." Hayse's arm was later amputated.[27]

Just before he was ready to give the order to advance, Bross noticed hundreds of Confederate troops emerging from the shallow ravine 350 yards to the west. It portended a counterattack, and he planted the flag of the 29th USCT in the ground. Bross offered a promotion to any man who safely carried the colors back to the rear and shouted "Rally, my brave boys, rally!" He was immediately hit by a bullet "in the left side of the head." Murmuring "O, Lord," Bross fell dead. Two of his men tried to drag his body into the captured works but could not because the assembly of troops quickly broke apart and retired into the breach.[28]

Many Federals saw Bross die and witnessed the abrupt end of the third effort by black troops to expand out of the breach. Freeman Bowley heard some of his men shout, "The rebels are charging! Here they come!" He looked westward and saw "a splendid line of gray" emerging from the ravine on the run.[29]

Mahone's Division

Those Confederates belonged to William Mahone's division and had finally made their appearance on the battlefield by about 9 A.M. Mahone's counterattack completely altered the nature of the fighting on July 30 and spelled the end of Burnside's tenuous hold on the captured works.

Born in Monroe, Virginia, in 1826, Mahone was less than five years old when Nat Turner's Rebellion swept across several counties of southeastern Virginia. His father saved the family members by moving them onto a boat on the Nottoway River where they rode out the only serious slave uprising in Southern history. Mahone graduated from Virginia Military Institute in 1847 and became a civil engineer, laying tracks in the railroad boom that swept the country in the 1850s. Most of his work centered in the Petersburg and Norfolk area. He was president of the Norfolk and Petersburg Railroad when the Civil War broke out and became colonel of the 6th Virginia before his promotion to brigadier general. Mahone commanded a Virginia brigade, seeing service at Seven Pines, Malvern Hill, and Second Manassas (where he was badly wounded). His greatest battlefield accomplishments took place in 1864. Assuming command of his division after the Wilderness, Mahone engineered the repulse of Grant's Second Offensive at Petersburg on June 22 by taking three brigades along a route familiar to him from his prewar experiences in the area and driving back the 2nd Corps effort to extend Federal lines west of the Jerusalem Plank Road.[30]

Mahone's division held the extreme right of Lee's line at Petersburg, his own left resting at Rives's Salient near the road and the line extending about one mile west. Mahone and several of his subordinates insisted that an order arrived from Lee's headquarters about midnight of July 29 warning that an attack was expected somewhere along the lines. All units were to be on the

William Mahone. RG6675, vol. 72, p. L3599, Massachusetts Commandery, Military Order of the Loyal Legion and the U.S. Army Military History Institute

alert and ready by 3 A.M. Mahone sent out instructions accordingly but nothing happened. Some of his men went back to sleep while others remained awake, still expecting an attack. Ironically Lee's staff officers later verified that no such order originated from Lee. Richard H. Anderson probably issued that order from 1st Corps headquarters. Mahone's was the only division of Lee's army south of the Appomattox River that day, and the order was not issued to the divisions of Beauregard's command.[31]

A group of men in Company G, 12th Virginia, sat atop the parapet west of the Jerusalem Plank Road waiting for something to happen. One of them finally "called out aloud lets go back to sleep, they are not going to do anything." Just then there came "a grumbling sound like distant thunder," but it sounded odd. "I never heard thunder like that," commented a Virginian. Other members of the division thought it might have been an earthquake. "Earthquake, the mischief," snorted William S. Hubbard of the 16th Virginia, "It is old Grant blowing up our line somewhere."[32]

The explosion was loud enough to awaken men sleeping in the house and barn of the Wilcox Farm, near Mahone's trenches. Although the explosion was some two miles away, many Confederates heard it as "a deep, rumbling sound" and could see it if they happened to be in the right place at the right time. William H. Stewart, commander of the 61st Virginia, described it as "a mountain of curling smoke."[33]

David A. Weisiger, who led Mahone's Virginia brigade, also heard the mine explosion. "We all conjectured about what it was as we had heard that such a thing was in contemplation." Maj. Richard Watson Jones, commander of the 12th Virginia, had spent the previous night in Petersburg with family members. The explosion woke him too, "the house shook as if by an earthquake," and Federal shelling began to strike some homes nearby. Jones put his women relatives in the cellar and sped back to the regiment. The mine also woke up men in Matthew R. Hall's Georgia brigade, next to Weisiger's. The "dreadful chorus of artillery" that ensued immediately after the explosion exacted some casualties. A round took off the legs of three men in the 41st Virginia who were standing in a group.[34]

Not long after the commotion, Capt. Murray F. Taylor brought Hill's order to send troops to Pegram's Salient. Mahone ordered Weisiger and Hall to pull their men out of the trenches singly or in small groups, so as not to attract Federal attention. These two brigades were on Mahone's far right and thus could more easily be spared. Weisiger's men gathered in the peach orchard and a cornfield on the Wilcox Farm, taking their full gear and personal belongings with them. The sharpshooter battalion of Weisiger's brigade went along. It had been relieved on the picket line the night before by members of the 6th Virginia, and there was no time to change places with these men before setting out for the salient. Capt. Wallace Broadbent of the 16th Virginia commanded the sharpshooters. They were nearly as numerous as any regiment in the brigade and essentially made up for the detachment from the 6th Virginia, which reduced that regiment's contribution to the fight to only ninety-eight men.[35]

Weisiger's position was two miles from the crater, on a direct line, but he would have to march along a circuitous route of two and a half miles to avoid observation by the Federals. The sharpshooters headed his column, followed by the 6th Virginia, while the 12th Virginia brought up the rear. Mahone and Venable rode at the head of Weisiger's troops as Mahone asked questions of Lee's staff member to glean all he could of the course of the battle. One of A. P. Hill's staff members, Capt. Norbonne Starke, also accompanied the column. D. M. Bernard of the 12th Virginia chatted with him on the way. The two loved the same girl, but Bernard had possession of her daguerreotype in a locket. Whenever he and Starke met, Starke was eager to see the photograph and tried to persuade Bernard to give it to him for keeps. Given the mission of the brigade, Bernard knew his chances of surviving the day were slimmer than usual. The two made an agreement; in exchange for recovering and burying Bernard's body, Starke would take possession of the locket.[36]

Weisiger stopped at the Ragland House, located west of the Jerusalem Plank Road, after marching half a mile. Mahone had noticed that the men were carrying their knapsacks and other belongings. He ordered both brigades to halt and drop their gear, leaving men to guard the property. They did so in the apple and peach orchard near the house, except the 12th Virginia, which had already done this at its regimental camp. Sporadic artillery fire descended on the area around the Ragland House; one round took off the leg of a sergeant in the 41st Virginia, who later died. Before the two brigades resumed their march, Mahone told Venable of a decision he had made. "I can't send my brigades to Gen. Johnson," he confided, "I will go with them myself."[37]

The Confederates left the Ragland House and entered a ravine to the rear of Rives's Salient that led into the valley of Lieutenant Run. Here they were sheltered by the high ground to the right from Federal view. Artillery rounds continued to drop near, forcing some members of the 12th Virginia to dodge. The two brigades continued along the run, passing an ice pond, until they encountered "a military footpath" that ran up a deep ravine to the right, toward the Jerusalem Plank Road. On the east side of the road, at this point, lay the major ravine that drained toward the Confederate line north of Pegram's Salient. Venable told Mahone enough information about the topography of the battlefield so that he aimed to bring his reinforcements through the covered way that snaked along inside this wide ravine.[38]

At some point, when the head of Weisiger's column neared the western approach to the Jerusalem Plank Road, Venable and Mahone left the command. Venable wanted to return to Lee and report the movement of fresh troops toward the battlefield. He found the army commander with Hill at a traverse close to Rives's Salient, and Lee was pleased that Mahone was personally leading the two brigades into battle. Soon after, Lee made his way to the Gee House to more closely observe the fight.[39]

Mahone left the column to get more information about the battlefield before the troops arrived on the scene. As he rode toward Bushrod Johnson's headquarters, he met some troops moving away from the battlefield and asked them what was wrong. "Hell is busted back thar," was all he could get out of them. Mahone reached Johnson's headquarters about 8:15. He had no interest in consulting Johnson but had been told Hill would be here. Disappointed in that expectation, he found Beauregard and was pleased when the general suggested that he take charge of efforts to recover the captured works, a suggestion that Johnson happily endorsed. Mahone was not impressed by Johnson, who seemed about ready to eat his breakfast. When he asked him how much of his division line the Yankees had captured, Johnson inaccurately told him the "retrenched cavalier." Mahone answered, "In *feet,* I want to know, Gen.

Johnson, that, as you may imagine, I may determine the face of my attacking force." Johnson again replied inaccurately, "About one hundred yards." When Mahone asked Johnson to show him how to get there, the latter dispatched Lieutenant Harris of his staff to show him the way. Mahone and Harris mounted and rode back along the Jerusalem Plank Road; leaving their horses at the entrance to the covered way, Harris pointed down the roadway and left as Mahone walked down the slope.[40]

Mahone found another of Johnson's officers to fill him in on the intricate nature of the battlefield. Fitz William McMaster received a message from one of Johnson's staff officers to meet Mahone at Elliott's headquarters, where the shallow ravine occupied by Smith's and Crawford's men joined the covered way. Mahone had just arrived when McMaster reached the place and asked the South Carolinian how to arrange his men. McMaster suggested the shallow ravine, which was big enough to accommodate two understrength brigades in addition to Smith's and Crawford's men.[41]

Mahone walked into the shallow ravine, toward the south, and went up the eastern slope until he could peer at the crater only 350 yards away. "For the moment I could scarcely take in the reality," he recounted. "My heart almost went into my mouth." Mahone could tell the Federals were there in large numbers but "greatly disordered." He needed more men and sent courier Jimmy Blakemore with a message for Brig. Gen. John C. C. Sanders to bring his Alabama brigade from the division line. Then he told Capt. Victor J. B. Girardey of his staff how to position Weisiger and Hall in the small ravine and waited a few minutes for the head of his column to appear.[42]

As Weisiger's men neared the battlefield, a few stragglers from McMaster's brigade made their appearance. The Virginians chided them for going to the rear. "Ah, boys, you have hot work ahead," a Carolinian retorted. "They are negroes and show no quarter." Weisiger's men were surprised; Lee's infantry had never fought black Federal soldiers before this day. The news enraged the Virginians. "I never felt more like fighting in my life," recalled William H. Stewart. "Our comrades had been slaughtered in a most inhuman and brutal manner, and slaves were trampling over their mangled and bleeding corpses. Revenge must have fired every heart and strung every arm with nerves of steel for the Herculean task of blood."[43]

The two brigades marched a bit along the Jerusalem Plank Road when they left the military footpath in order to reach the entrance to the covered way east of the road. This occurred near the Hebrew Cemetery at Blandford, and Johnson's headquarters was also nearby. The covered way had two dogleg turns before it entered the deeper part of the ravine, and negotiating these sharp turns exposed the men to Federal view. They were told to run past to lessen the danger.[44]

Mahone remained at the entrance to the ravine where a bank of earth had been erected to offer some protection. He continued to consult with McMaster and called for John Haskell to ask him further information about the placement of Confederate artillery in the area. Haskell was utterly delighted to see Mahone and his troops arrive on the battlefield. He had worried all morning, but now there seemed to be a different spirit animating the defense. "There was no better division and no better commander," Haskell wrote. "Everything changed at once."[45]

Federal signal officers, some of them perched on observation towers, failed to detect the movement of Weisiger and Hall to the battlefield. As the head of Weisiger's column neared the junction of the covered way and the ravine, Weisiger saw Mahone "stooping down" as McMaster drew "a diagram of the works on the ground, Mahone looked up & asked me if I understood it, I told him I did, he then ordered me to move my Brigade" into the shallow ravine and report when ready to attack.[46]

As the Virginians left the covered way and marched up the shallow ravine, Mahone stood at the junction and shouted encouragement. "Give them the bayonet," he told the 12th Virginia. "Remember your homes, remember old Norfolk. You have got to fight negroes," he said as the 61st Virginia passed him. Mahone told John T. Woodhouse of the 16th Virginia, "Now, Major, I want to take those lines without firing a gun. I want to take it with the bayonet." McMaster also watched the brigade move by and added his own encouragement to Mahone's. "Show them no quarter, boys, they raised the black flag on us and showed none."[47]

The Virginians moved all the way up the ravine, which initially was more than deep enough to hide a standing man, until it became so shallow that one had to lie down to remain concealed. A tree marked the extreme right flank of Weisiger's brigade on July 30, and there is a tree similarly situated today. The ravine was more than big enough to accommodate Weisiger's eight hundred men. Each regiment lay down as soon as it reached its assigned spot; those on the center and far left had to move forward a few yards to be near the eastern edge of the ravine slope. The sharpshooters held the most exposed position on the far right, followed by the 6th Virginia, 16th Virginia, 61st Virginia, 41st Virginia, and 12th Virginia. J. Edward Whitehorne of the 12th noticed that the brigade line was not straight but curved forward at both ends. He was told to oblique sharply to the right during the attack and avoid going straight ahead. This was to get the regiment aligned for a direct strike at the crater rather than at the captured works north of the hole.[48]

David Addison Weisiger oversaw the deployment of his brigade as quickly as possible. A forty-six-year old Virginian and veteran of the Mexican War, Weisiger had worked as a businessman in Petersburg before the war broke out and as captain of a militia company had witnessed the hanging of John Brown. He had commanded the 12th Virginia for several years and had led the brigade since May 6, 1864. Weisiger ordered his eight hundred men to fix bayonets.[49]

Almost none of the Virginians, least of all Mahone or Weisiger, mentioned that any other troops occupied the shallow ravine before they arrived. Smith's 26th South Carolina and Crawford's three companies of the 17th South Carolina, plus the 25th North Carolina, had held this position for three hours and had repelled at least three efforts by the Federals to advance out of the captured works toward the ridge crest 177 yards to the rear. These Carolinians had performed essential service in containing the breach with little help other than artillery and mortar support. The Virginians took position "a little in advance of my detachment," McMaster later wrote. Johnson ordered the rest of the 17th South Carolina under Capt. James F. Steele to reinforce Crawford's three-company detachment in the ravine, intending to reunite the regiment and add a bit more strength to Mahone's attack, but it is likely that the men did not reach the ravine in time. Johnson also sent instructions for McMaster to remain with Mahone and continue to offer him assistance, leaving his own brigade in the hands of the next-ranking officer. Mahone failed to even mention McMaster in any way after the war, much less acknowledge his assistance. And McMaster himself never gave the 25th North Carolina credit for helping his men repel the Federal attacks. George Bernard of the 12th Virginia noted that some artillerists manned one or two mortars in the shallow ravine behind a slight line of earthworks that they apparently had dug that morning with bayonets.[50]

Several members of Weisiger's brigade crawled up the ravine slope to peer at the objective, and they were not encouraged by the sight. D. M. Bernard of the 12th Virginia realized how difficult the task would be when he counted twenty-one regimental flags in the captured works. He felt "that my earthly career was approaching its close." John T. West of the 61st Virginia saw the flags and "commended myself to God and resolved to die as a man and a soldier." Weisiger himself remembered the sight of the crater as "a grand though ominous spectacle," whereas William Stewart focused only on those Federal banners, seven in number, which seemed to be exactly opposite his 61st Virginia. "Boys, we must have all of those flags," he told his men.[51]

If Mahone felt apprehension at the prospects ahead, he was careful not to show it. The division commander oversaw the deployment of Weisiger's brigade "as if he were laying out a railroad," thought Richard Owen Whitehead. When Weisiger was ready, he sent his aide-de-camp, Drury A. Hinton, to inform Mahone. By now the division leader had moved from the bank of earth at the junction of the covered way and the ravine to take some shade under an arbor only thirty yards from Weisiger's left flank, probably where Elliott had his headquarters. Mahone instructed Hinton to tell Weisiger he should wait until either himself or Girardey gave the order to go in.[52]

Mahone was waiting for Hall's brigade to take position on Weisiger's right to cover the five-hundred-yard segment of Confederate works occupied by the enemy. Before he saw to Hall's deployment, the division leader walked into the ravine to give detailed directions to Weisiger's regimental officers and encouragement to the rank and file. The men of his old brigade had implicit faith in him. "Wherever he led or placed them, they always felt a moral certainty that they were being properly led or placed, either to inflict the most damage on the enemy or to have the enemy inflict the least damage on them." Mahone offered "minute and particular directions as to the manner of advancing" to William Stewart, which included a warning not to allow anyone to skulk around in the ravine or covered way, not to fire until reaching the captured works, and to freely use the bayonet when they reached the objective. The rank and file heard every word as well. William J. Murphy of the 41st Virginia now regretted that he had thrown away his bayonet sometime before July 30, for "I felt the need of it then, though I had never felt like that before."[53]

Officers and men remembered bits of advice and encouragement that Mahone offered in the few minutes before the attack began. He told them they would have to fight "negro troops" and encouraged them to take no prisoners. Mahone reminded the troops that, despite the daunting nature of the task ahead, they had performed difficult assignments before. He reminded them of his long tenure as their commander and of their personal connection with Petersburg. "I want the Old Brigade to save the city,'" he told them.[54]

Weisiger and the regimental officers took up Mahone's cue and encouraged their men as well. The brigade leader walked along the line and warned them to be ready for hand-to-hand combat in the captured works. Stewart "put a great deal of enthusiasm in the boys by telling us that we were bound to take those works, as we had always been good soldiers," recalled A. W. Grandy. Maj. Richard Watson Jones was so impressed by Mahone's message that he gave an impassioned talk to the 12th Virginia. "I reminded them that we were literally fighting for our homes, and that every man was expected to do his whole duty." The speech had an effect. Thomas Emmett Richardson of Company K stood in front of the regiment "with hat in hand and said, 'Boys, if you ever want to do anything for the old Cockade City, now is the time. Follow me.'"[55]

As they were screwing up their courage, the men of Weisiger's brigade received some scattering fire from the Federals ensconced in the Confederate works 350 yards away. The regiments on Weisiger's left wing lost several men while waiting for the order to charge, and J. Edward Whitehorne insisted that the men "were rapidly becoming demoralized" as a result. Lt. John T. West was "speaking words of encouragement" to his men in the 61st Virginia when he heard someone say, 'They are going to charge us.'" Drury Hinton looked toward the east and saw Bross trying to coax the Federals out of the captured works. They were trickling out "indifferently," he thought, but most remained in the safety of the entrenchments. A few Virginians fired at the Yankees, which tended to make them even more reluctant to stand in the open, even though Bross struck an impressive figure with his flag. A man of the 12th Virginia spoke the sentiments of many when he said, "Boys they are coming let us meet 'em."[56]

Mahone became aware of the Federal attempt to organize an attack when Girardey yelled, "Gen'l, they are coming." He turned his head and quickly took in the situation. Yelling loudly so that the men could hear as well, Mahone said to Girardey, "Tell Weisiger to forward." Girardey felt there was no time to go through channels. He raised his sword, placed himself in front of the brigade's left wing, and gave the order himself. Born in France, Girardey had grown up in Augusta, Georgia, and New Orleans. He had prewar experience in the militia and had served on the staff of Ambrose R. Wright's brigade, the same now commanded by Matthew Hall, when he secured a position on Mahone's division staff in May 1864. Mahone wanted Girardey to replace Hall as brigade commander, and Lee fully endorsed the idea, writing of the Frenchman, "I consider Capt. Girardey one of our boldest & most energetic officers." Girardey demonstrated his effectiveness by completely bypassing the brigade commander and initiating the charge himself.[57]

Weisiger remembered the start of the attack differently. Even though he had commanded the brigade for many months, he felt overshadowed by Mahone. Perhaps that is why Weisiger tried to garner credit for initiating the charge. When the Federals appeared from the captured works, he claimed to have asked Girardey if the brigade had not better go in immediately. The Frenchman, according to Weisiger, said he should wait until Hall was in place, but Weisiger insisted until Girardey agreed. Then Weisiger, not Girardey, gave the order to advance. Unfortunately for the brigade leader, only Drury Hinton supported his story. Everyone else agreed that Girardey bypassed Weisiger to lead the brigade forward. Sgt. Thomas E. Richardson of the 12th Virginia spoke for many when he asserted, "I heard no command from Gen. Weisiger." He further noted that the attack began on the brigade's left wing, where both Mahone and Girardey were located, and spread to the right. The 61st Virginia was the third regiment from the left and the guide for the brigade. Stewart instructed the color guard and the left and right general guides of the regiment to prepare to move forward twenty paces in preparation for the attack. Before he could follow through and order these men to move forward, regimental adjutant

W. A. S. Taylor saw Girardey "raise his hands above his head and shout 'Charge!'" He assumed the order came from Mahone, and everyone obeyed. Some men heard no order to attack from anyone; they just went along with their unit when it moved out. William J. Pate of the 61st Virginia heard Stewart say, "Now is your time, boys." Said Pate, "That was all the order I heard to charge."[58]

Hall's Georgia brigade had just begun to pass by to the rear of the Virginians when Weisiger's men started out on their counterattack. After telling Girardey to get the Virginians started, Mahone muttered, "I will go it with the old brigade, alone."[59]

12

WEISIGER ATTACKS

Weisiger's eight hundred men were ready to advance against ten thousand Federals who jammed the captured works 350 yards to the east. The Virginians had a slight descent, for the ground at the shallow ravine was about three feet higher than the ground occupied by Pegram's Salient.[1]

A few hundred troops from other commands joined Weisiger. Smith's 26th South Carolina and Crawford's three companies of the 17th South Carolina were available to participate in the attack, but it is unclear how many of them did so. Neither Smith nor Crawford had orders to go in. A member of the 17th South Carolina estimated that between twenty and thirty men of his company advanced with the Virginians. Smith Lipscomb of the 18th South Carolina was on his way to the rear through the covered way when the attack began. He asked the Virginians for permission to accompany them, and they agreed. Lipscomb wanted to see if he could get into the crater and dig out comrades still buried there.[2]

Observers convincingly claim that the 25th North Carolina from McAfee's brigade participated in the attack. The South and North Carolinians formed to the left of Weisiger's brigade, in the deepest part of the ravine. The 48th Georgia and half of another regiment in Hall's brigade also joined in Weisiger's charge. The 61st North Carolina of Hoke's division arrived at the ravine about the time that Weisiger did, but it did not take part in the attack conducted by the Virginia brigade. The 56th North Carolina, also from Hoke's division, arrived after Weisiger went in. A few Virginians mentioned that some members of McMaster's brigade went in with them, but not in an organized body.[3]

Weisiger began his charge just when the vanguard of Lt. Col. Matthew R. Hall's Georgia brigade arrived. One and a half regiments had entered the ravine when the Virginians set out, and Girardey ordered them to go in to the

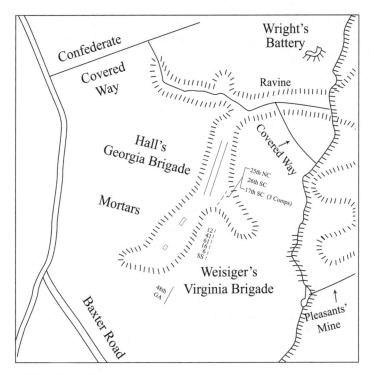

Weisiger's attack

right of Weisiger. Hall formed the rest of his brigade in the ravine and awaited further orders.[4]

Before they started at 9 A.M., some members of Weisiger's brigade took pot shots at the Federals. Corp. Virginius S. Kilby of the 16th Virginia claimed that he fired at the Federal officer who stood with raised sword encouraging his black troops to advance and brought him down. If so, Kilby was the Rebel responsible for shooting John Bross of the 29th USCT.[5]

Weisiger's Virginians "grandly and beautifully swept onward over the intervening space with muskets at trail," their officers "with uncovered heads and waving hats" in their front. This was the image that William H. Stewart wanted to remember decades later. George Bernard of the 12th Virginia glanced down the line as Weisiger started and remembered how beautifully the brigade emerged from the ravine. The Virginians began with a compact formation 150 yards wide but soon loosened their line so that it stretched 100 to 200 feet longer. They began the attack at the double-quick and kept up the pace nearly the entire distance.[6]

Partway across the space between the ravine and the captured works, Weisiger's right began to receive heavy fire coming from the defenders of the crater. This caused the right wing to wheel a bit to the left, skewing the brigade's line of advance. The Virginians received the heaviest fire from the crater when halfway across the open space. Henry E. Chase, a member of the sharpshooter battalion on the far right, described it as "a withering fire." He glanced to the left and saw that it "had a staggering effect for an instant, resembling a windrow in a wheat field, the men untouched closed, touched elbows and went ahead apparently with redoubled pace."[7]

Since they were nearing the enemy, the officers dropped back to rejoin the line when about one hundred yards from the captured works, but the Virginians were true to their instructions not to stop and shoot. Fifty yards from the Federals, the fire continued strong from the crater. Capt. John Wallace of the 61st Virginia was hit in the thigh. He fell but refused offers of help to the rear, shouting to his men, "Go on; go forward."[8]

Many Confederates witnessed the charge from afar. Artillery commander William Pegram and his adjutant, Capt. W. Gordon McCabe, watched through bullet holes in the wall of the Gee House. "Pegram and I yelled and clapped our hands and ran back and told our men," McCabe recalled. "It was the first good news we had to tell that day." Lee and Beauregard also witnessed the

Modern view of the ground over which Weisiger attacked. Earl J. Hess

attack from the Gee House, the latter finding it "an imposing, striking spectacle." Lee guessed Mahone led with his old Virginia brigade and simply stated, "I thought so" upon receiving confirmation. Both Lee and Beauregard regretted that Mahone was unable to bring all his brigades to attack at once, for they were confident that he would have quickly restored the breach to Rebel control.[9]

Weisiger was unable to cover all the captured Confederate works, and his brigade shied away from the area around the crater itself. Despite their cramped condition, the Federals inside the hole put up a spirited defense in contrast to the troops crammed in the cavalier and the maze of bombproofs north of the crater, who as yet offered no fire at all. Howard Aston of the 13th Ohio Cavalry (dismounted) estimated that up to six hundred Federal troops crowded the rim of the crater to fire at Weisiger's men; about one hundred of them were black troops. Sgt. Wesley Stanley and his comrades of the 14th New York Heavy Artillery fired one of Pegram's recovered howitzers at Weisiger, loading the piece with canister. William H. Powell characterized the Confederate attack as "feeble; more in the way of a reconnaissance than a charge," but only because of the way the Confederate right wing avoided a direct confrontation with the withering fire from the crater.[10]

When the Confederates drove within thirty yards of the captured works, many black soldiers stood up and yelled, "Remember Fort Pillow!" Still others added, "and show the D—— rebels no quarter." Some Virginians had breath enough to retort, "remember 'Beast Butler,'" referring to Federal Maj. Gen. Benjamin Butler's controversial administration of occupied New Orleans in 1862. Other Confederates fired their muskets, one of them bringing down "a big yellow negro" who had just climbed up on a traverse.[11]

Closing in, the Virginians opened a volley at the packed Federals in the entrenchments. Most were only a few feet from their enemy. Given the crowded conditions, it was not necessary to aim. Amnon Peek of the 61st Virginia stood just outside the captured works as his comrades handed him five or six guns to fire in rapid succession. Another member of the 61st recalled that he "could see the powder burn their clothes" as he fired his musket into the mass. Many Federals "seemed to drop down in the breastworks." If they tried to return fire, they were too frightened to aim properly and shot into the air. "The smoke of their guns went straight up," recalled Calvin Peek of the 61st Virginia. Peek then knew "we were safe and I felt cool and collected as I would have been under ordinary circumstances."[12]

It is likely that the Federals who fired wildly were mostly the inexperienced black troops rather than the hardened veterans of the white divisions. In other ways many of the blacks could not stand the shock. Those men who had followed Bross out of the captured works recoiled so quickly that they disrupted everyone inside the entrenchments, crowding them even further and interfering with attempts to oppose the Rebels. Col. Stephen Weld was so jammed that he "literally could not raise my hands from my side." He heard the Rebel yell, saw a Confederate flag as it appeared outside the captured works, and realized he could actually touch it if his arms were free. Then he saw the musket barrels appear and felt the blast of the discharge on his face. Fortunately for Weld, the bullets sailed over his head.[13]

Richard B. Davis of the 12th Virginia saw a Federal officer trying to force his black enlisted men to resist. The officer threatened to shoot anyone who attempted to surrender, yet many blacks crouched in the trenches with hands raised, crying for mercy. Some Confederates, in an effort to break resistance more quickly, yelled, "Shoot the officers!" Maj. William Etheredge thought the black troops did not have the experience or stamina to resist Mahone's veterans. He claimed that the white Federals fired as best they could, and he lost many men to that fire.[14]

After the first exchange, Weisiger's brigade jumped into the captured works to clear them out in close fighting. The 12th Virginia, on Weisiger's far left, reached the entrenchments a few seconds before the rest of the brigade, and James Eldred Phillips glanced to the right to see his comrades move up. "I never saw such a grand sight in all of my experience," he wrote. The 12th Virginians got into the entrenchments and fired obliquely to the right to help pave the way for the rest of the brigade to do the same.[15]

In the brigade center, members of Stewart's 61st Virginia led the way into the entrenchments. Lt. John T. West saw that the works were packed and estimated that about half of the Federals were blacks. He demanded they surrender and some "dropped their guns and squatted down in the ditch." A few black soldiers, without guns, bolted through the ranks of the 61st and headed for the Confederate rear, since it seemed all but impossible to run in the other direction. One of them shouted to West as he passed by, "Let me come, boss, I done." A Rebel tried to shoot him, but West saved his life by saying, "There are plenty in front to shoot. Let him go." The lieutenant then saw that two white Federals a few feet away were trying to level their muskets at him. West jumped across other Yankees and landed squarely on his assailants, grabbing one musket with his left hand and knocking the other away with his sword and his right hand. He then started "to whack them over the head" until they surrendered.[16]

West performed his acrobatic stunt in an instinctive manner to save himself, but James Eldred Phillips demurred when Stewart told him to "climb over" the earthworks, preferring to go through a passageway to the left. Several men who followed him were shot, but even some of the Rebels who vaulted over the works were killed while doing so. Enough Federals offered resistance to make the task of entering the captured works a dangerous assignment. Pvt.

Edmund Curling of the 61st Virginia initially fired his musket and "killed my man;" he then jumped into a ditch and landed astride a musket held by a black soldier. Curling's lieutenant managed to disable the black man with his sword as Curling killed another Yankee.[17]

When Weisiger's right wing closed on the captured works, Capt. W. W. Broadbent, commander of the brigade sharpshooters, led his men into the entrenchments with his hat in one hand and his sword in another. "Follow me men," he shouted as he plunged into a ditch crammed with white Federals. Because the right wing had veered left during the advance, the sharpshooters on the extreme right did not reach as far as the crater. In fact, Broadbent took his men into a section of entrenchments at least forty yards north of the hole. Here a long traverse extended all the way to the rear edge of the maze of bombproofs, offering convenient flank protection for the sharpshooters from the hail of Union fire coming from the crater.[18]

Some Rebels had difficulty getting into the dubious shelter of the entrenchments. J. Frank Cutchin of the 16th Virginia tripped when his foot caught the bayonet of a musket held by the man behind him and fell headlong into the ditch. He looked up to see a Federal officer about to hit him with a sword, and managed to lunge upward with his bayonet and stab him in the side. The weapon penetrated the officer just under his ribs; the Federal fell on Cutchin and "covered me with blood." Another member of the 16th Virginia, however, had an easy time entering the works. He jumped into the ditch and saw many black soldiers, "lying flat down in the bottom," offering no resistance.[19]

The fire from the crater took out the commander of the Virginia brigade. Weisiger was hit by a bullet "across my stomach," just as his men neared the captured works. Weisiger remained on the ground but sent for Col. George T. Rogers of the 6th Virginia, the next-ranking officer in the brigade. When Rogers came to him, Weisiger confessed his fear that he was mortally wounded and gave him command of the brigade.[20]

Blacks Panic and Retreat

Many Federals scrambled for the rear as soon as the Virginians entered the works. Lt. W. F. Baugh of the 61st Virginia was struck by the sight: "As far as the eyes could reach, it was one fleeing & retreating mass . . . rushing pell mell away from us."[21]

From the Federal side, the scene was anything but pleasing. "What a lamentable sight to see the Negroes come back like a flock of black sheep," moaned Capt. Levi Brackett of Willcox's staff. Brackett admitted that he saw some white soldiers join the retreat, but he claimed that most stood their ground and allowed the mass to pass by. Most white officers in the black regiments also felt ashamed of the way their men reacted. James H. Rickard of the

19th USCT "struck several upon the head but could not stop them." The enlisted black troops ran "in perfect disorder, horrible slaughter," commented Capt. Albert Rogall. Pvt. Joseph Trevan of the 28th USCT was trampled in the rush and suffered "a permanent injury to his spine."[22]

The black retreat swamped the right wing of the 100th Pennsylvania, causing serious injury to a captain in the regiment. William Taylor, another officer in the 100th, claimed that white troops shot down some panic-stricken blacks in an effort to stem the rout. An officer of the 35th Massachusetts tried to rally the fleeing blacks by standing up and waving his sword, but the regimental adjutant suggested it would be better to let them go to the rear.[23]

In their first reaction to Weisiger's attack, many black soldiers of Thomas's brigade jumped into a traverse occupied by the 9th New Hampshire. Sgt. Newell Dutton ungenerously described their reaction as they crowded into the overfilled trench. "If you can imagine a mass of worms crawling over each other, you will have a very good idea of the condition of things in that traverse." The white soldiers of the 9th reportedly were "bayoneted, crushed, and trampled" by the blacks. A New Hampshire private mostly managed to deflect the bayonet of one black soldier with his gun, but the weapon nicked him in the abdomen anyway. Dutton, who was in charge of the regimental flag, climbed over the black soldiers and got out of the traverse, making his way to the crater.[24]

Quite a few whites either deliberately retreated to the Union line with the blacks or were swept along in the crowd. Officers re-formed as many as 450 men of Marshall's brigade in the forward Union line, but they never made an attempt to rejoin their comrades in the captured works. [25]

Weisiger's attack and the mass retreat arrested all Federal efforts to push more troops into the captured works and widen the breach. Eighteenth Corps staff members were in the covered way leading to the Fourteen Gun Battery when the blacks surged past. Thomas Livermore grabbed one man and then another, ordering them to stand, but they ran away as soon as he turned his back. Livermore looked desperately for a flag to rally the blacks but could find none. He realized that his frenzied oaths were overheard by fellow staff members who later poked fun at him, but Livermore and the others also found a source of amusement in Ord's brother and aide-de-camp, a "rather weak sister," as they described him. Ord was knocked down and trampled by the blacks, surviving without serious injury. But when he told the story later, "with a melancholy face, bearing not even the trace of humor in it, and in rather weak, slow accents," his fellow staff members found his demeanor so funny that they arranged for him to retell the story to Potter's staff as well.[26]

Joseph B. Carr also was caught in the middle of the black rush. He was walking from the forward Union line through the right-side covered way when the surge of retreating men hit him. "I was lifted from my feet by the rushing mass and carried along with it ten or fifteen yards in the covered way," he related. Carr and some of his staff members then managed to stop and re-form a few of the black troops, aided by Potter, who also happened to be in the covered way when the blacks retreated.[27]

Turner's division of the 10th Corps was caught in the middle of its advance. Bell's brigade was only twenty feet outside the Confederate line, attempting to advance northward to widen the breach. The retreating blacks completely disrupted his column. "We used our sabers freely on the cowards," Bell wrote home, "but could not stop them and were all driven back—pell mell." Other officers also tried to arrest their flight, but they "might as well have tried to stop a tornado." Elias A. Bryant, who had been wounded in the thigh, was being carried on a stretcher across Poor Creek valley when the black throng surged past. Bryant encouraged them to stop, but it did no good. They crowded into the covered way until "it was packed solidly full." His stretcher bearers carried him along the open ground, managing to get Bryant back to the rear safely.[28]

Turner lost all control of his division for a while. "He seemed to be very much distressed about it," according to an observer. Moreover the retreat of Bell's brigade enabled McAfee's North Carolina troops to more easily fire down the length of the main Confederate trench and help to drive the Federals out of the maze of works north of the crater.[29]

Coan's brigade was in the process of advancing across no-man's-land in a complex formation when the blacks retreated. Coan tried to rally the fugitives, but they paid no attention to him. The retreating blacks took his left wing along to the rear, while one hundred men of the 97th Pennsylvania and a portion of the 48th New York, on his right, held fast behind a shelf of ground for another hour before retiring to the Union line.[30]

Curtis's brigade was just taking position outside the forward end of the right-side covered way when the blacks arrived. Curtis had carefully formed his brigade in regimental columns just behind the forward Union line. The 3rd New York and 117th New York fixed bayonets and managed to corral a lot of retreating black soldiers, but the surging mass of troops arrived just as Curtis's last regiment, the 112th New York, was leaving the covered way. "My heart sunk within me as I saw the utter recklessness of men and officers in that stampede," reported Orrin S. Allen. That portion of the 112th New York which had cleared the covered way was forced back a bit by the mob. The retreating blacks "ran over us and made to the rear," as J. C. Rowland put it. That portion which was still moving out of the covered way was stopped by a mob of black soldiers, "crowding, swearing, yelling, making frantic endeavors to get through; some were down and others treading over them; and those in front were pushed on by the dense mass behind." Capt. Ephraim A. Ludwick jumped out of the covered way and called on his men to follow him across the open ground. He lost fourteen men who were shot while thus exposing themselves, but the rest avoided the uncontrollable mob and made it to the relative safety of the forward Union line.[31]

The black retreat did not extend far enough to engulf the 51st New York, 2nd New York Mounted Infantry, or the four companies of the 97th Pennsylvania that lay between the two New York regiments in the captured Rebel skirmish line at the mouth of the ravine. These units, however, became the target of a push forward by McAfee's skirmish line. Emboldened by Weisiger's attack and the subsequent retreat of Ferrero's troops, the Confederates gathered in the ravine, out of sight of the 51st New York, and then "came down on us like a whirlwind," according to George Washington Whitman. The New York and Pennsylvania troops fell back to the Union position, but the Confederates did not advance beyond their reclaimed picket line. The Rebel advance "was one of the boldest and most desperate things I ever saw," Whitman reported.[32]

"I was literally insane over our defeat," recalled Capt. D. E. Proctor of the 30th USCT. He walked slowly while accompanying his men in the retreat. "Demoralization seized me" upon seeing an artillery projectile disembowel an enlisted man, and "I reached cover as soon as possible, and all this in a minute." A signal officer reported to Benjamin F. Butler at 9:20 A.M. that he could see the massed retreat as well as a lot of Union prisoners being escorted to the Confederate rear. "The black troops are not doing well," B. C. Ludlow accurately told Butler, "but there are many reasons for their not acting well." Indeed many of the black troops soon rallied behind cover. Division commander Ferrero once again ducked into Surgeon Chubb's bombproof, where he and Ledlie obtained more stimulants. Sigfried also stopped briefly at the bombproof on his way to the rear. Ferrero left soon after, but Ledlie dallied half an hour longer before retiring to the rear.[33]

Many black troops stayed in the captured works and offered resistance to the Confederates. Others stayed in the captured works only because they did not have an opportunity to run. Those hundreds of blacks who caused so much disruption in their retreat were those who happened to be close to the rear of the Union position inside the captured works; those who stayed were too close to the enemy, or too determined to fight. Henry G. Thomas later reported that a group of his men held inside the captured works and fought for about fifteen minutes to hold the enemy at bay while the rest retired. After a while Thomas ordered them to pull back. Some did, but the rest were "nearly all shot away."[34]

Hand-to-Hand Combat

One of the most intense episodes of hand-to-hand combat that ever took place in the Civil War occurred in the captured works north of the crater. "Our men would drive the bayonet into one man, pull it out, turn the butt and knock the brains out of another," recalled Maj. William Etheredge. It was a close, personal form of battle that engendered enormous passion and desperate struggles for life.[35]

On Weisiger's far left, members of the 12th Virginia hit the captured works at a place that the Federals did not occupy. They were able to enter the entrenchments freely and turn to the right, making their way through the maze until coming upon the enemy. Three black soldiers tried to club Sgt. James L. Wilton with their musket butts. Thomas Emmett Richardson came to his rescue, breaking the wooden butt of his own musket on one Yankee's head and using the barrel to deal with the other two. Richardson, remembered as "a tall, strong, athletic fellow," killed a total of five Federals in the maze of bomb-proofs.[36]

D. Meade Bernard of the 12th Virginia entered a crooked traverse that led directly to the main Confederate trench, preceded only by a young soldier of Elliott's brigade. They encountered some wounded and demoralized black troops before meeting resistance. A black soldier tried to bayonet the South Carolinian; Bernard attempted to bayonet him, but his weapon merely glanced off the Yankee's hip. A white Federal officer appeared, demanded Bernard's surrender, and held a pistol close to his face. Bernard managed to deflect the discharge with his arm. By then, help arrived and another Virginian bayoneted the officer as the South Carolinian beat the black soldier over the head with a pistol. Bernard then took cover around a bend in the traverse and nearly shot a Confederate officer in the back, mistaking him for a Federal. Another member of Bernard's company knocked out a black soldier who had "the most fiendish countenance that I have ever seen." He dreamed of that face several times in later years.[37]

George Bernard, also of the 12th Virginia, had missed the news that black troops were in the captured works and was doubly surprised when he saw a uniformed Negro stand in front of him. At a glance, Bernard also saw dozens of blacks and whites in the works thirty feet behind him, "as closely jammed and packed together as we sometimes see pedestrians on the crowded sidewalk of a city, and seemingly in great confusion and alarm. I distinctly noticed the countenances and rolling eyes of the terror-stricken negroes." Bernard could also see the caps of other Federals taking cover in the works farther to the rear.[38]

Bernard fired his gun and ducked into a traverse that happened to be nearly empty, except for a black soldier who leveled his musket at him with a grin that the Rebel remembered for the rest of his life. Bernard's musket was empty and there was no time to reload, so he ducked into a recess for cover. Here he found another black soldier, who pleaded for his life, offering to be his slave if he spared him. "Old man, I do not intend to kill you, but you deserve to be killed," Bernard told him. The black began to fan a wounded member of Elliott's brigade, who was lying in the recess, to ingratiate himself with Bernard. The Virginian reloaded his gun and looked down the traverse. His adversary was nowhere in sight, but Bernard saw the muzzles of several muskets sticking around an angle in the traverse, indicating the enemy were no more than five feet away. He peeked across the top of the ground and saw that the crater was but seventy-five yards away. Bernard also saw more Federal troops crowded close by and took potshots at them, joined by a comrade who made his way into the recess. Soon more Rebel troops entered the traverse in continued efforts to clear out the captured works, and Bernard and his comrade were safe.[39]

Sgt. John Crow of the 12th Virginia cleared out one bombproof that contained a white officer and fourteen blacks. They readily surrendered but then were threatened by Capt. James Piper Cox of the 41st Virginia. Cox was maddened by the thought of fighting black troops and seemed about to kill the captives when a black man went to his knees and pleaded, "Master! Master! Please don't kill me! I'll be your nigger!" Cox relented, and Crow managed to get the prisoners to the rear in safety.[40]

As the 12th Virginians penetrated the maze of bombproofs, the fighting intensified to a fever pitch. "I saw men slam their bayonets in the Enemy and fire the guns off in them," remembered James Eldred Phillips, and "then I also saw them knock the enemy on the heads with the but of their guns, & others Cut them with swords." Within ten minutes bodies littered the floor of the works, "in some places in such numbers that it was difficult to make one's way along the trench without stepping upon them."[41]

The 61st Virginia, in the center of the brigade, put up a spirited offensive behind the inspired leadership of William Stewart. The colonel stood up on a parapet and called on "the Norfolk County boys" to follow him into the entrenchments. As his men fought their way into the works, they often met demoralized Federals who only wanted to save themselves. Many blacks called out, "Master please do not kill us," and Stewart cautioned one of his men not to harm prisoners after they gave themselves up. A white officer also tried to surrender and "appealed to me for protection," as Stewart recalled. "I said, 'You must drop your arms and run to the rear. The excitement is too great for me to be responsible for you if you remain here.'"[42]

But Stewart's men also encountered blacks and whites who fought to the death. One black soldier fired at Pvt. A. W. Grandy and missed. He then threw his musket at Grandy, but the Rebel dodged it by dropping to his knees and shot the Yankee in the mouth. When a second black soldier ran at him, Grandy sidestepped his lunge and bayoneted him as another Confederate shot the Yankee. Grandy finished him off with a second bayonet thrust, yelling in his excitement, "D—— him. I fixed him." Grandy later saw a black man smash comrade John Lee on the nose, breaking it badly, only to be bayoneted by another Confederate.[43]

Pvt. William J. Pate of the 61st Virginia thrust his bayonet so deeply into a Federal soldier that he had difficulty retrieving it. This gave an opportunity for a black soldier to smack him on the cheek and arm with his musket, but Pate was saved by a comrade who came up in time to kill the Federal. When Laban Godwin began to hit a wounded black man in the face with his gun as the Federal tried to rise up, Amnon Peek told him to stop, as the black man was obviously dying.[44]

After a few minutes of heated combat, the 61st Virginia cleared out the westernmost layer of works. At least one man, John W. Robertson, stood on the edge of a ditch and repeatedly fired into the Federals taking shelter farther east, as two or three comrades handed him loaded weapons. Stewart continued the charge into those eastern works, yelling, "Who will follow me over into the next line[?]" Pvt. William Wright bayoneted a black soldier in the side, but he could not pull the bayonet out because the victim grabbed the musket barrel. Wright dropped the weapon, picked up an abandoned rifle nearby, and was about to stab the man again, but two officers stopped him. Wright was so worked up that he hit the Federal with his fist, and he hit another black soldier who refused to give up.[45]

Many members of the 61st Virginia experienced similar episodes of enraged combat in the confined spaces of the works. Capt. John West fought two blacks with his sword; a comrade tried to help him but accidentally stabbed West in the shoulder with his bayonet. Many men on both sides "pierced each others hearts and crushed each others skulls until the entire place seemed a veritable hell," as West put it. Lt. Julius J. Bilisoly "cut down a color bearer, and grabbed two flags," but other Federals retrieved one of them. With the aid of James Denby, who bayoneted one of the Federals, Bilisoly was able to take away the other Union color.[46]

Within the ranks of the 41st Virginia, Maj. William Etheredge was among the first to jump into the captured works. The "Yanks were as thick as they could stand," and he quickly encountered two white soldiers with bayonets. Etheredge grabbed and held them as a shield, for a third Federal tried to shoot him. He "clubbed their heads together" and squatted a bit behind them, because he was taller than both. The third Yankee hesitated long enough for more Confederates to come to Etheredge's aid. The major yelled, "Kill the man in front of me," and Peter Gibbs of Company E stepped aside and shot him. Etheredge then took the first two prisoner. Other members of the regiment experienced similar fights. Capt. John W. Beaton was slashing about with his sword when a Federal officer fired his pistol at a range of only four feet. He missed and was killed by one of Beaton's men. Pvt. Virgil B. Dunford of Company I discarded his bayonet, as it got in the way, and used the butt of his musket. Despite the desperate nature of the struggle, James Alfred Ritter "seemed in exuberant spirits . . . and whenever he gained an advantage over his adversary he would break out in a loud laugh."[47]

On the brigade's right wing, the 16th Virginia entered the entrenchments later than the rest of Weisiger's command. J. H. Parker grabbed the upraised bayonet of a lunging Federal soldier with his hand and pushed it aside to avoid a fatal wound, but the Federal also pulled the trigger and the gun went off, sending its ball into Parker's arm. He managed to continue holding the bayonet until a comrade shot the Yankee. Pvt. Robert E. Norfleet "was beginning to get nervous" as he fought a black soldier with his bayonet and saw another adversary approach. Then he heard comrade John F. Lotzy say, "Old boy, I have saved your life, go ahead." Some black soldiers put up stiff resistance for a while, then gave up, saying, "We will surrender. Where is the rear?" The boys of the 16th Virginia responded, "There is no such thing as a rear. Remember Beast Butler."[48]

The North Carolinians, South Carolinians, and Georgians who attacked with Weisiger fought as well as the Virginians. Lt. Col. Matthew Norris Love of the 25th North Carolina reported that his men freely used their bayonets after entering the captured works. "We was not very particular whether we captured or killed them," he wrote, referring to the black soldiers. The 48th Georgia participated in the fight, along with half of another regiment from Hall's brigade. "The Bayonet was plunged through their hearts & the muzzle of our guns was put on their temple & their brains blown out," as James Paul Verdery put it. The flag of the 48th Georgia was rent by 103 bullets, and the staff was severed during the close-range combat.[49]

Yet many black soldiers stood and fought like tigers beside their white comrades. Confederate soldier Henry Bird praised them by writing, "They fought like bull dogs and died like soldiers." Ervin Case of the 9th New Hampshire saw a black man deliberately stand up and shoot a Rebel, clubbing two others until the butt of his gun broke into pieces, and then duck into shelter. During the fighting retreat of the 43rd USCT, Lt. James W. Steele noticed that a Virginian grinned "diabolically, and [shook] his head" every time he reloaded. Steele assumed "he was on a 'nigger' hunt, and it made me mad." The lieutenant stood up and rapidly fired his pistol four times at the man but never knew if he hit him. A bullet nicked Steele's shoulder and he tried to run as someone called out, "Come in heah, Yank, or we gwine to kill yeh," but Steele made it to safety.[50]

In the 30th USCT, Corp. Samuel Hall lost his life desperately fighting to save the regimental colors. A Virginian knocked down the color-bearer and Hall shot him, grabbing the flag before it hit the ground. Hall waved it vigorously and called for his comrades to rally, but a bullet smashed into his arm. He shifted the flag staff to his left hand, but another ball hit that arm and penetrated his body as well, killing him.[51]

Freeman Bowley reported that the 30th USCT tried to retire south toward the crater as a group, but then broke apart. Bowley made his way to the crater, followed by about a dozen of his men. He could see the Virginians jump into the works just vacated, only twenty yards behind the retreating blacks. Capt. William H. Seagrave of Company K, earlier wounded in the knee, could not get away and killed several Confederates before being shot and bayoneted. A group of his loyal black soldiers remained behind to help and were all killed. Seagrave was taken prisoner but died at his home a few months after the end of the war.[52]

When it became apparent that the captured works could not be held, members of the white regiments made frantic efforts to save their colors. In the 31st Maine and 11th New Hampshire, Virginians and Federals fought for control of the flags, "tearing them to pieces and breaking the staves" in the process. Most of the regiments in Simon Griffin's brigade brought their flags back; Sgt. Leander A. Wilkins of the 9th New Hampshire recaptured the colors of the 21st Massachusetts.[53]

Sgt. James W. Lathe of the 9th New Hampshire shot a Rebel officer at close range in the melee. He vividly remembered the look on the Virginian's face when the bullet hit his chest. Lathe shot four other Confederates before he was hit in the hand and retired amidst a shower of balls across the lip of the crater. He ran back across no-man's-land and counted four bullet holes in his clothes when he reached the forward Union line. Lathe also lost three fingers because of the hand wound.[54]

Capt. Theodore Gregg, who commanded the 45th Pennsylvania, fought off a large Virginian who grabbed him by the throat and put a revolver to his head. Gregg wrestled the pistol away and shot the Rebel. Later Gregg rescued Capt. R. G. Richards when a Confederate officer tried to compel him to surrender. Richards recalled that the Rebel stared at him for several seconds without firing, long enough for Gregg to arrive and disarm him.[55]

The Federals saw ample evidence that the enemy had no intention of taking black prisoners. Capt. Frank Kenfield of the 17th Vermont heard the Rebels call out to "save the white men but kill the damn niggers." He survived the battle and recalled with "a cold shudder . . . how those poor colored men were butchered in cold blood." For their part, Rebel survivors of the battle claimed that "our men were in a hot rage and hardly knew when to give quarters."[56]

A group of 12th Virginians witnessed a particularly horrifying incident that amounted to nothing less than cold-blooded murder. A black noncommissioned officer was tormented by two Confederates. One beat him with a ramrod while the other shot him at close range in the hip. The black man begged for mercy as the Rebel calmly reloaded and held the muzzle of his gun to his stomach and pulled the trigger. "It was a brutal, horrible act," recalled George Bernard, "and those of us who witnessed it from our position in the trench a few feet away could but exclaim: 'That is too bad! It is shocking!'"[57]

Decades later, aged Confederate veterans recalled the brutal fighting. "I recollect killing two negroes—one I killed with the bayonet, and the other I shot," testified George White of the 61st Virginia. William Pate of the same regiment could not tally the number of blacks he dispatched with gunfire but knew he killed three with the bayonet. Joshua Denby was certain he sent five or six Federals of all races to their maker. Henry Bird of the 12th Virginia reported soon after the battle that orders went out to kill all prisoners and that the men executed those orders until "our Genl. Sickened of the slaughter and ordered it to be stayed." There is no evidence to support Bird's contention; the killing seems to have been the work of the rank and file. William Stewart, commander of the 61st Virginia, "sought so far as I could to prevent unnecessary killing," but a lot of it took place anyway.[58]

The intense, hand-to-hand fighting lasted about twenty minutes before the Yankees were cleared out of the captured works north of the crater. It seemed "an incredibly short time" to some Confederate survivors, but others thought it lasted up to three hours. Many of Weisiger's men fired into the forty-yard space separating their hard-won position from the crater and drove the Federals out of that area and into the hole.[59]

The crater became the only Federal stronghold inside the breach. Sgt. Howard Aston estimated that about eight hundred whites and two hundred blacks took shelter there as refugees. Other estimates place the total number of Union troops in the hole at six hundred. The Federals evacuated the trench south of the crater as well. Hartranft asked Byron Cutcheon, who had returned from his visit to the Union lines, to bring his 20th Michigan north to help stem the disorderly retreat of Ferrero's division. Cutcheon tried but could do little; in fact a few of his men took part in the retreat to the Union line. Cutcheon settled the rest of his regiment inside the intact portion of Pegram's battery emplacement, where he also found members of the 1st Michigan Sharpshooters and the 2nd Michigan.[60]

Freeman Bowley led about twenty members of the 30th USCT into the crater from the north, facing Federal fire from the hole as they jumped in. "A full line around the crest of the crater were loading and firing as fast as they could," he recalled, "and the men were dropping thick and fast, most of them shot through the head. Every man that was shot rolled down the steep sides to the bottom, and in places they were piled up four and five deep."[61]

Weisiger's attack acted on the Federals like a cold, wintry blast, taking the will to fight out of many black and white troops. George Bernard admitted that the ill-organized Union forces were vulnerable to an attack, even by an outnumbered brigade. As E. Porter Alexander put it, Weisiger's charge "decided the day, which was still easily anybody's battle."[62]

Cleaning Up

When the hand-to-hand fight ended, Stewart took the lead in consolidating control of the recaptured works north of the crater. He created details to clear the entrenchments of bodies so the Virginians could use them as shelter and move in any direction as needed. Details of six men from each regiment began the work, piling the bodies outside the trenches and traverses where they would also serve as added protection against enemy fire. The men used gun slings to pull the bodies out. Black prisoners were also put to work at this gruesome task. If gun slings were not available, four men took hold of one corpse and lifted it out of the works, piling white and black, blue and gray indiscriminately. Blood saturated the floor of every trench and traverse where numbers of men had fallen. It ran "nearly shoe sole deep" in some spots, making what William J. Murphy called "a bloody muck."[63]

The Confederates discovered another gruesome sight when they cleaned out the works. Capt. William W. Broadbent of the 16th Virginia, commander of Weisiger's sharpshooters, had been killed in the hand-to-hand fight and mutilated in the heat of battle rage. One amazed Rebel reported that he had "nearly every conceivable kind of wound upon him that a soldier can receive in battle." His head was "beaten to a pulp," and as many as fifteen bayonet cuts appeared on his body. William Stewart concluded that Broadbent, who had been born in New Jersey but sided with the South because of his prewar residence in Sussex County, Virginia, had been "mercilessly murdered."[64]

William Mahone had waited in the shallow ravine after Weisiger began his attack to place Hall's Georgians and instruct them to advance as soon as it became evident that Weisiger needed help. He then moved into the recaptured works very soon after the hand-to-hand fight ended, braving a stout fire laid across the intervening space by the Federals in the crater. He told George Rogers, who now led the brigade, how to dispose his men in the recaptured works. Mahone also wanted Rogers to lay down fire on no-man's-land between the contending lines. While inspecting the area, he became a target of the Federals in the crater. Stewart warned him to take care and the division leader replied, "No, I do not want to get shot now as the worst of it is over."[65]

But Mahone realized there was much more to do. He told Capt. William A. S. Taylor, adjutant of the 61st Virginia, that "the work is not over and . . . *we* must retake the balance of the line." He then advised Taylor to tally the regiment's losses and gave him responsibility for shepherding prisoners to the rear. Mahone soon returned to the shallow ravine to organize mortar support for further action.[66]

Some of Weisiger's men set up firing positions and began to pepper nearby Federal targets. John Edgar Foreman of the 61st Virginia fashioned a sharpshooter's embrasure and recruited two men to reload for him. He estimated that he shot up to ten Federals during the course of the next three hours. It was impossible for the entire brigade to find suitable positions from which to harass the enemy, who by now were well hidden inside the crater.[67]

Those Federals unlucky enough to be caught by Weisiger's command now faced an uncertain future. Frank Kenfield of the 17th Vermont lost his sword, gold watch, and chain to his captors, who also confiscated his revolver and hat. A Virginian asked Col. Stephen Weld "what do you'uns come down here and fight we'uns for?" Weld also lost his hat and sword to his captors, but a diary he had kept since the first day at the Wilderness was secure inside his bootleg. Weld and some black prisoners were forced to head west out of the recaptured works, even though Federal fire from the crater blanketed the area. Along the way two Confederates decided to kill a wounded Negro who walked slowly in front of Weld, shooting him at point-blank range as if he were an animal. A Federal signal officer perched on top of a tower behind 9th Corps lines saw the group of prisoners as they approached the ridge crest that Burnside had so desperately sought to capture all morning.[68]

Ironically a few Confederates also were taken prisoner in Weisiger's attack. Lt. Francis M. Whitehurst of the 6th Virginia tried to lead a charge against the crater, but all around him were shot down. Whitehurst took shelter until two Yankees emerged from the hole and approached near enough to call on him to give up. Tension developed between the whites and blacks over whether he should be shot in cold blood, and Whitehurst appealed to an officer for help. The Federal sent him to the Union rear for safety. Whitehurst made it across no-man's-land and survived many months in different prisons. Pvt. R. H. Holland of the 6th Virginia also became a prisoner during the hand-to-hand fight, although he was shot first and then taken away by the Federals.[69]

The Union flags that so intimidated the Virginians were either in Confederate hands or safely in the crater. Pvt. Leonidas D. Dean and Pvt. Thomas

Valentine had "each picked out and pointed to a stand of Federal colors and said he meant to have it" as the brigade prepared to charge. Dean was killed and Valentine was seriously wounded in the attempt. The flag of the 12th Virginia, which was fairly new and yet untouched by bullets, was severely handled during the hand-to-hand fighting. The color-bearer had planted it on the works, but it was knocked down three times, and he spliced the staff with a ramrod to keep it flying. By the end of the fight, amazed members of the regiment counted seventy-five bullet holes through the fabric, and nine balls had hit the staff. A bullet broke the staff of the 61st Virginia color as well. It fell on Pvt. LeRoy McC. West's head, hurting him more than a flesh wound in the shoulder he had earlier suffered.[70]

Weisiger's men took stock after the hand-to-hand fight. Pvt. John Edgar Foreman scrounged around in the recaptured works for food, filling his haversack with Federal rations, but Stewart stopped him because enemy fire was too heavy to expose oneself. Before he stopped, Foreman also came across "a large Newfoundland dog" lying dead in the works. He assumed it "belonged to some Federal officer."[71]

The Virginians took care of their wounded as best they could. Weisiger lay for some time near the recaptured works until Drury Hinton organized a stretcher party and carried him away. They found Mahone standing under the arbor at Elliott's headquarters, just after he returned from his visit to the recaptured works. Upon reaching the Jerusalem Plank Road, Weisiger encountered Beauregard and at least one staff member, who had left the Gee House to get closer to the action. Col. Samuel Paul glowingly told Weisiger, "Colonel, you all have covered yourselves with glory." Beauregard confirmed his staff officer's compliment with "a profound bow," as Hinton remembered. Weisiger's stretcher party later encountered the vanguard of Sanders's brigade as the Alabamians approached the entrance to the covered way to reinforce Weisiger and Hall. The Battle of the Crater was not yet over.[72]

13

HALL ATTACKS

Soon after Weisiger's brigade launched its attack, the Federal high command lost all hope of continuing the offensive. Warren sent word to Meade that he could not obey his order to attack Davidson's battery after all. Grant, who witnessed the panicked retreat of Ferrero's regiments, reached Meade's headquarters about 9:15 A.M. and confirmed that there was no hope of pursuing the offensive. Meade therefore sent a message to Burnside at 9:30, telling him he had better pull his men out of the captured works but allowing him to wait until dark to withdraw more safely. In subsequent messages, Meade made it clear that the Federals should not hold any captured ground longer than necessary to allow the troops to pull out.[1]

Meade also instructed Ord to place 18th Corps troops behind Burnside's position and told Hancock to fill the trenches formerly held by two of Ord's divisions with 2nd Corps units that were not yet in the works. Hancock informed army headquarters that a brigade of Mott's division, holding works well north of the crater, raised their hats on their ramrods to see what the Rebels would do and received a hail of infantry fire. This demonstrated that the lines were still held in force.[2]

Grant had seen enough of operations that morning to know how badly things had gone for the Federals. As he rode from Meade's headquarters to City Point, the general in chief said little except to inform his staff that if he had been in charge of a division or corps that morning he would have been in the front directing everything personally. This was his roundabout way of criticizing 9th Corps officers, including Burnside. On reaching his headquarters, Grant reported the bad news to Halleck. The mine had opened up a gap in Rebel defenses that was easily seized, but not easily evacuated. Grant assumed responsibility for the decision to call off the offensive, "not being willing to take the chances of a slaughter sure to occur if another assault was made." Holding the captured position was not feasible because it "would be a very bad one for us, being on a side hill, the crest on the side of the enemy."[3]

Grant also informed Lincoln that he could meet him at Fortress Monroe the next day, and then he fished about for something to do while the grand tactical situation was still in a state of flux. He instructed Meade to send an infantry corps and the army's cavalry to tear up twenty miles of the Weldon and Petersburg Railroad the next day, before Lee's divisions returned to the south side of the Appomattox. They were to hit the rail line as close to Petersburg as possible. Sheridan had finished crossing to the south side of the James River at Deep Bottom by dawn of July 30 and was in place on Meade's left by 10 A.M. Grant also suggested that if Sheridan could move mounted troops around the Confederate right flank before Burnside pulled out of the crater, Petersburg might fall. Meade discounted the latter idea, but he liked the thought of raiding the railroad with the 18th Corps. Ord believed he could get Turner's 10th Corps division and Ames's 18th Corps troops ready for the move but needed to keep the rest of his command in the trenches until Burnside relieved them. When Meade consulted other subordinates, however, he found little enthusiasm for the project.[4]

News arrived from Maryland on the afternoon of July 30 that changed Grant's mind about the railroad operation. The Federal pursuit of Early was hampered by conflict of command emanating from Washington, and a Rebel cavalry force crossed the border to burn Chambersburg, Pennsylvania. Grant decided to send more cavalry to Maryland and to dispatch Sheridan to take charge of operations there, canceling the raid on the Weldon and Petersburg Railroad by 5 P.M. that day.[5]

At the epicenter of conflict, Burnside hesitated and brooded for half an hour after receiving Meade's order to retire. He was loath to admit defeat and pull out, and he contemplated either advancing or staying put in the captured works. Hartranft sent word to Willcox at 9:18 A.M. that "we can hold this position, but cannot advance." It is possible Burnside was privy to this message and that it might have fueled his desire to salvage something from the fiasco. He sent for Potter at about 10 A.M. and asked the division leader's opinion. Potter believed his men capable of holding the crater but thought there was no point in doing so if the army was not going to send troops to help. Potter suggested that Bliss's brigade attack Wright's battery to relieve some pressure. Burnside and Ord rode to Meade's headquarters to discuss whether they should continue the offensive or hold the captured ground, arriving at 10:30 A.M.[6]

What followed was an embarrassing incident that did neither commander any good. Burnside later tried to put the best face on it, claiming that he told Meade calmly "that I did not think that we had fought long enough that day:

that I felt that the crest could still be carried if a decided effort were made to carry it." Meade recalled that Burnside pleaded for the opportunity to attack but could not explain how he might capture the ridge. Ord, who accompanied the 9th Corps leader to army headquarters, completely sided with Meade, much to Burnside's irritation. In Meade's words, Ord claimed that "it would be nothing but murder to send any more men forward" into the captured works.[7]

A more colorful, and perhaps accurate, description of the meeting came from the pen of Theodore Lyman. Burnside was "much flushed" as he approached Meade and "used extremely insubordinate language." Lyman noted that Burnside was incapable of explaining how he could capture the crest after several hours of futile attempts. When Meade reiterated his order to retire, Burnside turned on Ord and snapped, "You have 15,000 men concentrated on one point. It is strange if you cannot do something with them." "Flourishing his arms," according to Lyman, Ord retorted, "You can fight if you have an opportunity; but, if you are held by the throat, how can you do anything?" After calming down a bit, Burnside admitted within Lyman's hearing that "I certainly fully expected this morning to go into Petersburg!"[8]

Burnside sent a telegram to Julius White ordering the troops to retire and rode back to the Fourteen Gun Battery. White had earlier recommended that the corps stay where it was and hold on to the captured works for good, but Burnside now told him the order to retire was "peremptory . . . I have no discretion in the matter." White endorsed Burnside's telegram with the recommendation that division leaders consult their subordinates in the crater as to the best mode of withdrawing. Potter read this and was on his way to the crater when one of Burnside's aides intercepted him with the news that the corps leader wanted all division commanders to meet him at the battery. Potter, Willcox, Ledlie, and Ferrero attended, and Burnside told them to dig covered ways between the Union line and the captured works and prepare to evacuate the position after dark.[9]

There was little satisfaction in disengaging from a bloody failure, and Burnside continued to fume out of anger and frustration. Meade evacuated the old 9th Corps headquarters site at 11:30 A.M., allowing corps staff to return to that spot. Cyrus Comstock hung around for some time after Meade left. Burnside told him of his troubled relations with the army commander and that "he thought he had better leave. I suppose resign." Comstock "attempted to quiet him," but Burnside could not be soothed. He turned on Comstock, asking the staff officer if Grant "had left me to see that orders were obeyed," and if so, "he wished [Grant] would send some other staff officer to him." Comstock felt pity rather than anger at Burnside's remarks. "He is not competent to command a corps, & I have spoken freely of him—some one has repeated it. Poor Burn."[10]

Hall Attacks

Burnside's plans to pull back after nightfall depended, of course, on Confederate actions, and William Mahone had no intention of allowing the Federals such luxuries. After he inspected Weisiger's brigade in its new position, inside the Confederate works north of the crater, Mahone made his way back to the shallow ravine where Hall's Georgia brigade was gathering. The division leader relayed his instructions for the coming attack. Matthew Robert Hall was a twenty-seven-year-old officer who had worked his way up from captain to become lieutenant colonel of the 48th Georgia. Relatively new to brigade command, he readied his 370 men and moved out of the ravine about 10 A.M.[11]

The Virginians opened fire from the reclaimed works north of the crater to support Hall's advance. This did not prevent the Federals, who were protected by the lip of the crater, from laying down a withering fire at the Georgians. The infantry lined the rim; some of them had stockpiled several loaded weapons nearby for rapid firing. Stanley and his improvised gun crew also opened with canister from two Napoleons of Pegram's battery.[12]

The effect of this fire was decisive. Hall's men wavered, broke ranks, managed to close them again, but in the end veered north to escape the hail of gunfire. Instead of heading directly for the crater, Hall's troops duplicated the line of attack by Weisiger's brigade, crowding into the reclaimed works north of the hole. Some Georgians turned and retired to the shallow ravine, while others on Hall's extreme right flank entered the cavalier behind the crater and gave themselves up to the few Federals who occupied that trench. Some of Hall's men cowered at the foot of the cavalier. Howard Aston took pity on one Georgian and called on his comrades not to fire. "He'll surrender," Aston assured them. But the Rebel tried to run away instead. "Come here, you d—d fool, or I will shoot," Aston called out, and the frightened man went into the crater. The Federals shoved all the prisoners into the bottom of the hole to get them out of the way.[13]

Hall's attack was nearly a complete failure. It is possible that he occupied some of the forty yards or so of Confederate works immediately north of the crater that Weisiger's men had not taken, but that was far from a decisive close of the battle. It was not feasible to pull the Georgians out and try again, so Mahone relied on Sanders's Alabama brigade to finish the job.[14]

The Georgia brigade received a black star for its performance on July 30, and Matthew Hall tried to explain away the failure. After newspaper reports disparaging the brigade's performance began to appear, he wrote a letter for publication in the *Petersburg Express*. Hall pointed out that a portion of his command had gone in with the Virginia brigade and had contributed to Weisiger's success. The rest of the brigade did its best. It "was as well represented on the edge of the immense hole, caused by the explosion, as any brigade on the line." In fact, Hall argued, one of his regiments planted its flag on the edge of the crater.[15]

Several observers tried to account for the brigade's failure that day. Some pointed to the 64th Georgia as the culprit. The regiment had been raised in the spring of 1863 and had performed occupation duty in Florida and provost duty in Petersburg before it joined Hall's brigade. It had suffered a serious desertion problem just before the battle, according to some reports. Other observers pinpointed Hall himself for bad leadership, and still others noted that if the entire brigade had been able to deploy to Weisiger's right in the shallow ravine and had attacked in full with the Virginians, it probably would have been able to maintain a steady course toward the crater. William Etheredge of the 41st Virginia claimed Hall's men stopped during their advance to fire a volley and re-form their ranks, neutralizing the momentum of their advance. Lee and Beauregard witnessed the attack from the Gee House and thought it was a sudden, snap movement that was ill prepared. After witnessing its result, the two commanders grew very worried because they knew how few reserves were available to try another attack.[16]

Despite Hall's failure to end the battle, the Confederates had Sanders on the way. They also repositioned units on the field and added more artillery to their resources. Weisiger's attack had compelled the Federals to abandon about 150 yards of the Confederate main trench line south of the crater. This allowed the 26th Virginia of Goode's brigade to move northward again, at least up to the traverse located thirty yards south of the hole. All the other regiments of Goode's command also extended northward. As the 46th Virginia did so, a shell hit the works and lopped off the top of a post, which flew so fast it killed a man by hitting him on the head. North of the crater, Capt. Thomas A. Brander's Letcher Artillery of Virginia placed four Napoleons on Cemetery Hill, next to Crenshaw's Virginia battery (commanded by Capt. Thomas Ellett), which also had four Napoleons. These eight guns added weight to the stream of Confederate artillery fire already directed on the Union position.[17]

Weisiger's men continued firing at the Federals after Hall's attack. A young soldier of the 41st Virginia was so excited at one of his shots that he yelled, "I killed that d—d Yankee! I saw him fall!," but the boy was instantly hit in the forehead and died. In another part of the reclaimed works, Sgt. W. W. Tayleure and Pvt. William C. Johnson of the 12th Virginia exchanged some heated words when Tayleure asked why Johnson was not firing away. Their exchange was cut short when a comrade, Joseph B. Sacrey, was killed by a ball in the head and fell at their feet.[18]

Many Confederates began to notice that, oddly enough, a few black and white Federals were wandering behind Rebel lines. These men had either gotten lost in the confusion or had been taken prisoner but had not been escorted to the rear. McAfee's North Carolinians told them to go to Petersburg on their own, for no fighting man could be spared from the trenches. Most of the Yankees were searching for water and gathered at the spring located in the ravine about 150 yards up from the main line. Some of these Federals were wounded; they died while at the spring and dammed up the rivulet that issued from the ground until the water flowed over and around their bodies.[19]

At some point during the fight, William R. J. Pegram visited the battlefield and witnessed a desperate fight between a black Federal and a white Confederate behind the Rebel line. He surmised that the Rebel had told the black he intended to kill him in cold blood, and the Yankee managed to grab a musket to defend himself. "They fought quite desperately for a little while with bayonets, until a bystander shot the negro dead."[20]

Inside the Crater

Although the Federals retained possession of the crater in the face of Hall's attack, their situation was critical. The high command had decided that the ground was not worth holding, and the occupants faced the difficult job of holding on in the sunbaked crater and the small space of Confederate works north of it until darkness offered them an opportunity to retreat.

The few Unionists left in the Rebel works north of the hole were caught between the Confederates and the imposing rim of the crater. Capt. R. G. Richards of the 45th Pennsylvania found himself in charge of a detachment in those works after his regimental leader took a group of prisoners into the crater. Richards had no more than a handful of men and could see Confederate troops only fifty feet away. He wrote a note asking for entrenching tools, wrapped it around a stone, and threw it into the hole. Meanwhile his men used bayonets and tin cups to make a barricade across the covered way that connected them to the Confederates. The sun was hot, his men were exhausted and thirsty, but they worked hard despite the hail of bullets that flew overhead. Looking toward the crater for signs of relief, Richards saw only a pile of up to twenty dead men, who had been shot as they emerged from the hole in an attempt to retreat to the Union line. Before Richards and his men completed their barricade, the Rebels advanced through the covered way and overwhelmed the small group, wounding and capturing Richards.[21]

Not long after Hall's failed attack, the only Federals left in the captured works were those crammed into the crater. Initially they maintained a spirited fire at Weisiger's men to the north, aided by the sharpshooting of several Native Americans who served in Burnside's corps. Nearly everyone in Company K, 1st Michigan Sharpshooters, was Ottawa, Ojibwa, Delaware, Huron, Oneida, or Potawatomi, and they used Sharps breech-loading rifles. The Indians impressed everyone with their coolness and careful aim, peeking across the crater rim to see if their shot took effect. There were Seneca Indians in the 14th New York Heavy Artillery and the 37th Wisconsin as well. On the other side, some Catawba Indians served in the 17th South Carolina of Elliott's brigade.[22]

Stanley's cannon fire ceased after Hall's attack, probably because of lack of ammunition or exhaustion among the improvised gun crew. A captain in the 19th USCT thought it was well that the guns fell silent; he believed they did little good except "to concentrate [Confederate artillery] fire, if possible, at this point more intensely."[23]

Some Federals in the crater kept up small-arms fire for some time. A sergeant in the 31st Maine planted himself at the rim and fired rifles handed up to him by others, cheering and exposing himself in a reckless manner until a bullet mangled the fingers of his left hand. Then the Maine sergeant screamed and ran back, shouting, "Oh, my hand! Oh-h-h, my hand!" Some of the black soldiers caught the spirit of resistance, crying out, "I'se done killed one" and "Glory! I'se done got another." One black man became so excited that he carelessly exposed himself and was shot in the head.[24]

Whether or not they posted themselves on the rim, the Federals inside the crater increasingly took casualties as time wore on. Col. Mark Wentworth of the 32nd Maine was hit by two balls; one went on to wound Sgt. Ray Eaton. Another bullet penetrated the shoulder of Capt. James L. Hunt and went on to kill a private behind him as well.[25]

The Confederates began to fire down the length of their own trench into the crater, so Bartlett instructed some men nearby to build a breastwork for protection. Freeman Bowley took on the responsibility of directing this work, using his own black troops. They gathered hard dirt clods, but these did not work very well. Someone suggested using the bodies of the slain, and it was done. Bowley's men gathered Union and Confederate dead, as well as any debris they could grab, and piled the dirt clods on top of them.[26]

Inside the crater, Bowley recalled that the blacks gathered in the right of the hole and the whites in the center and left. But the hard experience of dying was shared by all, regardless of color or ethnicity. Howard Aston recalled "a light haired boy, apparently under 18," who fired steadily for more than an hour at the rim. A bullet smashed into the young man's forehead, and he "fell with his head against my feet, his blood gushing over them." Aston covered the boy's face and continued firing.[27]

Those who were wounded cried out for water. At times they would stop and "hold their breath for a few minutes, then all shriek together." Aston noticed that many black soldiers made their way up to the rim to a point where two flags were planted. Here they fired away until shot. Aston counted twenty-one blacks who were shot at this spot in one hour, their bodies rolling and tumbling down the steep slope. "Blood was everywhere," Aston wrote years later, "trickling down the sides of the crater in streamlets, and in many places ponds of it as large as an ordinary wash basin."[28]

Aston described his own condition, using the present tense although writing many years later, after firing at the rim for some time. "My tongue is swollen and lips cracked, from the powder in biting cartridges. My gun at times gets so hot that I have to stop firing, once it went off prematurely just as I had loaded it. The discharge burnt my eyelashes and brows. Earlier in the day a shell burst close to my head and I was tumbled over unconscious for a few seconds. At another time my ramrod was shot from my hand, and twice I was hit on the hand."[29]

Conditions inside the crater worsened when Maj. John C. Haskell began dropping mortar fire into the hole. There were two Coehorn mortars, "juvenile implements of death," as Mahone called them, in the shallow ravine where Weisiger and Hall had started their attacks. Designed for siege warfare, small enough to be carried by four men and to be placed in constricted areas, they were ideal for this type of work. Mahone suggested that Haskell advance them into the recaptured works and fire at close range. Haskell directed Capt. James N. Lamkin's gunners to plant them among members of the 16th Virginia and use powder charges of only one and a half ounces, just enough to plop the projectiles over the crater rim fifty yards away.[30]

The sky was clear, and the Federals could see the small projectiles reaching the height of their trajectory when Haskell opened fire about 11 A.M. They began to calculate where the bomb would land and adjust their position accordingly. Many of the shells buried themselves in the jumbled clay floor of the crater and showered the inhabitants with dirt, causing little harm, and some failed to explode at all. But those that burst in midair began to exact a draining cost in life and limb among the Federals.[31]

One shell exploded near a group of fifteen or twenty men huddled in the intact corner of Pegram's battery emplacement, hitting only one of them on the neck with a fragment. Hartranft survived, without a scratch, a mortar shell that exploded six feet away. Another shell arched toward Byron Cutcheon and another man who were working on a covered way to link the crater with the Union line. Both men saw it in time to take cover before the shell buried itself in the ground two yards away, nearly covering them with dirt but harming neither man. Another mortar round fell into the earth near the large clay boulder that had been tossed out by the mine explosion, where a group of officers from the 19th USCT were taking shelter. It threw sand all over them. "What's the matter, Fletcher? Don't you like it?" asked Capt. James O. Blakeley of Capt.

Frederick K. Fletcher. "Yes, . . . I like it well enough, and it tastes well enough, but I don't know how long I am going to live, and I don't want to wear my teeth all out chewing sand.'"[32]

One could afford to joke as long as the mortars failed to hit a mark, but when they did, the effect was horrific. A shell hit Lt. Richard Craven of the 100th Pennsylvania squarely as he lay down, "blowing him to pieces." Freeman Bowley watched as a Maine officer was decapitated and his body "fell sloping downwards, and the blood rushed out as from an overturned bucket." Bowley also reported seeing a mortar shell that penetrated the crater floor and dug up two bodies that had been buried by the mine explosion. The Confederates, waiting in the reclaimed works, and the Federals inside the Union line could see body parts flying into the air as a result of hits by the mortar shells. Blood and brains flew so freely through the air that many men, including Simon Griffin, were "completely covered" with them.[33]

William Bartlett became the victim of a mortar round, but it did him no bodily harm. The shell exploded fifty feet away, and a fragment knocked a large clod of clay against his artificial leg, smashing it to pieces. "Put me any place where I can sit down," he told the men who lifted him up. They assumed he was hurt and told him he would not be able to sit. "Oh no!" he replied, *"it's only my cork leg that's shattered!"*[34]

Despite the ability of Bartlett and some other Federals to make the best of this horrible situation, Haskell's mortar fire had a devastating effect on the morale and physical endurance of the crater's occupants. The relentless pounding did more than anything else to break the spirit of Union resistance and prepare the way for Sanders's attack.

Looking to the Rear

Some Federals made strenuous efforts to connect the small Union enclave in the captured works with their own lines in order to allow the men to retreat with some safety. It was a daunting task, because they had to dig a covered way 125 yards long in hard-baked clay under fire. When staff officer William Powell went back to the Union line and asked Ledlie for entrenching tools, the division leader viewed the project coldly. Powell could find no tools, anyway. Yet Burnside ordered Ferrero to begin digging a covered way, informing him that one had already been started from the crater. Willcox reported that he gave orders for Ferrero and 18th Corps troops to start not one but three covered ways. Most members of the 35th Massachusetts had left the crater by noon, taking their tools and guns with them. They had begun a covered way to the right of the mine entrance, aiming for a point to the right of the crater, but the panicked retreat of Ferrero's troops had put a stop to that work.[35]

Efforts to work backward from the crater availed little. Men of the 20th Michigan started a covered way near the house-sized block of hard clay that had been spewed out by the mine explosion, but Haskell's mortar fire prevented the diggers from accomplishing much. It was difficult even to dig a way out of the crater; Howard Aston recalled that some men tried to dig a passageway through the lip, but too many men were hit at that spot and the work was abandoned.[36]

Covered way or not, many Federals made their way back to Union lines singly or in small groups, ignoring efforts by brigade leaders in the crater to exert some control over the process. Lt. Col. Martin P. Buffum of the 4th Rhode Island authorized his men to return if they so desired, and everyone except himself, four other officers, and eighteen men took their chances. Albert E. Sholes recalled that the ground between the lines was "carpeted with dead and wounded." Federals seeking shelter among the clay boulders near the captured works called out to him, "Lie down! Don't try to go across! You'll be killed if you do." Members of the 9th New Hampshire also braved the dangers of no-man's-land, and some of them found safety in the forward Union trench.[37]

As time passed, the intensity of Confederate fire directed across the open space of ground was such that chances of making it through dimmed by the minute. James Lathe of the 9th New Hampshire believed one out of three men who attempted the passage was hit; Howard Aston thought the ratio was three out of four. Aston could find only two other men of his company left in the crater by 11 A.M., Sgt. John L. McGlade and Pvt. Samuel Ehrman. All three agreed that it would be best to leave, but no one wanted to initiate the movement, so they all stayed and continued firing as best they could.[38]

George Bradford Carpenter of the 4th Rhode Island somehow made it across no-man's-land even with a dreadful wound. One of Haskell's mortar rounds nearly cut his arm off. It hung to his body "by a few cords at the back side, the bone having been severed." A quick-thinking soldier tore a strip from a rubber blanket and used it as a tourniquet, saving Carpenter's life. Despite encouragement to stay, because no one thought he could ever survive the journey back, Carpenter had enough presence of mind to figure out that if he started from the crater when the shell burst was loudest (given the time lapse in transmission of sound), he could avoid the worst fallout of fragments. Carpenter ran across the open space and plopped into the Union works, counting seven marks of bullets in his clothing and equipment. Despite his grievous wound, Carpenter walked a mile to the rear, drinking whiskey and brandy offered by Christian and Sanitary Commission agents, before climbing into an ambulance for a two-mile ride to the field hospital, where a surgeon trimmed off his dangling limb.[39]

Sgt. Franklin J. Burnham of the 9th New Hampshire fired more than one hundred rounds, using two or three guns, before he escaped to the Union line unscathed. Burnham ran when a canister charge hit the ground, stirring up a cloud of dust that hid him as he sprinted across no-man's-land. A private of the same regiment did not attempt the dangerous passage until after he was hit above the knee by a ball. Even so, the lucky man survived the trip although bullets perforated his hat, cut his shoelace, and nicked his instep.[40]

The flow of traffic was mostly out of the captured Confederate works and back to the forward Union line, but some of it went in the opposite direction. Hartranft sent a request for more ammunition, and Willcox brought cartridge boxes to the forward Union line so that troops of the 51st Pennsylvania could carry them into the crater. Many of these brave men were shot in the process, but at least ten thousand rounds were delivered in this way. Members of the 35th Massachusetts also participated in this flow of supplies, although they were too exhausted to carry entire boxes. The engineers piled cartridge packets into shelter tents and slung them over their shoulders for the run into the crater.[41]

Water was more important to the men in the hole than ammunition. The heat was intense, and many wounded soldiers were dehydrated. Several men loaded themselves with empty canteens and volunteered to get water. Few observers were willing to bet on their chance of success, and they saw several of these Samaritans hit on the way to the rear. Some of the volunteers made it back, receiving cheers for their effort. "It was to me the most striking exhibition of heroism and true courage that I saw during the whole war," commented Simon Griffin. One water carrier was hit by a spent ball in the forehead just as he climbed over the crater's lip on his way back. He rolled into the hole and lay unconscious for a while, then woke up and found that he was not badly hurt after all.[42]

The brigade leaders who were in the crater tried to organize their men for an orderly withdrawal from the captured works, but it proved impossible. After his stormy consultation with Meade, Burnside had made it clear to White that "it may be best to entrench where we are for the present, but we must withdraw as soon as practicable and prudent." White's endorsement confirmed that "officers on the line" should "consult and determine the time of evacuation." For reasons that are unclear, this message did not reach the crater until about 12:30 P.M. With full authority to go at any time, Hartranft called a meeting to consider the options. Bartlett, Griffin, and Byron Cutcheon attended. Even though he was in the crater, Marshall was apparently not part of the group.[43]

Hartranft wrote his ideas as an endorsement on the back of the message from White, recommending that Burnside organize an attack aiming to the north and south of the crater to cover the withdrawal. "The men here are a rabble," he continued. "They are suffering very much for water, & the troops can not well be organized." Griffin wrote, "I concur in the above," and Bartlett also agreed, writing his endorsement at 12:40 P.M. Regardless of how the withdrawal took place, everyone agreed that it would be accompanied by chaos and heavy losses. Cutcheon volunteered to go to the Union line and secure entrenching tools so that more serious efforts to dig a covered way could be made. Hartranft supported the idea, although he probably held little hope for its success. Cutcheon dashed across the stormy space of no-man's-land but found it very difficult to find, much less secure, tools. Sigfried, who was taking shelter in a bombproof near the mine entrance, lent him one of his aides, who took a message to Willcox. Cutcheon could do little more than wait for a reply.[44]

"The day was excessively hot," recorded a brigade leader in Warren's corps, and careful measurement proved the point. Warren's medical inspector noted that the high temperatures had been in the seventies and eighties throughout July, but on this day it was already eighty degrees at 6 A.M. and ninety-nine degrees at noon. William H. Powell wrote with little exaggeration that the sun "caused waves of moisture produced by the exhalation" of the troops in the captured works "to rise above the crater. Wounded men died there begging piteously for water, and soldiers extended their tongues to dampen their parched lips until their tongues seemed to hang from their mouths."[45]

Conditions worsened with the passage of time and the increasing heat. "No air was stirring within the crater," wrote Charles H. Houghton of the 14th New York Heavy Artillery. "It was a sickening sight; men were dead and dying all around us, blood was streaming down the sides of the crater to the bottom, where it gathered in pools for a time before being absorbed by the hard red clay." Recalling the scene before he left, Byron Cutcheon noted that the "slaughter became monotonous until it ceased to horrify."[46]

Discouragement became widespread. Men who had fired at the rim of the crater now gave up and "sat down, facing inwards, and neither threats nor entreaties could get them up into line again." Freeman Bowley argued that from then on, black troops mostly carried on the firing, along with white officers who took muskets from their men. Neither the thought that the Rebels would kill everyone, white and black, nor the sight of their comrades slaughtered by their side roused these disheartened men to action. The Native Americans in the 1st Michigan Sharpshooters continued to fire methodically, but when hit, they prepared themselves as best they could for death. Pulling their shirts across their face, the Indians chanted a death song and died with dignity amid the atmosphere of bloody terror that permeated the crater.[47]

14

SANDERS ATTACKS

As Mahone arranged for Sanders to come up, William Stewart worried that the division leader might ask Weisiger's brigade to attack the crater. "We have but a handful left," responded William Etheredge when Stewart confided in him, "but if they order the old brigade to take the other side, I am ready to go."[1]

Bushrod Johnson made his first appearance on the battlefield after Hall's attack, meeting McMaster and Mahone in the shallow ravine. The three coordinated plans for an attack spearheaded by Sanders's brigade. Johnson told McMaster to put the rest of the 17th South Carolina into the ravine to attack with Sanders. Fragments of Elliott's brigade would cooperate with elements of Goode's Virginians south of the crater, closing in on the hole as Sanders advanced. The three officers fixed 1 P.M. as the time for launching what they hoped would be the final attack of the battle.[2]

Brig. Gen. John Caldwell Calhoun Sanders was only twenty-four years old, yet commanded one of the best brigades in Lee's army. He had left his senior-year studies at the University of Alabama to become a captain in the 11th Alabama and had participated in nearly every major battle of the Army of Northern Virginia. He rose in rank and survived a wound suffered at Frayser's Farm during the Seven Days campaign and another wound at Gettysburg. Sanders had commanded the brigade since Spotsylvania and was destined to "make his mark if the war continues," thought an admiring officer. His brigade was the last fresh unit the Confederates could spare south of the Appomattox River.[3]

When Mahone's staff officer brought word to pull out of the entrenchments and move toward the battlefield at 11 A.M., Sanders left his battalion of sharpshooters in the skirmish line and assembled the rest of his brigade in a ravine to the rear. The men formed a column and set out for the battlefield, five hundred strong. Only eight regiments were left behind to cover the division sector.[4]

The Federals detected Sanders's move. A signal officer perched atop a tower observed what he thought were two brigades marching toward the 9th Corps position. The report apparently made no impression on anyone.[5]

Sanders pushed his men until he entered the covered way in the ravine, placing them single file to negotiate the zigzags. Mahone directed him to move them into the shallow ravine, stooping so as to conceal their presence as long as possible. The 9th Alabama led the way and formed on the right of the brigade line. Sanders's men were stunned to see black prisoners moving to the rear, their first indication that blacks were involved in the fight. They were "as black as the ace of spades," recalled a captain of the 9th Alabama, "and in every sense of the word equipped as soldiers." Wounded men from Hall's and Weisiger's commands told the Alabamians that the blacks had raised the cry "No quarter. Remember Fort Pillow."[6]

As soon as the brigade formed in the ravine, Mahone walked along the formation and gave instructions similar to those he had previously given Weisiger's and Hall's men. The Alabamians were to advance at 1 P.M. without firing a shot and open only when the Federals began firing. Mahone impressed on everyone that the attack had to seal the breach in the Confederate line, that there were no other available troops, and that Lee was watching the result. The division leader even threatened that Lee would personally command a second attack by Sanders's men if their first one failed. A soldier retorted when he heard this, "If the old man comes down here, we will tie him to a sapling while we make the fight." An officer in the 8th Alabama remembered that this was the first and only occasion during the war when his comrades were told what was expected of them before a battle.[7]

Sanders would have help from a diverse group of units. To his left assembled the 61st North Carolina of Hoke's division and a portion of the 17th South Carolina from Elliott's brigade. Parts of the 22nd and 23rd South Carolina also assembled south of the crater, given word of the general plan of attack by Johnson, who had to take a wide detour through the Confederate trench system to reach this area. One account indicated that no more than sixteen men of Elliott's brigade were in close support of Sanders, referring to all that could be assembled from the 17th South Carolina. This is quite possible, because Thomas J. LaMotte was the only man of his company available to take part in the charge. Capt. John Featherston of the 9th Alabama recalled one of Elliott's men, covered in dirt and powder, who told him, "I want to even up with them." The South Carolinian asked Featherston to take down his name and inform his captain if he was killed, but Featherston had no opportunity to do so. He thought the brave man was a "rough diamond."[8]

The men of the 61st North Carolina had not yet been engaged, having hurried two miles to arrive at the battlefield "greatly exhausted" because their legs had cramped owing to long spells of crouching inside trenches. They had waited in the ravine for some time, suffering from the hot sun with little water to drink, before Sanders showed up. Some of the Tar Heels had fainted as a result, and others were hit by shell fire, but the regiment had 140 men ready to go in.[9]

Sanders waited for some time in the shallow ravine for the signal to attack, his men suffering from the broiling sun. Capt. George Clark, his assistant adjutant general, made his way forward to consult with William Stewart about conditions in the reclaimed works. Stewart showed him all he could of the situation to help Sanders prepare for the attack. Clark returned to the brigade and reiterated Mahone's earlier instructions.[10]

Sanders launched his attack at 1 P.M. with about 630 Alabamians, Tar Heels, and South Carolinians. They moved at common time at first, then picked

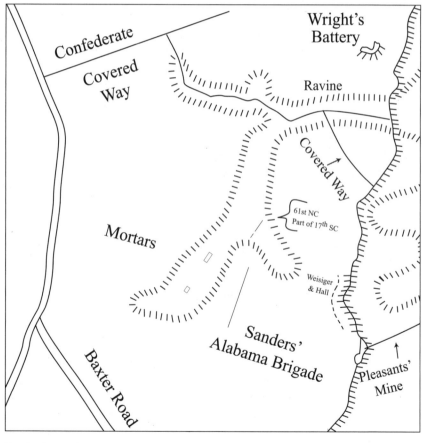

Sanders's attack

up the pace as they crossed the open, exposed ground between the shallow ravine and the Confederate works. Glancing ahead, John Featherston could see sunlight flashing on the burnished steel of Federal musket barrels as the enemy leveled them over the rim of the crater. The first Union fire took down many Confederates, but the rest kept moving forward. Weisiger's men intensified their own fire from the recaptured works to suppress the defenders. Artillery in the Union line attempted to fire at Sanders's formation but could not stop the Rebels either. The two artillery pieces inside the captured works were silent.[11]

Federal resistance paled in comparison to the hail of fire that had met Hall's attack. Many Unionists were too exhausted and demoralized by this stage of the battle, especially because of the intense heat and the pounding of Haskell's mortars, to offer much resistance. Staff officer Powell reported that only about one hundred Federals could fire from the rim anyway, because of lack of room, and they had to move a bit to the rear and lie on their backs against the wall of the crater to reload. Howard Aston was among those who shot at Sanders's men, having fired eighty rounds during the course of the battle. The rest of the Unionists huddled in the hole, "about as much use there as so many men at the bottom of a well," as Ord put it.[12]

Federal officers realized that there was little chance of resisting the assault. When Sanders's men were only one hundred feet from the crater, Hartranft gave the order to retreat. He and Griffin led the way out of the breach. They were helped somewhat by Charles Houghton, who had run the gauntlet a bit earlier to organize those men of the 14th New York Heavy Artillery who were in the Union line to fire as rapidly as possible to cover the retreat. Seeing this flight, some of the better shots among Weisiger's men climbed to the top of traverses to fire at the running Yankees. The officers made it safely, although members of the 6th New Hampshire, who had lain prone between the lines most of the morning, fully expected Griffin to be hit as he stopped to survey the field after clambering across the crater rim and then "stepped off briskly toward our lines." Behind Hartranft and Griffin came a number of officers and enlisted men, among them color-bearers of the 9th New Hampshire, bringing both the state and national flags of the regiment back to safety, although four men were shot in the process.[13]

As Sanders closed in on his objective, the Confederate left wrapped around and into the mostly vacated works that stretched forty yards north of the crater, which had not yet been fully occupied by Weisiger's or Hall's men. The Alabama brigade had guided correctly; its left flank breezed past the traverse that marked the right flank of Weisiger's command. Thomas J. LaMotte of the 17th South Carolina found the works that his regiment knew well to be covered with dead and dying; he had to walk on them to make his way toward the crater. Some of the Virginians and Georgians moved south to help Sanders's men, closing in on the Federals in the hole and shooting down anyone who ran out. Some Georgians threw large dirt clods over the rim to annoy the Yankees if they could not get a shot at them, and Sanders's men could hear Federal officers exhorting their black soldiers to "remember Fort Pillow."[14]

For several minutes, a strange kind of stalemate ensued around three sides of the crater. The Confederates had brought enough men to this point to contend with those Federals who remained in the breach on a level of numerical equality, yet the twelve-foot-high clay rim served as the final barrier to Confederate success, and as the last refuge of the exhausted, frightened inhabitants of the hole. For a time no one knew what to do about that barrier. Confederate flag bearers raised their colors high enough so that Freeman Bowley could see the tips of three flags rise above the rim, then disappear, apparently as a way to show the Yankees what confronted them.[15]

Then someone on the Confederate side had the idea to use bayoneted muskets as spears, or as Bowley put it, in "harpoon style." Some of Sanders's men tossed abandoned rifles with bayonets attached across the rim, hoping they might injure or at least disconcert the Federals. They would not have been able to do this if all the Unionists had ranged around the rim and opened fire, but very few Yankees dared to expose themselves above the clay wall. Bowley, however, claimed he fired his pistol across the rim, shooting at least two Rebels. The Confederates also threw shell fragments into the hole, and sometimes received similar missiles thrown back by the Yankees.[16]

Bartlett was the only brigade commander left in the crater, but he was immobilized by his crushed artificial leg. Marshall huddled for safety just on the Union side of the hole. Bartlett wanted to see what was going on and asked Benjamin A. Spear to help him up to the rim. There a bullet pierced Bartlett's cap and "cut a gash about one-and-a-half inches long in his scalp." Bartlett was stunned for a while but soon recovered.[17]

A little "cur" dog that Sanders and his staff had adopted as a pet accompanied the brigade on its charge. It was excited by the noise and found a passage into the crater, "barking most fiercely. But he soon came out with a 'flea in his ear' and ran off yelping and limping." The dog might have found what Capt. G. I. Turnley of the 10th Alabama remembered as a three-foot-wide depression in the rim. Sanders encouraged Turnley to enter this gap and break the stalemate, and the good captain attempted it, but Union fire drove his men back. Lt. John Francis then grabbed a musket and yelled, "Boys, come on and let's go in there." Before Turnley could stop him, a Federal ball ended Francis's life and he fell, blocking the entrance to the gap. After that, wherever there was a depression in the rim or a crevice in the wall owing to the position of a chunk of clay, enterprising Federals stuffed them with shirts and haversacks to prevent the Rebels from firing through.[18]

Mahone had no patience with the stalemate and sent a courier to find out what was wrong. Capt. William B. Young, of Sanders's staff, went back to the shallow ravine to inform the division leader of the problem. Mahone asked, "Why do the men not jump over on them and end the fight?" Young explained that the Federals were "so thick in there that if men jumped over they would jump into a bayonet and the men know it." Mahone suggested that the officers call for volunteers to do this. "It is of *vital* importance to have our lines reestablished at once," he assured Young.[19]

The captain made his way back to the fight but did not have the heart to ask men to risk their lives in this way. He devised a different approach, and he called out to the Federals to give up. "Why don't you fools surrender?" he yelled. "You will all be killed if you do not." Surprisingly a Federal officer replied that they would do so if the Rebels stopped firing. Young managed to silence the men near him, but could do nothing with those farther away. He finally told the officer to come out toward the sound of his voice, and he would personally guarantee their safety. Several Federals did so and quickly made their way to the Confederate rear. This allowed the Rebels to cross the rim at the same place and begin to enter the hole. Young glanced rearward and saw that some of the Federals were hit by their own artillery fire on their way to the ridge crest.[20]

After Young returned to the fight, Mahone left the ravine and went forward to call for volunteers to enter the hole. He later claimed that more than one hundred men volunteered, but other Confederates around the crater had devised a better way to cross the rim, and Mahone's volunteers never had to undergo their perilous mission.[21]

Many Rebels around the rim came up with a simple expedient to cross the wall: raising hats on bayonets to draw Federal fire and then racing across the rim as fast as possible before the enemy could reload. Freeman Bowley heard a Rebel officer tell his subordinates, "Every man get his gun loaded, give one spring and go right over; they are out of ammunition, they won't fight." There was a price to be paid for cracking the last Union stronghold on the battlefield. Sgt. Andrew McWilliams of the 9th Alabama was shot through the mouth as he crested the wall. He died instantly, his body falling across the rim with his head hanging down the inner slope.[22]

As soon as the Confederates entered the crater, they engaged Federals who still had some willingness to fight. This prompted many other Unionists to rush out of the hole and head for the Federal line. Howard Aston and his two comrades of the 13th Ohio Cavalry (dismounted) were among those who headed for the rear. Aston covered his comrades as they made their way, one of them injured by a shell burst but able to continue by leaning on the other. Aston could not remember his journey across no-man's-land. He only recalled waking up from a blackout, lying across the parapet of the forward Union trench as some-one pulled him across by tugging on his leg.[23]

Inside the crater many Federals fought desperately for their lives. P. M. Vance of the 11th Alabama engaged in a tussle with a black soldier who shot him in the leg and then tried to stab him. Vance saved his life by grabbing the Yankee and holding his arms until others could stab and beat him into submission. After firing one shot upon entering the crater, other Confederates "went down in the hole amongst them clubbing them out with the butts of our guns." A sort of "delirium all soldiers have felt" settled among the combatants in this confined space, as one side fought for life and the other fought to complete a magnificent victory. The Confederates probably had an added spur. Many of them had heard the Federal cry of "No quarter," raised by the specter of Fort Pillow, and had no intention of allowing their enemy to put that resolution into practice. As a result, "We kild asite of nigers an thay fought us till the veary last," as John M. Lewis of the 61st North Carolina put it.[24]

The hand-to-hand combat lasted from fifteen minutes to half an hour, according to various accounts. How to give up became a touchy problem. According to one story, Adjutant Morgan Smith Cleveland of the 8th Alabama called out to the Federals, "Why in the h—— don't you fellows surrender?" A Union officer replied, "Why in the h—— don't you let us?" This broke the ice, and resistance collapsed. According to another account, some Federals raised "a dirty Confederate shirt on a ramrod" as a token of surrender. When those Federals in the larger part of the irregular crater were subdued, those in the smaller part were still armed. They began to cross the ridge separating the two sections upon hearing the Confederates call on them to surrender, but a couple of Unionists fired their weapons and the Rebels shot them instantly. "They are showing us no quarter, let us sell our lives as dearly as possible," yelled those Federals who remained. Only when the Confederates explained that they should drop their guns first and then come slowly out did about thirty Unionists emerge from the small part of the crater.[25]

Unfortunately many Confederates could not bring themselves to stop fighting even after the enemy gave up. "Some of the men went to work knocking them in the head with their guns," reported one man. Frank Kenfield, a captain in the 17th Vermont, was horrified when he heard the Rebels yell, "Save the white men but kill the damn niggers." For several minutes there ensued a frenzy of cold-blooded murder as many unarmed black soldiers were bayoneted and beaten to death. The sight horrified Kenfield, who remembered for the rest of his life "how those poor colored men were butchered in cold blood."[26]

Incredibly a handful of white Union officers participated in the killing, hoping to prove to their captors that they deserved to live. George L. Kilmer of the 14th New York Heavy Artillery heard some Union officers boast of doing so.

John Cheves Haskell, who had given up his mortar firing and entered the crater, saw a Federal officer kill a black soldier. Haskell's orderly wanted to kill the officer out of anger; Haskell also was appalled and allowed him to do so.[27]

Bartlett had encouraged the black troops to give up when it became apparent that all was lost, but as soon as the Rebels began to bayonet wounded blacks, those who could do so grabbed weapons and resumed fighting. Only when a Confederate officer intervened and promised to take care of all prisoners did this cease. A few other Rebel officers also tried to stop the killing, shouting, "Hold on there; they have surrendered." On the other hand, some Rebel officers actually encouraged their men to kill more. Reportedly one man in Sanders's brigade cut the throat of a disarmed black soldier with his pocket knife even after he was ordered to stop killing.[28]

Alfred Lewis Scott of the 9th Alabama tried to explain the emotions of the hour by noting that this was the first time his comrades had fought black troops, and they were incensed at the cry of "No quarter" heard just before entering the crater. Scott claimed that he tried to stop the killing. "Oh boys, let the poor devils alone; if I had it in me to kill a man after he was unarmed and at my mercy, I would kill the white men who armed them and brought them in here, like that scoundrel there," he said, pointing to Bartlett, who Scott assumed was an officer of a black regiment. Bartlett "looked at me very steadily but said nothing."[29]

In the end the blood lust expended itself as dozens of unarmed and sometimes wounded black soldiers died needlessly in the steaming hole. Just as the battle came to an end, remnants of the 22nd and 23rd South Carolina moved from the south into the crater to add weight to the Confederate victory, helping the Alabama brigade to round up prisoners. Elements of Goode's Virginia brigade "closed into the left slowly" to support that move. Sanders had brought an end to the bloody Battle of the Crater. He lost perhaps 90 men out of the approximately 630 engaged from his own brigade and the supporting Tar Hell and South Carolina units, excluding those fragments of the 22nd and 23rd South Carolina. Stunned Federals in the 18th Corps could see "several rebel flags flying" in the crater where only moments before the Stars and Stripes had waved.[30]

15

AFTERNOON AND EVENING, JULY 30

The battlefield presented a horrific sight to those who surveyed the landscape soon after the Federals surrendered. The dead and wounded were piled up, white and black, Confederates and Federals intermingled. Stretching for at least one hundred yards north of the crater, the Rebel works were filled with the dead and dying, some lying across the parapets, shot as they attempted to escape the fighting. Inside the trenches and covered ways, they lay so thick it was impossible not to tread on them when making one's way through the works.[1]

Inside the crater, engineer Edwin Wise reported 133 bodies of "negroes, indians, and whites," but "very few" Confederates. The Rebel dead were mostly victims of the mine explosion, their bodies partly exposed above ground and their clothing burned. Looking about, many Confederates were stunned to see the traverse made with Federal dead that Freeman Bowley had constructed during the battle. With the bodies piled eight deep in the hole, a group of Elliott's men dug down and found that blood permeated the sandy clay as much as five inches deep. Some bodies of the South Carolinians had been thrown seventy-five yards from the crater, yet a handful of the mine victims were still alive after the battle ended. One was partly protected by a board and thus had a pocket of air to breath even though he was buried by the explosion.[2]

Everyone who witnessed the scene was shocked. Hundreds of dead and wounded lay in an area not much more than 250 yards long and 100 yards wide. Mahone told his men that he had never seen the killed and wounded lie so thick on any battlefield. The intense heat and the horrible smell of dead bodies overcame G. I. Turnley of the 10th Alabama. He fainted and his comrades fanned his face and poured water to revive him. William H. Stewart called the crater "a veritable inferno filled with sounds of suffering and paved with the rigid dead." Beyond the hole, no-man's-land was also strewn with casualties.

The wounded who lay between the lines cried out for relief and were "tossing their arms about as if appealing for help," according to Alfred Lewis Scott of the 9th Alabama.[3]

The Federals had to view the battlefield from afar. The medical inspector of the 5th Corps saw Confederates firing on the wounded between the lines, and within their works he could see them "robbing the dead." A Federal who used a telescope to gain a closer view wrote, it "puts all humanity to shame. Sun exceedingly hot and flies blowing our wounded."[4]

After barely escaping the horrors of the crater, Howard Aston recovered a bit in the advanced trench before making his way back to Poor Creek, where a dozen or more swollen bodies, covered with flies, lay on the bank and in the shallow water. Their blood created a "crimson stream" that "followed the meanderings of the current." After washing his "slight wounds," Aston staggered through the covered way, still crowded with the troops of Ames's division. They assumed he was badly hurt because his clothes were saturated with blood. As he passed division headquarters at about 3 P.M., Aston noticed a thermometer hanging under a shade bower that registered 110 degrees.[5]

Prisoners

Lee reported that Mahone took prisoner 855 enlisted men and 74 officers in the battle, most of them from the crater itself. The first experience of the captives was to be disarmed and have their military equipment taken away. Rebel officers directed them to the rear by the covered way because, "you 'un's men is shelling right smart," as one said to Freeman Bowley, but the prisoners were robbed of their personal possessions along the way. A South Carolina lieutenant grabbed Bowley's haversack and hit him with the flat of his sword. He forced the Federals to leave the covered way and move across open ground to the rear, where several were hit by Union artillery fire. Once the prisoners were out of danger, the robbery continued. Two Confederates forcefully took Bowley's watch, but he prevented a third from taking his cap. Lt. Col. Buffum of the 4th Rhode Island lost his good felt hat to a Rebel who replaced it with his own dilapidated headgear. Many other captives lost "hats, boots, socks, blouse, moneys, watches, swords," according to William Baird of the 23rd USCT, who managed to retain only the shirt and pants that he wore. Seeing the situation, Frank Kenfield of the 17th Vermont hid his gold watch and chain in his boot, using it during his long captivity to buy food, which kept him alive in prison.[6]

Bartlett impressed many Southerners when he emerged from the crater with his cork leg dangling, using guns as crutches. "By God!" cried one Rebel, "there's a plucky Yankee! One leg shot off & look at him hoofing it along on the stump!"[7]

The prisoners assembled about a mile from the battlefield, where their captors began separating the blacks from the whites. Some USCT officers tore off their insignia, afraid of ill treatment if identified as commanding black troops. Bowley saw this and debated his own action. After careful thought, he decided he could not disgrace the bravery of his men by disowning them. Lt. Charles B. Sanders agreed, and both owned up to their full identity. They "saw the words 'negro officer' written opposite our names in the list." Lt. Lemuel D. Dobbs of the 19th USCT identified himself with bravado as an officer of the "Nineteenth Niggers, by ____," and the Rebels shook his hand to reward his bravery. So few whites admitted to serving in black regiments that Mahone called on black captives to identify their officers, and many of them did so. According to a general order issued in 1862, any Confederate unit that captured Union officers of black troops had to report their names and units to Richmond. A. P. Hill forwarded the names of eleven such men captured on July 30, including Bowley, Sanders, and Dobbs.[8]

If some white officers of black regiments were apprehensive, even more black soldiers were terrified. Fort Pillow was uppermost in their minds, and now that there was no opportunity to flee or fight, many black prisoners began to act in abjectly servile ways in order to save their lives. They claimed that the Yankees had forced them to enlist and then treated them cruelly. "My God, massa, I nebber pinted a gun at a white man in all my life," declared an "old cornfield chap" to William H. Stewart; "dem nasty, stinking Yankees fotch us here, and we didn't want to come fus!" One prisoner claimed the Federals enlisted him by placing the barrel of a pistol to his head, forcing him to leave his master's mule in the field. A handful of Rebels realized that a declaration such as this was little more than a "pitiful lie" and assumed that if the blacks had been victorious "they would have sung an entirely different song." But most Confederates relished hearing such stories. In fact, an officer of Sanders's brigade forced a black prisoner to fire toward the Union line six or seven times before disarming him. Going farther than most prisoners, some blacks sought to ally themselves with Confederates they had known earlier when they were slaves. Alfred Lewis Scott of the 9th Alabama, formerly of Fredericksburg, Virginia, heard his name called from among the black prisoners. The man had formerly been owned by one of Scott's neighbors, and he pleaded to be taken in as Scott's servant so as to avoid prison.[9]

The Confederates could not stop killing blacks even after they had surrendered. Many white Rebels were infuriated because they received wounds inflicted by black adversaries. As the rage of battle merged with racial anger, the killing continued. Many Southerners stalked among the death-filled bombproofs, looking for blacks who were still alive. Even as the prisoners were moved to the rear, some Southerners took advantage of their helplessness. Isaac

Gaskins of the 29th USCT was shot after he surrendered by a Rebel who "said he did not recognize any damn negro as a prisoner of war and that I would never get back to my brother Yankees alive." The close-range blast tore away Gaskins's cartridge box and seriously injured his hip, but he survived. One observer believed that not more than half of the black prisoners taken in the crater ever reached the rear areas. John C. Haskell managed to save at least one prisoner when he noticed a Confederate who seemed about to shoot a black sergeant. The man refused to stop when ordered, and Haskell called on other Rebels nearby for help. They stopped the man and placed him under arrest. Black bodies lay along the line of march taken by the Federal prisoners, according to Willie Pegram.[10]

The Confederates Settle In

What had once been a battery emplacement was now a ragged hole in the ground lined with dead and wounded. Mahone told officers of Weisiger's and Sanders's brigades to establish firing positions and clean out the hole. They dug out a deep passage through the rim of the crater for safer entry and tried to gouge out a firing step near the top of its rim, facing the Federals. The diggers used whatever material they could find as a substitute for shovels, and they uncovered bodies and pieces of artillery equipment in the process.[11]

While this went on, the wounded inside the crater, still mingled among the dead, raised pitiful cries for water in the broiling heat. The Confederates worked to remove them as soon as possible, but it was a task made difficult by the rim that surrounded the hole. Meanwhile some men who were working on creating firing positions could hear muffled cries just under the surface, coming from South Carolinians who had been buried in bombproofs by the explosion and had survived by breathing air filtering in through crevices. At least one Rebel and one black soldier seemed alive, both in a posture to fire at the enemy on different parts of the battlefield. In reality, both had been transfixed by instantaneous rigor mortis and presented a sight that confused and startled passersby.[12]

The Federals Regroup

The Federals concentrated on adjusting their positions and coping with the stunning defeat they had just endured. When a flag bearer raised the colors inside the forward Union line as a show of bravado, a mortar shell landed so close it took a hand off one man and splattered dirt over everyone within reach. The bearer meekly lowered the flag.[13]

Potter reported to corps headquarters that his division was "nearly annihilated and cannot therefore possibly reoccupy the position from which it advanced this morning." The other three divisions in Burnside's command were in

Confederate position inside the crater. Robert Underwood Johnson and Clarence Clough Buel, *Battles and Leaders* (New York: Century Company, 1887–88), 4:557

similar circumstances, but Meade relied on the 9th Corps to hold its assigned sector. Meanwhile a circular went out from army headquarters requesting casualty reports.[14]

Ord's command cooperated with Burnside in adjusting troop positions following the battle. Turner kept two-thirds of his division and Ord kept Carr's two divisions on the 9th Corps sector until Burnside could relieve them. By late that evening, Butler became anxious to have his men back. Burnside, however, had difficulty accommodating that desire. Hancock prepared to put his 2nd Corps into the 18th Corps sector that night to fill the void, but that plan was dropped. Willcox found enough troops to relieve two of Carr's brigades, but the rest had to hold 9th Corps trenches all that night and all day of July 31. So Hancock returned that night to the position his corps had held before the move to Deep Bottom. Butler's engineers had dismantled the new pontoon bridge at Deep Bottom on the morning of July 30, leaving the old one intact to support Foster's brigade on the north bank of the James.[15]

The first indication that Lee was shifting troops south of the Appomattox arrived a bit after noon on July 30, and increasing signs appeared before 4 P.M. Meade feared an attempt to turn his left flank. He instructed Warren and Sheridan to get ready and urged Hunt to remove all the siege artillery and mortars that had been planted to support Burnside's attack. Only enough field artillery would be left for defensive purposes. Artillery officers scrambled that night to effect a gargantuan task, moving fifty-two heavy pieces of ordnance an average of eight miles to Broadway Landing on the Appomattox in thirty-six hours. All attendant equipment, from ammunition to platforms and mant-lets, were carried away as well. That left thirty-three guns and mortars on the Bermuda Hundred front and twenty-nine outside Petersburg. Actually Lee had no intention of attacking the Federals.[16]

Meade could not know Lee's plans, and he still worried about a Confed-erate flank movement. He also had to admit that he could not rely on Burnside to relieve Cutler's division in time for Warren to prepare for a Confederate attack, because "I do not know in what condition either his force or his works are." Communications between the 9th Corps and army headquarters com-pletely broke down during the afternoon, evening, and night of July 30. Burn-side had become so angry at the decision to call off the attack, and what he considered Meade's lack of support for extricating his men from the captured works, that he threw aside a message from the army commander asking for confirmation of a report that his men had been driven from the crater. Burnside later admitted that this was not proper of him, but he did the same with two more messages received that evening. About 6 P.M., Meade received reports of Federal wounded lying unattended between the Union and Confederate lines. He assumed that Burnside still held the crater and wondered why they had not been removed. "I had to go to bed that night without knowing whether his troops were in the crater or whether they were not."[17]

It was certainly wrong of Burnside to keep this information from his supe-rior, but also wrong of Meade not to send a staff officer to ascertain the condi-tion of affairs in the absence of dispatches from him. Meade was careful to give the impression that he had no information of any kind as to whether Burnside continued to hold the crater for the rest of the day, but Theodore Lyman received confirmation from an engineer officer at 3:30 P.M. that the 9th Corps had been driven out. It is difficult to believe that Lyman did not relay this crit-ical news to his chief. Relations between Meade and Burnside had reached such a stage that neither could hope to work effectively with the other.[18]

Grant relayed more information to Meade just before leaving City Point to meet Lincoln at Fortress Monroe. He might have to send a division of Sheridan's cavalry to Washington to deal with Early. Moreover he warned that it was "by no means improbable" that two more infantry corps might have to be sent as well. One of those corps was the 19th, recently arriving in stages from Louisiana.[19]

Before leaving, Grant wrote a perceptive note to Meade about the results of Burnside's attack. "Our experience of to-day proves that fortifications come near holding themselves without troops." The lesson reinforced fear that Lee might try to turn the left flank, for he could leave a small force in his trenches while assembling a mobile column west of the Jerusalem Plank Road. "With a reasonable amount of artillery and one infantryman to six feet I am confident either party could hold their lines against a direct attack of the other."[20]

The agenda for Grant's conference with Lincoln centered on choosing a commander for the new department to be created by consolidating the four existing departments around Washington. Grant had suggested such a reorganization on July 25, and Lincoln had asked for a meeting to discuss it sometime after the 28th. Grant had postponed the conference until the results of his Third Offensive were known. During the nearly daylong meeting, several men, including Meade himself, were discussed, but the president essentially left the decision up to Grant. He chose Sheridan, returned to City Point on the evening of July 31, and announced the appointment the next day.[21]

But the participants of the conference at Fortress Monroe had to commiserate about the miserable failure of July 30. "Grant felt badly," reported Assistant Secretary of the Treasury George Harrington, and Lincoln "was very much disturbed, but after an interview with Grant was reassured and consequently felt much better. Grant says he will have both Petersburg and Richmond. He disliked to see the prize slip through his fingers because of the poor execution of his orders."[22]

The Confederates

Lee had witnessed Sanders's attack from the Gee House and left as soon as the fighting ended, but Beauregard remained there and at Johnson's headquarters until nearly all firing around Pegram's Salient had stopped at about 2:30 P.M. Lee sent a brief report of the battle to the secretary of war at 3:25, followed by a more detailed report at 6:30. The next day Lee explained to the authorities in Richmond that he had known "for weeks" of the Federal mine, but his engineers had failed to intercept it.[23]

Johnson, whose hands-off attitude during the battle was noted by more than one observer, appeared at Goode's brigade for the first time immediately after the fighting ended. Goode recalled that he ambled into the trench with his "coat on his arm" and announced that Lee had sent him to report on conditions in the crater. According to Goode, Johnson asked him to go into the hole and find out what he could. The brigade commander did so "and witnessed a sickening scene." He reported to his division leader, who quickly left.[24]

After the battle ended, sniping and artillery fire continued with sometimes devastating results. Capt. Edwin V. Harris of the 49th North Carolina was hit when his regiment moved back to its original position. He was walking past a more exposed part of the work when a bullet narrowly missed Major Davis and struck him in the neck. As a stream of blood gushed out, Harris staggered to Davis, held out his arm as if to say goodbye, and "gave the Major a look in which all the emotions of his soul seemed concentrated." He died later that day. Henry Philips of the 17th North Carolina was hit in the back by a Federal shell "and literally torn to pieces, a hand full of his intestines falling on my head ten feet away," reported J. M. Cutchin. Philips was so decimated that "his remains were taken up by the shovelful and carried away."[25]

Fitz William McMaster stepped and crawled over many dead on his way to his sleeping quarters after the battle, and he found two wounded black soldiers inside the bombproof. One had used a book, William Paley's *The Principles of Moral and Political Philosophy,* as a pillow, staining it with his blood. McMaster later found two bullets on the battlefield that had met in midair and fused together. He kept it as a souvenir and saw other soldiers pick up at least three more examples of this strange phenomenon.[26]

Hugh Douglas examined the crater and connecting works on the evening of July 30. He found the ground between the main line and the cavalier "heaved up, forming a Crater," and measured it with a tape at 125 feet long, 50 feet wide, and 20 to 25 feet deep. He and Edwin N. Wise could not find the end of Pleasants's gallery because the crater was still filled with dead. They discovered at least two bodies in Shaft No. 2.[27]

Carriers brought tools into Pegram's Salient after dusk on July 30, allowing the Confederates to dig a proper fire step around the rim of the crater. They also began the gruesome task of burying the dead that littered the crater floor and the connecting works. The wounded had been carried out by this time, and the bodies were simply rolled to the deepest part of both sections of the crater, where dirt was shoveled over them from above. The digging uncovered several bodies of South Carolinians who had been buried in the mine explosion. In one spot, eight men were "lying side by side with their coats under their head. They seemed never to have moved after the explosion." More Confederates, superintending work details of captured black soldiers, opened a burial trench one hundred feet behind the crater to inter bodies removed from the connecting works.[28]

The total number of burials that night is uncertain. Lt. Thomas Smith of the 16th Virginia superintended interment inside the crater and detailed Sgt. John Sheppard to tally them. Sheppard recorded 177 burials, about equal numbers of Union and Confederate. He estimated that about 20 percent of them were black soldiers. Adding those Confederates killed in the mine explosion, more than 200 bodies were buried in the crater.[29]

Surprisingly, in the midst of this carnage, signs of life appeared. One South Carolinian emerged from the rim of the hole, having been buried by falling earth when the mine went up. He managed to survive all day by breathing air through a crevice. For several hours the man worked his way out until he

Earliest known photograph of the crater. RG985–CWP27.27, U.S. Army Military History Institute

emerged, his hair matted with red clay, but very happy. On the surface, a burial detail was surprised as a live Federal soldier, who had been playing possum, finally revealed himself when dirt began to fall around his head.[30]

The dead inside the crater were covered by barely a foot of dirt, and those Rebels who had to hold the excavation were forced to "endure a horrible stench." The smell was so strong that Weisiger's men could not eat the rations their commissary brought forward.[31]

Wounded, Dead, and Captive

Willcox was the first Federal officer to urge that a truce be arranged to allow the two sides to succor the wounded who lay between the lines and to bury the dead. Meade was willing, but he preferred it be worked out locally and informally. The army commander warned, however, that Beauregard had refused such a truce on an earlier occasion during the campaign. When the first Federal request went across no-man's-land at about 2:30, Beauregard passed it on to Lee. There is no evidence that anything was done with it from that point on. Meanwhile pickets ceased firing in the vicinity of Pegram's Salient. This allowed soldiers to peek across their parapets and examine the intervening space, which was covered with bodies and wounded. Some of the latter managed to raise pieces of tents or blankets on guns to shield themselves from the baking rays of the sun, while others waved futilely at their comrades for assistance that could not come until the details of the truce were worked out. But no word came from the Confederate side, and firing resumed well before evening. Grant, meanwhile, gave Meade full authority to organize any truce he could to help the sufferers.[32]

The Federals taken prisoner in the crater bivouacked in an open lot close to Petersburg for the night. The darkening skies offered some relief to those who were suffering from heat exhaustion, but the Confederates did not feed the prisoners all evening. Brigade leader Marshall lost a fine pair of boots, with a spread eagle stitched into them with white silk, even though he slept with the pair under his head. The boots were later found and returned, but Marshall's loss provided some little humor to lighten the predicament of other prisoners.[33]

Inside the crater, hungry and tired but exultant, Weisiger's men settled in for whatever rest they could find amid the recently buried dead. Some of them, unable to sleep after their most exciting and deadly day of battle, amused themselves by picking up abandoned muskets and firing the ramrods across no-man's-land toward the Federals.[34]

16

JULY 31 AND AUGUST 1

The Federals lost 504 killed, 1,881 wounded, and 1,413 captured or missing, for a total of 3,798. Burnside's 9th Corps suffered the lion's share of these casualties; only about 300 of the losses occurred in other units, and Ferrero's division suffered more than one-third of all losses among the five divisions involved in the battle. Burnside reported 15,272 men available on July 20 and lost 3,434 of them ten days later. All told, 16,772 Federal troops were involved in the battle.[1]

The 9th Corps lost 23 regimental commanders and 2 brigade leaders, Bartlett and Marshall. Griffin's brigade lost all regimental officers above the rank of captain and had only 400 men left. In the 9th New Hampshire, four companies were commanded by sergeants, and only 5 men out of 23 in Company F survived the battle. Ord reported that Turner's division of the 10th Corps, and sporadic hits among 18th Corps units, accounted for 33 killed, 281 wounded, and 50 missing, for a total of 364 casualties.[2]

The most unusual aspect of Federal statistics involved the black troops. Ferrero's division lost 423 killed, 744 wounded, and many captured, according to a recent calculation. This amounted to about 1,240 men. Survivors of the battle were aware of the discrepancy between the number of blacks who were missing and the number reportedly held captive by the Confederates and explained it by assuming the difference represented those who were killed after surrendering on the field. There is little doubt that the slaughter of unarmed blacks accounted for the unusually high casualty rate among Ferrero's regiments, even though some Confederates refused to admit that the slaughter took place when they recorded their memories of the fight.[3]

Confederate losses have been estimated at 1,140 (400 killed, 700 wounded, and 40 missing), although some sources place them as high as 1,612. These losses occurred in a force that probably totaled 9,400 men. Weisiger lost nearly one-third of the 800 troops he took into the battle, and Sanders lost about 14 percent. Elliott's brigade suffered about 45 percent casualties among 1,500 men involved in the engagement. Goode's brigade lost 25 killed and 86 wounded, and the 61st North Carolina lost 40 killed and wounded out of 140 men engaged.[4]

Care of the Wounded

A total of 1,393 officers and men were admitted to 9th Corps hospitals on July 30–31, and Ord reported that 157 wounded were admitted to field hospitals from Turner's division. Surgeons had begun preparing for this flood early on the day of battle by moving all the wounded back to City Point. Conrad Noll of the 20th Michigan was shot in the thigh at about 9 A.M. Helped to the rear by a comrade, he was admitted to a 9th Corps hospital but did not have his wound dressed until 6 P.M. Noll reported the conditions at City Point to be excellent, but it was only a temporary stay for the Michigan soldier. Shipped by steamer, he arrived at Washington, D.C., on the morning of July 31, where he recovered without the amputation of his leg.[5]

Surg. Francis Minot Weld of the 27th USCT began treating the wounded at 8 A.M., not long after Ferrero's attack. "I never left the operating table," he reported home, "except for a hasty meal at dinner and supper, till half-past-one the next morning—making seventeen hours and a half of incessant cutting and sawing." He then slept until 5 A.M., except to be consulted regarding a wounded officer. Then Weld ate breakfast and operated until 10 P.M. of July 31, another seventeen hours. All told, he worked thirty-four and a half hours, and slept only three and a half hours, out of forty-one. "You can imagine what a back I have." Weld continued to work in long spurts for the next couple of days, tending to about two hundred wounded men and performing forty amputations.[6]

Weld praised the wounded black soldiers for acting "like heroes. I took out half the upper jaw of one poor boy, without chloroform, and he just sat right up, and never uttered a word or a groan during the whole operation, which took half an hour, as it was all smashed to pieces. It was impossible to give chloroform or aether, as he would swallow the blood and choke."[7]

Sgt. James Lathe of the 9th New Hampshire was placed on the waiting list at the field hospital because he had suffered only an injury to his hand. He wandered about, observing that the wounded exhibited all sorts of injuries, from simple bullet holes to powder burns and bayonet gashes. Some had their bowels exposed to the air or had faces so smashed they were nearly unrecognizable. Lathe's clothes were covered not only with blood but also "scraps of flesh, brains, and everything else that could fly from men that had been torn to pieces by shot and shell." He eventually lost only three fingers.[8]

Col. William J. Bolton of the 51st Pennsylvania had been shot relatively early in the battle. Carried by two of his men through the covered way, his regimental surgeon probed for the ball but could not find it at the division hospital. At dusk Bolton was taken by ambulance to City Point and boarded a steamer unassisted the next day. Admitted to Georgetown Seminary Hospital at Washington, D.C., on August 1, the surgeons still could not find the bullet. His hometown doctor in Norristown, Pennsylvania, also could not locate the missile when Bolton went home. The colonel recovered enough to return to the regiment in late September, but his wound caused so much pain that he could not resume duty. The regimental surgeon performed a major operation, cutting forty incisions, and still could not find the projectile. Bolton, however, resumed command of the regiment on October 16.[9]

The touching case of Lt. James J. Chase of the 32nd Maine epitomized the suffering of Federals wounded at the crater. His face had been torn by a bullet. Carried to the rear, he was left at a field hospital with a canteen of water and the hot sun shining directly on him, the amputating table nearby. Not until late on the evening of July 30 was he placed on the table and given chloroform. Five days later, Chase was taken by steamer to Washington, his sword and bloody clothes still on his body. His father arrived from Auburn, Maine, to tend him until he was able to travel home. Reaching Auburn on August 18, Chase was stunned when a woman passenger pleaded that he not be allowed to enter the conveyance that was to take him home. "Don't let him come in here; I can't ride with such a horrid looking creature." She blocked the door and forced the poor man to use a different carriage. Chase's bandages were removed the next day for the first time since the battle. His entire family looked at him with pity and pain, and when Chase looked in a mirror he understood for the first time what the lady in the carriage meant. It devastated the young man.

But time healed a great deal of the injury, although Chase's face remained badly scarred for the rest of his life. He retained some degree of humor about his situation; "having been endowed by nature with a nose of monstrous size, it stood the test much better than I had anticipated." Chase recovered enough to volunteer for duty in the Coast Guards for the remainder of the war. He continued to suffer a lot of pain after the war but married and fathered children. On December 10, 1872, however, Chase began to suffer sharp pain in the one good eye he had left. It worsened during the day, and he began to lose his vision that night. One of the last sights Chase recalled was that of his daughter holding up her favorite doll. "Papa can see my dolly," repeated the three-year-old. Inflammation resulting from his wound robbed Chase of sight that night. He was only twenty-five years old.[10]

Wounded Left on the Field

Although the Federals strained to take care of those wounded who made it to Union lines, some remained immobile in no-man's-land. Their groans and calls for help could be heard all night. A few daring men braved a "scattering fire" and crawled out under cover of darkness. They managed to get water to some, even dragging a few others back, but most wounded remained beyond the reach of friendly hands. Willcox estimated that about fifty were left alive in no-man's-land, scattered among two hundred to three hundred dead.[11]

The weather continued "bright and beautiful" the day after the battle. As the sun rose, the wounded suffered even more and the dead emitted a suffocating odor. Some Confederates took pity on their enemy and offered aid that night. Members of the 12th Virginia heard a wounded black man plead for mercy, saying he was "tired of fighting," and the Confederates helped him across their parapet. Other Rebels pushed a cupful of water to another wounded black man, but he died immediately afterward.[12]

Behind Confederate lines, doctors strained to treat the wounded prisoners. Five captured Union surgeons were rounded up to help, and nurses were detailed from among the captives. The wounded prisoners were treated at Central Park Hospital in Petersburg; many of them lay on the grass because of a shortage of space inside the building. When Chief Surgeon James W. Claiborne inspected the hospital on July 31, he was shocked to find 150 black wounded prisoners lying on the ground, suffering terribly from neglect. Captured Union surgeons refused to treat them, claiming to be "sick, and tired, and disgusted, and that they were prisoners of war, and were not in duty bound to do any work." When Claiborne threatened to ship them to Andersonville, the surgeons relented but complained of the food, exposure to Federal shelling, and many other things. John C. Haskell recalled coming across a group of 50 wounded black prisoners who had settled, unattended, in the branch of a ravine behind the Jerusalem Plank Road. Unwounded black prisoners refused to help them, and the Confederate surgeon at Locust Grove Hospital also turned them away, pleading lack of space. Haskell finally located a Rebel surgeon who agreed to find transportation to haul them to a hospital and promised to take care of them.[13]

The view of this situation from the other side of the fence was a bit different. Surg. Francis J. D'Avignon of the 96th New York, one of the captured Federal surgeons, willingly took on the job of treating 130 black prisoners on August 2. "This lot of wounded were looked upon by the Rebels with a great deal of hatred & with an earnest desire to degrade them," he reported. The Confederates had mixed them with white prisoners, which helped spread communicable diseases. "I gave my attention to the Black & to the white soldiers, uniformly alike, to the great annoyance & regret of the Southerners."[14]

Souvenirs and Flags

Mahone's division collected nineteen Union flags from the battlefield; the lion's share—fifteen—were picked up by members of Weisiger's brigade. The Virginians collected the national colors of the 11th New Hampshire, 100th Pennsylvania, 28th USCT, 57th Massachusetts, and 31st Maine and the state flag of the 58th Massachusetts; the rest were not identified. Sanders's brigade collected the national flags of the 2nd and 20th Michigan, and another that was not identified, and Hall's brigade claimed the national flag of the 58th Massachusetts. Some of the ten unidentified flags probably belonged to the 23rd, 29th, and 30th USCT, which also lost state or national colors. Five color-bearers in the 29th USCT were shot; the last was Lieutenant Colonel Bross.[15]

In fact many of the flags Mahone's men claimed were actually taken from the hands of an enemy soldier were simply picked up after the Federals lost control of them. David Barnes of the 16th Virginia found a black soldier lying on a Union flag in a ditch and demanded the emblem. "I will give it to you. Don't kill me. My people used to live near you," the black man cried. Barnes took the flag and left, but another Rebel bayoneted the frightened soldier. Julius H. Tyler of the same regiment came across a Massachusetts flag partially buried in the bottom of a trench after the battle. He dug it up and turned it in but recalled that he never received credit for the find. The importance placed on capturing enemy flags was so great that many Confederates cheated in order to garner glory. At least two flags were turned in to the adjutant of the 17th South Carolina by members of Elliott's brigade, but the adjutant lay them down to attend to other business and later found they had been stolen by some of Mahone's men. Beauregard officially forwarded but three flags captured by his command, making an official total of twenty-two Union standards captured on July 30. Only one Confederate flag was taken into Union lines, by Capt. Thomas Wright of the 31st USCT.[16]

Many of the Federal colors that were saved by their units had been torn nearly to shreds during the battle. Members of the 4th New Hampshire in Bell's brigade counted fifty-one bullet holes and one large tear caused by an artillery round in their standard.[17]

The Confederates also collected two thousand small arms from the battlefield, and many individuals snatched up personal possessions as souvenirs. A member of Weisiger's sharpshooter battalion found "a very handsome sword" and gave it to Mahone, who "seemed to be about the happiest man I ever saw, for all things were going his way splendid." James Paul Verdery of the 48th Georgia garnered a welcome lode of sugar, light bread, flour, and an inkstand from the captives. Dorsey N. Binion of the same regiment "captured" a watch, knife, portfolio, envelopes and paper, and a handful of cigars from the Federals. "Our Boys are great on plundering dead y[ankee]s," he bragged to his sister. Reuben L. Whitehurst of the 16th Virginia found a diary on the body of a man belonging to the 100th Pennsylvania. He kept the book and wrote, "The last of the 'poor' Yankee" at the end of the last entry.[18]

Eventually twenty-four Congressional Medals of Honor were awarded to Federal soldiers for their actions in the Battle of the Crater. Four were given to members of Ferrero's division, three to whites and one to a black man, Sgt. Decatur Dorsey of the 39th USCT. Fifteen members of Weisiger's brigade, and four more men from other units, were listed on the Confederate Roll of Honor for their actions in the battle.[19]

Prisoners

The Confederates sought to humiliate their captives by parading them through the streets of Petersburg on July 31, placing black men in alternate files among the white officers. Bartlett rode "a very sorry looking nag without any saddle." It is not clear if this was Mahone's horse, which the Confederate general had lent Bartlett so he could move from the battlefield to the rear areas the day before. The assemblage of Federal prisoners moved slowly through many streets, "taunted by the women, stoned by the boys, and cursed by the men," as Freeman Bowley put it. "See the white and nigger equality soldiers!" shouted a civilian. "How do you like it, Yanks? Yanks and niggers sleep in the same bed." When an elderly woman stuck her head out of a window and shouted, "Birds of a feather will flock together," a lieutenant of the 32nd Maine replied, "Yes, but we don't mix in the nest as you do down here." A nearby guard threatened to shoot him for insulting Southern womanhood, but the Federal challenged him to fire "and then boast you have killed a Yankee as you will never kill one by going to the front." The Rebel guard took the insult in silence and continued marching.[20]

The torrent of insults from the civilians stemmed from weeks of Federal shelling and the anger felt over the use of black troops in the battle. It extended to threats as well. Some civilians shouted that the prisoners ought to be blown to atoms by artillery fire. "They are going to take you down to Andersonville" was a more ominous threat. "They are dying down there three or four hundred a day; you will never live to see home again." Some guards who escorted the prisoners through Petersburg were considerate, but others were less than kind. One man of the 17th Vermont was jabbed in the side with a bayonet "because he could not keep up" with the procession. Guards hit several other Federals with the flat sides of swords or knocked them down with musket butts.[21]

The Confederates segregated the whites and blacks after the parade, placing the former on Merchant's Island in the Appomattox River, where they received some hardtack and a piece of raw bacon on the night of July 31, their first rations in more than twenty-four hours. The prisoners remained on the island until August 3, often fed cornbread and bacon that was infested with maggots. Most of the black prisoners able to do physical labor were sent to various work sites. Douglas used up to ten black prisoners to dig shafts in his effort to find Pleasants's gallery in the crater.[22]

Confederate authorities also allowed captured blacks to be reclaimed by their former owners and placed advertisements to let citizens know of this opportunity. There seems to be no final accounting of the number of Union soldiers who thus returned to slavery, but officers of the 19th USCT reported that two regimental members captured at the Battle of the Crater eventually were sold to a Mr. De Vaughan of Powhatan County, Virginia, and to a Richmond slave trader named John Sedgewick, who later sold him to James Cobb of Shelby, North Carolina. More than one black captive sought out his former master and offered to return to slavery voluntarily in order to avoid going to military prison.[23]

Federal Moves, July 31

Still worried about a Confederate effort to turn his flank, Meade instructed Burnside and Warren to hold their corps fronts with as few men as possible and accumulate a reserve to move to any threatened point. But Meade had no idea of conditions in the 9th Corps. Potter could put only two of his regiments in the trenches on July 31, yet he was to relieve all units of other divisions and resume the full length of his division line by dusk. Ord had been waiting for hours for 9th Corps troops to relieve Turner's division and two divisions of the 18th Corps. When Meade asked him to report which of his units were detained by Burnside's tardiness, "as I get no reports from that officer," Ord sought to deflect further anger at Burnside by assuring him that he could "get along without pressing Burnside for these men."[24]

Turner's division left the 9th Corps works early on the morning of July 31. Marching during the oppressive heat, many men dropped out because of exhaustion, but the rest reached the Bermuda Hundred line late that day. Turner reported that at least three of his men died of heat exhaustion, and he needed thirty ambulances to haul many others along the way.[25]

On the army's left flank, Burnside still had not yet relieved some of Warren's units by the evening of July 31. Burnside had no more than ten thousand men left in his command, barely enough to relieve Ord's units, much less Warren's, but he made a solid effort to get the job done that evening. Burnside also had to rebuild damaged defenses and hold the same line with nearly four thousand fewer troops.[26]

The ill feeling between Meade and Burnside crested once again on the evening of July 31. In a brief message sent at 6:40, Burnside mentioned losing forty-five hundred men, mostly after the order to retire from the crater was issued. Meade took offense at the insinuation that his actions were to blame for these losses and demanded an explanation. He also reminded Burnside that he had not received a detailed report of conditions in the 9th Corps since almost noon of July 30. Burnside expressed surprise that the army commander did not understand that the withdrawal order depressed morale among the Federals inside the crater and contributed to the hasty and unorganized manner of withdrawing. Meade responded with an assertion that 9th Corps troops should not have executed the order with haste or lack of care and suggested that a court of inquiry investigate the matter.[27]

Confederate Moves on July 31

Conditions inside the crater on July 31 were still bad. The Confederates had to keep low in the hole to avoid heavy picket firing, and "many arms and legs and hands could yet be seen protruding from different parts" of the crater floor. Black prisoners were at work on the Confederate defenses all day. They helped to uncover three or four Confederates who had been underground since the mine explosion; they "were still alive, though some of them died almost immediately after." A few Confederate dead were also dug up during the process of reconstructing the works.[28]

The heat began to abate and a sprinkle fell on the area by the evening of July 31, but it failed to dampen the awful stench of death that emanated from bodies lying between the lines. The wounded among them continued to scream in pain, dying slowly during the course of the day. Meade wrote to Lee to arrange a formal truce, but that would take more time than if Burnside could negotiate with the local commander. Meanwhile several other officers became alarmed at the suffering they witnessed in no-man's-land. Warren urged Meade to open fire on the Confederates if they did not allow the Federals to succor their own wounded and refused to send out help themselves. He thought their neglect was attributable to racial prejudice, for many of the wounded were blacks.[29]

Consummating the deal proved difficult. The Federals raised a white flag that morning and the Confederates ceased firing. Sanders sent out his adjutant, George Clark, with a handkerchief tied to a ramrod to consult with Major Lydig of Burnside's staff. Clark accepted Burnside's request for an informal, local truce and passed it on to Sanders, who forwarded it up the chain of command. Meanwhile everyone waited and tried to do what they could for the sufferers. The Confederates did not allow the wounded to be removed, but Byron Cutcheon, who served as officer of the day in this sector, helped arrange for shelter tent halves and blankets to be erected as shade for some of them.[30]

At noon the Confederates replied that they could not consider a truce until Meade wrote a formal request to Lee, but they allowed the Federals to continue tending the wounded. The truce flag flew off and on during the remainder of July 31, and a few Confederates crossed their parapet and delivered water to a handful of suffering Federals. The Unionists could also get a clearer view of Pegram's Salient and observed what a "mass of ruins" it appeared to be, "but being diligently repaired by the Rebels." They could also see civilians from Petersburg among the gray-clad figures who stood up on the parapet whenever the truce flag was in effect.[31]

Burnside reported that the flag flew for a total of three hours that day, and still no arrangement was made to bring proper help to the wounded. He estimated that no more than twenty Federals remained alive between the lines; he had been able to forward water and whiskey to at least some of them, but the Confederates insisted on resuming fire later in the day. Meade agreed with the Rebels; he had never intended the truce flag to fly longer than was needed to arrange matters. The Confederates would inform Burnside when Meade's letter to Lee had wound its way through the proper channels. Many Federals wondered why it took so long and assumed it was because of Confederate resentment at use of black troops in the attack. Lee forwarded Meade's request to Beauregard, because the latter's troops were responsible for that sector. Beauregard received and approved the request late on July 31 but suggested the truce begin early the next day and last for four hours. This was acceptable to the Federals.[32]

Firing ceased at 5 A.M. August 1 as the Confederates established a line of sentinels halfway across no-man's-land. No Federals were allowed on the Rebel side of that line, and only members of the burial details were allowed on the Union side of it. Black prisoners were used to gather the dead from the Confederate half of no-man's-land and carry them to the sentinel line, where the Federals took charge of them.[33]

As soon as the firing stopped, men on both sides popped out of the trenches to watch the proceedings. The "two armies rose up as out of the ground and the face of the earth seemed to be peopled with men," recalled an officer of Sanders's brigade. Joseph A. Hobbs of the 32nd Maine was a member of the burial detail. He recalled the bodies were "swollen out of all human shape, and whites could not be told from blacks, except by their hair." The clothes had burst, emitting an awful stench that "penetrated the clothing and impressed the senses," according to the historian of the 35th Massachusetts. To Henry Pippitt "it peared every time I drawed my breath it would nock me down." Flies had deposited eggs in exposed flesh, and many bodies were crawling with maggots. Concerned comrades were able to identify some bodies by looking at personal belongings on them, but most were too badly decomposed to allow for removal to the Union line.[34]

Anywhere from four to twenty men were found yet alive in no-man's-land. One survivor elicited the admiration of his comrades. When asked if he regretted serving in the army, he replied, "I don't know that I have."[35]

The burial details dug a couple of trenches thirty feet long and four feet deep between the lines. They then rolled or dragged the corpses in when possible, and "shoveled" them onto stretchers when necessary. After piling them in, there was room for only about a foot of covering dirt. The black prisoners brought forward piles of dismembered body parts, and the Federals put them into the pits as well. They interred white and black bodies together. Major Etheredge of the 41st Virginia was impressed with how methodically the Federals worked at the task, divided into three details for digging, interring, and covering the pits. Lee's artillery chief, William Nelson Pendleton, thought the white Federals in the burial details gathered "the offensive remains of their African soldiers" with "loathing," but there is no supportive commentary for this notion.[36]

A member of the Christian Commission had piled ice and stimulants on a hand-drawn cart for the wounded men found alive. He apparently reached the scene too late and offered the goods to the burial details. One Union officer suggested the restoratives be offered to the black prisoners working on the Confederate side of the sentinel line. They received the iced drinks with "grave, silent courtesy." Col. Henry G. Thomas also offered some to Confederate officers who superintended the process.[37]

Because everything took place within the bare expanse of no-man's-land, the burial was witnessed by hundreds of Union and Confederate soldiers of all ranks. "It was our first chance to stand up and look over since the beginning of the siege," commented W. A. Day of the 49th North Carolina. The Confederates who crowded on top of their parapet seemed to Theodore Lyman like "malevolent spirits, towering to an unnatural height against the sky." A Virginia artilleryman, however, noted that many of those towering figures were rear-area men too timid to appear near a raging battle but who now hurried forward to gawk at the aftermath of combat. For many, it was their first and only chance to examine the crater in detail.[38]

Among the crowds of men in gray observing the burial, as well as the forward Union line, were Beauregard and Gracie, apparently dressed in private's uniforms to hide their identities. Maj. James C. Coit took advantage of the truce to draw a sketch of no-man's-land, obviously for intelligence purposes.[39]

Sketch of the crater by Maj. James C. Coit. Robert Underwood Johnson and Clarence Clough Buel, *Battles and Leaders* (New York: Century Company, 1887–88) 4:555

Capt. John C. Featherston of the 9th Alabama visited with Potter, and the Yankee offered him a cigar and a drink from his canteen. Featherston had recovered some papers belonging to Ferrero when the Confederates recaptured the crater; Potter wanted to call Ferrero so as to "guy" him about it. Featherston declined, wanting nothing to do with a man who commanded black troops. When Potter asked Featherston to point out Confederate generals, the captain spied Gracie, A. P. Hill, and Mahone, all standing on the crater's rim. Sanders was the only Rebel general who came into no-man's-land. When Potter saw the diminutive Mahone, the author of many 9th Corps misfortunes on July 30, he remarked, "Not much man, but a big general."[40]

Featherston took pride that the Yankees "acknowledged we had whipped them badly and caught them in their own trap," but most bantering between blue and gray involved a good deal of give and take. William Olin of the 36th Massachusetts concluded that "they feel as we do—wishing the war would end. They said, they hated to see us coming up to be slaughtered, and admit that but for mismanagement on our part we would have been victorious." The men conversed pleasantly and traded coffee for tobacco. "A man jumped upon the works and sung out; 'Let's all go home!'" Yet one of Lee's staff officers thought there was "too much intimacy." Walter Taylor complained, "I could not have approached the creatures whilst immediately before my eyes were hundreds of black soldiers, no doubt the majority of them having once owned masters in happy Virginia homes."[41]

Henry G. Thomas circulated freely among the crowd, searching for the remains of Lt. Christopher Pennell, who had been shot while trying to rally the 31st USCT to advance out of the captured works. He offered one hundred dollars to any Confederate who could recover the body, because Pennell was the son of a good friend. Word circulated and produced a report that Pennell might have been buried inside the crater on the night of July 30. Recalling the shower of bullets that descended on that part of the field, Thomas also thought that Pennell's body might have been shot to pieces. At any rate he was unable to find him. Thomas became disoriented at the end of the truce period and wandered into the Confederate picket line. At first he pretended to be a private seeking a trade, then a Christian Commission worker, but his captors recognized him because of his interactions with the Rebels during the truce. Thomas insisted on being released because his capture resulted from the truce itself, but he was told to wait until the Confederates could report his presence and receive instructions.[42]

Although Thomas claimed he was not a spy, he did recall having in his possession a sketch of the crater. Remembering this, the Federal surreptitiously took it out of his pocket, along with a cigar, and brought both items to his mouth. While pretending to smoke, he managed to eat the paper with the incriminating evidence on it. Transported to Johnson's headquarters, where he ate a badly made Irish stew, Thomas was then taken to a prison in Petersburg. On the way he was shaken down not only by one of Beauregard's staff officers but also by the private who escorted him to jail. Thomas managed to retain possession of most of his belongings, however, and eventually bribed a guard to deliver a note to Lee pleading for his release. But before a response to that missive arrived, a series of misadventures took place as he attempted more than once to escape his prison cell, bothered by drunken Confederate soldiers picked up by the provost guard and incarcerated in the room above him, with loud noises and urine dripping through the floorboards into his compartment. Thomas also sent notes to Otway P. Hare, whom he had helped recover most of the possessions from his house in late June, and to Lt. Col. R. O. Whitehurst of the 16th Virginia. But Lee responded late that night with an order to release the troubled Yankee. A Confederate officer escorted him to the picket line and spread the word until everyone on both sides of no-man's-land understood what was to happen. Then Thomas walked "from bondage into liberty" at 4 A.M. on August 2.[43]

The Federals interred anywhere from two hundred to three hundred bodies during the four-hour truce on August 1. Many reports indicate that most of them were black soldiers. The Confederates found up to a dozen of their own dead in no-man's-land. Near the end of the truce, Mahone noticed that the dirt piled on top of the bodies was higher than the natural level of the earth, and he protested that this could be used as cover for an advance. He forced the Federals to level it, thus reducing the fragile covering for the dead even more and contributing to their exposure within a few weeks.[44]

Although one South Carolina soldier reported that the area was "cleaned up and order restored" by the end of the truce, other men reported the stench continued "almost unendurable even after burial, as so much blood covered the ground." Moreover, in an incident reminiscent of Henry Thomas's, Pvt. James Meyers of the 43rd USCT, a member of the burial detail, somehow crossed into Confederate lines and was taken prisoner. Why and how this happened was never explained, but the Confederates used Meyers as a laborer for the rest of the war. He returned to his unit in April 1865.[45]

Harman Bower of the 44th New York found a German-language testament and an envelope addressed to a lady in Pennsylvania, both lying near a dead man in no-man's-land who apparently had laid them out to be found by someone. Bower sent both to the woman, telling her of the pitiful circumstances of their discovery.[46]

Although those buried in the truce were interred with no ceremony, members of the 24th New York Cavalry (dismounted) held a service for sixty-three of their comrades on August 2. The burial took place with preaching and music provided by the regimental band.[47]

The men of Weisiger's brigade pined for an opportunity to leave the salient and return to their former position west of the Jerusalem Plank Road. They finally received their wish after dusk on August 1.[48]

17

AFTERMATH

Grant was thoroughly disgusted with the results of the mine attack, calling it a "fizzle" and lamenting, "So fair an opportunity will probably never occur again for carrying fortifications." The general in chief also termed it "the saddest affair I have witnessed in the war." A member of his staff reported that Grant grew "sicker at heart" when he learned further details of the failure. "I regret not having made better progress in whipping out the rebellion," he admitted to an old friend. When the troops failed to push out of the breach in Rebel lines and the defenders recovered, Grant said, the Federals found "that we had the wolf by the ears. He was hard to hold, and more dangerous to let go." Meade and Butler felt the same deep disappointment.[1]

"Never before have I felt that the Army of the Potomac was disgraced," lamented Charles Wainwright. "Failed it has frequently, and botches its commanding generals have made of more than one piece of work, but the army itself has always come out with honour." Morale dropped so low that a "feeling of despair almost of ever accomplishing anything" pervaded, according to another member of Warren's staff.[2]

Ninth Corps troops felt worse about the attack than anyone, believing that they "had utterly failed—had missed a great opportunity," as Byron Cutcheon put it. Everyone felt demoralized, "down in the mouth," as another man wrote, with "nothing to do but bear it." Potter sent a bottle of forty-year-old brandy to Zenas Bliss and asked him to "prefer charges against certain officers, or furnish him with information on which he could base them." But Bliss "declined to do so."[3]

Members of the 48th Pennsylvania boasted that if Pleasants had led the attack with their regiment, the Federals would have succeeded, "or there would have been no Forty-eighth left to hear of it." For his part, "Pleasants was awful mad all day when he saw how things were going on," reported Henry Heisler.[4]

Adelbert Ames refused to blame individuals but "took no pains to conceal his contempt for the management in general." Ord wrote movingly to his wife of the disgust he felt while watching good men die for nothing. Louis Bell, in Turner's division, could not look on his suffering command "with out feeling sick at heart," and other members of the Army of the James admitted to feeling "tired in body and depressed in spirit" after the battle.[5]

In Washington, D.C., stories and rumors circulated like a storm, "some of them absurdly wild and ridiculous," according to Secretary of the Navy Gideon Welles. Lincoln left for Fortress Monroe on July 31, before the flurry of rumors had settled down, but he returned in time to call a cabinet meeting on August 2. The Battle of the Crater was a major topic of conversation. Welles came away from the meeting despondent and afraid that Grant might not be the man for the job. Welles had harbored doubts about Grant's generalship before and now feared that the heavy losses of the Overland campaign had been wasted if Grant was stymied beyond hope at Petersburg. Word that the lead division had been drawn by lot further upset everyone at the meeting. "A blight and sadness comes over me like a dark shadow when I dwell on the subject," Welles confided to his diary.[6]

The failure of July 30 cast a gloom over the civilian population of the North comparable to that which affected the Federal troops at Petersburg. It was the first major sign of doubt among Northerners about the eventual success of Grant's campaign against Lee. The "moral effect was intensely calamitous," wrote a friend of the slain Colonel Bross. "It was widely felt, as a result, that we were making no progress in the war, and were likely to make none."[7]

The emotional effect of the mine battle was succeeded by a worse shock to the faithful supporters of Lincoln: the adoption of a peace platform by the Democratic Party and the nomination of the former general George B. McClellan as the party's candidate in early August. As time slipped by, it appeared more likely that McClellan would win the presidency on the basis of his party's assertion that the Republican war effort was a bloody failure. The pall cast by the result of Burnside's attack reinforced that view among many potential voters.[8]

Confederate Reaction

Not surprisingly a mixture of joy and relief characterized Southern reaction to the Crater Battle. Rebel survivors were amazed that, taken by surprise and fighting a largely superior force, they had saved Petersburg and Lee's army. The men of Weisiger's, Hall's, and Sanders's brigades achieved results "unparalleled in the history of the war," as Mahone put it in a congratulatory order. Other Confederates referred to "a peculiar joy" when they contemplated the ordeal.[9]

Many participants and observers commented on the Federal use of black troops. "This day was the jubilee of fiends in human shape," noted the adjutant of the 46th Virginia. Many Confederates bragged in letters home that their comrades had slaughtered the blacks without mercy. Noting that many of the slain were buried in the crater, Samuel S. Watson reported "they cant get out of thare I don' think. We put a few Yanks in with them for commanders." Another Rebel who did not participate in the fight correctly noted the racial-ethnic composition of the Federal attackers by writing that "many a bayonet was wet with African, Yankee, Dutch, Indian blood."[10]

James Otey had no reason to celebrate the Crater Battle; he faced court-martial proceedings for deserting his command early in the fight. Davidson's battery was in shambles as a result of its pounding on July 30. When John Hampden Chamberlayne took command of the unit that afternoon, he found that the men were "scattered, undisciplined & disorganized." While Chamberlayne put it back together, Otey was tried, found guilty, and sentenced to be shot. Alexander was responsible for making the arrangements, but influential citizens pleaded for mercy and Jefferson Davis reduced his death sentence to dismissal from the army in early September 1864.[11]

The Federals Recover

It took some time for 9th Corps troops to recover from their trial on July 30. Byron Cutcheon called the next two weeks "the most depressing experience of the whole war." The only commissioned officers left in the 17th Vermont were the adjutant and two surgeons. "One more fight, and goodbye the Seventeenth," wrote the regimental quartermaster. In the 9th New Hampshire, discipline suffered enormously after the battle. "With no punishments for neglect of duty, no reprimands from any source that is felt, nearly all are doing about as they choose." Such neglect of duty was not tolerated in Hartranft's brigade, however; when twenty men of Company F, 13th Ohio Cavalry (dismounted), refused an order to return to the trenches, they were arrested and forced to carry logs in front of brigade headquarters. The men eventually relented, and Hartranft gave them "a little fatherly advice" before they stepped back into the works.[12]

Ninth Corps troops eventually recovered their spirit and commitment to duty. If nothing else, as Hartranft told his wife, the corps had proven that it could endure the worst and survive. Meanwhile inspections were held in all units to discover what was needed in terms of replacement equipment. Given the heavy losses, army headquarters told Burnside to plan a modification of his line so it could be held with fewer men.[13]

Making Sense of the Crater Battle

The Federals endlessly discussed who was to blame for the unexpected failure to break Lee's line on July 30. Grant set the tone by telling everyone that leadership was the problem. He did not refer to Meade, but to Burnside and Ledlie. It was a line of reasoning that resonated with nearly everyone in the Federal armies operating against Petersburg. As Turner put it, there were "too many men, too few generals" at the point of contact. "I do not see the use of Grant's planning movements and battles, and his plans are admirable, when nobody will execute them," Butler complained to his wife.[14]

Grant also created another line of thought to explain the failure of July 30. He spread the word in private conversations that, in the words of cavalry commander James H. Wilson, "the inability of our officers, to force their men to assault even a demolished line of works," was the cause. Theodore Lyman of Meade's staff echoed the idea by writing, "the men did not fight hard enough," and even a member of Burnside's staff concurred with this line of reasoning.[15]

Ninth Corps troops refused to admit to not fighting hard enough, but they readily agreed that mismanagement had caused their failure. "It was botched and bungled and bedeviled from the beginning," Cutcheon wrote of the charge. Burnside became the most visible target of criticism. Many soldiers in the Army of the Potomac recalled the disaster at Fredericksburg, when Burnside had led the army in its futile attack against Lee's defensive position and lost more than thirteen thousand men to no effect. The fact that he selected the lead division by chance astonished many true soldiers, and the fact that he did little to modify the Union works for easy crossing also struck them as negligent. Warren blamed Burnside for mismanaging his troops, and Ord wrote his wife that "it made me almost sick to think of it." "Fredericksburg over again from the same inefficient head," recorded a staff member in the 2nd Corps journal. When draftsman Charles W. Reed sketched the battlefield on August 2, he also drew a sketch of Burnside and labeled it "Bungling Blunderer."[16]

Ledlie also came in for considerable blame, but he was a less visible target than the corps commander. First Division staff officer Charles J. Mills told Lyman "what a miserable man Gen. Ledlie was; how he was drunken and entirely incapable." Simon Griffin spared no invective when he wrote: "Judas Ledlie a poor drunken imbecile."[17]

Many soldiers, especially 9th Corps troops, were highly critical of Meade for not attempting to widen the breach before advancing toward the Jerusalem Plank Road. As Willcox put it, there was a "fatal error" in attempting "to plunge so many thousand men through such a bung hole." Hartranft complained that

Meade's order to retire undermined the spirit of resistance among crater occupants, destroying their ability to resist Sanders. Other 9th Corps men thought Meade should have compelled Warren to advance against Davidson's battery or against the lightly defended Rebel line west of the Jerusalem Plank Road.[18]

Many soldiers believed that liquor must have played a role in the attack. As a member of the 11th New Hampshire put it, "a bottle of whiskey got in some way between the cogs & stoped" the well-planned attack. Although no one reported rumors as to who was drunk, there seemed to be a widespread feeling that "Whiskey was the Gen. in command" on July 30.[19]

The black troops became an obvious target of criticism. This was their first major defeat in the East, and their panicked retreat greatly contributed to turning the tide in favor of the Confederates. "They ran like sheep," asserted one of Ledlie's staff members, who lost all confidence in making soldiers out of African Americans. Some 9th Corps whites pledged never to go into battle with blacks again. Conservative newspapers, such as the *Louisville Daily Journal,* pointed to the bungled battle as proof of the "infatuation, the delusion, the criminality of bringing the negro into the war for white men's rights."[20]

Some Federal observers defended, or at least tried to explain, the behavior of Ferrero's troops. A member of Turner's division argued that they fought well, all things considered, and some 9th Corps men pinpointed the difficult tactical situation as the prime cause for their retreat. They correctly pointed out that the failure on July 30 was not primarily the result of what Ferrero's division did or failed to do. As an officer of the 31st USCT put it while writing to the New York *Evening Post,* the blacks moved forward after the attack had stalled and fled from a fire that drove many whites out of the breach as well. "If there be any disgrace in that, it does not belong exclusively nor mainly to the negroes," the officer wrote. Ferrero wanted to write a public letter to defend his men, but Burnside did not allow it. Lower-ranking officers, however, did so. Chaplain White of the 28th USCT argued that the only running was done by former slaves, rather than troops recruited from among the free black population of the North.[21]

After several days of recuperation following the battle, many black troops had regained their self-confidence. They boasted to their white comrades that, if given another chance, they could take and hold the salient for good. The blacks also blamed their white officers for not allowing them to cap their guns or fix their bayonets during the charge on July 30, as if that was a reason for their failure.[22]

The Confederates viewed the participation of Ferrero's men in the Battle of the Crater with anger. Their astonishment at meeting black troops on the battlefield gave way to rage, which resulted in nothing less than a killing frenzy. It was "*a perfect Massacre nearly* a Black flag fight," wrote a survivor of Hall's brigade. News that Ferrero's troops had shouted "No quarter! Remember Fort Pillow!" further incensed the Rebels. A. T. Fleming, who had not participated in Sanders's charge because of illness, reported that his comrades had dispatched the blacks as if they were "killing hogs." He saw the bodies on the battlefield and thought them "the Blackest greaysest [greasiest] negroes I ever saw in my life."[23]

Memories of John Brown, Harpers Ferry, and abolitionist attempts to incite a race war in the South were among the reasons why Southerners were incensed by the thought of confronting black opponents on the battlefield. Some Confederates felt tainted by the need to face members of the lowest rung of Southern society on the field of honor. Moreover, if blacks fought well, it would weaken the notion of racial inferiority that underpinned the institution of slavery in the South. In fact the willingness of the former slaves to enlist in the Union army was a denial of the self-serving idea that slavery was a benevolent institution and that blacks were content to live within it.[24]

The shock of seeing blacks in blue on July 30 was accentuated by fear of what they might do to white Southerners if they had the chance. John Calton had spoken with a returned prisoner of McAfee's brigade who had been guarded by black soldiers in the North. When the man had asked a guard what he was fighting for, the answer was chilling. In Calton's words, "his reply is too mean for me to repete but in amild manner to Seduce your Sister." As a result, "the Ide[a] [of] fighting negros" had "rased the dander" in McAfee's brigade, and everyone thought it was best to fight to the bitter end. It is no wonder that many Rebel survivors of the battle portrayed the thin gray line as the only thing standing between Ferrero's "drunken, depraved blacks, with guns in their hands" and the innocent women and children of Petersburg.[25]

Ironically some Confederates felt sorry for Ferrero's men, believing them to have been deluded into enlisting. A few Southerners were surprised that the blacks fought as well as they did, but they explained it away by assuming the whites simply pushed them into it and even shot them down in the heat of the fighting. Although many Rebels admitted their comrades had acted cruelly in killing unarmed blacks, they refused to condemn such action and hoped the example of July 30 would dispel any Yankee notion that blacks could make effective soldiers.[26]

Support Arms

Even though Hunt had amassed a powerful artillery force, the Union guns failed to give an advantage to Burnside's infantry. The Confederate artillery emplacements that pounded Burnside's men remained untouched. Guns belonging to the 9th Corps fired 3,587 rounds during the day, and their crews lost but one killed and two wounded. Fifty-four guns and mortars belonging to the 18th Corps fired 1,776 rounds and also lost only two men wounded, whereas Abbot's heavy ordnance fired 3,833 rounds, amounting to seventy-five tons of metal. One mortar battery alone fired 238 rounds, weighing 10,948 pounds of iron, and 600 to 700 pounds of powder.[27]

The Federal guns were largely ineffective because of the careful positioning of key Rebel guns and their protection by well-designed earthworks. About twenty-five field guns and a dozen mortars deteriorated the Union hold on Pegram's Salient, demonstrating how a small amount of light artillery could play a decisive role in battle. Wright's battery fired five hundred to six hundred rounds during the battle, ammunition that had to be carried into the emplacement by hand under Union fire. Wright's guns, however, were saved by heavy traverses between each piece, and the tree cover that Burnside never cut down also helped to shield his position. The light mortars also proved their worth on July 30. Designed for quick placement in crowded conditions, they tore up and demoralized the occupants of the crater during the final phase of the engagement.[28]

The cavalry played a minor role in the Battle of the Crater. Sheridan's two divisions did not reach the army's left flank until after the fighting ended, but Wilson's division moved out under orders from Meade toward several points well to the west of the Jerusalem Plank Road, including Ream's Station and Globe Tavern, along the Weldon and Petersburg Railroad. The troopers engaged in no significant action.[29]

Prisoners

The Confederates dispersed their prisoners to several camps across the Atlantic states. Many of the officers boarded cars for a hot and dirty trip to Danville, Virginia, where three hundred prisoners were crammed into the first floor of a warehouse on August 2. William F. Bartlett had lost his crutches and had to be helped everywhere. He also suffered from diarrhea. A week later some officers traveled from Danville to Columbia, South Carolina.[30]

The prisoners endured enormous suffering while in captivity. Held in the Richland County Jail in Columbia, Frank Kenfield of the 17th Vermont tried to survive on a steady diet of cornmeal and sorghum, living in a room swarming with vermin. The inmates, seventeen men in a room twenty feet square, made the best of the situation by dreaming of food and playing cards and checkers. William Baird of the 23rd USCT spent some time in a tobacco warehouse at Saulsbury, North Carolina, eating "half cooked" cornbread and drinking water that was tainted by sewage. This treatment gave him the impression that the Confederates meant to "kill us off in any manner."[31]

The Confederates in Virginia captured a large number of black Union soldiers for the first time at the crater. In compliance with a general order issued by the Confederate Adjutant and Inspector General's Office in 1862, A. P. Hill forwarded the names of eleven white officers who commanded black troops. The Rebel government had initially considered putting such officers on trial for inciting slave rebellion, but this was not done. Nevertheless racial issues bedeviled the black prisoners for the duration of their captivity. Pvt. Isaac Gaskins of the 29th USCT, although wounded, was punched in the side with the butt of a musket wielded by a Rebel guard at Danville. This brutal blow caused internal injuries from which Gaskins never recovered. Moreover he suffered frostbite while working barefoot on Confederate fortifications during the winter of 1864–65. The black prisoner-workers received "vile stuff" to eat and could not maintain their strength.[32]

Butler put several Confederate prisoners to work on his Dutch Gap Canal as retaliation when some of his own black soldiers, who had been captured during the Fifth Offensive at Petersburg in late September, were used to build Rebel defenses. Confederate authorities investigated and found that sixty-eight black prisoners, all of them supposedly captured on July 30, had also been sent to labor on fortifications by October 2. Reports indicated that eleven of those sixty-eight were free blacks, but the rest were slaves. This last was an important point to the Confederates, for they treated any black prisoners who had been slaves before enlistment as if they were still slaves. If their masters did not come forward to claim them, the Confederate government exercised a right to use them as laborers. Of course the Union authorities could not accept this, but there was comparatively little that could be done about it.[33]

Despite the breakdown of the exchange cartel between North and South in 1864, many of the prisoners taken in the Battle of the Crater were released before the end of the war. Secretary of War Edwin M. Stanton asked that Stephen Weld and another officer be released on parole so they could coordinate the shipment of clothing and other needed articles to ease the suffering of captives in Southern prisons. Grant and the Confederate commissioner in charge of prisoner exchange made the arrangements.[34]

When the war ended, most surviving prisoners captured on July 30 returned thin, emaciated, and ill. Seven of the eighteen men captured from the 17th Vermont died in prison, many from wounds that were improperly treated by the Confederates. Benjamin Spear of the 57th Massachusetts recalled that about half of his acquaintances in prison never made it back home.[35]

Squabbling, Finger Pointing, and Judgment

It was obvious to many that Meade or Burnside had to go before the army could put the disaster behind itself and move forward. Meade had "been in long enough, he is tired out!" remarked an officer in the 2nd Corps who assumed that Hancock would be "the next *victim*" to be put in charge of the Army of the Potomac. Ninth Corps men thought Meade was jealous of Burnside and therefore did not support his attack strongly enough. When he read rumors of his impending dismissal in the *New York Herald*, Meade cracked a joke about it: "Oh, that's bad; that's very bad! I shall have to go and live in that house in Philadelphia; ha! ha! ha!" But there also were plenty of rumors that the 9th Corps would be broken up or moved back to the West, while its commander would be shelved for incompetence.[36]

"I am in the midst of my row with Burnside," Meade informed his wife on August 3. He deliberately brought matters to a head by requesting an investigation of the "recent miserable failure," preferring charges against Burnside and even asking to be relieved of the army command. The key point with Meade was Burnside's intemperate response to his demand for an explanation as to why his men were not moving out of the breach, a demand the 9th Corps leader "chose to construe into an imputation on his veracity." The army's provost marshal general characterized the general as "very hard & unfeeling," saying there was "no sympathy in his disposition" toward Burnside. Willcox tried to mediate the conflict. Meade explained the true meaning of his demand for an explanation as having nothing to do with Burnside's truthfulness, but he had no intention of explaining this to Burnside. When Willcox relayed this news to the 9th Corps leader, Burnside refused to believe it. When another mutual friend told him the same thing, Burnside visited Grant at City Point for advice and decided to withdraw his response to Meade's demand. By then the army commander's charges had been announced, however, and it was too late.[37]

The Court of Inquiry

In the end Meade's request to be relieved and his charges against Burnside were ignored, but Grant agreed to mount an investigation. Meade was able to pack the court of inquiry with officers who tended to see things his way. Hancock, Ayres, and Nelson A. Miles constituted the panel, and Edmund Schriver, Meade's inspector general, acted as recorder. When the court met on August 2, the first order of business was to report that it had convened without higher authority than the army command. Meade asked Grant to intercede with Lincoln for the highest authority possible, and that was done. Burnside asked Lincoln to appoint officers from outside the Army of the Potomac, but the president felt comfortable with Meade's nominees and confirmed them.[38]

A number of officers involved in the attack spoke on the first day, August 8, their testimony recorded by a phonographer named Finley Anderson. Meade began by stating that he did not want to assign blame but wanted to discover the facts regarding why the attack had failed. Because he still did not have an official report from anyone in the 9th Corps, he had "been groping in the dark" since July 30. Burnside availed himself of a lawyer, who cross-examined the army commander, but Meade felt that he had given him "as good as he sent."[39]

Burnside did not want to testify, but friends in the army urged him to do so in order to put pressure on Meade. The corps commander did all he could to protect himself and his subordinates. He argued that the chief cause of failure lay in Meade's change of plan to go straight ahead rather than widening the breach.[40]

When the court took a break from August 13 to August 28 to accommodate the Fourth Offensive at Petersburg, Burnside left the army. Lyman rode to 9th Corps headquarters on August 13 and was surprised to find a party in progress. As a brass band played, Potter, Willcox, and Ferrero enjoyed a drink, and Burnside's staff packed their leader's papers and belongings for a thirty-day leave of absence. Lyman correctly assumed the leave would extend itself into permanent separation from the army. Burnside set out for the North that night, leaving Willcox temporarily in command. Meade was "intensely angry" that Grant allowed Burnside to take many of his staff members with him, but Willcox did not have to worry long; John Parke, Burnside's trusted chief of staff, returned to duty by August 14 and soon after was assigned to command the 9th Corps.[41]

After the court resumed hearings on August 28, a long string of army officers testified that they lacked faith in many aspects of the operation, implicating Burnside as the linchpin of failure. Adelbert Ames summed up the implied criticism of Burnside by arguing that lack of overall direction was the fundamental cause of failure. "Everybody appeared to be acting for himself with no particular determination to go any farther than he was compelled to," Ames said.[42]

After meeting seventeen days, from August 6 to September 9, and hearing testimony from thirty-two officers, the court of inquiry concluded that the formation of the attacking force had been poorly planned. Rather than moving forward by the flank, all units should have moved up in battle line. The court faulted Burnside for not preparing the forward Union line so that his men could advance in lines. The officers also noted Burnside's underutilization of engineer officers and troops, his dismal lack of leadership on the division level, and the fact that no officer of higher authority was close enough to the scene to push things along at the critical moment. Burnside bore the brunt of this, but the court also cited Ledlie, Ferrero, and Willcox for various levels of failing to do all they could. The court even criticized Bliss for hanging back with half of his brigade in the Union position. The court's only left-handed criticism of Meade lay in its finding that he should have named someone to command all troops rather than relying on army headquarters to coordinate everything.[43]

As Meade hoped, the weight of court disapproval landed on Burnside. Parke's 9th Corps subordinates had to take their medicine too. Zenas Bliss was miffed by the court's finding and argued that he was no farther from the crater than Potter had been. Potter sympathized with Bliss but advised him not to request a court of inquiry to clear his name. Potter told him that "the Board did not amount to anything" and the brigade leader ought to forget about it.[44]

After vacationing in the White Mountains of New Hampshire, Burnside returned to his home in Providence by late August, just before the court of inquiry finished its deliberations. He wanted a new assignment, but Grant advised him to wait and to send his staff members back to the field in the meantime. By mid-October, Grant admitted that he did not want to send Burnside back to the Army of the Potomac, considering the bad feelings existing between him and Meade, but he also could not spare the 9th Corps from the lines at Petersburg. Burnside's connection with the corps he had created and led for nearly the entire war had ended. Grant permitted Burnside to visit the Army of the Potomac in mid-November but conveniently left to visit his wife in New Jersey, thereby avoiding a personal interview. While trying to track down the general in chief, Burnside ran across Meade at City Point, but the two pointedly said nothing to each other. Burnside told Willcox that he was willing to apologize to Meade for accusing him of ungentlemanly conduct in their heated exchange of dispatches on July 30, but only *after* he received a new command. Burnside wanted to either be put to use in the field or to resign, but Grant and Lincoln were unable to accommodate either request until the end of the war gave Burnside an opportunity to leave the army.[45]

Ledlie gave no testimony before the court of inquiry. Granted a twenty-day sick leave on August 4, he left the army five days later. "Ledlie is gone! Hurrah!" exulted one of his staff officers. "I never met anyone more thorough[ly] black-guard, in a responsible place, or one who had less sense of his duty." Because of chronic diarrhea, Ledlie did not report for duty until December 8. Meade had no interest in assigning him to a command and asked Grant to send him away. Grant readily agreed, and Ledlie returned north. He offered his resignation several times before it was finally accepted in March 1865. Ledlie suffered from a number of debilitating ailments throughout the remainder of his life, endured the death of his son, and carried on an active career as a civil engineer, especially in the railroad industry. He succumbed to his many health problems on August 15, 1882, while living in St. Mark's Hotel on Staten Island, New York.[46]

In December 1864 Senator Henry Anthony of Rhode Island introduced a resolution calling for an investigation of the battle by the joint congressional committee known as the Committee on the Conduct of the War. It had wide-ranging authority to look into almost any aspect of the war effort, and Anthony was concerned about countering the negative publicity accorded Burnside, a resident of Providence. The committee responded, for its members had long identified Meade as a politically conservative general, whereas they admired Burnside's readiness to use black troops in a prominent role on the battlefield. Committee members traveled to Petersburg to begin hearings by late December. Meade girded for his second confrontation with the politicians, following their investigation into his handling of the Gettysburg campaign, because he knew they were "prejudiced and biased" against him and believed that their examinations were "not conducted with fairness."[47]

The committee members, Senators Zachariah Chandler (Republican of Michigan) and Benjamin F. Harding (Democrat of Oregon) and Representatives Benjamin F. Loan (Republican of Missouri) and George W. Julian (Republican of Indiana), met at Meade's headquarters to begin testimony on December 17. They listened to fourteen people, half of them 9th Corps officers. Burnside began by asserting his faith in the black troops; Meade criticized the lack of "vim" with which the 9th Corps attacked. When Hunt and Duane finished their testimony, they came away "laughing" because, as Meade explained it, the committee members "stopped them and said that was enough" when they began to say anything "unfavorable to Burnside." Meade wanted to find an ally in the Senate to counteract the fallout from this investigation but then decided to wait until he could have a face-to-face consultation with the secretary of war.[48]

The committee resumed its hearings in Washington, D.C., on January 13, and the first to step forward was Henry Pleasants. He had not appeared before the court of inquiry because he had feared repercussions for himself, and for certain generals, if he spoke his mind to the officers of that court. Instead Pleasants had requested a leave of absence to attend to personal business, and Meade had granted it. In fact Pleasants was already out of the army by the time he appeared before the committee, having been discharged following the expiration of his term of service the previous month. Pleasants spoke forcefully in Burnside's favor, criticizing Meade and Duane for not believing in the mine.[49]

The Committee on the Conduct of the War concluded that the first and greatest cause for the disaster of July 30 was Meade's change of Burnside's plan of attack. The members also faulted Burnside for choosing the replacement unit by lot.[50]

The 9th Corps troops and Burnside's friends agreed with the committee findings when they were published in early February 1865, but Meade tried to save his reputation. He asked Grant to talk to Stanton when the general in chief visited Washington a few days later; Grant conveniently forgot to do so. To counteract this "severe censure upon me," Meade requested that the findings of the court of inquiry be published as well. Grant assured Meade that he sympathized with the army commander's frustration. "Gen Burnsides evidence apparently has been their guide," Grant wrote of the congressmen, and "to draw it mildly he has forgotten some of the facts." The court's opinion was published in the *Army and Navy Journal* by early March, and Meade felt it completely vindicated him in the eyes of the public. Through all of this, Meade assured a friend in the Senate that he held "no personal feeling against Burnside, and no desire to injure him."[51]

Meade's wife assumed Grant had testified against her husband when she read the committee report, but Meade assured her that the congressmen had "distorted his testimony, my own, and that of every one who hold the truth." In fact Grant blamed himself in his testimony because he knew that Ledlie was the worst division leader in the 9th Corps and had not done anything about it before July 30.[52]

In 1878 Grant also criticized Warren to a newspaper reporter for losing a golden chance to win on July 30, saying, "But when he should have been in the works he was worrying over what other corps would do. So the chance was lost." Grant said he felt he should have relieved Warren of 5th Corps command as a result but "did not like to injure an officer of so high rank for what was an error of judgment." A few years later, Grant carefully discussed the Battle of the Crater in his memoirs. In a self-serving fashion, he printed nearly the full text of his July 24 order to Meade, which gave detailed instructions about how the attack should be conducted. Grant blamed Meade for forcing Burnside to replace Ferrero with a white division (ignoring his own role in supporting Meade's viewpoint), but he also blamed Burnside for not removing obstructions in front of the Union line. He further blamed Ledlie and Ferrero but praised Ord, Potter, and Willcox. He also praised Warren for fulfilling his orders, even if he did not go beyond them. Grant shaped many aspects of his memory of the Crater Battle to coincide with the dominant political line rather than with his own viewpoints at the time of the attack.[53]

It is probably true, as historian Bruce Tap has suggested, that the committee's well-established antagonism toward Meade influenced the army commander to take Ferrero's division from the vanguard of the attack, fearful of the political fallout resulting from a slaughter of black troops within the context of military failure. In that sense the political influence committee members sought to wield backfired. Whether one was a partisan of Meade or Burnside, it was easy to criticize the judgment of civilians, public officials, and newspapermen alike over a matter that military men could best understand. "Meanwhile, the immaculate, patriotic, self-sacrificing, heroic public will eat their good dinners & make their cent per cent," complained Willcox to his wife, "while they curse that infernal blunder & those blundering generals at Petersburg."[54]

CONCLUSION

Pegram's Salient

Sanders's and Weisiger's brigades held Pegram's Salient until the night of August 1, when they returned to Wilcox Farm on the far Confederate right. Except for a few days, Elliott's South Carolinians held the salient until March 15, 1865. What was left of Pegram's Virginia battery took position on a secondary line to the rear of the salient for the remainder of the campaign and only one gun, a twenty-four-pounder howitzer, was emplaced in the battery's former position. Crew members of Kelly's South Carolina battery of Coit's battalion manned the piece.[1]

The crater was a difficult assignment for weeks following the battle. Gases from the buried bodies inside the hole seeped up through the ground and created a horrible smell. The South Carolinians spread lime to disinfect the area, and green flies buzzed around. "Every attempt to eat or even open one's mouth caused nausea," remembered a man in the 23rd South Carolina. The Confederates continued to find bodies of their companions, killed and buried in the mine explosion, for days after the battle, but they also feasted on the contents of Union haversacks left behind when the owners were shot or marched away as prisoners. J. Warren Pursley of the 18th South Carolina lived well on crackers, potatoes, onions, coffee, and sugar. He also found eating utensils and pulled "a mighty good pair of shoes" from the feet of "an old dead yankee."[2]

The Confederates reworked fortifications in and around the jagged hole. Beginning August 10, they constructed a new cavalier immediately on the Confederate side and made loopholes in the parapet north and south of the crater as well, using gabions, sandbags, and blocks of wood faced with iron plating. (The cavalier still stands, up to ten feet tall and ninety yards long.) The Confederates also moved their main line back a few feet for about fifty yards on both sides of the crater to take better advantage of the landscape. They dug a line of works in the shallow ravine west of the crater, the staging area for the counterattacks on July 30, to serve as yet another line of defense.[3]

The Confederates had no skirmish line immediately in front of the salient before the battle, but they dug one forty feet from the crater by mid-September. An archaeological dig of a twenty-foot-long section of the trench in 1985 found that the compacted earth of the floor held two fire pits. The diggers found five logs studded with ninety-six bullets. Hundreds of percussion caps littered the floor, and melted lead slag around the fire pits indicated the Confederates might have been trying to make usable bullets from fired Union balls. Presumably the burial trenches were located between the fortified Confederate skirmish line and the forward Union trench; erosion soon exposed parts of bodies because not more than a foot of dirt had been used as cover.[4]

The Confederates recovered one of the two guns blown out of the left side of the salient by the mine explosion, the one that landed twenty yards forward, by the end of August. The piece that landed forty yards away required more time to recover. Coit reported that both guns were reached by digging saps toward them. They were refurbished and placed in position near the Gee House.[5]

The smell of death never completely went away inside the crater, and the thought of resting "on hundreds of negroes every night" unnerved many men. Officers of the 17th South Carolina preferred to sleep in bombproofs to the rear, but the rank and file had no such option. They curled up in their blankets on the firing step to avoid the floor of the crater. As time went by, erosion softened the contour of the hole and filled it up a bit. An English engineer officer who visited the Confederate lines reported the hole was only ten feet deep and fifty yards by thirty yards in diameter by November. Like the Federals who dug the gallery, the Confederates made crosses and hearts out of the raw clay of the crater and sent them home as souvenirs.[6]

Rebel engineers wanted to find the Union gallery because they were afraid the Federals might use it for another blast. Lt. Edwin Wise and ten men started a new shaft inside the south side of the crater on the morning of July 31. When another detail of ten men arrived at noon, he started a second shaft at the north end. On August 1, Wise hit several cavities at the bottom of the northern shaft, twenty-four feet below the top of the Confederate parapet. He assumed they were evidence of the Union gallery or powder chambers. The men stopped working for fear of a cave-in because the earth was unstable owing to the mine explosion.[7]

Maj. W. W. Blackford, who took charge of countermining at Pegram's Salient on August 1, supervised Wise's work. He did not believe Wise when the lieutenant reported his men fainted from the gas seeping through fissures into

Visitors to the crater soon after the war. Vol. 1, 45, Massachusetts Commandery, Military Order of the Loyal Legion and the U.S. Army Military History Institute

his shaft from decomposing bodies. Wise also reported that one could still smell gunpowder in the shaft, left over from the explosion on July 30. Black-ford went down with a candle and a rope tied around his waist to see for him-self. He hardly reached the bottom of the shaft when the candle nearly flickered out and he breathed a lungful of gas. Men on the top had to pull him out, and Blackford did not get all of the gas out of his system for days. Blackford was convinced; he obtained fans from Richmond used in blowing the chaff from wheat and rigged a canvas tube with hoops to improvise a ventilation system.[8]

The cavities that Wise had discovered on August 1 were inconclusive evi-dence of the Union gallery. The Confederates continued to dig until hitting the gallery with certainty by September 25. The Engineer Bureau in Richmond was interested in the Union mine, requesting as much information, "in the Engi-neering point of view," as local officers could provide.[9]

Ironically the Confederates had some reason to worry that the Federals might reuse the gallery. On August 5, Potter reported to Burnside that the gallery was intact up to the tamping. He suggested new branch galleries could be run from the intact section diagonally to the Confederate line north or south of the crater. Burnside forwarded this information to army headquarters with his recommendation to try it, arguing that the new branches could be finished in "a few days." Understandably Meade ignored the suggestion.[10]

Federal prisoners warned the Rebels that more mines could be expected; this contributed to a growing fear among the rank and file that peaked in early August. A private in the 41st Alabama developed a boring tool that could be used to dig a small hole many feet into the ground to intercept a mine gallery. As soon as a number of these borers were manufactured, dozens of Confederate soldiers used them along the trench line. From his position north of the crater, Gracie noticed that the Federals were "bringing dirt from under the hill near Elliott's left" and worried that another mine attack was under way.[11]

The Confederates exploded a mine of their own soon after the Crater Battle, but it was a defensive move rather than an attack designed to break open the Union line. The Federals had extended a sap into no-man's-land near Gracie's Salient to gain access to some slightly advantageous ground near the Rebel picket line. Confederate engineers could not be certain of their intentions, so they decided to extend the gallery of a countermine at that location and blow up the sap. Hugh T. Douglas was in charge of the operation. He prepared the mine by the morning of August 1, but the burial truce caused a delay. When it ended, Douglas and two civilian miners in his employ tried to spring the mine, but it failed to detonate because of a defective safety fuse.[12]

Douglas dismantled the preparation and extended the gallery even further before exploding the charge. He created two powder chambers, each filled with 425 pounds of explosives, and tamped the gallery only up to the level of the powder barrels, leaving two feet of clear space. Douglas created a cotton tubing to hold the powder train. He set off the mine at 6:30 P.M., August 5. The explosion, occurring forty yards in front of the left wing of the 18th Corps line, failed to damage the head of the sap. Both sides exchanged artillery and small-arms fire for a half hour afterward, which led to some casualties, but the mine itself caused no damage. Federal observers were puzzled as to its purpose, even though they were ready for a follow-up attack.[13]

The August 5 mine nearly ended Douglas's bright career as an engineer officer. Under great pressure, perhaps depressed over his failure to intercept Pleasants's mine, Douglas lost his temper when Col. Thomas M. R. Talcott of the 1st Confederate Engineers pushed him to work faster in preparing the powder chamber on August 5. Retorting that he "was not a miner," Douglas failed to tamp the gallery all the way to the top. Talcott filed charges because of his insubordinate attitude. Douglas later apologized for his actions and was allowed to resign his engineer's commission. He finished the war as a civilian engineer employed by the Confederate army.[14]

The Crater battlefield was the scene of two small fights after July 30. Grant gave up frontal attacks for the time and concentrated on extending the Union line west of the Jerusalem Plank Road. During the Sixth Offensive, on October 27, the major thrust of operations lay far to the west, but 2nd Corps troops

Another image depicting a visit to the crater soon after the war. Vol. 110, 5664, Massachusetts Commandery, Military Order of the Loyal Legion and the U.S. Army Military History Institute

mounted a small attack against the emplacement formally held by Davidson's battery. It was now occupied by elements of Goode's Virginia brigade and often referred to as Fort Crater by the Federals. Ordered to mount a demonstration to draw Confederate attention, a strike force of one hundred men was assembled from the 148th Pennsylvania. It sallied forth that evening and quickly took the fort, capturing seventeen men and an artillery piece. A supporting regiment failed to advance, so the Federals fell back after holding the earthwork for twenty minutes. The strike force lost more than a third of its number in this futile capture.[15]

The Confederates mounted a retaliatory raid in front of Pegram's Salient on the night of November 5. Two hundred men of the Holcombe Legion, of Elliott's South Carolina brigade, gathered in the Rebel picket line that had been constructed two months before. They sallied forth and captured a section of the picket line the Federals had constructed, but found it was untenable. The Yankees had cut away the counterscarp of the trench so they could fire into it from their main line if the Rebels occupied the work. The Carolinians brought up tools, but bullets flew too freely to rework the trench; the Legion men evacuated the trench before dawn.[16]

On January 29 the Confederates raised a flag of truce and asked that three commissioners pass through the lines at Pegram's Salient to discuss peace terms with representatives of Lincoln's government. Willcox, who was responsible for this part of the line, referred them to Parke, and eventually the three men were allowed through to meet Lincoln at Hampton Roads. The

Peace Commission foundered on Confederate refusal to accept the abolition of slavery as a precondition for further negotiations.[17]

The Petersburg campaign ended with heavy fighting miles west of the crater on April 2, causing Lee to evacuate Petersburg that night. James Coit waited until the infantry pulled out, then he sent Kelly's South Carolina gunners on their way and spiked the twenty-four-pounder howitzer because it was too heavy to quickly take it out of the salient. "Not a Confederate was to be seen as we marched down the line and through the covered way to Petersburg," Coit recalled.[18]

The next day Meade and a group of staff officers visited the salient. As Lyman put it, their examination made painfully apparent "what a short distance lay between the 'crater' and that wished for crest!"[19]

Three Veterans

There is no evidence that three men intimately associated with the mine ever visited Petersburg again. Jacob Douty, who risked his life to help Henry Reese repair the disrupted fuse, made a living as a boilermaker after the war. The leg injury he suffered during the East Tennessee campaign, plus a stiff shoulder, inhibited his ability to work, and Douty received a government pension in the amount of $4.25 per month from 1882 until his death thirteen years later.[20]

Henry Reese received a lieutenant's commission in October 1864 and led Company E, 48th Pennsylvania, in the 9th Corps attack on the Confederate works along the Jerusalem Plank Road on April 2, 1865. He was hit by grapeshot on the right arm and injured. Parke recommended him for a Medal of Honor because of his bravery in entering the mine gallery, but there is no indication he received it. The Welshman left the army in July 1865.[21]

Reese served as a bodyguard for a mining boss during the Mollie Maguire disturbances in Pennsylvania from 1876 to 1878, but he also operated a saloon and worked as a butcher. For many years he served as a police officer in Shamokin, Pennsylvania. While arresting a prisoner in 1885, a pistol held by a friend of the accused accidentally went off. The bullet broke Reese's left index finger. When he applied for a pension a few years later, Reese claimed that his April 2 wound, plus asthma, reduced his ability to make a living, but the examining physicians did not believe this to be true. They found the former miner to be in good shape and noticed that he suddenly pretended weakness in his right arm partway through the examination. Reese died in 1893 after he developed complications from an abscessed tooth. He had been widely known as Snapper after the war, because he seemed to have no fear.[22]

Before his death Reese spoke candidly of his experiences on July 30 to James Guthrie, who reproduced his commentary in a book on African Americans in the Civil War. "If I had known what a blunder was going to be made in the assault after the mine had been made such a success," Reese said, "I never would have gone into it to relight the fuse." Reese felt sorry that the black troops were shoved into the breach after the operation had degenerated into chaos, but, he said, "they went in cheering as though they didn't mind it, and a great many of them never came back." The Confederates who had been blown up in their sleep and the Federals trapped in the crater elicited Reese's sympathy. The former may have thought "it was only a nightmare that ailed them," he said, but the latter died "hemmed in and shot down with their eyes open" and therefore "had a worse lot."[23]

Henry Pleasants endured a period of depression following the mine attack. While serving as general of the trenches on August 5, he became "beastly intoxicated" and ordered members of the 6th New Hampshire to drop their guns and charge the Confederate position with sharp knives. Pleasants called them cowards when they refused and boasted that his 48th Pennsylvania would do it. Pleasants also was serving as temporary commander of Griffin's brigade at the time. Officials drafted court-martial charges and specifications, but he was never tried. Instead Pleasants received a twenty-day leave of absence on August 20 and was mustered out following the expiration of his term of service on December 18, 1864. He was brevetted brigadier general of volunteers in March 1865 as a reward for his mine work. Parke also recommended brevets for Lt. Col. Theodore Gregg of the 45th Pennsylvania, Lt. Col. Percy Daniels of the 7th Rhode Island, Capt. Peleg E. Peckham of Bliss's staff, Col. Delevan Bates of the 30th USCT, Col. Charles S. Russell of the 28th USCT, and Capt. George A. Hicks of Ferrero's staff because of their actions on July 30.[24]

Pleasants's war experience had been clouded by personal tragedy, according to his family. He had married Sallie Bannon of Pottsville, Pennsylvania, in 1860, but her death a short time later plunged him into deep grief. His aunt suggested he go to war to help deal with the trauma, and Pleasants confided to his uncle after he returned home that he had "recklessly exposed" himself many times in action in the hope of being killed.[25]

Pleasants continued his career in the coal fields after the conflict. His controversial monument to coal mine engineering lay in the Pottsville Shafts, one mile north of town, begun in 1874 to reach veins that lay more than eleven hundred feet below the surface. Pleasants disagreed with many who thought coal veins that deep would be crushed by the weight above and rendered useless for mining. His two shafts enabled the Reading Coal and Iron Company to obtain fifty million tons of good-quality coal, even though critics continued to argue that similar deposits of shallow coal could have been found. Pleasants remarried and fathered three children. He died of an undisclosed illness on April 1, 1880. Characterized as "energetic, resolute, and self-reliant" in his

Reclaiming land north of the crater after the war. Vol. 6, 290, Massachusetts
Commandery, Military Order of the Loyal Legion and the U.S. Army Military
History Institute

civilian career, it also seemed to many that he was "impatient of advice and
never cared to consult with anybody on plans or details."[26]

What Went Wrong, What Went Right

Opinions about why the Union attack failed have never ceased to intrigue students since the guns fell silent on July 30. Meade often received the lion's share
of the blame because he compelled Burnside to change what seemed to be a
good plan and because he issued the order to pull out of the captured works
after several hours of forcing more troops into it. The pullout order, unaccom-
panied by efforts to support the withdrawal, contributed to heavy losses as
Burnside's men were left on their own hook. All of the accusations have merit,
except that, considering their performance when attacked by Weisiger, using
the black troops to lead the attack was no guarantee of victory.[27]

   The chief blame for the failure of July 30 must rest with Burnside. It was not
Meade's fault that Burnside elected to choose the lead division by drawing lots,
and it was not Meade's fault that Burnside apparently confused his division
leaders while giving them instructions for the next day. It also was not Meade's
fault that a thoroughly incompetent officer had been allowed to command
Burnside's 1st Division for weeks. All of those issues were the responsibility of

the 9th Corps commander. Critics tended to blame Burnside for the wrong things; it was not important that he failed to tear away the Federal abatis or that he failed to provide a better method for his men to cross the forward Union line. Neither impediment delayed the Union advance in any significant way. The seeds of failure were planted at 9th Corps headquarters on the night of July 29.

Ledlie's refusal to share his men's fate in the captured works was deplorable, but there is every reason to believe that the attack would have failed even if he had done so. An incompetent commander probably should stay in the rear and let his subordinates handle the situation. There is no doubt that Ledlie took a few drinks to steady his nerves during the battle, but there is no evidence that he was inebriated. Nevertheless it is difficult to imagine that Ledlie would have restarted the advance if he had entered the crater.

While the chances of success were severely crippled by command failures, one wonders if the attack would have succeeded if those failures had not taken place. There were many other factors that impeded success over which Meade, Burnside, and Ledlie had no control. Pleasants could not demolish the cavalier, traverses, and bombproofs connected to the salient. Even the part of the Confederate fortifications he did blow up was replaced by an enormous hole, which served as a physical obstruction to the organized movement of troops. In short, the mine explosion could not make a clear path for the rapid advance of Burnside's men. Despite much postwar commentary, there is little evidence that Ledlie's men were paralyzed by the shock of stepping foot into this hole; they remained there because their commanders thought that was what they were supposed to do.

Would there have been any advantage to the Federals to hold the breach rather than evacuate it (or, as happened, to be driven out of it)? Neither Grant nor Meade thought so, but Charles Venable of Lee's staff said he believed "it would have been a very serious disaster had the enemy even simply held the captured salient until nightfall," because that would have broken "the integrity of our lines." If Burnside's men could have held the breach long enough to rework the ground and prepare a strong position, they might have drained Lee's manpower by compelling him to launch major counterstrikes to reclaim the ground.[28]

The history of military mining did not favor success on July 30. Willcox made this point in his testimony before the Committee on the Conduct of the War and in his unpublished memoirs. "Assaults with mining and countermining are generally considered as a series of partial, though desperate, attempts in a siege, rather than counted on as finalities, and are limited to gaining or destroying some important part of the work." He noted that Federal mining failed to break the Confederate defense line at Vicksburg. In fact, Grant's army was in the process of planting at least six mines for a final

The crater, overgrown with brush, ca. 1890. Taken by Bvt. Lieut. Col. George A. Bruce, 13th New Hampshire. RG 6415–MOL-PA 13.29, Civil War Library and Museum, MOLLUS, Philadelphia, Pennsylvania

attempt before the defenders surrendered. The Federals started mine galleries at Port Hudson, at Cold Harbor (after the failed attack of June 3), and at Kennesaw Mountain (after the failed attack of June 27) but did not push any of them very far.[29]

While Northerners discussed what went wrong, Southerners extolled what went right. The only cross words involved who deserved credit for creating victory. Survivors of Elliott's brigade argued that they set up success by holding Burnside's troops in the breach for four hours. It is unfortunate that the Virginians were loath to honor their South Carolina comrades, for the two phases of the Confederate battle depended on each other. Weisiger's attack would not have succeeded if Elliott's men had not contained the enemy, and the Carolinians needed help to repair the breach. Victory was bought by cooperative effort from Johnson's and Mahone's men, as well as from artillerymen and mortar crews. Ironically the Georgians and Alabamians who helped seal the breach never joined their Virginia comrades in aggressively claiming credit for July 30, a claim greatly motivated by postwar politics in Virginia.[30]

What had the Confederates averted by throwing back Burnside's troops and repairing the hold in their long line? That important question can only be answered with qualified confidence. To fully break Lee's line, the Federals probably needed to gain the ridgelike feature on which the Jerusalem Plank Road ran out of Petersburg. It is doubtful, however, that such a break would have led immediately to the end of the war. Lee had fallback options in a case like this; Beauregard had planned to retire across the Appomattox River and hold a strong position along Swift Creek, between Petersburg and Richmond, when his troops were battling Meade's army during the first round of fighting in mid-June. Holding Petersburg was not essential to holding Richmond, for Lee could still supply his army by way of railroads entering the Confederate capital from the west and northwest without the lines that entered Petersburg from the south. Lee gave up Richmond and retreated west when he lost Petersburg to Grant on April 2, 1865, because Sherman was bringing sixty thousand Union veterans of the western campaigns toward the city to help Grant deal with the Army of Northern Virginia. He had to move or be trapped in the capital, a threat that the Army of the Potomac and the Army of the James could not offer him in July 1864. The Battle of the Crater held the potential to end the Petersburg campaign, but probably not the war, in a single stroke.[31]

In the end the Federals wasted the Third Offensive's potential for ending the campaign in a Union victory, and the Confederates were graced with a temporary period of self-confidence because of their ability to hold the line at Petersburg. How long that period could last remained to be seen.

APPENDIX 1
After the War

The crater became an object of curiosity for visitors after the war. Journalist John T. Trowbridge found that sections of the Union gallery had caved in by September 1865. Weeds, discarded bayonets, canteens, shell fragments, and graves littered the battlefield. Black residents were collecting bullets to sell to the curious, for four cents per pound. "It was hard work, but they made a living at it," Trowbridge asserted. Lieutenant Colonel Whitehurst of the 16th Virginia visited the site soon after the war and vividly recalled seeing the hand of a skeleton sticking aboveground, with faded gray cloth indicating he had been a Rebel soldier.[1]

Landowners began to reclaim their property for agricultural purposes, stripping the wooden revetments from the Confederate works and drying them in the sun before reusing the timbers. They also started to level the connecting works north and south, isolating the crater on the battlefield. The federal government began to exhume the dead buried on the battlefield in July 1866. Crews uncovered 669 bodies in the crater area, at least 300 of them inside the crater itself, and reburied them in Poplar Grove National Cemetery a few miles to the west. They failed to clean up the bits of uniform, wasted equipment, and bones that lay around for years to come.[2]

The Griffith family, which owned the land around the crater, exploited its tourist potential. William H. Griffith fenced in the hole by 1867 and charged twenty-five cents for admission, listing visitors such as James Longstreet, Fitzhugh Lee, and Edward Porter Alexander in his record book. He also built the Crater Saloon to sell refreshments and set up a small museum at the entrance to the site, displaying relics picked up on the battlefield. A wide variety of artifacts, including broken muskets, a shovel with bullet holes in it, cooking utensils, and two bullets that met and fused in midair, were on display.[3]

When William Griffith died in 1873, he passed the property to his son Timothy Rives Griffith. Timothy had witnessed the Petersburg campaign as a twelve-year-old boy. He saw Harris and Jones stake out the Harris Line on June 17, and Pegram's battery take up its position that evening. On July 30 Timothy went perilously close to the fighting, standing near the Gee House to watch Weisiger charge and pull the lanyard of a nearby mortar. He also

Group of visitors, probably veterans, viewing the crater in 1887. Vol. 106, 5181, Massachusetts Commandery, Military Order of the Loyal Legion and the U.S. Army Military History Institute

witnessed the burial truce. Griffith continued to operate the crater as a tourist attraction. Veterans of the battle often were allowed in free, but some of them resented the fact that anyone had to pay admission.[4]

As time passed, more and more survivors of the battle visited the site to refresh their memories. Freeman Bowley, who had survived imprisonment as well as the engagement, came in 1888 to find that bullets still littered the ground. Griffith allowed trees to grow at the crater's edge, plus "a good-size peach tree" on the bottom, and grass stabilized the soil and arrested further erosion. Sgt. James W. Lathe of the 9th New Hampshire visited the crater with his son in 1893 and toured the site with Griffith and two Confederate veterans. "Looking back now it seems like a horrible dream," he wrote.[5]

Griffith constructed a frame house only twenty yards behind the crater for his family. He kept the entrance to Pleasants's gallery closed by allowing brush to grow in front of it, and brush also filled one of the two Union covered ways that had served as avenues of attack. The other covered way was gone by 1904. The spring at the junction of the main Confederate covered way and the branch ravine still provided water at the turn of the century.[6]

The Griffith family sold the land by 1918. Seven years later the Crater Battlefield Association acquired it and constructed a clubhouse near the hole and an eighteen-hole golf course nearby. Workers uncovered the remains of twenty-nine men while making the greens. They were Federal soldiers, many with crushed skulls, and the paper of their cartridges was still intact. The association also dug out the Union gallery in 1926, put in new wooden stairs and electricity, and opened a section leading toward the Federal line from the crater. Bankruptcy forced the association to close the golf course in 1934, and the federal government began to acquire the battlefield two years later, adding it to the Petersburg National Military Park, which had been created in 1932.[7]

The park used a house the association built near the hole as a visitor center and museum until 1955. Thirteen years later a new visitor center was constructed at Battery No. 5 of the Dimmock Line. Park officials dismantled the association's golf course and closed the crater entrance to Pleasants's gallery, although they retained the entrance as a landmark until maintenance problems forced them to cover it up in 1946. In 1963 the government constructed a tour road within the park, linking the crater area with the rest of the holdings by constructing a bridge over the Norfolk and Petersburg Railroad (now called the Norfolk and Western Railroad) and extending that road to link with Jerusalem Plank Road. The Union end of Pleasants's gallery was cleared up and marked by 1967, and a vista was opened up between Fort Morton and the crater in the mid-1970s. How long Davidson's battery site survived the war is unclear, but it would have been destroyed, at any rate, during construction of the interchange at Interstate 95 and Route 460 in the mid-1960s.[8]

A number of archaeological digs took place in and around the crater to determine exact locations and measurements of various features associated with the battle. The Civilian Conservation Corps conducted one such effort in 1937, and National Park Service personnel managed digs in 1958 and 1962. A more extensive effort was undertaken by Historic Conservation and Interpretation of Paterson, New Jersey, under contract with the park service, in 1975. This dig uncovered more evidence of the 1920s development of the gallery as a tourist attraction than evidence of Civil War construction. A series of auger holes bored into the crater failed to go deeper than the area of earth that had been disturbed by the mine blast.[9]

Pleasants's gallery still has several sections that are caved in, allowing the interested visitor to trace its course from the entrance to the crater. No remnant of the firing step constructed by the Confederates inside the crater is visible, although the new cavalier dug after the engagement is well preserved. A monument to the 48th Pennsylvania stands where the gallery enters the crater today, and flank markers erected by veterans of the 2nd Pennsylvania Provisional Heavy Artillery stand just in front of the postbattle Confederate cavalier. The Petersburg chapter of the United Daughters of the Confederacy erected a monument, in November 1910, at the northern end of the cavalier to denote the right flank of Weisiger's brigade after its charge. The Petersburg chapter also erected an obelisk to honor Mahone on the Confederate side of the cavalier, and the South Carolina Division of the UDC erected a monument to Elliott's brigade north of the crater in 1923. The citizens of Petersburg commemorated the battle by erecting an obelisk-like monument on July 30, 1964, and the State of Massachusetts erected a monument where the park service road joins Jerusalem Plank Road to honor all units from that state that served in the Army of the Potomac and the Army of the James during the war.[10]

Cultural Legacy

William Mahone became identified with the battle of the crater more than any single person on the Confederate side. He lived in Petersburg after the war, engaging in the railroad business and becoming a conservative member of the state's Republican Party. He favored Reconstruction but not the disenfranchisement of former Confederates, nor the granting of black rights. His support for Reconstruction was tied mostly to his desire to promote business and economic development. By the 1870s Mahone had become the leader of the

Another view of the crater in 1887. Vol. 101, 5185, Massachusetts Commandery, Military Order of the Loyal Legion and the U.S. Army Military History Institute

Readjustors, who sought to adjust the state government's obligation to pay Virginia's war-derived debt, as opposed to the Funder faction, which advocated the raising of more money to pay all of the debt. The Readjustors dominated Virginia politics from 1879 to 1883, using a coalition of black and white political support.[11]

Mahone's controversial stand on postwar politics made him a target of Lost Cause advocates, who held no room for Reconstruction in their hearts. But he also became the target of resentment by David Weisiger, who had survived the wound he received while leading Mahone's brigade forward on July 30. Weisiger claimed that he selected the ground for placing the troops and adjusted their position before the attack. When Mahone learned of this claim in 1872, he chose to ignore it. But eight years later, in the midst of his Readjustor triumph, the scrappy general took on Weisiger in the Richmond *Whig*. Referring to his former subordinate's "singular arrogance," he claimed for himself and Girardey credit for preparing the attack. The Richmond *Commonwealth* responded by printing a letter Weisiger had written in 1876, in which he claimed credit for ordering the brigade to start its attack. Veterans of the brigade published statements in the Richmond *State* to prove that Mahone gave the order. Weisiger and Mahone wrote fresh statements of their positions in response to this paper war.[12]

Mahone and many of his partisans used the Crater Battle as the centerpiece of a campaign to glorify the Confederate cause. The fact that they had saved Petersburg, not just from Yankee hordes but from brutal blacks, was the focus of this creation. Joseph T. Wilson heard Mahone give a talk on the battle in 1883; seven years later Wilson published a book about black soldiers in America's wars. Wilson thought it wiser to let former Rebels "tell the stories of their butcheries than for me to attempt them" and noted with bitter irony that one orator had whipped up his audience to such a fever pitch that the Rebel yell rang out in the lecture hall. Not even First Bull Run "elicited so much comment and glorification among the confederates as that of the crater," Wilson concluded.[13]

Mahone commissioned a painting to depict the attack of his Virginians on July 30. John Adams Elder of Fredericksburg had studied in Germany and endured the Federal bombardment of his native town in mid-December 1862. After that, he served as an aide in the Confederate army and witnessed the Crater Battle. He made a good living painting scenes of war and Southern life. *The Battle of the Crater*, completed in 1870, and *After Appomattox* (ca. 1880) came to be his most famous works. His earlier painting of the crater fight, completed during the war, had been destroyed in the evacuation of Richmond. Mahone displayed the Elder painting at his home, and visitors often commented on it.[14]

Although one observer who had served in the Confederate army called Elder's painting of the battle a "ghastly, but most effective picture," most viewers found it thoroughly praiseworthy. Someone signing himself J.D. thought Elder had "entered into the battle itself," praising his character studies, detail, and use of light and dark shades. J.D. thought it would have been an even more successful work if painted in "a more subdued tone," but he believed Elder had portrayed "*battle* in its very self." John D. Young, who had not participated in the engagement, criticized Elder for not portraying Mahone or any other well-known participants. But decades later Carter R. Bishop, a civil engineer at Petersburg, argued that the Confederate who is depicted as striking down a Yankee with his clubbed musket was modeled after Emmett Richardson of the 12th Virginia. There is also evidence that the Rebel flag depicted in the painting is that of the 12th Virginia. That regiment's flag, whose staff was repaired with a ramrod after the battle, is today held by the Siege Museum at Petersburg.[15]

The survivors of Mahone's brigade held their first reunion in May 1875 at the crater, where Mahone walked across the hallowed field with his former comrades. They met again at Petersburg two years later. Federal veterans from a Grand Army of the Republic post in Newark, New Jersey, visited the crater in October 1883, and a group of thirty veterans from the 51st Pennsylvania met there two years later, visiting Mahone at his home as well. Veterans of

John A. Elder's *The Battle of the Crater.* Robert Underwood Johnson and Clarence Clough Buel, *Battles and Leaders* (New York: Century Company, 1887–88), 4:566

Students touring the crater, ca. 1930. Petersburg Museums

the 57th and 59th Massachusetts arrived in May 1887 and listened to a talk by Mahone.[16]

In the years following Mahone's death in 1895, William H. Stewart, former commander of the 61st Virginia, was "stung" by the apparent absence of credit given the brigade for its role in the battle. He organized another reunion of brigade veterans at the battlefield for November 6, 1903, and preserved details of the unit's history by collecting statements from as many participants as he could. Weisiger's veterans gathered in the shallow ravine, where they knelt to pray and listened to a long speech by Stewart, extolling their role in saving "the inhabitants of dear old Petersburg from the brutal malice of negro soldiers in the flush of success." With anywhere from ten thousand to twenty thousand spectators present, the Virginians reenacted a portion of their advance out of the ravine, and young members of the state militia carried on the charge all the way to the crater. Five companies of militiamen pretended to be Federals defending the hole. After the half-hour fight, everyone who participated received a silver medal. Of course, given the predominance of segregation in the early twentieth century, no blacks took part in the reenactment. Seventeen-year-old Douglas Southall Freeman was among the spectators; he was so impressed with the event that it played a role in forming his desire to write about the history of the Confederate war for independence. Stewart tried to stage a reenactment again in September 1905, but bad weather wrecked plans to hold another sham battle. It did not prevent the pugnacious colonel from giving another talk, which became famous as the "Field of Blood" speech, to the assembled veterans in a hall.[17]

The United Daughters of the Confederacy erected a monument honoring Mahone on July 30, 1927. The group initially wanted to place it inside Petersburg, but Mahone's memory had become controversial enough to force it out of town and to the crater, where it connoted war deeds rather than political causes. Carter Bishop continued to portray the "Petersburg boys" as "the only line between their homes and the thousands of drunken negroes making that cry ["No Quarter"] and they must be stopped or life would not be worth living." Another reenactment, held on April 30, 1937, involved three thousand participants from the U.S. Marines, the Virginia National Guard, and the cadets of the Virginia Military Institute. Douglas Southall Freeman, now an accomplished journalist and historian, addressed fifty thousand spectators. Only four Confederate veterans of the battle were in attendance.[18]

The Virginians played the dominant role in shaping the historical memory of the Crater Battle, much to the belittlement of veterans from four other states who had participated in the fight. That dominance continued as long as the Virginia veterans lived.

APPENDIX 2
Order of Battle

Armies of the United States:
Lt. Gen. Ulysses S. Grant

Army of the Potomac: Maj. Gen.
George G. Meade

9th Corps: Maj. Gen. Ambrose E.
Burnside

*1st Division: Brig. Gen. James H.
Ledlie*

1st Brigade: Brig. Gen. William F.
Bartlett
21st Massachusetts
29th Massachusetts
56th Massachusetts
57th Massachusetts
59th Massachusetts
100th Pennsylvania
2nd Brigade: Col. Elisha G. Marshall
3rd Maryland Battalion
14th New York Heavy Artillery
179th New York
2nd Pennsylvania Provisional Heavy
Artillery
35th Massachusetts (designated engineer regiment of division)

*2nd Division: Brig. Gen. Robert B.
Potter*

1st Brigade: Col. Zenas R. Bliss
36th Massachusetts
58th Massachusetts
2nd New York Mounted Rifles
51st New York

45th Pennsylvania
48th Pennsylvania
4th Rhode Island
2nd Brigade: Brig. Gen. Simon G.
Griffin
31st Maine
32nd Maine
2nd Maryland
6th New Hampshire
9th New Hampshire
11th New Hampshire
17th Vermont
7th Rhode Island (designated
engineer regiment of division)

*3rd Division: Brig. Gen. Orlando B.
Willcox*

1st Brigade: Brig. Gen. John F.
Hartranft
8th Michigan
27th Michigan (1st and 2nd
Companies, Michigan
Sharpshooters attached)
109th New York
13th Ohio Cavalry (dismounted)
51st Pennsylvania
37th Wisconsin
38th Wisconsin (5 companies)
2nd Brigade: Col. William Humphrey
1st Michigan Sharpshooters
2nd Michigan
20th Michigan
24th New York Cavalry (dismounted)

46th New York
60th Ohio (9th and 10th Companies,
    Ohio Sharpshooters attached)
50th Pennsylvania
17th Michigan (designated engineer
    regiment of division)

*4th Division: Brig. Gen. Edward
    Ferrero*

1st Brigade: Lt. Col. Joshua K. Sigfried
27th USCT
30th USCT
39th USCT
43rd USCT
2nd Brigade: Col. Henry G. Thomas
19th USCT
23rd USCT
28th USCT
29th USCT
31st USCT

**Corps Artillery Brigade: Lt. Col. J.
    Albert Monroe**

2nd Battery, Maine Light Artillery
3rd Battery, Maine Light Artillery
7th Battery, Maine Light Artillery
11th Battery, Massachusetts Light
    Artillery
19th Battery, New York Light Artillery
34th Battery, New York Light Artillery
Battery D, Pennsylvania Light Artillery
3rd Battery, Vermont Light Artillery
Mortar Battery (2nd Pennsylvania
    Provisional Heavy Artillery
    detachment)

**Army of the James: Maj. Gen. Benjamin
    F. Butler**

10th Corps: Maj. Gen. David B. Birney

*2nd Division: Brig. Gen. John W.
    Turner*

1st Brigade: Col. N. Martin Curtis
3rd New York
112th New York
117th New York
142nd New York
2nd Brigade: Lt. Col. William B.
    Coan
47th New York
48th New York
76th Pennsylvania
97th Pennsylvania
3rd Brigade: Col. Louis Bell
13th Indiana (3 companies)
9th Maine
4th New Hampshire
115th New York
169th New York

**Department of Southern Virginia and
    North Carolina: Lt. Gen. Pierre G. T.
    Beauregard**

*Johnson's Division: Maj. Gen.
    Bushrod R. Johnson*

Ransom's Brigade: Col. Lee M.
    McAfee
24th North Carolina
25th North Carolina
35th North Carolina
49th North Carolina
56th North Carolina
Elliott's Brigade: Brig. Gen. Stephen
    Elliott (W)-Col. Fitz William
    McMaster
17th South Carolina
18th South Carolina
22nd South Carolina
23rd South Carolina
26th South Carolina
Wise's Brigade: Col. J. Thomas Goode
26th Virginia
34th Virginia

46th Virginia
59th Virginia

Hoke's Division: Maj. Gen. Robert F. Hoke

Clingman's Brigade: Brig. Gen. Thomas L. Clingman
61st North Carolina

Artillery: Maj. James C. Coit
Halifax Virginia Battery: Capt. Samuel T. Wright
Petersburg Virginia Battery: Capt. Richard G. Pegram

Army of Northern Virginia: Gen. Robert E. Lee

3rd Corps: Maj. Gen. Ambrose P. Hill

Anderson's Division: Brig. Gen. William Mahone

Mahone's Brigade: Col. David Weisiger (W)-Col. George T. Rogers
6th Virginia
12th Virginia
16th Virginia
41st Virginia
61st Virginia
Wilcox's Brigade: Col. John C. C. Sanders
8th Alabama
9th Alabama
10th Alabama
11th Alabama
14th Alabama
Wright's Brigade: Lt. Col. Matthew R. Hall
3rd Georgia
22nd Georgia
48th Georgia
64th Georgia

1st Corps Artillery: Lt. Col. Frank Huger
Haskell's Battalion: Maj. John C. Haskell
Branch North Carolina Battery: Capt. Henry G. Flanner
Nelson Virginia Battery: Capt. James N. Lamkin
13th Battalion Virginia Light Artillery: Maj. Wade H. Gibbs (W)
Company A, Otey Battery: Capt. David Norvell Walker
Company B, Ringgold Battery: Capt. Crispin Dickenson
Company C, Davidson's Battery: Lt. James C. Otey
Mortar Battery: Lt. Jack Langhorne

3rd Corps Artillery: Col. Reuben L. Walker
Pegram's Battalion: Lt. Col. William J. Pegram
Crenshaw's Virginia Battery: Capt. Thomas Ellett
Letcher Virginia Light Artillery: Capt. Thomas A. Brander

NOTES

Abbreviations

AAS	American Antiquarian Society
ALPL	Abraham Lincoln Presidential Library
BHL-UM	Bentley Historical Library, University of Michigan
BPL	Boston Public Library
CWM	College of William and Mary
CWURM	Civil War and Underground Railroad Museum
DC	Dartmouth College
ECU	East Carolina University
EU	Emory University
GA	Georgia Archives
HCLA-PSU	Historical Collections and Labor Archives, Pennsylvania State University
HSSC	Historical Society of Schuylkill County
KC	Knox College
LC	Library of Congress
LOV	Library of Virginia
LSU	Louisiana State University
Maine-HS	Maine Historical Society
Mass-HS	Massachusetts Historical Society
MCL-DU	Medical Center Library, Duke University
MMF	Moravian Music Foundation
MOC	Museum of the Confederacy
NARA	National Archives and Records Administration
NCDAH	North Carolina Division of Archives and History
NHHS	New Hampshire Historical Society
NYPL	New York Public Library
NYSL	New York State Library
OHS	Ohio Historical Society
OR	*The War of the Rebellion: A Compilation of the Official Records of the Union and Confederate Armies.* 70 vols. in 128. Washington, D.C.: U.S. Government Printing Office, 1880–1901.

PNB	Petersburg National Battlefield
RCCW	*Report of the Committee on the Conduct of the War on the Attack on Petersburg on the 30th Day of July, 1864.* Washington, D.C.: Government Printing Office, 1865.
RIHS	Rhode Island Historical Society
RU	Rutgers University
SCHS	South Carolina Historical Society
SCL-DU	Special Collections Library, Duke University
SHSN	State Historical Society of Nebraska
SHSP	*Southern Historical Society Papers*
SU	Stanford University
TSLA	Tennessee State Library and Archives
UA	University of Alabama
UCB	University of California, Berkeley
UCSB	University of California, Santa Barbara
UNC	University of North Carolina
UNH	University of New Hampshire
USAMHI	U.S. Army Military History Institute
USC	University of South Carolina
UVA	University of Virginia
Ver-HS	Vermont Historical Society
VHS	Virginia Historical Society
WHS	Wisconsin Historical Society
WLC-UM	William L. Clements Library, University of Michigan
WLU	Washington and Lee University
WRHS	Western Reserve Historical Society
YU	Yale University

Preface

1. Quotation taken from Grant to Meade, August 1, 1864, report of court of inquiry, *OR,* vol. 40, pt. 1, 134. Saussy, "Story of the Crater, 99; James W. Steele to H. Seymour Hall, n.d., in H. S. Hall, "Mine Run to Petersburg," 239–40; William Hannibal Thomas to Jervey, July 30, 1911, box 251, folder 6, Theodore Dehon Jervey Papers, SCHS; James L. Sherman to Gould, August 14, 1876, and Asst. Surgeon Hubbard to Sherman, August 1, 1876, John Mead Gould Papers, SCL-DU.

1. I Think We Might Do Something

1. Bosbyshell, "Petersburg Mine," 212.
2. Ibid.; Bosbyshell, *48th in the War,* 165.
3. Potter testimony, December 20, 1864, *RCCW,* 97; Potter to Parke, June 22, 1864, *OR,* vol. 40, pt. 2, 319.
4. Potter to Parke, June 24, 1864, *OR,* vol. 40, pt. 2, 396–97.
5. Pleasants testimony, January 13, 1865, *RCCW,* 126; Burnside testimony, August 10, 1864, report of court of inquiry, *OR,* vol. 40, pt. 1, 58.
6. Pleasants testimony, January 13, 1865, *RCCW,* 126; Burnside to Humphreys, June 25, 1864: Meade to Burnside, June 25, 1864, *OR,* vol. 40, pt. 2, 417; Burnside to

Williams, August 13, 1864, *OR,* vol. 40, pt. 1, 523–34; Meade testimony, August 8, 1864, and Burnside testimony, August 10, 1864, report of court of inquiry, *OR,* vol. 40, pt. 1, 45, 58.

7. Bosbyshell, "Petersburg Mine," 211–12; Bosbyshell, *48th in the War,* 163–64; Pleasants and Straley, *Inferno at Petersburg,* 10–19.

8. Bosbyshell, "Petersburg Mine," 211–12; Cavanaugh and Marvel, *Battle of the Crater,* 4; Bosbyshell, *48th in the War,* 163, 165; Haas, "Famous 48th," 53–55, 58; Pleasants and Straley, *Inferno at Petersburg,* 20–29.

9. Nevins, *Diary of Battle,* 352, 406; M. D. Howe, *Touched with Fire,* 116.

10. Marvel, *Burnside,* 389–90; Powell, "Battle of the Petersburg Crater," 559.

11. Powell, "Battle of the Petersburg Crater," 545; Cutcheon, "Twentieth Michigan Regiment," 130; Crater, *Fiftieth Regiment Penna.,* 70; Cavanaugh and Marvel, *Battle of the Crater,* 5; Wallace and Olsen, "Study of the Taylor House Remains," 1–2, PNB; Orr, "Archaeology of Trauma," 26.

12. Barnwell, "A View on the Crater Battle," 177. Henry Goddard Thomas, who led a black brigade in the mine attack, later characterized the salient as "protruding like the ugly horn of a rhinoceros." Thomas, "Colored Troops at Petersburg," 563.

13. Gallagher, *Fighting for the Confederacy,* 432, 435, 442.

14. T. J. Howe, *Wasted Valor,* 1–105.

15. Ibid., 107–8; Hilary P. Jones letter, May 11, 1891, and Richard G. Pegram letter, August 26, 1892, Bernard, *War Talks,* 205n, 207–8.

16. Pegram letter, August 26, 1892, Bernard, *War Talks,* 207–8.

17. T. J. Howe, *Wasted Valor,* 110–33; Harris diary, June 19, 1864, William Hamilton Harris Papers, NYPL; Knowles diary, June 18, 1864, Francis W. Knowles Papers, June 18, 1864, ECU.

18. Pegram letter, August 26, 1892, Bernard, *War Talks,* 208; Gallagher, *Fighting for the Confederacy,* 442; Ord testimony, December 20, 1864, *RCCW,* 119; Day, "Battle of the Crater," 355; Barnwell, "A View on the Crater Battle," 177.

19. Coit, "Battle of the Crater," 124; Cavanaugh and Marvel, *Battle of the Crater,* 146; Robinson, "Artillery in Battle of the Crater," 165.

20. Warner, *Generals in Gray,* 157–58; Welsh, *Medical Histories of Confederate Generals,* 116–17; Cummings, *Yankee Quaker,* 10.

21. Elliott, *Elliott's Brigade,* 3–6, 28; Warner, *Generals in Gray,* 81–82, 324; Conrad, "From Glory to Contention," 35–38.

23. Simpson, *A Good Southerner,* 278–80; T. J. Howe, *Wasted Valor,* 72; Sifakis, *Who Was Who in the Civil War,* 253; Warner, *Generals in Gray,* 253–54.

2. Underground War

1. Gould, *Story of the Forty-eighth,* 271–72; muster and descriptive rolls, Henry Reese service record, 48th Pennsylvania, RG94, NARA; Adjutant General's Office to Commissioner of Pensions, September 16, 1880: Henry Reese death certificate: Elizabeth Reese declaration for widow's pension, June 28, 1912: affidavit, March 7, 1917, Henry Reese pension file, 48th Pennsylvania, RG94, NARA; Haas, "Famous 48th," 61; Cavanaugh and Marvel, *Battle of the Crater,* 5–6.

2. Bosbyshell, "Petersburg Mine," 213; Bosbyshell, *48th in the War,* 168; Henry Reese interview, in "Petersburg Mine," *Philadelphia Weekly Times,* April 24, 1880.

3. Potter to Van Buren, June 28, 1864, *OR,* vol. 40, pt. 2, 484; entries of June 26, 29, 1864, Samuel A. Beddall Diary, Civil War Miscellaneous Collection, USAMHI; Pleasants to not stated, August 2, 1864, *OR,* vol. 40, pt. 1, 556–57; James C. Fitzpatrick dispatch, July 27, 1864, *New York Herald,* August 1, 1864; Pleasants testimony, January 13, 1865, *RCCW,* 126–27; William Baird memoirs, 19, BHL-UM; "Petersburg Mine," *National Tribune,* January 17, 1884; transcript of Pleasants to Barnard, July 7, 1864, John Gross Barnard Papers, SCL-DU; Aston, "Crater Fight Reminiscences," in Aston, *History and Roster,* 95.

4. Bosbyshell, *48th in the War,* 167–68; Pleasants to not stated, August 2, 1864, *OR,* vol. 40, pt. 1, 557; James C. Fitzpatrick dispatch, July 27, 1864, *New York Herald,* August 1, 1864; transcript of Pleasants to Barnard, July 7, 1864, John Gross Barnard Papers, SCL-DU; "Petersburg Mine," *National Tribune,* January 17, 1884; Davis, *Death in the Trenches,* 90, has a photograph of two bottles used as candleholders that were retrieved from the mine many decades ago.

5. Pleasants to not stated, August 2, 1864, *OR,* vol. 40, pt. 1, 557; Potter to John G. Parke, July 2, 1864, Ambrose E. Burnside Papers, RG94, NARA; Burnside to Humphreys, July 2, 1864, and Potter to Parke, July 2, 1864, *OR,* vol. 40, pt. 2, 590–91; Inners, "Military Geology of the Petersburg Mine," 7. Long after the war, Henry Reese related a story about a member of Meade's staff who did not believe the report of quicksand and deliberately stepped into it. Two men pulled him out and he lost his boots in the muck. The staff officer had to borrow an old pair of shoes to get back to headquarters. Both Burnside and Pleasants had a good laugh over the incident. Henry Reese interview, in "Petersburg Mine," *Philadelphia Weekly Times,* April 24, 1880.

6. Agassiz, *Meade's Headquarters,* 194–95; Bosbyshell, *48th in the War,* 168; Jackman, *History of the Sixth New Hampshire,* 310–11; Hartranft to wife, August 18, 1864, John F. Hartranft Papers, Helen L. Shireman; Way, "The Battle of the Crater," *National Tribune,* June 3, 1904; Sargent to wife, July 27, 1864, Ransom Sargent Papers, DC. A photograph of a Ninth Corps badge made of marl from the gallery is reproduced in Cavanaugh and Marvel, *Battle of the Crater,* 61.

7. Inners, "Military Geology of the Petersburg Mine," 3–5, 7. Inners notes on page 3 that the exact edge between the Atlantic coastal plain and the Piedmont is twelve miles west of Petersburg.

8. Hartranft to Sallie, August 18, 1864, John F. Hartranft Papers, Helen L. Shireman; Culver, "Petersburg Mine," *National Tribune,* September 4, 1919.

9. Pleasants to not stated, August 2, 1864, *OR,* vol. 40, pt. 1, 558; Pleasants testimony, January 13, 1865, *RCCW,* 126; James C. Fitzpatrick dispatch, July 27, 1864, *New York Herald,* August 1, 1864; "Petersburg Mine," *National Tribune,* January 17, 1884.

10. Pleasants to not stated, August 2, 1864, *OR,* vol. 40, pt. 1, 557–58; Inners, "Military Geology of the Petersburg Mine," 7; Pleasants and Straley, *Inferno at Petersburg,* 68–69; James C. Fitzpatrick dispatch, July 27, 1864, *New York Herald,* August 1, 1864.

11. Entries of July 7, 11, 1864, Samuel A. Beddall Diary, Civil War Miscellaneous Collection, USAMHI.

12. Duane, *Manual for Engineer Troops,* 207–37; Duane testimony, September 3, 1864, report of court of inquiry, *OR,* vol. 40, pt. 1, 112.

13. Duane, *Manual for Engineer Troops,* 207, 217; Pleasants testimony, January 13, 1865, *RCCW,* 127.

14. Duane, *Manual for Engineer Troops,* 233–34.

15. Ibid., 228–29.

16. Ibid., 231–32.

17. Gallagher, *Fighting for the Confederacy,* 442–44.

18. Ibid., 442–43, 603n.

19. Ibid.

20. Ibid., 445–46.

21. McDonald to Richard H. Anderson, July 4, 1864, Marshall McDonald Papers, SCL-DU; Potter to Richmond, July 11, 1864, Ambrose E. Burnside Papers, RG94, NARA; pay vouchers: Stephen W. Presstman to George W. Randolph, May 2, 1862: Delaware Kemper to Randolph, May 4, 1862: index card of Confederate records: Jeremy F. Gilmer to Randolph, October 6, 1862, Hugh Thomas Douglas service record, 1st Confederate Engineers, M258, Roll 93, RG109, NARA.

22. Douglas, "Petersburg Crater," Petersburg Crater Collection, UVA.

23. E. N. Wise to editor, November 1905, unidentified newspaper clipping, n.d., in Stewart, comp., "Charge of the Crater," unpaginated, MOC; E. N. Wise to Daniel, November 14, 1905, John Warwick Daniel Papers, UVA.

24. Special requisition, July 9, 1864, Hugh Thomas Douglas service record, 1st Confederate Engineers, M258, Roll 93, RG109, NARA; Douglas to John Postell, July 13, 14, 15, 1864, *OR,* vol. 40, pt. 3, 772, 774, 778–79; Douglas, "Petersburg Crater," Petersburg Crater Collection, UVA.

25. Douglas's regulations, July 15, 1864, *OR,* vol. 40, pt. 3, 777–78.

26. Douglas to Stevens, July 16, 17, 18, 1864, *OR,* vol. 40, pt. 3, 776–77, 779–81.

27. Stevens to Hill, July 12, 1864: Douglas to Postell, July 13, 15, 1864: Douglas's regulations, July 15, 1864: Douglas to Stevens, July 16, 1864, *OR,* vol. 40, pt. 3, 771–72, 776–80.

28. Douglas, "Petersburg Crater," Petersburg Crater Collection, UVA; Douglas to Stevens, July 19, 1864, *OR,* vol. 40, pt. 3, 784–85.

29. Douglas to Stevens, July 20, 1864, *OR,* vol. 40, pt. 3, 789.

30. Ibid., July 22, 23, 24, 1864, *OR,* vol. 40, pt. 3, 791–92, 795, 797.

31. Ibid., July 25, 1864, *OR,* vol. 40, pt. 3, 801; Douglas, "Petersburg Crater" and "Confederate Countermining in Front of Petersburg: Experience and Recollection," Petersburg Crater Collection, UVA.

32. Receipt, July 28, 1864, Hugh Thomas Douglas service record, 1st Confederate Engineers, M258, Roll 93, RG109, NARA.

33. Fred Harris to uncle, July 31, 1864, David B. Harris Papers, SCL-DU; E. N. Wise to Daniel, November 14, 1905, John Warwick Daniel Papers, UVA.

34. William Benyaurd to Duane, July 14, 1864, J. C. Duane Letter Book, UVA; entries of July 14, 18, 1864, Samuel Beddall Diary, Civil War Miscellaneous Collection, USAMHI; *History of the Thirty-sixth Regiment Massachusetts,* 232; Bliss reminiscences, 122, 125–26, Zenas R. Bliss Papers, USAMHI.

35. Burnside to Williams, August 13, 1864: Pleasants to not stated, August 2, 1864, *OR,* vol. 40, pt. 1, 524, 557; Burnside to Williams, July 16, 1864, *OR,* vol. 40, pt. 3, 283.

36. Meade to Grant, July 17, 1864: Burnside to Williams, July 17, 1864, *OR,* vol. 40, pt. 3, 290, 300–310; Pleasants testimony, January 13, 1865, *RCCW,* 127.

37. Bosbyshell, *48th in the War,* 168–69.

38. Potter to Richmond, July 19, 1864: Pleasants to Potter, July 20, 1864, Ambrose E. Burnside Papers, RG94, NARA; Warren to Williams, July 19, 1864: Burnside to Williams, July 19, 1864: Potter to Richmond, July 19, 1864: Pleasants to Potter, July 20, 1864, *OR,* vol. 40, pt. 3, 336–37, 354; Pleasants to not stated, August 2, 1864, *OR,* vol. 40, pt. 1, 557; Pleasants testimony, January 13, 1865, *RCCW,* 127. Historian Alfred P. James believes the Federals tried to avoid the Rebel countermine by digging "a downward incline to the left at an angle of forty-five degrees and carried forward the desired distance. Then a shaft was dug upwards and work begun again on a higher level." This is not consistent with Pleasants's report. Apparently, James's only source is stories associated with a ladder that was discovered in the mine in the twentieth century and which was on display at the Petersburg Museum. It is probable that the feature James described was dug after the war by people exploring what was left of the gallery—it was opened more than once after 1865. Moreover, since both branches were destroyed in the explosion, this feature had to be in the gallery, further proving that it was made after the war, because Pleasants did not suspect the Confederates were countermining until after the gallery was finished. See James, "Battle of the Crater," 355n.

39. "Petersburg Mine," *National Tribune,* January 17, 1884; Burnside to Williams, July 17, 1864, *OR,* vol. 40, pt. 3, 301; Jackman, *History of the Sixth New Hampshire,* 310.

40. William H. Bolton journal, June 27, 1864, CWURM; Van Den Bossche, "War and Other Reminiscences," 140; Charles J. Mills to father, July 4, 1864, "Civil War Letters of Major Charles J. Mills," 120, Gregory A. Coco Collection, USAMHI; Heisler to sister, July 20, 26, 1864, Henry C. Heisler Papers, LC; Sheahan to father, July 6, 1864, John Parris Sheahan Collection, Maine-HS; William Barker to Luther, July 15, 1864, Lunt Family Collection, Maine-HS; Pleasants to uncle, July 25, 1864, quoted in Pleasants and Straley, *Inferno at Petersburg,* 95–96.

41. Morton to Ma and Pa, July 14, 1864, William Goodridge Morton Papers, VHS; Tower, *Lee's Adjutant,* 175–77; Scott, *Forgotten Valor,* 556.

42. Bliss reminiscences, 126–28, Zenas R. Bliss Papers, USAMHI; John C. Hackhiser to Sarah, July 27, 1864, Earl J. Hess Collection, USAMHI; William Hamilton Harris Journal, July 23, 26, 1864, VHS; Meade to Grant, July 5, 1864, Simon, *Papers of Ulysses S. Grant,* 11:175n.

43. Reese interview, in "Petersburg Mine," *Philadelphia Weekly Times,* April 24, 1880.

44. Pleasants to not stated, August 2, 1864, *OR,* vol. 40, pt. 1, 557–58; entries of July 23–24, 1864, Samuel Beddall Diary, Civil War Miscellaneous Collection, USAMHI; "Sketch of Mine in front of 2d Div., 9 Corps, near Petersburg, Va.," Dr. 150–58, RG77, NARA.

3. The Third Offensive

1. Hickenlooper, "Vicksburg Mine," 540–42.

2. Grant to Meade, July 3, 1864, Simon, *Papers of Ulysses S. Grant,* 11:167–68, 168n; Meade to Burnside, July 3, 1864: Burnside to Meade, July 3, 1864: Burnside to Meade, July 4, 1864: Meade to Burnside, July 4, 1864, *OR,* vol. 40, pt. 2, 608–9, 629–30; Burnside testimony, August 10, 1864, report of court of inquiry, *OR,* vol. 40, pt. 1, 58–59.

3. Meade to Burnside, July 3, 1864, *OR*, vol. 40, pt. 1, 161; Meade to Grant, July 3, 4, 1864, Simon, *Papers of Ulysses S. Grant*, 11:168n, 173–75n; Meade to Hunt, July 3, 1864: Meade to Grant, July 4, 1864, *OR*, vol. 40, pt. 2, 600, 619–20.

4. Hunt to Williams, October 31, 1864: Meade to Hunt, July 3, 1864: Hunt and Duane to Humphreys, July 6, 1864: Hunt and Duane to not stated, July 10, 1864: Williams to Hunt and Duane, July 11, 1864, *OR*, vol. 40, pt. 1, 279, 285–87; Journal of the Siege of Petersburg, June 26, 29, 30, July 2–6, 1864, Henry Jackson Hunt Papers, LC; Meade to Grant, July 5, 1864, Simon, *Papers of Ulysses S. Grant*, 11:175n; Longacre, *Man behind the Guns*, 205.

5. Grant to Meade, July 5, 1864, Simon, *Papers of Ulysses S. Grant*, 11:173; John G. Barnard to Burnside, July 5, 1864, Ambrose E. Burnside Papers, RG94, NARA; transcript of Barnard to Burnside, July 3, 1864: transcript of Pleasants to Barnard, July 7, 1864, John Gross Barnard Papers, SCL-DU; Barnard to Burnside, July 5, 1864, *OR*, vol. 40, pt. 3, 12; Barnard to Pleasants, July 3, 1864, *OR*, vol. 40, pt. 2, 610–11; Pleasants and Straley, *Inferno at Petersburg*, 60–63.

6. Bosbyshell, *48th in the War*, 176–77.

7. Transcript of Barnard's evaluation of the mine attack, August 6, 1864, John Gross Barnard Papers, SCL-DU. The story that the engineer officers of Meade's army had no faith in Pleasants's mine circulated widely in the Ninth Corps. See Loving, *Civil War Letters*, 126.

8. Gibbon, *Personal Recollections*, 252–53; Sumner, *Diary of Cyrus B. Comstock*, 278, 283; Nevins, *Diary of Battle*, 439.

9. Burnside to Humphreys, July 9, 1864, *OR*, vol. 40, pt. 3, 109; Duane testimony, September 3, 1864, report of court of inquiry, *OR*, vol. 40, pt. 1, 112.

10. Michler to Williams, October 20, 1864, *OR*, vol. 40, pt. 1, 293; Pleasants to uncle, July 25, 1864, quoted in Pleasants and Straley, *Inferno at Petersburg*, 96.

11. Grant to Meade, July 7, 1864: Meade to Grant, July 7, 1864: Humphreys to Burnside, July 7, 1864: Grant to Meade, July 8, 1864, *OR*, vol. 40, pt. 3, 61–62, 66, 72–73.

12. Hunt to Williams, October 31, 1864: Hunt to Humphreys, April 16, 1864: unnumbered orders, Headquarters, Army of the Potomac, July 9, 1864, *OR*, vol. 40, pt. 1, 279, 283–84, 286; Journal of the Siege of Petersburg, July 9, 10, 1864, Henry Jackson Hunt Papers, LC; Duane and Hunt to Humphreys, July 10, 1864, and Meade's endorsement, *OR*, vol. 40, pt. 3, 125–27.

13. Meade to Duane, July 14, 1864: Duane to Meade, July 14, 1864, J. C. Duane Papers, LOV; Meade to Grant, July 16, 17, 1864, *OR*, vol. 40, pt. 3, 276–77, 290.

14. Michler to Williams, October 20, 1864, *OR*, vol. 40, pt. 1, 291.

15. Grant, *Personal Memoirs*, 2:606, 608; Sumner, *Diary of Cyrus B. Comstock*, 279–80; transcript of Barnard's evaluation of mine attack, August 6, 1864, John Gross Barnard Papers, SCL-DU.

16. Grant, *Personal Memoirs*, 2:608.

17. Weitzel to Barnard, July 1, 1864, *OR*, vol. 40, pt. 1, 677; Suderow, "Glory Denied," 18; Cavanaugh and Marvel, *Battle of the Crater*, 137; Maxfield and Brady, *Roster and Statistical Record of Company D*, 36; Longacre, *Army of Amateurs*, 163–65; Frassanito, *Grant and Lee*, 303–4.

18. Suderow, "War along the James," 12–14.

19. Dunlop, *Lee's Sharpshooters,* 131–33; Caldwell, *History of a Brigade of South Carolinians,* 167–68.

20. Lee to Ewell, July 6, 1864, *OR,* vol. 40, pt. 3, 745; Suderow, "War along the James," 14–16, 18.

21. Weitzel to Grant, July 21, 1864: Terry to Weitzel, July 21, 1864: Weitzel to Grant, July 22, 1864: Hill to Fox, July 22, 1864, *OR,* vol. 40, pt. 3, 377, 381, 400, 407; Suderow, "Glory Denied," 18; Longacre, *Army of Amateurs,* 184–85.

22. Taylor to Anderson, July 23, 1864: Lee to Ewell, July 24, 1864: Kershaw to Ewell, July 24, 1864: Ewell to Kershaw, [July 27, 1864], *OR,* vol. 40, pt. 3, 795–96, 811; Suderow, "Glory Denied," 18–19; Dunlop, *Lee's Sharpshooters,* 137; Caldwell, *History of a Brigade of South Carolinians,* 169; *Story of One Regiment,* 224.

23. Sumner, *Diary of Cyrus B. Comstock,* 283; Meade to Duane, July 24, 1864: Duane to Meade, July 24, 1864, *OR,* vol. 40, pt. 3, 427–28.

24. Duane, Comstock, and Weitzel to not stated, July 23, 1864: Meade to Grant, July 24, 1864, *OR,* vol. 40, pt. 3, 416, 424–25.

25. Duane, Comstock, and Weitzel to not stated, July 23, 1864: Grant to Meade, July 24, 1864, *OR,* vol. 40, pt. 3, 416, 424–26.

26. Grant to Meade, July 25, 1864: Sigfried to Richmond, July 25, 1864: Willcox to Richmond, July 25, 1864, *OR,* vol. 40, pt. 3, 437–38, 446–47.

27. Meade to Benham, July 25, 1864: Meade to Hancock, July 25, 1864: Meade to Sheridan, July 25, 1864, *OR,* vol. 40, pt. 3, 442, 443, 448; Sheridan, *Personal Memoirs,* 1:446; Feis, *Grant's Secret Service,* 256; A. A. Humphreys, *Virginia Campaign,* 251.

28. Burnside to Williams, July 24, 1864, *OR,* vol. 40, pt. 3, 429; Gallagher, *Fighting for the Confederacy,* 435–36, 441; Johnson journal, June 25, 1864, *Supplement to the Official Records,* 7:279; Beauregard statement, in C. M. Wilcox letter to editor, *New Orleans Times,* January 1, 1872, clipping in Mahone Family Papers, LOV; "Notes of Genl. Beauregard on W. J. Marrin's acct. of the explosion of the Federal Mine at Petersburg Va. July 30th 1864," July 17, 1876, Pierre G. T. Beauregard Papers, ALPL; McMaster, "Elliott's Brigade," 12, 14; McMaster to Beauregard, February 14, 1872, in Roman, *Military Operations of General Beauregard,* 587.

29. Johnson journal, July 1, 11–12, 1864, *Supplement to the Official Records,* 7:280–81; Johnson to Brent, July 4, 1864, *OR,* vol. 40, pt. 2, 714; Johnson to Faison, July 13, 1864: Foote to Goode, July 13, 1864: Johnson to Goode, July 14, 1864: Johnson to Faison, July 15, 1864, *OR,* vol. 40, pt. 3, 773, 775, 779; Andrews, *Sketch of Company K,* 20–21; Cummings, *Yankee Quaker,* 294–95.

30. Johnson to Moseley, July 12, 1864: Johnson to Brent, July 19, 1864, *OR,* vol. 40, pt. 3, 770, 783–84.

31. Beauregard statement, in C. M. Wilcox letter to editor, *New Orleans Times,* January 1, 1872, clipping in Mahone Family Papers, LOV; Johnson statement, in Roman, *Military Operations of General Beauregard,* 583; Johnson to Brent, June 30, 1864, *OR,* vol. 40, pt. 2, 703–4; Stevens to Hill, July 12, 1864, *OR,* vol. 40, pt. 3, 771; Johnson journal, June 29, and July 1, 9, 1864, *Supplement to the Official Records,* 7:279–80; Day, "Breastworks at Petersburg," 174; Stewart, *Pair of Blankets,* 155; Roulhac, "Forty-ninth N.C. Infantry," 72; Stewart, "Carnage at 'The Crater,'" 41; Stewart, "Charge of the Crater," 80; Fred Harris to uncle, July 31, 1864, David B. Harris Papers, SCL-DU; R. N. Doyle to W. H. P. Steerer, July 15, 1864, Ambrose E. Burnside Papers, RG94, NARA.

32. Stewart, "Carnage at 'The Crater,'" 41; Stewart, "Charge of the Crater," 80; Gallagher, *Fighting for the Confederacy*, 436.

4. Deep Bottom

1. Circular, Headquarters, Second Corps, July 25, 1864: orders, Headquarters, Second Corps, July 26, 1864, *OR*, vol. 40, pt. 3, 443, 465–66.

2. Hancock to Williams, November 11, 1864, *OR*, vol. 40, pt. 1, 308–9; Hancock to Humphreys, July 26, 1864: Humphreys to Hancock, July 26, 1864, noon: Butler to Hancock, July 26, 1864: Humphreys to Hancock, July 26, 1864, 4:15 P.M.: Hancock to Meade, July 26, 1864: Humphreys to Warren, July 26, 1864, 5 P.M.: Humphreys to Burnside, July 26, 1864, *OR*, vol. 40, pt. 3, 464–65, 467, 478; entry of July 26, 1864, Charles W. Ford Diary, BHL-UM; Sheridan, *Personal Memoirs*, 1:446–47; F. C. Floyd, *History of the Fortieth (Mozart) Regiment*, 229–30; Billings, *History of the Tenth Massachusetts Battery*, 231.

3. Hancock to Williams, November 11, 1864: memoranda of Second Corps, *OR*, vol. 40, pt. 1, 308–9, 321; Weitzel to Foster, July 26, 1864: Hancock to Meade, July 27, 1864, 12:30 A.M. and 1:30 A.M.: Meade to Hancock, July 27, 1864: Hancock to Morgan, July 27, 1864: Hancock to Meade, July 27, 1864, received 5:40 A.M.: Sheridan to Humphreys, July 27, 1864, *OR*, vol. 40, pt. 3, 496, 509–11, 531–32; Billings, *History of the Tenth Massachusetts Battery*, 231; Walker, *History of the Second Army Corps*, 560; Cavanaugh and Marvel, *Battle of the Crater*, 29–30, 33; Longacre, *Army of Amateurs*, 185–86.

4. Foster to Birney, July 26, 1864: Foster to Weitzel, July 26, 1864: Weitzel to Foster, July 26, 1864, *OR*, vol. 40, pt. 3, 495–96; Maxfield and Brady, *Roster and Statistical Record of Company D*, 39–40; *Story of One Regiment*, 229.

5. Suderow, "Glory Denied," 23; Sommers, *Richmond Redeemed*, 14–15; Horn, *Destruction of the Weldon Railroad*, 10.

6. Grant to Burnside, July 26, 1864: Meade to Burnside, July 26, 1864: Burnside to Grant, July 26, 1864: Humphreys to Burnside, July 26, 1864: Burnside to Humphreys, July 26, 1864, *OR*, vol. 40, pt. 3, 474–76.

7. Burnside to Humphreys, July 26, 1864, *OR*, vol. 40, pt. 3, 476–77.

8. Meade to Grant, July 26, 1864, noon: Grant to Meade, July 26, 1864, 12:30 P.M.: Grant to Meade, July 26, 1864, 3 P.M., *OR*, vol. 40, pt. 3, 458–59.

9. Meade to Grant, July 26, 1864, 5:30 P.M.: Grant to Meade, July 26, 1864, 9:30 P.M., *OR*, vol. 40, pt. 3, 459–61.

10. Stanton to Grant, July 26, 1864: Grant to Stanton, July 26, 1864, 9 P.M., *OR*, vol. 40, pt. 3, 456–57.

11. Suderow, "Glory Denied," 21–22.

12. Ibid.; Cavanaugh and Marvel, *Battle of the Crater*, 143.

13. Hancock to Williams, November 11, 1864: memoranda of Second Corps, July 27, 1864: Miles to Bingham, October 10, 1864: itinerary of Hardaway Light Artillery Battalion, July 27, 1864, *OR*, vol. 40, pt. 1, 309, 321, 329–30, 800; Hancock to Meade, July 27, 1864, *OR*, vol. 40, pt. 3, 511; Walker, *History of the Second Army Corps*, 562–63; Suderow, "Glory Denied," 22, 27; Cavanaugh and Marvel, *Battle of the Crater*, 30–31.

14. Billings, *History of the Tenth Massachusetts Battery*, 232; itinerary of Hardaway Light Artillery Battalion, July 27, 1864, *OR*, vol. 40, pt. 1, 800; Suderow, "Glory Denied," 22.

15. *Story of One Regiment*, 227, 229.

16. Walker to Barlow, July 27, 1864: Walker to Mott, July 17, 1864, *OR*, vol. 40, pt. 3, 516–17; Hancock to Williams, November 11, 1864, *OR*, vol. 40, pt. 1, 309; Sheridan to Rawlins, May 13, 1866, *OR*, vol. 36, pt. 1, 800; F. C. Floyd, *History of the Fortieth (Mozart) Regiment*, 230; Walker, *History of the Second Army Corps*, 563; Sheridan, *Personal Memoirs*, 1:447; Suderow, "Glory Denied," 23; Cavanaugh and Marvel, *Battle of the Crater*, 31–32.

17. Hancock to Meade, July 27, 1864, 7:25 A.M. and 7:50 A.M.: Meade to Hancock, July 27, 1864, *OR*, vol. 40, pt. 3, 511–12; memoranda of Second Corps, July 27, 1864, *OR*, vol. 40, pt. 1, 321.

18. Walker to Foster, July 27, 1864, *OR*, vol. 40, pt. 3, 547; Sumner, *Diary of Cyrus B. Comstock*, 284; Comstock to Grant, July 27, 1864, Simon, *Papers of Ulysses S. Grant*, 11:326n; H. Porter, *Campaigning with Grant*, 259.

19. Walker, *History of the Second Army Corps*, 564; Hancock to Williams, November 11, 1864, *OR*, vol. 40, pt. 1, 310; Grant to Hancock, July 27, 1864: Hancock to Grant, July 27, 1864, *OR*, vol. 40, pt. 3, 512–13; Cavanaugh and Marvel, *Battle of the Crater*, 31.

20. Seddon to Lee, July 27, 1864: Ewell to Cooper, July 27, 1864: Ewell to Kershaw, [July 27, 1864], and July 27, 1864, 11:30 A.M. and 12:30 P.M., *OR*, vol. 40, pt. 3, 807–11; Pfanz, *Richard S. Ewell*, 404–5, 408–9; Suderow, "Glory Denied," 23, 26.

21. Grant to Meade, July 27, 1864, and 8:10 P.M.: Meade to Grant, July 27, 1864, 8 P.M. and 9 P.M.: Sheridan to Hancock, July 27, 1864, 4:17 P.M., 4:40 P.M., and 5 P.M.: Hancock to Meade, July 27, 1864: Meade to Hancock, July 27, 1864, 10 P.M. and 10:30 P.M.: Weitzel to Hancock, July 27, 1864: Sheridan to Humphreys, July 27, 1864, *OR*, vol. 40, pt. 3, 503–4, 513–15, 532; Hancock to Williams, November 11, 1864, *OR*, vol. 40, pt. 1, 309; Walker, *History of the Second Army Corps*, 564–65.

22. Grant to Halleck, July 27, 1864: Meade to Burnside, July 27, 1864: Hancock to Williams, July 29, 1864, *OR*, vol. 40, pt. 3, 502, 528, 598.

23. Lee to Anderson, July 27, 1864, in Dowdey and Manarin, *Wartime Papers of R. E. Lee*, 826; Anderson to Taylor, n.d., 1865, *Supplement to the Official Records*, 7:252; Cavanaugh and Marvel, *Battle of the Crater*, 32.

24. Grant to Meade, July 28, 1864: Hancock to Meade, July 28, 1864: Hancock to Grant, July 28, 1864: Meade to Hancock, July 28, 1864: Foster to Birney, July 28, 1864: Birney to Foster, July 28, 1864: Birge to Foster, [July 28, 1864], *OR*, vol. 40, pt. 3, 552, 560, 584–86; Hancock to Williams, November 11, 1864: memoranda of Second Corps, July 28, 1864, *OR*, vol. 40, pt. 1, 310–11, 322–23; Cavanaugh and Marvel, *Battle of the Crater*, 32; Suderow, "Glory Denied," 27.

25. Caldwell, *History of a Brigade of South Carolinians*, 169–70; Dunlop, *Lee's Sharpshooters*, 137–38; Suderow, "Glory Denied," 21, 27; Cavanaugh and Marvel, *Battle of the Crater*, 32–34.

26. McDaid, "'Four Years of Arduous Service,'" 301; Harris, *Historical Sketches*, 53; Caldwell, *History of a Brigade of South Carolinians*, 170–72; Dunlop, *Lee's Sharpshooters*, 138; Speer to Hale, July 31, 1864: Bost to Hale, August 3, 1864, *Supplement to the Official Records*, 7:296–97, 299–300; Suderow, "Glory Denied," 21.

27. H. A. Hall, Besley, and Wood, *History of the Sixth New York Cavalry*, 199; Sheridan, *Personal Memoirs*, 1:447; Sheridan to Rawlins, May 13, 1866, *OR*, vol. 36, pt.

1, 800; Gregg to Williams, November 23, 1864: Gregg to Humphreys, August 3, 1864: Randol to Weir, August 3, 1864, *OR*, vol. 40, pt. 1, 613, 615–16; Speer to Hale, July 31, 1864: Calais to Hale, July 29, 1864, *Supplement to the Official Records*, 7:296–97, 301–2; Cavanaugh and Marvel, *Battle of the Crater*, 34.

28. Caldwell, *History of a Brigade of South Carolinians*, 171–72; Dunlop, *Lee's Sharpshooters*, 138–39; McDaid, "'Four Years of Arduous Service,'" 301–2.

29. Caldwell, *History of a Brigade of South Carolinians*, 171–72; Dunlop, *Lee's Sharpshooters*, 139; McGill to Hale, July 29, 1864: Calais to Hale, July 29, 1864, *Supplement to the Official Records*, 7:295, 301–2; McDaid, "'Four Years of Arduous Service,'" 302; H. A. Hall, Besley, and Wood, *History of the Sixth New York Cavalry*, 199; Cheney, *History of the Ninth Regiment*, 207; Wesley W. Darling to father, August 1, 1864, Darling Family Papers, WRHS; Sheridan to Rawlins, May 13, 1866, *OR*, vol. 36, pt. 1, 800; Cavanaugh and Marvel, *Battle of the Crater*, 34; Suderow, "Glory Denied," 28.

30. Davies to Bibber, November 21, 1864, *OR*, vol. 40, pt. 1, 618–19; Caldwell, *History of a Brigade of South Carolinians*, 172–74; Shore to brother and sister, August 2, 1864, Augustin E. Shore Papers, EU; Harris, *Historical Sketches*, 53; McDaid, "'Four Years of Arduous Service,'" 303; Dunlop, *Lee's Sharpshooters*, 141; H. A. Hall, Besley, and Wood, *History of the Sixth New York Cavalry*, 199; Cheney, *History of the Ninth Regiment*, 207; Grant to Halleck, July 28, 1864, 3:30 P.M. and 9 P.M.: Sheridan to Humphreys, July 28, 1864: DuBois to Pease, July 28, 1864, *OR*, vol. 40, pt. 3, 551, 569; Suderow, "Glory Denied," 29.

31. Hancock to Grant, July 28, 1864: Walker to Gibbon, July 28, 1864: Sheridan to Gregg, July 28, 1864, *OR*, vol. 40, pt. 3, 561, 563, 569–70; Hancock to Williams, November 11, 1864: memoranda of Second Corps, July 28, 1864, *OR*, vol. 40, pt. 1, 310–11, 322–23; Gibbon, *Personal Recollections*, 248–49.

32. Hancock to Grant, July 28, 1864: Walker to Barlow, July 28, 1864: Birney to Weitzel, July 28, 1864: Foster to Weitzel, July 28, 1864: Foster to Birney, July 28, 1864, 2:15 P.M. and 4:30 P.M.: Birney to Foster, July 28, 1864, *OR*, vol. 40, pt. 3, 561, 563–64, 583–84, 586–88; Hancock to Williams, November 11, 1864: memoranda of Second Corps, July 28, 1864, *OR*, vol. 40, pt. 1, 310–11, 322–23; Cavanaugh and Marvel, *Battle of the Crater*, 35.

33. Grant to Meade, July 28, 1864, 11:30 A.M. and 12:20 P.M.: 12:20 P.M.: Meade to Grant, July 28, 1864, noon and 1 P.M.: Comstock to Hancock, July 28, 1864: Grant to Butler, July 28, 1864, *OR*, vol. 40, pt. 3, 553–54, 562, 575; Sumner, *Diary of Cyrus B. Comstock*, 284; memoranda of Second Corps, July 28, 1864, *OR*, vol. 40, pt. 1, 323.

34. Anderson to Taylor, n.d., 1865, *Supplement to the Official Records*, 7:252–53.

35. Weitzel to Comstock, July 28, 1864, 12:10 P.M., 1:10 P.M., and 3:20 P.M.: Hancock to Butler, July 28, 1864: Weitzel to Hancock, July 28, 1864, *OR*, vol. 40, pt. 3, 573–75.

36. F. C. Floyd, *History of the Fortieth (Mozart) Regiment*, 230; Foster to Weitzel, July 28, 1864: Birney to Foster, July 28, 1864, *OR*, vol. 40, pt. 3, 589.

37. Grant to Halleck, July 28, 1864, 9 P.M.: Lincoln to Grant, July 28 and 29, 1864: Grant to Lincoln, July 28, 1864: Lincoln to Grant, July 29, 1864, *OR*, vol. 40, pt. 3, 551, 590.

38. Grant to Meade, July 29, 1864: Meade to Grant, July 29, 1864, 10:30 A.M. and 2:30 P.M., *OR*, vol. 40, pt. 3, 591, 593; Feis, *Grant's Secret Service*, 256.

39. Grant to Hancock, July 29, 1864: Hancock to Grant, July 29, 1864, *OR*, vol. 40, pt. 3, 599; Gibbon, *Personal Recollections*, 249–51; Cavanaugh and Marvel, *Battle of the Crater*, 36.

40. Grant to Butler, July 29, 1864, *Private and Official Correspondence of Gen. Benjamin F. Butler*, 4:556–57.

41. Meade to Hancock, July 29, 1864: Weitzel to Hancock, July 29, 1864: Hancock to Butler, July 29, 1864: Ludlow to Hancock, [July 29, 1864]: Hancock to Meade, July 29, 1864, *OR*, vol. 40, pt. 3, 600–602; Hancock to Williams, November 11, 1864: memoranda of Second Corps, July 29–30, 1864, *OR*, vol. 40, pt. 1, 311, 323; Washburn, *Complete Military History and Record*, 82; Bowen, "Diary of Captain George D. Bowen," 201; Grant, *Personal Memoirs*, 2:611; Cavanaugh and Marvel, *Battle of the Crater*, 36.

42. Hancock to Williams, August 3, 1864, *OR*, vol. 40, pt. 1, 312–13; entry of July 29, 1864, Charles W. Ford Diary, BHL-UM.

43. Gallagher, *Fighting for the Confederacy*, 454; Ewell to wife, July 30, 1864, quoted in Pfanz, *Richard S. Ewell*, 409.

44. Anderson to Taylor, n.d., 1865, *Supplement to the Official Records*, 7:253; Gallagher, *Fighting for the Confederacy*, 452, 454; Comstock testimony, August 30, 1864, report of court of inquiry, *OR*, vol. 40, pt. 1, 83.

45. Walker, *History of the Second Army Corps*, 566; Cavanaugh and Marvel, *Battle of the Crater*, 143–44.

5. Preparing, July 27–29

1. Warner to Burnside, July 15, 1864: Burnside to Williams, July 21, 1864: Grant to Meade, July 25, 1864: Burnside to Humphreys, July 25, 1864, *OR*, vol. 40, pt. 3, 266, 369, 438, 445.

2. Burnside to Humphreys, July 26, 1864, report of court of inquiry, *OR*, vol. 40, pt. 1, 137; Burnside to Comstock, July 26, 1864: Warner to Burnside, July 26, 1864: Burnside to Warner, July 26, 1864, *OR*, vol. 40, pt. 3, 473–74.

3. Burnside testimony, August 10, 1864, report of court of inquiry, *OR*, vol. 40, pt. 1, 59–60; Gibbon, *Personal Recollections*, 252.

4. Agassiz, *Meade's Headquarters*, 196n; Meade testimony, August 8, 1864, report of court of inquiry, *OR*, vol. 40, pt. 1, 46; Edie to Schaff, July 26, 1864: Humphreys to Burnside, July 26, 1864, *OR*, vol. 40, pt. 3, 463, 479; C. B. Comstock to Burnside, July 26, 1864, Ambrose Everts Burnside Collection, RIHS.

5. William H. Randall Reminiscences, July 30, 1864, BHL-UM; Sheahan to father, July 27, 1864, John Parris Sheahan Papers, Maine-HS; Burnside to Humphreys, July 26, 1864, appendix to report of court of inquiry: Pleasants to not stated, August 2, 1864, *OR*, vol. 40, pt. 1, 137, 557, 561; James C. Fitzpatrick dispatch, July 27, 1864, *New York Herald*, August 1, 1864.

6. Burnside to Humphreys, July 26, 1864, report of court of inquiry: Pleasants to not stated, August 2, 1864, *OR*, vol. 40, pt. 1, 137, 557; Meade to Burnside, July 27, 1864: Burnside to Meade, July 27, 1864: Burnside to Warner, July 27, 1864: Burnside to Williams, July 27, 1864: Van Buren to Potter, July 27, 1864, *OR*, vol. 40, pt. 3, 526–30; Allen, *Forty-six Months with the Fourth R.I.*, 281–82; Meade to Burnside, July 27, 1864: Burnside to Meade, n.d., Ambrose Everts Burnside Collection, RIHS; Sheahan to father, July 27, 1864, John Parris Sheahan Papers, Maine-HS.

7. Entries of July 27–28, 1864, Samuel Beddall Diary, Civil War Miscellaneous Collection, USAMHI; Burnside to Humphreys, July 26, 1864, appendix to report of court of inquiry: Pleasants to not stated, August 2, 1864, *OR*, vol. 40, pt. 1, 137, 557; Potter report, August 5, 1864, Ambrose E. Burnside Papers, RG94, NARA; Pleasants testimony, January 13, 1865, *RCCW*, 127–28; Burnside to Humphreys, July 28, 1864: Burnside to Loring, July 28, 1864: Burnside to Van Buren, July 28, 1864, *OR*, vol. 40, pt. 3, 565–66; "Petersburg Mine," *National Tribune*, January 17, 1884.

8. Duane, *Manual for Engineer Troops*, 230–31.

9. Burnside testimony, December 17, 1864: Pleasants testimony, January 13, 1865, *RCCW*, 18, 23–24, 128–29; Burnside to Humphreys, July 26, 1864, appendix to report of court of inquiry, *OR*, vol. 40, pt. 1, 137. J. B. Culver of the 48th Pennsylvania later recalled that Pleasants tested his fuse by burying a section one hundred feet long in a trench. Lighting it, and seeing how well and long it burned, he felt confident of the actual detonation. Culver, "Petersburg Mine," *National Tribune*, September 4, 1919. Newspaper correspondent Fitzpatrick characterized the fuse as one of "the regular 'sure fire,' coal mining fuses of Pennsylvania." James C. Fitzpatrick dispatch, July 27, 1864, *New York Herald*, August 1, 1864.

10. Pleasants testimony, January 13, 1865, *RCCW*, 128; "Petersburg Mine," *National Tribune*, January 17, 1884; Pleasants to not stated, August 2, 1864, *OR*, vol. 40, pt. 1, 557; Burnside to Williams, July 28, 1864, *OR*, vol. 40, pt. 3, 566; James C. Fitzpatrick dispatch, July 27, 1864, *New York Herald*, August 1, 1864.

11. Burnside to Humphreys, July 26, 1864, appendix of report of court of inquiry, *OR*, vol. 40, pt. 1, 136; Cavanaugh and Marvel, *Battle of the Crater*, 16; E. A. Miller, *Black Civil War Soldiers of Illinois*, 60.

12. Burnside testimony, December 17, 1864, *RCCW*, 14; Burnside testimony, August 10, 1864, report of court of inquiry, *OR*, vol. 40, pt. 1, 58–59; H. S. Hall, "Mine Run to Petersburg," 246.

13. Forstchen, "28th United States Colored Troops," 84–85; E. A. Miller, *Black Civil War Soldiers of Illinois*, 49; James H. Payne letter, August 12, 1864, in *Christian Recorder*, August 20, 1864; Redkey, *Grand Army of Black Men*, 114; W. G. Robertson, "From the Crater to New Market Heights," 176; Thomas, "Colored Troops at Petersburg," 563n; Cavanaugh and Marvel, *Battle of the Crater*, 17.

14. Burnside to Williams, August 13, 1864, *OR*, Vol. 40, Pt. 1, 524; J. T. Wilson, *Black Phalanx*, 426; W. G. Robertson, "From the Crater to New Market Heights," 187; Stevens, *As If It Were Glory*, 178–79.

15. Thomas, "Colored Troops at Petersburg," 563, 567n; Joshua K. Sigfried to H. Seymour Hall, September 28, 1889: Hall to Sigfried, October 17, 1892, Albert D. Wright Congressional Medal of Honor File, RG94, NARA; Rickard, *Services with Colored Troops*, 26; Delevan Bates statement, January, 1891, in Bernard, *War Talks*, 183; Bowley, "Petersburg Mine," 28–29; Cavanaugh and Marvel, *Battle of the Crater*, 18; Ferrero testimony, August 31, 1864, report of court of inquiry, *OR*, vol. 40, pt. 1, 93; H. S. Hall, "Mine Run to Petersburg," 220–21; Way, "Battle of the Crater," *National Tribune*, June 3, 1904. Burnside testified that officers in the black regiments had told him they crossed their units over earthworks during training to familiarize the men with the type of terrain difficulties they would encounter in the attack. Burnside testimony, August 10, 1864, report of court of inquiry, *OR*, vol. 40, pt. 1, 59.

16. Scott, *Forgotten Valor,* 555; Thomas, "Colored Troops at Petersburg," 563; Delevan Bates statement, January, 1891, in Bernard, *War Talks,* 182; Sigfried to Hall, September 28, 1889, Albert D. Wright Congressional Medal of Honor File, RG94, NARA.

17. Meade testimony, August 8, 1864: Grant to Meade, July 28, 29, 1864: Meade to Grant, July 28, 1864, report of court of inquiry, *OR,* vol. 40, pt. 1, 46, 133–34; Grant to Butler, July 29, 1864, *OR,* vol. 40, pt. 3, 619–20.

18. Grant to Butler, July 20, 1864: Special Orders No. 64, Headquarters, Armies of the United States, July 21, 1864, *OR,* vol. 40, pt. 3, 355–56, 361; Butler to Smith, June 23, 1864, *OR,* vol. 40, pt. 2, 369; Longacre, *Army of Amateurs,* 188.

19. Burnside testimony, August 10, 1864, report of court of inquiry: Burnside to Williams, August 13, 1864, *OR,* vol. 40, pt. 1, 60–61, 524; Burnside testimony, December 17, 1864, *RCCW,* 17.

20. Meade testimony, August 8, 1864, report of court of inquiry, *OR,* vol. 40, pt. 1, 46; Grant testimony, December 20, 1864, *RCCW,* 125; Forstchen, "28th United States Colored Troops," 110, 112–13.

21. Humphreys to Burnside, July 29, 1864, *OR,* vol. 40, pt. 3, 608; Meade testimony, August 8, 1864: Burnside testimony, August 10, 1864, report of court of inquiry: Burnside to Williams, August 13, 1864, *OR,* vol. 40, pt. 1, 47, 61–62, 524; A. A. Humphreys, *Virginia Campaign,* 254.

22. Burnside testimony, August 10, 1864, report of court of inquiry, *OR,* vol. 40, pt. 1, 62.

23. Grant to Meade, July 29, 1864: Meade to Grant, July 29, 1864: Meade to Burnside, July 29, 1864, 5 P.M., *OR,* vol. 40, pt. 3, 590–91, 609; Meade testimony, August 8, 1864, report of court of inquiry, *OR,* vol. 40, pt. 1, 45.

24. Burnside testimony, August 10, 1864, report of court of inquiry, *OR,* vol. 40, pt. 1, 61; William Hamilton Harris Journal, July 29, 1864, VHS.

25. Potter, "General Robert B. Potter and the Assault at the Petersburg Crater," 481; Rickard, *Services with Colored Troops,* 26.

26. Orders, Headquarters, Army of the Potomac, July 29, 1864, *OR,* vol. 40, pt. 3, 596–97.

27. Circular, Headquarters, Ninth Corps, July 29, 1864, *OR,* vol. 40, pt. 3, 611–12; William Hamilton Harris Journal, July 29, 1864, VHS.

28. Burnside testimony, August 10, 1864, report of court of inquiry, *OR,* vol. 40, pt. 1, 61–62; Burnside to Williams, August 13, 1864, *OR,* vol. 40, pt. 1, 530; William Hamilton Harris Journal, July 30, 1864, VHS; Cavanaugh and Marvel, *Battle of the Crater,* 128.

29. Thomas W. Clarke account, 1865, Anderson, *Fifty-seventh Regiment of Massachusetts,* 203–4; Osborne, *History of the Twenty-ninth Regiment of Massachusetts,* 315–16; Powell, "Battle of the Petersburg Crater," 549n-550n.

30. Ledlie to Richmond, August 4, 1864, *OR,* vol. 40, pt. 1, 535; Powell, "Battle of the Petersburg Crater," 550; Willcox testimony, August 31, 1864, report of court of inquiry, *OR,* vol. 40, pt. 1, 94; Scott, *Forgotten Valor,* 556; Cavanaugh and Marvel, *Battle of the Crater,* 23, 115; Marvel, *Burnside,* 399–400.

31. Osborne, *History of the Twenty-ninth Regiment of Massachusetts,* 315–16; Joseph H. Barnes letter, Anderson, *Fifty-seventh Regiment of Massachusetts,* 213–14; Weld, "Petersburg Mine," 207.

32. Thomas W. Clarke account, 1865, Anderson, *Fifty-seventh Regiment of Massa-* *chusetts,* 204; Kilmer, "Dash into the Crater," 774.

33. Potter testimony, August 30, 1864, report of court of inquiry, *OR,* vol. 40, pt. 1, 88–89; Griffin to Benedict, n.d., Benedict, *Vermont in the Civil War,* 2:515; White, "Charging the Crater," *National Tribune,* June 21, 1883; Bliss reminiscences, 131, Zenas R. Bliss Papers, USAMHI. After the war, when Griffin wrote to Benedict in the second source cited in this note, he misremembered his instructions and stated that he was supposed to turn right and "double up the enemy's line" while keeping close enough to Ledlie to protect his right flank. This would have been impossible to do, but it shows how the confusion between the Burnside plan and the Meade plan continued to plague the participants of the attack for years to come.

34. William Baird Memoirs, 19–20, BHL-UM.

35. J. M. Miller, *North Anna Campaign,* 101, 171n; Hartranft to Sallie, July 12, 1864, John F. Hartranft Papers, Helen L. Shireman.

36. Warner, *Generals in Blue,* 277; James H. Ledlie obituary, *New York Times,* August 16, 1882; Thomas Ward letter, October 19, 1888: William E. Mercer affidavit, January 24, 1889: John C. Kelton to Commissioner of Pensions, October 24, 1888, James H. Ledlie Pension File, RG94, NARA; McWhiney and Jenkins, "Union's Worst General," 30, 32, 35–36; Burnside to Grant, June 5, 1864, *OR,* vol. 36, pt. 3, 619; J. M. Miller, *North Anna Campaign,* 100–105; Marvel, *Burnside,* 387; T. J. Howe, *Wasted Valor,* 93–104; Cavanaugh and Marvel, *Battle of the Crater,* 116; Simon Goodell Griffin, "Civil War Recollections," 22, DC.

37. Warner, *Generals in Blue,* 24–25; Welsh, *Medical Histories of Union Generals,* 21–22; Henry Ropes to father, April 25, 1862, 20th Massachusetts Regimental Collection, BPL; Morris Schaff, "Oration," in *Record of the Dedication of the Statue,* 61–62; Weld, *War Diary and Letters,* 344; Palfrey, *Memoir of William Francis Bartlett,* 110, 112, 117–18; Burnside to Williams, July 21, 1864, *OR,* vol. 40, pt. 3, 370–71; entry of July 26, 1864, Henry White Diary, AAS; LoPiano, "Gallantry in the Crater," 18–19; Thomas W. Clarke account, 1865, Anderson, *Fifty-seventh Regiment of Massachusetts,* 203.

38. Warner, *Generals in Blue,* 191–92, 382; Welsh, *Medical Histories of Union Generals,* 265–66; Cutrer, "Bliss, Zenas Randall," 594.

39. Warner, *Generals in Blue,* 211–12, 558–59; Welsh, *Medical Histories of Union Generals,* 155, 369.

40. *New York Times,* December 13, 1899; Ferrero, *Art of Dancing,* 13–181; Warner, *Generals in Blue,* 150–51, 502; Cavanaugh and Marvel, *Battle of the Crater,* 16–17; Gallagher, *Fighting for the Confederacy,* 329; Grant to Stanton, July 15, 1864, Simon, *Papers of Ulysses S. Grant,* 11:250; Delevan Bates to father, May 16, 1864, Saint, "The Civil War Letters of Delevan Bates," Nebraska Genealogical Project, http://files.usgw archives.org/ne/state/military/cwletter.txt; Welsh, *Medical Histories of Union Generals,* 337.

41. Burnside to Williams, July 3, 1864, *OR,* vol. 40, pt. 2, 609; White to Burnside, July 9, 1864: Burnside to Meade, July 29, 1864: Williams to Burnside, July 29, 1864: General Orders No. 34, Headquarters, Ninth Corps, July 29, 1864, *OR,* vol. 40, pt. 3, 111, 609–10, 612; Cavanaugh and Marvel, *Battle of the Crater,* 24; Marvel, *Burnside,* 403.

6. Night of July 29

1. Hunt to Williams, October 31, 1864, *OR*, vol. 40, pt. 1, 280; Hunt to Abbot, July 28, 1864: Hunt circular, July 29, 1864, *OR*, vol. 40, pt. 3, 581, 597; Nevins, *Diary of Battle*, 439–40, 444.

2. Hunt to Williams October 31, 1864, *OR*, vol. 40, pt. 1, 280; Hunt circular, July 29, 1864, *OR*, vol. 40, pt. 3, 597.

3. Nevins, *Diary of Battle*, 442–43.

4. Burnside to Williams, July 26, 1864: Hunt to Burnside, July 28, 1864: Hunt to Abbot, July 28, 1864, *OR*, vol. 40, pt. 3, 473, 566, 581; Cavanaugh and Marvel, *Battle of the Crater*, 25; Abbot testimony, September 2, 1864, and Monroe testimony, September 3, 1864, report of court of inquiry, *OR*, vol. 40, pt. 1, 110, 117; Nevins, *Diary of Battle*, 448–49; Bernard comment on Walker to Bernard, August 2, 1892, Bernard, *War Talks*, 204n, 230; Case, "Battle of the Mine," 21; Marvel, *Burnside*, 396.

5. Sheridan, *Personal Memoirs*, 1:450; Sheridan to Rawlins, May 13, 1866, *OR*, vol. 36, pt. 1, 800; Grant to Meade, July 29, 1864, report of court of inquiry: Humphreys to Wilson, July 29, 1864, 10 A.M. and 3:15 P.M., *OR*, vol. 40, pt. 1, 134, 155–56.

6. Weld, *War Diary and Letters*, 354–55; Meade testimony, December 20, 1864, *RCCW*, 39; Potter testimony, August 30, 1864, report of court of inquiry, *OR*, vol. 40, pt. 1, 88. Historians have consistently written of the need to use sandbags to construct steps out of the trench as the way to prepare the Union works for the passage of Burnside's infantry, but this view is not supported by the primary sources. Ledlie positioned his division on the open ground behind the forward Union line before the attack; he needed a method to get the men *across* the trench, not back into and out of it again, and the only way to do that was to completely fill in the trench. See, for example, Cavanaugh and Marvel, *Battle of the Crater*, 26.

7. Burnside testimony, August 11, 1864: Willcox testimony, August 31, 1864, report of court of inquiry, *OR*, vol. 40, pt. 1, 68–69, 94; Scott, *Forgotten Valor*, 555–56.

8. Burnside to Williams, August 13, 1864, *OR*, vol. 40, pt. 1, 524; Burnside testimony, August 11–12, 1864, report of court of inquiry, *OR*, vol. 40, pt. 1, 69, 71; Agassiz, *Meade's Headquarters*, 203; Chase, *Charge at Day-Break*, 8; *History of the Thirty-sixth Regiment Massachusetts*, 233.

9. Ledlie to Richmond, August 4, 1864, *OR*, vol. 40, pt. 1, 535; B. A. Spear, "In Front of Petersburg," *National Tribune*, June 20, 1889; Palfrey, *Memoir of William Francis Bartlett*, 118–19; C. H. Houghton, "In the Crater," 561; Weld, "Petersburg Mine," 207–8.

10. Thomas M. Clarke account, 1865, Anderson, *Fifty-seventh Regiment of Massachusetts*, 205–6, 212; Robinson to Mills, August 3, 1864, *OR*, vol. 40, pt. 1, 541; C. H. Houghton, "In the Crater," 561. Houghton recalled that the 14th New York Heavy Artillery was organized for easier handling into two battalions of six companies each, with each of the two battalions "acting as an independent regiment."

11. Barnes to Mills, August 3, 1864, *OR*, vol. 40, pt. 1, 538; Weld, "Petersburg Mine," 207–8; Burnside testimony, August 12, 1864, report of court of inquiry, *OR*, vol. 40, pt. 1, 74; Beal to uncle, August 5, 1864, Caleb Hadley Beal Papers, Mass-HS; *History of the Thirty-fifth Regiment Massachusetts*, 265–66. Thomas M. Clarke account, 1865, Anderson, *Fifty-seventh Regiment of Massachusetts*, 205, claims that part of Bartlett's brigade had to stand in the covered way deployed in a battle line by the flank, but there is no support for that contention.

12. B. A. Spear, "In Front of Petersburg," *National Tribune*, June 20, 1889; Griffin to Benedict, n.d., Benedict, *Vermont in the Civil War*, 2:515; Powell, "Battle of the Petersburg Crater," 550.

13. Potter to Richmond, July 29, 1864, *OR*, vol. 40, pt. 3, 612–13; Potter testimony, August 30, 1864, report of court of inquiry, *OR*, vol. 40, pt. 1, 88; Chase, *Charge at Day-Break*, 8–9, 15–16; Case, "Battle of the Mine," 20–21; Lord, *History of the Ninth Regiment New Hampshire*, 495; Griffin to Benedict, n.d., Benedict, *Vermont in the Civil War*, 2:515; Kenfield, "Captured by Rebels," 231–32.

14. Potter to Burnside, July 30, 1864, *OR*, vol. 40, pt. 3, 665; Potter testimony, December 20, 1864, *RCCW*, 98–99; Allen, *Forty-six Months with the Fourth R.I.*, 284; Richards, "Forty-fifth in the Battle of the Crater," in Albert, ed., *History of the Forty-fifth Regiment Pennsylvania*, 151; Richards, "Blunder at the Petersburg Mine," *National Tribune*, June 18, 1925; *History of the Thirty-sixth Regiment Massachusetts*, 234. Bliss reminiscences, 132–33, Zenas R. Bliss Papers, USAMHI, tells a slightly different story of events, that Potter told Bliss his men would not have to participate in the attack at all if relief did not arrive in time.

15. Don E. Scott to mother, August 2, 1864, Scott Family Papers, UNC; Potter testimony, August 30, 1864, report of court of inquiry, *OR*, vol. 40, pt. 1, 91; Loving, *Civil War Letters*, 162; Heisler to sister, July 31, 1864, Henry C. Heisler Papers, LC; Hopkins, *Seventh Regiment Rhode Island*, 198; William Hamilton Harris Journal, July 29, 1864, VHS; Cavanaugh and Marvel, *Battle of the Crater*, 24.

16. Cutcheon, "Twentieth Michigan Regiment in the Assault on Petersburg," 129–31; Cutcheon autobiography, 284, Byron Cutcheon Papers, BHL-UM; entry of July 29, 1864, Conrad Noll Diaries, BHL-UM; entry of July 30, 1864, Hodskin diary, Charles Horace Hodskin Papers, BHL-UM.

17. Cutcheon, "Twentieth Michigan Regiment in the Assault on Petersburg," 129–31; Cutcheon autobiography, 285, Byron Cutcheon Papers, BHL-UM; Willcox to Richmond, August 6, 1864, *OR*, vol. 40, pt. 1, 574; Aston, "Crater Fight Reminiscences," in Aston, *History and Roster*, 96–97; William H. Randall Reminiscences, July 30, 1864, BHL-UM; entry of July 29, 1864, Coppernall diary, Hiram W. Coppernall Collection, WLC-UM.

18. Bowley, "Petersburg Mine," 29; H. S. Hall, "Mine Run to Petersburg," 221–22; H. Seymour Hall to Joshua K. Sigfried, October 17, 1892, Albert D. Wright Congressional Medal of Honor File, RG94, NARA.

19. Thomas, "Colored Troops at Petersburg," 563; Thomas testimony, September 1, 1864, report of court of inquiry, *OR*, vol. 40, pt. 1, 104–5; Cutcheon, "Twentieth Michigan Regiment in the Assault on Petersburg," 131; *Memorial of Colonel John A. Bross*, 16; Ferrero to assistant adjutant general, Ninth Corps, August 1, 1864, *OR*, vol. 40, pt. 1, 595.

20. Meade testimony, August 8, 1864: Duane to Williams, August 5, 1864, report of court of inquiry, *OR*, vol. 40, pt. 1, 45, 158; Meade to Grant, July 29, 1864, *OR*, vol. 40, pt. 3, 591; Robeson to mother, July 31, August 8, 1864, Andrew Robeson Letters, Mass-HS.

21. Special Orders No. 206, Headquarters, Department of Virginia and North Carolina, July 29, 1864: Special Orders No. 91, Headquarters, Eighteenth Corps, July 29, 1864, *OR*, vol. 40, pt. 3, 623, 634; Burnham to Russell, July 31, 1864: Carr to Russell, August 3, 1864, *OR*, vol. 40, pt. 1, 709, 723; Turner testimony, January 17, 1865, *RCCW*, 132–33.

22. Meade testimony, August 9, 1864: Mott testimony, September 2, 1864, report of court of inquiry, *OR,* vol. 40, pt. 1, 54, 111; Circular, Headquarters, Third Division, Second Corps, July 29, 1864: Ord to Meade, July 29, 1864: Orders (no number), Headquarters, Eighteenth Corps, July 29, 1864, *OR,* vol. 40, pt. 3, 604, 631, 633–34; Livermore, *Days and Events,* 383; Trobriand to Finkelmeier, September 26, 1864: Carr to Russell, August 3, 1864, *OR,* vol. 40, pt. 1, 393, 724.

23. Ord to Meade, July 29, 1864, 9:25 P.M.: Orders (no number), Headquarters, Eighteenth Corps, July 29, 1864, *OR,* vol. 40, pt. 3, 632–34; Cavanaugh and Marvel, *Battle of the Crater,* 25; Ord to Humphreys, August 3, 1864, *OR,* vol. 40, pt. 1, 706.

24. Circular, Headquarters, Second Division, Eighteenth Corps, July 29, 1864, *OR,* vol. 40, pt. 3, 634; Ord to Humphreys, August 3, 1864: Burnham to Russell, July 31, 1864: Ames to Russell, August 2, 1864: Carr to Russell, August 3, 1864, *OR,* vol. 40, pt. 1, 706, 709, 719, 724; Carr testimony, September 3, 1864, report of court of inquiry, *OR,* vol. 40, pt. 1, 119–20; Cavanaugh and Marvel, *Battle of the Crater,* 25.

25. Turner testimony, January 17, 1865, *RCCW,* 133; Price, *History of the Ninety-seventh Regiment, Pennsylvania,* 306–7; Bryant, *Diary of Elias A. Bryant,* 174–75; Curtis to Sealy, August 3, 1864, *OR,* vol. 40, pt. 1, 701; Nichols, *Perry's Saints,* 250; Cunningham, *Three Years with the Adirondack Regiment,* 139; H. F. Jackson and O'Donnell, *Back Home in Oneida,* 150.

26. Gibbon, *Personal Recollections,* 253; Walker, *History of the Second Army Corps,* 568.

27. Humphreys to Warren, July 26, 1864: Meade to Warren, July 27, 1864, 8 A.M., 9:30 A.M., and 10:30 A.M.: Warren to Humphreys, July 27, 1864: Warren to Humphreys, July 29, 1864, *OR,* vol. 40, pt. 3, 468, 517–19, 604–5; Meade to Warren, July 27, 1864: Humphreys to Warren, July 26, 1864, *OR,* vol. 40, pt. 1, 444; C. H. Porter, "Petersburg Mine," 229; William Hamilton Harris Journal, July 29, 1864, VHS.

28. Crawford, "Civil War Letters of S. Rodman and Linton Smith," 107; Meade to Warren, July 28, 1864, *OR,* vol. 40, pt. 3, 564–65; Circular, Headquarters, Fifth Corps, July 29, 1864: Warren to Humphreys, July 29, 1864, *OR,* vol. 40, pt. 3, 607–8; Circular, Headquarters, Fifth Corps, July 29, 1864, *OR,* vol. 40, pt. 1, 448.

29. William Hamilton Harris Journal, July 30, 1864, VHS; Burnside testimony, August 11, 1864, report of court of inquiry, *OR,* vol. 40, pt. 1, 68; Livermore, *Days and Events,* 383; Marvel, *Burnside,* 397; Thomas F. Rives map, 1892, Bernard, *War Talks,* 229.

30. Marvel, *Burnside,* 397; Cavanaugh and Marvel, *Battle of the Crater,* 25; Meade testimony, August 10, 1864, report of court of inquiry, *OR,* vol. 40, pt. 1, 55; H. Porter, *Campaigning with Grant,* 261–62; H. H. Humphreys, *Andrew Atkinson Humphreys,* 242.

31. McMaster, "Elliott's Brigade," 11; LaMotte, "Battle of the Crater," *Charleston News and Courier,* May 14, 1899.

32. Cavanaugh and Marvel, *Battle of the Crater,* 36.

33. LaMotte, "Battle of the Crater," *Charleston News and Courier,* May 14, 1899; McMaster, "Battle of the Crater," 120; McMaster, "Elliott's Brigade," 13–14; Beaty, "Battle of the Crater," in Hudson, *Sketches and Reminiscences,* 47; Johnson to Brent, August 20, 1864, *OR,* vol. 40, pt. 1, 787; Johnson statement, in Roman, *Military Operations of General Beauregard,* 583; John Floyd, "First Fighting at the Crater," *Confederate Veteran Papers,* SCL-DU; Haile to not stated, n.d., *OR,* vol. 40, pt. 1, 799; E. R. White to editors,

August 2, 1864, *Petersburg Express,* August 4, 1864, reprinted in Bernard, *War Talks,* 320; Coit, "Battle of the Crater," 125.

34. Barnwell, "A View on the Crater Battle," 176; John Thomas Goode to George S. Bernard, February 7, 1911, PNB; Johnson statement, in Roman, *Military Operations of General Beauregard,* 584.

35. Gallagher, *Fighting for the Confederacy,* 450; Bernard note and Thomas F. Rives map, 1892, Bernard, *War Talks,* 205n, 229; McCabe, "Defence of Petersburg," 286; Cavanaugh and Marvel, *Battle of the Crater,* 148.

36. Gallagher, *Fighting for the Confederacy,* 466; Walker to Bernard, August 2, 1892, and Thomas F. Rives map, 1892, Bernard, *War Talks,* 203, 229; Cavanaugh and Marvel, *Battle of the Crater,* 146.

37. Robinson, "Artillery in Battle of the Crater," 165; Walker to Bernard, August 2, 1892: Myers statement, August 26, 1892: Thomas F. Rives map, 1892, Bernard, *War Talks,* 206, 209–10, 229; Cavanaugh and Marvel, *Battle of the Crater,* 146–47.

38. Bushrod R. Johnson to E. Porter Alexander, June 29, 1864, Cameron Scrapbook, PNB; Cavanaugh and Marvel, *Battle of the Crater,* 147–48; Flournoy statement, August 2, 1892, and Myers statement, August 26, 1892, Bernard, *War Talks,* 206, 210; Weymouth, "Otey Battery Organized," *Ashland (Va.) Herald-Progress,* August 27, 1925.

39. Douglas to Johnson, July [26], 1864: Douglas to Stevens, July 26, 27, 28, 29, 1864, *OR,* vol. 40, pt. 3, 806–8, 813, 816.

40. Gallagher, *Fighting for the Confederacy,* 449–50; H. L. Jackson, *First Regiment Engineer Troops,* 73.

41. Charles I. Browne to editor, *Richmond Whig,* July 19, 1864, reprinted in *New York Daily Tribune,* July 26, 1864.

42. Palfrey, *Memoir of William Francis Bartlett,* 118.

43. Case, "Battle of the Mine," 18–19; Chase, *Charge at Day-Break,* 13; William H. Randall Reminiscences, BHL-UM.

44. Thomas, "Colored Troops at Petersburg," 564; Bates, "A Day with the Colored Troops," *National Tribune,* January 30, 1908; White to editor, August 8, 1864, and Payne to editor, August 12, 1864, *Christian Recorder,* August 20, 1864, reprinted in Redkey, *Grand Army of Black Men,* 111, 113.

45. Sumner, *Diary of Cyrus B. Comstock,* 284; Pleasants and Straley, *Inferno at Petersburg,* 95–96.

46. Coit, "Battle of the Crater," 125–26.

7. Springing the Mine

1. Pleasants to not stated, August 2, 1864, *OR,* vol. 40, pt. 1, 557; Potter to White, July 30, 1864, *OR,* vol. 40, pt. 3, 665; Bosbyshell, *48th in the War,* 169–70.

2. Meade testimony, August 8, 1864: Humphreys to Burnside, July 30, 1864: Burnside to Humphreys, July 30, 1864, report of court of inquiry, *OR,* vol. 40, pt. 1, 47, 139.

3. Reese account, Guthrie, *Camp-Fires of the Afro-American,* 528; Pleasants testimony, January 13, 1865, *RCCW,* 129. Unlike Reese, Jacob Douty had no apparent experience at mining. He had suffered a painful injury in his leg while jumping across a ditch in East Tennessee and had been shot through the shoulder during the siege of Knoxville. Muster rolls: Casualty Sheet, August 7, 1880: Douty to J. F. Anderson, December 14, 1863: Surgeon's Certificate, James Oliver, December 13, 1863, Jacob Douty service record,

48th Pennsylvania, RG94, NARA; William R. D. Blackwood affidavit, June 23, 1880: Blackwood to Pension Office, May 13, 1882: Douty pension claim, May 13, 1882: Douty declaration for pension application, June 7, 1879: report of Surgeon General's Office, July 23, 1881: Proof of Disability form, July 7, 1880, Jacob Douty pension record, 48th Pennsylvania, RG94, NARA.

4. Agassiz, *Meade's Headquarters*, 197–98; Meade testimony, August 8, 1864, report of court of inquiry: Humphreys to Burnside, July 30, 1864, 4:15 A.M., 4:25 A.M., 4:35 A.M.: Humphreys to Warren, July 30, 1864, *OR*, vol. 40, pt. 1, 45, 47, 139–40, 449; Humphreys to Mott, July 30, 1864: Humphreys to Warren, July 30, 1864, 4:40 A.M.: *OR*, vol. 40, pt. 3, 650; Sumner, *Diary of Cyrus B. Comstock*, 285.

5. Livermore, *Days and Events*, 383; Burnside testimony, August 10, 1864, report of court of inquiry, *OR*, vol. 40, pt. 1, 62; Marvel, *Burnside*, 398.

6. Cutcheon, "Twentieth Michigan Regiment in the Assault on Petersburg," 131; Carr testimony, September 3, 1864, report of court of inquiry: Roemer to Chapin, August 5, 1864, *OR*, vol. 40, pt. 1, 120, 609; Nevins, *Diary of Battle*, 444–45; Powell, "Battle of the Petersburg Crater," 550–51.

7. Randall testimony, September 3, 1864, report of court of inquiry, *OR*, vol. 40, pt. 1, 116; Weld, *War Diary and Letters*, 352–53, 355; Aston, "Crater Fight Reminiscences," Aston, *History and Roster*, 97.

8. Case, "Battle of the Mine," 23.

9. Pleasants to not stated, August 2, 1864, *OR*, vol. 40, pt. 1, 557; Burnside testimony, December 17, 1864: Potter testimony, December 20, 1864: Pleasants testimony, January 13, 1865, *RCCW*, 19, 101, 128–29; Reese interview, "Petersburg Mine," *Philadelphia Weekly Times*, April 24, 1880; Bosbyshell, *48th in the War*, 169–70. In his testimony before the Committee on the Conduct of the War, Potter speculated that the splice in the fuse probably had absorbed dampness from the air but likely was not really wet. In his own testimony, Burnside blamed the problem on either dampness or the fact that someone had failed to put enough powder at the splice.

10. Reese account, Guthrie, *Camp-Fires of the Afro-American*, 528–29.

11. Burnside testimony, August 10, 1864, report of court of inquiry, *OR*, vol. 40, pt. 1, 62–63; Burnside testimony, December 17, 1864: James L. Van Buren testimony, December 20, 1864, *RCCW*, 19, 108.

12. Pleasants to not stated, August 2, 1864, *OR*, vol. 40, pt. 1, 557–58; Pleasants testimony, January 13, 1865, *RCCW*, 128; Reese account, Guthrie, *Camp-Fires of the Afro-American*, 529; Bosbyshell, *48th in the War*, 169–70; Post, *Soldiers' Letters*, 431.

13. C. H. Houghton, "In the Crater," 561.

14. Thomas W. Clarke account, 1865, Anderson, *Fifty-seventh Regiment of Massachusetts*, 206; Livermore, *Days and Events*, 387n.

15. C. Wilson, "Petersburg Mine," *National Tribune*, July 3, 1919.

16. Weld, *War Diary and Letters*, 353; entry of July 30, 1864, Henry White Diary, AAS; Joseph Nelson account, Stevenson, *Account of the Battle of the Mine*, 7; Weld, "Petersburg Mine," 208.

17. C. Wilson, "Petersburg Mine," *National Tribune*, July 3, 1919: Weld, "Petersburg Mine," 208; Kilmer, "Dash into the Crater," 774, 776; Powell, "Battle of the Petersburg Crater," 551; Ethan S. Morehead to brother, August 4, 1864, reprinted in *Vicksburg Daily*

Herald, August 16, 1864, available online at http://www.100thpenn.com/esmoreheadlet
.htm (accessed November 23, 2009).

18. Case, "Battle of the Mine," 25; Don E. Scott to mother, August 2, 1864, Scott
Family Papers, UNC; Griffin to Benedict, no date, Benedict, *Vermont in the Civil War,*
2:516; Jackman, *History of the Sixth New Hampshire,* 312; Bliss reminiscences, 133–34,
Zenas R. Bliss Papers, USAMHI; Richards, "Blunder at the Petersburg Mine," *National
Tribune,* June 18, 1925; Richards, "Forty-fifth in the Battle of the Crater," 48; Allen,
Forty-six Months with the Fourth R.I., 285.

19. Aston, "Crater Fight Reminiscences," in Aston, *History and Roster,* 97; Cutcheon,
"Twentieth Michigan Regiment in the Assault on Petersburg," 131–32; Byron M. Cutcheon autobiography, 286, Byron Cutcheon Papers, BHL-UM.

20. H. S. Hall, "Mine Run to Petersburg," 235; Bowley, "Petersburg Mine," 29; White
to editor of *Christian Reorder,* August 20, 1864, Redkey, *Grand Army of Black Men,* 111.

21. Bryant, *Diary of Elias A. Bryant,* 176; Cunningham, *Three Years with the Adirondack Regiment,* 139.

22. A. Spear et al., *Civil War Recollections of General Ellis Spear,* 134–35; Herdegen
and Murphy, *Four Years with the Iron Brigade,* 296; Matthews, *149th Pennsylvania,* 189;
C. H. Porter, "Petersburg Mine," 234; Young to Delia, August 4, 1864, Henry F. Young
Papers, WHS.

23. Gibbon, *Personal Recollections,* 253.

24. Agassiz, *Meade's Headquarters,* 197; Ford, *Cycle of Adams Letters,* 2:171.

25. William Russell diary excerpts, in *Petersburg Progress-Index,* November 10, 1961,
clipping in William Russell Papers, SCL-DU; entry of July 30, 1864, William Russell Diary,
PNB; Goode to Pollard, July 26, 1912, and Ryland account, Pollard, "Edward Bagby,"
456–57; Longest to brother, August 4, 1864, Younger Longest Letters, VHS; Calvin T.
Dewese to father, August, n.d., 1864, Dewese Family Letters, LOV; Harrill, *Reminiscences,* 27.

26. Robinson, "Artillery in the Battle of the Crater," 165.

27. Cockrell and Ballard, *Mississippi Rebel,* 286; Enjolras to editors of Montgomery
Advertiser, August 17, 1864, in Shaver, *History of the Sixtieth Alabama,* not paginated.

28. LaMotte, "Battle of the Crater," *Charleston News and Courier,* May 14, 1899.

29. McMaster, "Battle of the Crater," 120; John Floyd to editor, *The State* (Columbia,
S.C.), no date, 1898, *History of the Darlington Rifles,* 15; D. B. Stone, *Wandering to
Glory,* 206; John Floyd, "First Fighting at the Crater," *Confederate Veteran* Papers, SCL-
DU; McMaster to Bernard, August 3, 1892, Bernard, *War Talks,* 193.

30. Hugh Toland to editor, *Republican* (Jacksonville, Ala.), September, n.d., 1878,
George S. Bernard Papers, SCL-DU.

31. Johnson to Brent, August 20, 1864: Whitner to Johnson, August 31, 1864, *OR,* vol.
40, pt. 1, 788, 795; Johnson statement, in Roman, *Military Operations of General
Beauregard,* 583; Stewart, *Spirit of the South,* 131; McMaster, "Elliott's Brigade," 12;
Cavanaugh and Marvel, *Battle of the Crater,* 52; Burnside testimony, August 12, 1864,
report of court of inquiry, *OR,* vol. 40, pt. 1, 72.

32. Smyth to Douglas, July 30, 1864, *OR,* vol. 40, pt. 3, 820; Douglas, "Petersburg
Crater," Petersburg Crater Collection, UVA; E. N. Wise to editor, November 1905, unidentified newspaper clipping, n.d., in Stewart, comp., "Charge of the Crater," unpaginated,

MOC; Gallagher, *Fighting for the Confederacy,* 450. E. N. Wise recalled that the shift in gallery No. 1 was relieved well before the mine explosion because one of the men was sick, and the gallery was too long to be worked by his seven comrades. This saved the entire shift from being "blown to atoms." Wise to Daniel, November 14, 1905, John Warwick Daniel Papers, UVA.

33. Joseph William Eggleston Autobiography, 43, VHS; Coit, "Battle of the Crater," 127; William R. J. Pegram to Jenny, August 1, 1864, Pegram-Johnson-McIntosh Family Papers, VHS; Cavanaugh and Marvel, *Battle of the Crater,* 146; Bernard diary, July 31, 1864, in Bernard, "Battle of the Crater," 20; Pegram to Bernard, August 26, 1892, in Bernard, *War Talks,* 209. Some estimates of Pegram's strength and losses differ from those used here. See Johnson statement, in Roman, *Military Operations of General Beauregard,* 584; Stewart, *Spirit of the South,* 131; Cavanaugh and Marvel, *Battle of the Crater,* 41.

34. Hugh Toland to editor, *Republican* (Jacksonville, Ala.), September, n.d., 1878, George S. Bernard Papers, SCL-DU; Bernard, "Battle of the Crater," 22; McMaster, "Elliott's Brigade," 14; Record of Events, Field and Staff, 18th South Carolina: Record of Events, Company H, 18th South Carolina, *Supplement to the Official Records,* pt. 2, vol. 65, 121, 128; Suderow, "Confederate Casualties at the Crater," 28. Other estimates of losses in the 18th South Carolina place the total at around eighty men. See Record of Events, Company H, 18th South Carolina, *Supplement to the Official Records,* pt. 2, vol. 65, 128 and Stewart, *Spirit of the South,* 131.

35. Stewart, *Spirit of the South,* 131; Andrews, *Sketch of Company K,* 21; Landrum, *History of Spartanburg County,* 556–59; McMaster, "Elliott's Brigade," 14; Record of Events, Company K, 22nd South Carolina, *Supplement to the Official Records,* pt. 2, vol. 65, 199; Suderow, "Confederate Casualties at the Crater," 28.

36. Johnson to Brent, August 20, 1864, *OR,* vol. 40, pt. 1, 788; Johnson statement, in Roman, *Military Operations of General Beauregard,* 584; Cavanaugh and Marvel, *Battle of the Crater,* 41; Bernard, "Battle of the Crater," 22. At some point after the war, the State of South Carolina tabulated the number of deaths in Elliott's brigade on July 30, 1864. It amounted to 262. Despite the title of the document cited, the number included the battle of July 30 in addition to the mine explosion and excluded the number wounded and captured. Guy, "Those Blown Up at Crater," PNB.

37. Henry Pleasants to not stated, August 2, 1864, *OR,* vol. 40, pt. 1, 558; E. N. Wise to editor, November 1905, unidentified newspaper clipping, in Stewart, comp., "Charge of the Crater," unpaginated, MOC; Stewart, *Spirit of the South,* 131. Hugh Thomas Douglas's reported dimensions of the crater were a bit different from those of Wise. He set them at 125 feet long, 50 feet wide, and 30 feet deep. Douglas, "Confederate Countermining in Front of Petersburg," Petersburg Crater Collection, UVA.

38. Loring testimony, December 20, 1864, *RCCW,* 104–5; entry of July 30, 1864, Henry White Diary, AAS; Stewart, *Spirit of the South,* 131; Gallagher, *Fighting for the Confederacy,* 456; C. H. Houghton, "In the Crater," 561.

8. The First Union Wave

1. Nevins, *Diary of Battle,* 445; Marvel, *Burnside,* 398; Grant, *Personal Memoirs,* 2:612; Cavanaugh and Marvel, *Battle of the Crater,* 41; Tapert, *Brothers' War,* 209. A National Park Service report written in 1934 indicated that the Federals fired a total of

203 artillery and mortar pieces in the postexplosion bombardment. Jackson, "Report on Artillery Operations in the Battle of the Crater," 2, PNB.

2. Cunningham, *Three Years With the Adirondack Regiment,* 139; Washburn, *Complete Military History and Record,* 82–83; Parker to father, July 31, 1864, Hilon A. Parker Papers, WLC-UM; Lewin to wife, July 31, 1864, William Henry Lewin Papers, VHS; Fowle to Eliza, July 31, 1864, George Edward Fowle Correspondence, Mass-HS; Nevins, *Diary of Battle,* 445;

3. Lapham, *My Recollections of the War of the Rebellion,* 135–36; Second Corps Headquarters Journal, July 30, 1864, *OR,* vol. 40, pt. 1, 323–24; Farquhar testimony, September 5, 1864, report of court of inquiry, *OR,* vol. 40, pt. 1, 121; Nevins, *Diary of Battle,* 445.

4. Burnham to Russell, July 31, 1864, *OR,* vol. 40, pt. 1, 709; Herdegen and Murphy, *Four Years with the Iron Brigade,* 297; Monks to Hattie, August 6, 1864, Zerah Coston Monks Papers, WRHS.

5. B. A. Spear, "In Front of Petersburg," *National Tribune,* June 20, 1889; Thomas W. Clarke account, 1865, Anderson, *Fifty-seventh Regiment of Massachusetts,* 206.

6. Thomas W. Clarke account, 1865, Anderson, *Fifty-seventh Regiment of Massachusetts,* 212; *History of the Thirty-fifth Regiment Massachusetts,* 267; Cutcheon, "Twentieth Michigan Regiment in the Assault on Petersburg," 132; C. H. Houghton, "In the Crater," 561–62; Kilmer, "Dash into the Crater," 774; Weld, "Petersburg Mine," 208; Powell, "Battle of the Petersburg Crater," 551.

7. Weld, "Petersburg Mine," 208–9; Weld, *War Diary and Letters,* 352, 356.

8. *History of the Thirty-fifth Regiment Massachusetts,* 267–68.

9. Powell, "Battle of the Petersburg Crater," 551; entry of July 30, 1864, John Alfred Feister Coleman Diary, Confederate Miscellany Collection I, EU; Record of Events, Company C, 22nd South Carolina, *Supplement to the Official Records,* pt. 2, vol. 65, 194.

10. Powell, "Battle of the Petersburg Crater," 551; C. H. Houghton, "In the Crater," 562; J. D. Lynch to Governor Montague, n.d., Stewart, "Field of Blood Was the Crater," 351.

11. Landrum, *History of Spartanburg County,* 556–59; Bacon, "Capt. George B. Lake," 153; H. H. Humphreys, *Andrew Atkinson Humphreys,* 243.

12. Gallagher, *Fighting for the Confederacy,* 456.

13. Ledlie to Richmond, August 4, 1864, *OR,* vol. 40, pt. 1, 536; Kilmer, "Dash into the Crater," 775; C. H. Houghton, "In the Crater," 562; Cavanaugh and Marvel, *Battle of the Crater,* 52.

14. Burnside to Williams, August 13, 1864: Robinson to Mills, August 3, 1864, *OR,* vol. 40, pt. 1, 527, 541; Powell, "Battle of the Petersburg Crater," 552; Stevenson, *Account of the Battle of the Mine,* 9. Some sources relayed wild stories of Federal units, such as the 100th Pennsylvania, advancing west out of the breach immediately after Ledlie's division entered it. One such account, by Joseph Nelson of Company F, claimed the 100th went so far it could "see into the streets" of Petersburg. This story is recounted in Stevenson, *Account of the Battle of the Mine,* 7–8. Another account, by Thomas W. Clarke of Marshall's staff, claimed Bartlett's brigade advanced up to the crest of the ridge west of Pegram's Salient. This is relayed in Livermore, *Days and Events,* 387n.

15. Palfrey, *Memoir of William Francis Bartlett,* 119; Thomas W. Clarke account, 1865, Anderson, *Fifty-seventh Regiment of Massachusetts,* 208; Weld, "Petersburg Mine," 209; Weld, *War Diary and Letters,* 353; Powell, "Battle of the Petersburg Crater," 552.

16. Powell, "Battle of the Petersburg Crater," 553.

17. Thomas W. Clarke account, 1865, Anderson, *Fifty-seventh Regiment of Massachusetts,* 208; Morrison to H. Warren, August 3, 1864, John W. Morrison, "Mine Explosion, Petersburg, Va., July 30th 1864," CWURM; Ledlie to Lewis Richmond, August 4, 1864, *OR,* vol. 40, pt. 1, 536; Weld, "Petersburg Mine," 209–10.

18. Robinson testimony, September 3, 1864, report of court of inquiry: Robinson to Mills, August 3, 1864, *OR,* vol. 40, pt. 1, 114, 541–42; Davis, *Death in the Trenches,* 76–78; Thomas W. Clarke account, 1865, Anderson, *Fifty-seventh Regiment of Massachusetts,* 207–9.

19. Burnside to Williams, August 13, 1864: Griffin to Wright, July 31, 1864, *OR,* vol. 40, pt. 1, 528, 567; Newell Dutton to Bragg, ca. August 29, 1864, in "Letters and Diary of Corporal Elmer Bragg, 1862–1864," 76, DC; Cavanaugh and Marvel, *Battle of the Crater,* 44.

20. Marvel, *Race of the Soil,* 261–62; Lord, *History of the Ninth Regiment New Hampshire,* 490–91, 496–97; Case, "Battle of the Mine," 27; entry of July 30, 1864, John B. Bailey Diary, NHHS; Houston, *Thirty-second Maine,* 363.

21. Kenfield, "Captured by Rebels," 232; Don E. Scott to mother, August 2, 1864, Scott Family Papers, UNC; Cavanaugh and Marvel, *Battle of the Crater,* 46.

22. Chase, *Charge at Day-Break,* 17–20.

23. Don E. Scott to mother, August 2, 1864, Scott Family Papers, UNC.

24. Griffin to Benedict, n.d., Benedict, *Vermont in the Civil War,* 2:516; Potter to Richmond, August 1, 1864, *OR,* vol. 40, pt. 1, 547; Potter testimony, December 20, 1864, *RCCW,* 99; Thomas S. Lamotte note, in Bernard, *War Talks,* 197; Cavanaugh and Marvel, *Battle of the Crater,* 45.

25. White, "Charging the Crater," *National Tribune,* June 21, 1883; Case, "Battle of the Mine," 27; Marvel, *Race of the Soil,* 262–63; Lord, *History of the Ninth Regiment New Hampshire,* 500–501.

26. Jackman, *History of the Sixth New Hampshire,* 318–19.

27. Ibid., 319–22.

28. Powell, "Battle of the Petersburg Crater," 553–54.

29. Cutcheon, "Twentieth Michigan Regiment in the Assault on Petersburg," 134; Hartranft testimony, September 1, 1864, report of court of inquiry, *OR,* vol. 40, pt. 1, 101–2; Cavanaugh and Marvel, *Battle of the Crater,* 46.

30. Willcox to Richmond, August 6, 1864, *OR,* vol. 40, pt.1, 574; Knowles reminiscences, 140–43, Francis W. Knowles Papers, ECU; Aston, "Crater Fight Reminiscences," in Aston, *History and Roster,* 98–99.

31. Hartranft to Hutchins, August 5, 1864, *OR,* vol. 40, pt. 1, 578–79.

32. Aston, "Crater Fight Reminiscences," in Aston, *History and Roster,* 99; Scott, *Forgotten Valor,* 556.

33. Willcox testimony, September 1, 1864, report of court of inquiry: Willcox to Richmond, August 6, 1864, *OR,* vol. 40, pt. 1, 99, 574–75; Cavanaugh and Marvel, *Battle of the Crater,* 46; Aston, "Crater Fight Reminiscences," in Aston, *History and Roster,* 100.

34. Thomas W. Clarke account, 1865, Anderson, *Fifty-seventh Regiment of Massachusetts*, 206–7; Cutcheon autobiography, 287, Bryon Cutcheon Papers, BHL-UM.

35. Although no document details these movements, it is safe to assume they took place at this juncture.

36. Thomas W. Clarke account, 1865, Anderson, *Fifty-seventh Regiment of Massachusetts*, 209–10.

37. Powell, "Battle of the Petersburg Crater," 553, 560.

38. Weld, *War Diary and Letters*, 356–57.

39. *History of the Thirty-fifth Regiment Massachusetts*, 268–70.

40. Entry of July 30, 1864, Grierson diary, John Grierson Papers, KC.

41. Chubb testimony, September 1, 1864, report of court of inquiry, *OR*, vol. 40, pt. 1, 103–4; Charles J. Mills to mother, July 31, 1864, "Civil War Letters of Major Charles J. Mills," 139, Gregory A. Coco Collection, USAMHI; Loring testimony, December 20, 1864, *RCCW*, 105.

42. Potter testimony, August 30, 1864, report of court of inquiry, *OR*, vol. 40, pt. 1, 91; Scott, *Forgotten Valor*, 558–59.

43. Ord testimony, August 30, 1864, report of court of inquiry, *OR*, vol. 40, pt. 1, 87.

44. Meade testimony, August 8, 1864: Farquhar testimony, September 5, 1864, report of court of inquiry, *OR*, vol. 40, pt. 1, 47, 121; William Hamilton Harris Journal, July 30, 1864, VHS; Meade to Burnside, July 30, 1864, *OR*, vol. 40, pt. 3, 657.

45. Meade testimony, August 8, 1864: Humphreys to Burnside, July 30, 1864, report of court of inquiry, *OR*, vol. 40, pt. 1, 48, 140; Marvel, *Burnside*, 401–2; Agassiz, *Meade's Headquarters*, 200.

46. Meade to Burnside, July 30, 1864: Sanders to Meade, July 30, 1864, *OR*, vol. 40, pt. 3, 658.

47. Humphreys to Burnside, July 30, 1864: Burnside to Meade, July 30, 1864, Ambrose E. Burnside Papers, RG94, NARA; Burnside testimony, August 10, 1864, report of court of inquiry, *OR*, vol. 40, pt. 1, 64, 141; Marvel, *Burnside*, 403–4.

48. Burnside to Williams, August 13, 1864, *OR*, vol. 40, pt. 1, 528; Burnside testimony, August 11, 1864, report of court of inquiry, *OR*, vol. 40, pt. 1, 70; Harris to Ledlie, Potter, Willcox, and Ferrero, July 30, 1864, *OR*, vol. 40, pt. 3, 666.

49. Meade to Burnside, July 30, 1864, *OR*, vol. 40, pt. 3, 659: Marvel, *Burnside*, 403–4.

50. Meade testimony, December 20, 1864, *RCCW*, 88.

51. Duff to Fisher, July 30, 1864, 5 A.M. and 6:20 A.M., *OR*, vol. 40, pt. 3, 643; Burnside testimony, August 10, 1864: Humphreys to Warren, July 30, 1864, 5:50 A.M. and 6 A.M., and Warren to Humphreys, report of court of inquiry, *OR*, vol. 40, pt. 1, 64, 148–49.

52. Ayres testimony, August 29, 1864: Humphreys to Warren, July 30, 1864: Warren to Humphreys, July 30, 1864, report of court of inquiry, *OR*, vol. 40, pt. 1, 77, 149–50; Livermore, *Days and Events*, 386; A. A. Humphreys, *Virginia Campaign*, 261–62.

53. Humphreys to James H. Wilson, July 30, 1864, *OR*, vol. 40, pt. 3, 671–72.

54. Humphreys to Hancock, July 30, 1864: Hancock to Humphreys, July 30, 1864: Trobriand to Mott, July 30, 1864, *OR*, vol. 40, pt. 3, 644–45, 650; Hancock to Williams, August 3, 1864, *OR*, vol. 40, pt. 1, 312–13.

55. Hancock to Humphreys, July 30, 1864, *OR*, vol. 40, pt. 3, 645; Hancock to Williams, August 3, 1864, *OR*, vol. 40, pt. 1, 312–13.

56. H. Porter, *Campaigning with Grant*, 262–63.

57. Ibid., 264; Thomas, "Colored Troops at Petersburg," 564.

58. H. Porter, *Campaigning with Grant*, 266–67; entry of July 30, 1864, Charles Hadsall Diaries, SHSN; Pippitt to mother, August 1, 1864, Henry Pippitt Papers, James M. Schoff Civil War Collections, WLC-UM; Ward, *History of the Second Pennsylvania Veteran Heavy Artillery*, 88.

59. Meade testimony, August 8, 1864: Comstock testimony, August 30, 1864: Comstock to Grant, report of court of inquiry, *OR*, vol. 40, pt. 1, 48, 82–83, 142; Grant to Butler, July 30, 1864: Butler to Grant, July 30, 1864, *OR*, vol. 40, pt. 3, 673; Butler to Birney, July 30, 1864: Butler to Grant, July 30, 1864, *Private and Official Correspondence of Gen. Benjamin F. Butler*, vol. 4, 563–64.

9. Holding the Line

1. Suderow, "Confederate Casualties at the Crater," 28.

2. LaMotte, "Battle of the Crater," *Charleston News and Courier*, May 14, 1899.

3. Ibid.; McMaster, "Battle of the Crater," 120.

4. McMaster, "Elliott's Brigade," 14; Beaty, "Battle of the Crater," in Hudson, *Sketches and Reminiscences*, 48; LaMotte notes in margin of McCabe, "Defence of Petersburg," in Bernard, *War Talks*, 197; Smith Lipscomb to Daniel, November 30, 1905, John Warwick Daniel Papers, UVA.

5. McMaster, "Battle of the Crater," 120; LaMotte, "Battle of the Crater," *Charleston News and Courier*, May 14, 1899; McMaster, "Elliott's Brigade," 15.

6. LaMotte, "Battle of the Crater," *Charleston News and Courier*, May 14, 1899; McMaster to Bernard, August 3, 1892, Bernard, *War Talks*, 197.

7. McMaster, "Elliott's Brigade," 15; McMaster, "Battle of the Crater," 121; Coit, "Battle of the Crater," 129; Johnson statement and McMaster to Beauregard, February 14, 1872, in Roman, *Military Operations of General Beauregard*, 584, 588; McMaster to Bernard, August 3, 1892, and LaMotte notes in margin of McCabe's "Defence of Petersburg," in Bernard, *War Talks*, 197, 199; LaMotte, "Battle of the Crater," *Charleston News and Courier*, May 14, 1899; Govan and Livingood, *Haskell Memoirs*, 74; Barnwell, "A View on the Crater Battle," 177–78.

8. McMaster, "Elliott's Brigade," 15–16; McMaster, "Battle of the Crater," 121; McMaster to Beauregard, February 14, 1872, in Roman, *Military Operations of General Beauregard*, 588; Smith Lipscomb to Daniel, November 30, 1905, John Warwick Daniel Papers, UVA; Lee, *Memoirs of William Nelson Pendleton*, 358; Coit, "Battle of the Crater," 129; LaMotte, "Battle of the Crater," *Charleston News and Courier*, May 14, 1899. B. L. Beaty, a member of the 26th South Carolina, claimed that Elliott's attack involved between 350 and 400 men, with losses amounting to 49 killed, wounded, and missing. Beaty reported that the attackers advanced seventy-five yards before they stopped. Elliott, according to Beaty, fell only thirty yards from the crater, and some attackers managed to make it to the hole itself, but there is no evidence to support Beaty's claims. Beaty, "Battle of the Crater," in Hudson, *Sketches and Reminiscences*, 49–50, 60.

9. McMaster, "Elliott's Brigade," 16; McMaster, "Battle of the Crater," 121; McMaster to Bernard, August 3, 1892, Bernard, *War Talks*, 196; Beaty, "Battle of the Crater," in Hudson, *Sketches and Reminiscences*, 50.

10. McMaster to Bernard, August 3, 1892, Bernard, *War Talks*, 196, 199; McMaster to Beauregard, February 14, 1872, in Roman, *Military Operations of General Beauregard*, 588–89; Smith Lipscomb to Daniel, November 30, 1905, John Warwick Daniel Papers, UVA.

11. Roulhac, "Forty-ninth N.C.," 71; Matthew Norris Love to mother, August 6, 1864, PNB; Day, "Battle of the Crater," 355; Day, "Breastworks at Petersburg," 174; Pearce, *Diary of Captain Henry A. Chambers*, 209.

12. Chambers, "Bloody Crater," 175;

13. Thrash, "Vivid Reminiscence," 509; Henry A. Chambers letter, July 31, 1864, Chambers, "Bloody Crater, 176; LaMotte, "Battle of the Crater," *Charleston News and Courier*, May 14, 1899; Johnson statement, in Roman, *Military Operations of General Beauregard*, 585.

14. Henry A. Chambers letter, July 31, 1864, Chambers, "Bloody Crater, 176; LaMotte, "Battle of the Crater," *Charleston News and Courier*, May 14, 1899; Dixon, "Additional Sketch Forty-ninth Regiment," 157; Johnson statement, in Roman, *Military Operations of General Beauregard*, 585; Day, "Battle of the Crater," 355; entry of July 30, 1864, Chambers diary, Henry A. Chambers Papers, UNC; Johnson to Brent, August 20, 1864, *OR*, vol. 40, pt. 1, 790; Roulhac, "Forty-ninth N.C.," 72; Day, "Breastworks at Petersburg," 174; Day, *A True History*, 82–83. Several accounts by members of McAfee's brigade mistakenly identified the cavalier as the ditch into which a portion of the 49th North Carolina moved; some even confused the branch ravine with the cavalier. The cavalier was not occupied by any Confederates after the Federals moved into the crater.

15. Graham, "Fifty-sixth Regiment," 372; Harrill, *Reminiscences*, 27; Burgwyn, "Thirty-fifth Regiment," 624;

16. Beaty, "Battle of the Crater," in Hudson, *Sketches and Reminiscences*, 51; McMaster to Bernard, August 3, 1892, Bernard, *War Talks*, 199–200.

17. McMaster, "Elliott's Brigade," 25; Beaty, "Battle of the Crater," in Hudson, *Sketches and Reminiscences*, 51; McMaster to Bernard, August 3, 1892, Bernard, *War Talks*, 196, 200.

18. John Thomas Goode to George S. Bernard, February 7, 1911, PNB; Pollard, "Edward Bagby," 456; Wiatt, *26th Virginia Infantry*, 28; Suderow, "Confederate Casualties at the Crater," 27.

19. McMaster to Bernard, August 3, 1892, Bernard, *War Talks*, 200; McMaster, "Elliott's Brigade," 18; Johnson to Brent, August 20, 1864, *OR*, vol. 40, pt. 1, 790–91; H. A. Wise, "Career of Wise's Brigade," 14; J. S. Wise, *End of an Era*, 366–67; Andrews, *Sketch of Company K*, 22–23.

20. LaMotte, "Battle of the Crater," *Charleston News and Courier*, May 14, 1899.

21. McMaster, "Elliott's Brigade," 16–17.

22. Ibid., 20, 22; Roulhac, "Forty-ninth N.C.," 72–73; Ward, "Personal Experience," Lowry Shuford Collection, NCDAH; McMaster to Beauregard, February 14, 1872, in Roman, *Military Operations of General Beauregard*, 589; Chambers, "Bloody Crater," 176.

23. Day, "Battle of the Crater," 355; Roulhac, "Forty-ninth N.C.," 72.

24. Johnson to Brent, August 20, 1864, *OR*, vol. 40, pt. 1, 789; Johnson statement, in Roman, *Military Operations of General Beauregard*, 585; McCabe, quoted in Bernard, "Battle of the Crater," 35n.

25. R. F. Hoke to George W. Brent, August 6, 1864, Robert F. Hoke Papers, NCDAH; Hoke to Brent, August 6, 1864, *Supplement to the Official Records,* pt. 1, vol. 7, 303–4.

26. R. F. Hoke to George W. Brent, August 6, 1864, Robert F. Hoke Papers, NCDAH; Hoke to Brent, August 6, 1864, *Supplement to the Official Records,* pt. 1, vol. 7, 303–4. Burgwyn, "Clingman's Brigade," 495, indicates that the 8th North Carolina also was detached from the brigade to help Johnson, and Barefoot, *General Robert F. Hoke,* 218, supports that contention, but there seems to be no evidence to back it up.

27. Coit, "Battle of the Crater," 126; Coit letter, October 1887, quoted in Powell, "Battle of the Petersburg Crater," 555; McMaster, "Battle of the Crater," 120; LaMotte, "Battle of the Crater," *Charleston News and Courier,* May 14, 1899. Federal engineer Francis Farquhar thought the Confederate artillery did not open fire until at least forty-five minutes after the explosion. Farquhar testimony, September 5, 1864, report of court of inquiry, *OR,* vol. 40, pt. 1, 121.

28. Pegram to Bernard, August 26, 1892, Bernard, *War Talks,* 208–9.

29. Flounoy statement, August 2, 1892, Bernard, *War Talks,* 206–7.

30. Robinson, "Artillery in the Battle of the Crater," 165; Govan and Livingood, *Haskell Memoirs,* 72–73.

31. McCabe to Bernard, n.d., Bernard, "Battle of the Crater," 35–36n.

32. Flanner, "Flanner's North Carolina Battery," 247.

33. Johnson to Brent, August 20, 1864, *OR,* vol. 40, pt. 1, 789; Joseph William Eggleston Autobiography, 43–45, VHS.

34. Joseph William Eggleston Autobiography, 45, VHS.

35. Smith to Bernard, August 16, 1892, Bernard, *War Talks,* 313; Cavanaugh and Marvel, *Battle of the Crater,* 147.

36. Robinson, "Artillery in the Battle of the Crater," 166; Pendleton to Taylor, February 28, 1865, *OR,* vol. 40, pt. 1, 760; Gallagher, *Fighting for the Confederacy,* 466; Alexander to wife, August 14, 1864, Edward Porter Alexander Papers, UNC; Lee, *Memoirs of William Nelson Pendleton,* 358; Cavanaugh and Marvel, *Battle of the Crater,* 146.

37. Walker to Bernard, August 2, 1892, Bernard, *War Talks,* 203; Robinson, "Artillery in the Battle of the Crater," 166; Goode to Pollard, July 26, 1912, in Pollard, "Edward Bagby," 456; John Thomas Goode to George S. Bernard, February 7, 1911, PNB.

38. Walker to Bernard, August 2, 1892, Bernard, *War Talks,* 204; Robinson, "Artillery in the Battle of the Crater," 166; John Thomas Goode to George S. Bernard, February 7, 1911, PNB; Cavanaugh and Marvel, *Battle of the Crater,* 147; Goode to Pollard, July 26, 1912: Samuel P. Ryland account, n.d.: Tom Kelly account, n.d., in Pollard, "Edward Bagby," 457. According to the Kelly account, Bagby was killed by an artillery round that took away part of his head.

39. Gallagher, *Fighting for the Confederacy,* 466.

40. Ibid., 461; Walker to Bernard, August 2, 1892, Bernard, *War Talks,* 204–6.

41. *Petersburg Express,* August 1, 1864, in Bernard, *War Talks,* 318.

42. Banister, "Incidents in the Life of a Civil War Child," 2–4, UVA.

43. "Notes of Genl. Beauregard on W. J. Marrin's acct. of the explosion of the Federal Mine at Petersburg Va. July 30th 1864," July 17, 1876, Pierre G. T. Beauregard Papers, ALPL.

44. "Notes of Genl. Beauregard on W. J. Marrin's acct. of the explosion of the Federal Mine at Petersburg Va. July 30th 1864," July 17, 1876, Pierre G. T. Beauregard Papers,

ALPL; McCabe, "Defence of Petersburg," 289; Charles S. Venable statement, April 10, 1872, *Reply to a Communication Published by Gen. C. M. Wilcox, in the New Orleans Times, of January 1st, 1872,* 21, Mahone Family Papers, LOV; Samuel B. Paul to William H. Stewart, October 21, 1903, in Stewart, comp., "Charge of the Crater," 102, MOC.

45. William H. Palmer to Stewart, November 3, 1903, and Jethro Raiford statement, September 23, 1903, in Stewart, comp., "Charge of the Crater,"unpaginated and 73, respectively, MOC; William A. Palmer to Mahone, February 27, 1872, *Reply to a Communication Published by Gen. C. M. Wilcox, in the New Orleans Times, of January 1st, 1872,* 26, Mahone Family Papers, LOV; McCabe, "Defence of Petersburg," 289, 289n.

46. William H. Palmer to Stewart, October 20 and November 3, 1903, in Stewart, comp., "Charge of the Crater," unpaginated and 100, MOC; McCabe to Bernard, undated, Bernard, "Battle of the Crater," 35n; Bernard, "Battle of the Crater," 6; "Notes of Genl. Beauregard on W. J. Marrin's acct. of the explosion of the Federal Mine at Petersburg Va. July 30th 1864," July 17, 1876, Pierre G. T. Beauregard Papers, ALPL; George W. Brent to G. T. Beauregard, November 28, 1871, LSU. One member of Mahone's division claimed that Lee rode all the way to the division sector west of Jerusalem Plank Road, but there is no corroborating evidence for this. Jesse A. Hamilton statement, August 12, 1903, in Stewart, comp., "Charge of the Crater," 48, MOC. Johnson's biographer believes Lee arrived at division headquarters at 8:30 A.M., but the earlier time cited seems more accurate. Cummings, *Yankee Quaker,* 298.

47. "Notes of Genl. Beauregard on W. J. Marrin's acct. of the explosion of the Federal Mine at Petersburg Va. July 30th 1864," July 17, 1876, Pierre G. T. Beauregard Papers, ALPL; Charles S. Venable statement, April 10, 1872, *Reply to a Communication Published by Gen. C. M. Wilcox, in the New Orleans Times, of January 1st, 1872,* 22, Mahone Family Papers, LOV; Joseph William Eggleston Autobiography, 47, VHS; McCabe, "Defence of Petersburg," 289; Gallagher, *Fighting for the Confederacy,* 464; R. O. Whitehurst to Stewart, October 23, 1903, in Stewart, comp., "Charge of the Crater," unpaginated, MOC. After the war, Whitehurst visited the battlefield and described the Gee House as "a white cottage surrounded by a young orchard."

48. W. Gordon McCabe to Mahone, July 17, 1872, *Reply to a Communication Published by Gen. C. M. Wilcox, in the New Orleans Times, of January 1st, 1872,* 18, Mahone Family Papers, LOV; Joseph William Eggleston Autobiography, 47–48, VHS.

49. Cummings, *Yankee Quaker,* 295–96.

10. The Second Union Wave

1. Bliss reminiscences, 135–36, Zenas R. Bliss Papers, USAMHI; Turner to Russell, August 5, 1864, *OR,* vol. 40, pt. 1, 698–99.

2. Bliss reminiscences, 136, Zenas R. Bliss Papers, USAMHI; Allen, *Forty-six Months with the Fourth R.I.,* 286; Cushman, *History of the 58th Regt. Massachusetts,* 14; Horton to Peckham, August 8, 1864, *OR,* vol. 40, pt. 1, 551.

3. Bliss reminiscences, 137, Zenas R. Bliss Papers, USAMHI; Raymond testimony, September 8, 1864, report of court of inquiry: Potter to Richmond, August 1, 1864: Bliss to Peckham, August 2, 1864, *OR,* vol. 40, pt. 1, 124–25, 547, 549–50; Potter to Burnside, July 30, 1864: Harris to Ledlie, Potter, Willcox, and Ferrero, July 30, 1864, *OR,* vol. 40, pt. 3, 666; Potter testimony, December 20, 1864, *RCCW,* 100; *History of the Thirty-sixth Regiment Massachusetts,* 234; Powell, "Battle of the Petersburg Crater," 554–55.

4. Gregg testimony, September 3, 1864, report of court of inquiry: Bucklin to Peckham, August 8, 1864, *OR,* vol. 40, pt. 1, 117–18, 564; Cushman, *History of the 58th Regt. Massachusetts,* 15.

5. Bliss reminiscences, 138–39, Zenas R. Bliss Papers, USAMHI; Raymond testimony, September 8, 1864, report of court of inquiry: Bliss to Peckham, August 2, 1864, *OR,* vol. 40, pt. 1, 124–25, 550.

6. Gregg testimony, September 3, 1864, report of court of inquiry: Gregg to Bliss, August 9, 1864, *OR,* vol. 40, pt. 1, 117–18, 554; Richards, "Forty-fifth in the Battle of the Crater," 50–51; Albert, *History of the Forty-fifth Regiment Pennsylvania,* 154; Cavanaugh and Marvel, *Battle of the Crater,* 47.

7. Horton to Peckham, August 8, 1864, *OR,* vol. 40, pt. 1, 551; Cushman, *History of the 58th Regt. Massachusetts,* 15; Allen, *Forty-six Months with the Fourth R.I.,* 287–88; Sholes, "Crater Fight Vividly Portrayed," *National Tribune,* January 12, 1928; Powell, "Battle of the Petersburg Crater," 554; Cavanaugh and Marvel, *Battle of the Crater,* 47.

8. Loving, *Civil War Letters of George Washington Whitman,* 127–28; *History of the Thirty-sixth Regiment Massachusetts,* 237; Potter to Richmond, August 1, 1864: Bliss to Peckham, August 2, 1864, *OR,* vol. 40, pt. 1, 547–48, 550; Cavanaugh and Marvel, *Battle of the Crater,* 47, 50.

9. Hopkins, *Seventh Regiment Rhode Island,* 198–99; Daniels to Peckham, August 7, 1864, *OR,* vol. 40, pt. 1, 566.

10. Powell, "Battle of the Petersburg Crater," 560; Bouton, *Memoir of General Louis Bell,* 22; Farquhar testimony, September 5, 1864, report of court of inquiry: Turner to Russell, August 5, 1864, *OR,* vol. 40, pt. 1, 121, 698–99; Turner testimony, January 17, 1865, *RCCW,* 133.

11. J. H. Clark, *Iron Hearted Regiment,* 147; Bryant, *Diary of Elias A. Bryant,* 175.

12. Ord testimony, August 30, 1864, report of court of inquiry, *OR,* vol. 40, pt. 1, 83; Turner testimony, January 17, 1865, *RCCW,* 135.

13. Turner testimony, January 17, 1865, *RCCW,* 133–34; Turner to Russell, August 5, 1864, *OR,* vol. 40, pt. 1, 698–99.

14. Burnside testimony, August 11, 1864: Ord testimony, August 30, 1864: Humphreys to Ord, July 30, 1864, report of court of inquiry: Ord to Humphreys, August 3, 1864, *OR,* vol. 40, pt. 1, 70–71, 83–84, 147, 706–8; Turner testimony, January 17, 1865, *RCCW,* 133–34.

15. Ord testimony, August 30, 1864, report of court of inquiry: Ord to Humphreys, August 3, 1864, *OR,* vol. 40, pt. 1, 86, 708; Turner testimony, January 17, 1865, *RCCW,* 133–34; Livermore, *Days and Events,* 384.

16. Ord testimony, August 30, 1864: Ord to Meade, July 30, 1864, report of court of inquiry: Ord to Humphreys, August 3, 1864, *OR,* vol. 40, pt. 1, 84–85, 148, 707–8; Humphreys to Ord, July 30, 1864, *OR,* vol. 40, pt. 3, 685; Bryant, *Diary of Elias A. Bryant,* 175.

17. Sigfried to Hicks, July 31, 1864, *OR,* vol. 40, pt. 1, 596; Bowley, "Petersburg Mine," 31.

18. John H. Offer speech, quoted in Stevenson, *Account of the Battle of the Mine,* 15, and Bowley, "Petersburg Mine," 31.

19. Thomas, "Colored Troops at Petersburg," 564.

20. Chubb testimony, September 1, 1864, report of court of inquiry, *OR,* vol. 40, pt. 1, 103.

21. Burnside testimony, August 10, 1864, report of court of inquiry: Burnside to Williams, August 13, 1864: Ferrero to assistant adjutant general, Ninth Corps, August 1, 1864, *OR,* vol. 40, pt. 1, 64, 528, 595–96; Loring testimony, December 20, 1864, *RCCW,* 105; Powell, "Battle of the Petersburg Crater," 556.

22. Bates, "A Day with the Colored Troops," *National Tribune,* January 30, 1908; Bowley, "The Crater," *National Tribune,* November 6, 1884; Bowley, "Petersburg Mine," 31–32; Bates statement, January, 1891, Bernard, *War Talks,* 183; Seagrave, *Boy Lieutenant,* 83; Schmutz, *Battle of the Crater,* 216–17.

23. Bowley, "Petersburg Mine," 33; Bates, "A Day with the Colored Troops," *National Tribune,* January 30, 1908. Charles G. Loring, Burnside's staff officer, claimed that Bates asked his advice about what to do when the 30th USCT was struggling into the crowded traverse, and Loring suggested the movement outside the main Confederate line that worked so well. See Post, *Soldiers' Letters,* 432.

24. H. S. Hall, "Mine Run to Petersburg," 222–23, 235, 237–38; Thomas, "Colored Troops at Petersburg," 564; H. Seymour Hall to Joshua K. Sigfried, October 17, 1892, Albert D. Wright Congressional Medal of Honor File, RG94, NARA; Beyer and Keydel, *Deeds of Valor,* 1:392; Cutcheon autobiography, 287, 308, Byron Cutcheon Papers, BHL-UM; Cavanaugh and Marvel, *Battle of the Crater,* 56. Forstchen, "28th United States Colored Troops," 125n, believes the division began its attack between 7:45 and 8:15 A.M.

25. Thomas, "Colored Troops at Petersburg," 567n; Hall to Sigfried, October 17, 1892, Albert D. Wright Congressional Medal of Honor File, RG94, NARA; H. S. Hall, "Mine Run to Petersburg," 223–24.

26. Thomas, "Colored Troops at Petersburg," 567n; H. S. Hall, "Mine Run to Petersburg," 224–25, 228–29, 235–37, 247; Hall to Sigfried, October 17, 1892: Hall to L. A. Grant, February 20, 1893: Wright to H. L. McLain, June 16, 1916, Albert D. Wright Congressional Medal of Honor File, RG94, NARA; Beyer and Keydel, *Deeds of Valor,* 1:392–93; Ferrero to Lydig, November 7, 1864, *Supplement to the Official Records,* pt. 1, vol. 7, 233. Duane recalled that the Confederate abatis consisted of a loose pile of limbs that the Rebels had "pitched over the parapet" and that they had added rails to it, inclining them forward. Duane testimony, August 29, 1864, report of court of inquiry, *OR,* vol. 40, pt. 1, 77.

27. H. S. Hall, "Mine Run to Petersburg," 236–37, 240; Beyer and Keydel, *Deeds of Valor,* 1:392–93; Hall to L. A. Grant, February 20, 1893, Albert D. Wright Congressional Medal of Honor File, RG94, NARA.

28. Entry of July 30, 1864, Albert Rogall Diary, OHS; William I. Brown to Chandler, August 7, 1864, George Henry Chandler Papers, NHHS; Potter testimony, December 20, 1864, *RCCW,* 100; Aston, "Crater Fight Reminiscences," in Aston, *History and Roster,* 101; Hartranft testimony, September 1, 1864, report of court of inquiry: Sigfried to Hicks, July 31, 1864, *OR,* vol. 40, pt. 1, 102, 596; Dutton account, Lord, *History of the Ninth Regiment New Hampshire,* 498; Marvel, *Race of the Soil,* 268; Cavanaugh and Marvel, *Battle of the Crater,* 56.

29. Van Buren testimony, December 20, 1864, *RCCW,* 109; Bowley, "Petersburg Mine," 33–34; Bates, "A Day with the Colored Troops," *National Tribune,* January 30,

1908; Delevan Bates to editor of *Otsego (N.Y.) Republican,* October 1, 1895, Saint, "Civil War Letters of Delevan Bates," Nebraska Genealogical Project, http://files.usgwarchives .org/ne/state/military/cwletter.txt; H. S. Hall, "Mine Run to Petersburg," 227, 240; Proctor, "Massacre in the Crater," *National Tribune,* October 17, 1907.

30. White letter, August 20, 1864, Redkey, *Grand Army of Black Men,* 111–12; Ferrero testimony, August 31, 1864: Thomas testimony, September 1, 1864, report of court of inquiry, *OR,* vol. 40, pt. 1, 93, 104–5; entry of July 30, 1864, Warren H. Hurd Diary, Michael A. Cavanaugh Collection, HSSC; William Baird Memoirs, 20, BHL-UM; *Memorial of Colonel John A. Bross,* 17; Holsinger, "Colored Troops at the Mine," *National Tribune,* October 19, 1905. Ferrero claimed that Humphrey's brigade attempted to advance at the same time as his division, cutting into Sigfried's column after the 43rd USCT left the covered way and delaying most of his regiments in their advance. There is no evidence, however, to support this. Ferrero to Hall, n.d., in H. S. Hall, "Mine Run to Petersburg," 242, 244.

31. Entry of July 30, 1864, Warren H. Hurd Diary, Michael A. Cavanaugh Collection, HSSC; Rickard to sister, July 31, 1864, James Helme Rickard Letters, AAS; Stevens, *As If It Were Glory,* 182; Thomas, "Colored Troops at Petersburg," 564; *Memorial of Colonel John A. Bross,* 33–34; Van Buren testimony, December 20, 1864, *RCCW,* 109; Bowley, "Petersburg Mine," 34.

32. Thomas W. Clarke account, Anderson, *Fifty-seventh Regiment of Massachusetts,* 210–11; Potter to Richmond, August 1, 1864, *OR,* vol. 40, pt. 1, 548; Loring testimony, December 20, 1864: Van Buren testimony, December 20, 1864, *RCCW,* 105, 108–9; Post, *Soldiers' Letters,* 432.

33. Van Buren testimony, December 20, 1864, *RCCW,* 108–9; Thomas W. Clarke account, Livermore, *Days and Events,* 387n; Ledlie to Richmond, August 4, 1864, *OR,* vol. 40, pt. 1, 536.

34. W. G. Robertson, "From the Crater to New Market Heights," 175; R. M. Gosney letter, July 31, 1864, *Indianapolis Daily Journal,* August 8, 1864; J. H. Clark, *Iron Hearted Regiment,* 148; James W. Steel recollections, in H. S. Hall, "Mine Run to Petersburg," 238–39; Landrum, *History of Spartanburg County,* 556–59.

35. Humphrey to Hutchins, August 4, 1864, *OR,* vol. 40, pt. 1, 586; Cutcheon, "Twentieth Michigan Regiment in the Assault on Petersburg," 133–34.

36. Cutcheon to Mathews, August 3, 1864: Serviere to Mathews, August 5, 1864, *OR,* vol. 40, pt. 1, 590, 591; William H. Randall Reminiscences, July 30, 1864, BHL-UM; Cutcheon autobiography, 322–23, Byron Cutcheon Papers, BHL-UM.

37. Cutcheon, "Twentieth Michigan Regiment in the Assault on Petersburg," 134–35; Cutcheon autobiography, 288, 309–11, Byron Cutcheon Papers, BHL-UM; William H. Randall Reminiscences, July 30, 1864, BHL-UM.

38. Cutcheon autobiography, 288, 323, Byron Cutcheon Papers, BHL-UM; Cutcheon, "Twentieth Michigan Regiment in the Assault on Petersburg," 135; Cutcheon to Mathews, August 3, 1864, *OR,* vol. 40, pt. 1, 590; Johnson statement, in Roman, *Military Operations of General Beauregard,* 585–86; Wiatt, *26th Virginia Infantry,* 28; Samuel Davis Preston to Ham Chamberlayne, May 4, 1875, Chamberlayne Family Papers, VHS; Knowles reminiscences, 143, Francis W. Knowles Papers, ECU.

39. Willcox to Richmond, August 6, 1864; Humphrey to Hutchins, August 4, 1864: De Land to Mathews, August 3, 1864: Serviere to Mathews, August 5, 1864, *OR,* vol. 40, pt.

1, 575–76, 586, 587, 591–92; Cutcheon autobiography, 313–14, Byron Cutcheon Papers, BHL-UM; William H. Randall Reminiscences, July 30, 1864, BHL-UM; Cavanaugh and Marvel, *Battle of the Crater,* 51.

40. Cutcheon autobiography, 288, Byron Cutcheon Papers, BHL-UM.

41. Willcox to Burnside, July 30, 1864, *OR,* vol. 40, pt. 3, 667; Powell, "Battle of the Petersburg Crater," 555; Bernard, "Battle of the Crater," 6; Stewart, "Spirit of the South," 132; Barnwell, "A View on the Crater Battle," 178; Bernard, *War Talks,* 334.

42. Turner testimony, January 17, 1865, *RCCW,* 134.

43. Turner testimony, January 17, 1865, *RCCW,* 135; Turner to Russell, August 5, 1864: Bell to Sealy, August 3, 1864, *OR,* vol. 40, pt. 1, 699, 704; Bryant, *Diary of Elias A. Bryant,* 176; Cavanaugh and Marvel, *Battle of the Crater,* 53.

44. Turner testimony, January 17, 1865, *RCCW,* 135; Nichols, *Perry's Saints,* 246–47, 251; Carr testimony, September 3, 1864, report of court of inquiry: Turner to Russell, August 5, 1864; Coan to Sealy, August 3, 1864, *OR,* vol. 40, pt. 1, 120, 699, 702; Price, *History of the Ninety-seventh Regiment, Pennsylvania,* 308–9.

45. Curtis to Sealy, August 3, 1864, *OR,* vol. 40, pt. 1, 701; Rowland, "Petersburg Mine," *National Tribune,* July 18, 1907; Cavanaugh and Marvel, *Battle of the Crater,* 53.

46. McMaster, "Elliott's Brigade," 20–21; Day, "Battle of the Crater," 355–56; Day, *A True History,* 82–83; Day, "Breastworks at Petersburg," 174; Johnson to Brent, August 20, 1864, *OR,* vol. 40, pt. 1, 791.

47. Turner testimony, January 17, 1865, *RCCW,* 135; Turner to Russell, August 5, 1864: Curtis to Sealy, August 3, 1864: Bell to Sealy, August 3, 1864, *OR,* vol. 40, pt. 1, 699, 701, 704. A member of the 112th New York spun a yarn about Curtis's brigade advancing up to the Confederate line, pouring fire into the Rebels, and capturing a section of trench. He even argued that Grant appeared among them in the captured works before the order to retire was issued. Rowland, "Petersburg Mine," *National Tribune,* July 18, 1907.

48. Ames testimony, September 2, 1864: Humphreys to Ord, July 30, 1864, report of court of inquiry: Ames to Russell, August 2, 1864, *OR,* vol. 40, pt. 1, 108–9, 148, 719. Ord kept a complete file of reports from both Ames's and Turner's divisions in his personal papers, all of which were published in the *OR.* See E. O. C. Ord Papers, UCB.

11. An End and a Beginning

1. The thirty-nine regiments that entered the breach were Bartlett's brigade—21st, 29th, 56th, 57th, 59th Massachusetts and 100th Pennsylvania; Marshall's brigade—3rd Maryland Battalion, 14th New York Heavy Artillery, 179th New York, 2nd Pennsylvania Provisional Heavy Artillery, 35th Massachusetts; Bliss's brigade—4th Rhode Island, 58th Massachusetts, 45th Pennsylvania; Griffin's brigade—31st, 32nd Maine, 2nd Maryland, 9th, 11th New Hampshire, 17th Vermont; Hartranft's brigade—8th, 27th Michigan, 109th New York, 13th Ohio Cavalry (dismounted), 51st Pennsylvania, 37th, 38th Wisconsin; Humphrey's brigade—1st Michigan Sharpshooters, 2nd, 20th Michigan; Sigfried's brigade—27th, 30th, 39th, 43rd USCT; Thomas's brigade, 19th, 23rd, 28th, 29th, 31st USCT.

2. Cushman, *History of the 58th Regt. Massachusetts,* 15–16; Davis *Death in the Trenches,* 80.

3. Chase, *Charge at Day-Break,* 21–26.

4. Cogswell, *History of the Eleventh New Hampshire,* 422; Abbot testimony, September 2, 1864, report of court of inquiry, *OR,* vol. 40, pt. 1, 110; Loring to Burnside, July 30, 1864, 7:40 A.M., *OR,* vol. 40, pt. 3, 660.

5. *History of the Thirty-fifth Regiment Massachusetts,* 271.

6. Thomas, Randall, and Smith testimony, September 1, 3, 1864, report of court of inquiry, *OR,* vol. 40, pt. 1, 105, 116, 119; Welsh, *Medical Histories of Union Generals,* 114, 200–201; Marvel, *Race of the Soil,* 264.

7. Smith testimony, September 3, 1864, report of court of inquiry, *OR,* vol. 40, pt. 1, 119; Cutcheon autobiography, 323, Byron Cutcheon Papers, BHL-UM; Powell, "Battle of the Petersburg Crater," 555–56.

8. Potter testimony, August 30, 1864, report of court of inquiry, *OR,* vol. 40, pt. 1, 91; Bliss reminiscences, 139–41, Zenas R. Bliss Papers, USAMHI.

9. Sumner, *Diary of Cyrus B. Comstock,* 284–85; Meade testimony, August 8, 1864, report of court of inquiry, *OR,* vol. 40, pt. 1, 48; Burnside to Meade, July 30, 1864, 7:20 A.M.: Meade to Burnside, July 30, 1864, 7:30 A.M.: Burnside to Meade, July 30, 1864, *OR,* vol. 40, pt. 3, 660.

10. Meade to Burnside, July 30, 1864, 7:40 A.M., and 8 A.M., *OR,* vol. 40, pt. 3, 660–61; Burnside testimony, August 10, 1864: Burnside to Meade, July 30, 1864, ca. 7:35 A.M., report of court of inquiry, *OR,* vol. 40, pt. 1, 63, 143.

11. Marvel, *Burnside,* 403–4.

12. Agassiz, *Meade's Headquarters,* 200; Ord to Humphreys, August 3, 1864, *OR,* vol. 40, pt. 1, 707–8; H. Porter, *Campaigning with Grant,* 266–67; Comstock to Grant, July 30, 1864, 7 A.M., 8 A.M., 9:15 A.M., *OR,* vol. 40, pt. 3, 637. Porter claimed that he and Grant pushed their way into the crowded covered way with the waiting troops of Turner's division, working up a sweat in the hot sun. Grant made his way to the forward Union line and then walked in the open toward the Fourteen Gun Battery and entered the work to tell Burnside, "The entire opportunity has been lost. There is now no chance of success. These troops must be immediately withdrawn. It is slaughter to leave them here." Grant and Porter then returned to Meade's headquarters. There is no evidence to support this story, and it is difficult to imagine that Burnside would have ignored the general-in-chief's visit to the Fourteen Gun Battery in his official report. It is far more likely that Grant was satisfied with telling Ord to relay his message to Burnside.

13. Warren testimony, August 30, 1864: Warren to Humphreys, July 30, 1864, 7:50 A.M., 8 A.M.: Humphreys to Warren, July 30, 1864, report of court of inquiry, *OR,* vol. 40, pt. 1, 80–81, 150, 450–51.

14. Warren to Humphreys, July 30, 1864: Humphreys to Warren, July 30, 1864, report of court of inquiry, *OR,* vol. 40, pt. 1, 151, 451.

15. Ayres testimony, August 29, 1864: Warren testimony, August 30, 1864: Burnside to Meade, July 30, 1864: Warren to Humphreys, July 30, 1864: Meade to Warren, July 30, 1864, report of court of inquiry, *OR,* vol. 40, pt. 1, 78, 80–81, 143, 151–52; Meade to Warren, July 30, 1864, 9:45 A.M., *OR,* vol. 40, pt. 3, 654; Warren testimony, December 20, 1864, *RCCW,* 94; Willcox to Burnside, July 30, 1864, Ambrose E. Burnside Papers, RG94, NARA; A. A. Humphreys, *Virginia Campaign,* 261–62.

16. Mott testimony, September 2, 1864, report of court of inquiry, *OR,* vol. 40, pt. 1, 111; Hancock to Burnside, July 30, 1864: Burnside to Hancock, July 30, 1864, *OR,* vol. 40, pt. 3, 647.

17. Mott testimony, September 2, 1864, report of court of inquiry, *OR,* vol. 40, pt. 1, 111; J. I. Robertson, *Civil War Letters of General Robert McAllister,* 470; Hoke to George W. Brent, August 6, 1864, Robert F. Hoke Papers, NCDAH.

18. John Floyd to editor of *The State,* 1898, in D. B. Stone, *Wandering to Glory,* 207–8; McMaster, "Elliott's Brigade," 17–18, 25.

19. Powell, "Battle of the Petersburg Crater," 556–57n.

20. Thomas testimony, September 1, 1864, report of court of inquiry: Thomas to Hicks, August 2, 1864, *OR,* vol. 40, pt. 1, 105, 598; Thomas, "Colored Troops at Petersburg," 565.

21. Thomas to Hicks, August 2, 1864, *OR,* vol. 40, pt. 1, 598; Thomas, "Colored Troops at Petersburg," 565; account by officer of 31st USCT in *New York Evening Post,* quoted in J. T. Wilson, *Black Phalanx,* 427; Cavanaugh and Marvel, *Battle of the Crater,* 57. Thomas described the brigade guidon that Pennell carried as a triangle with a green strip at the base along the staff. A cannon and anchor crossed in the center on the green field, representing the Ninth Corps badge, and the rest of the guidon was white. It was picked up on the battlefield by Pvt. John W. Niles of the 41st Virginia and stored in Richmond. The Federals recovered it when they occupied the capital on April 3, 1865. Thomas, "Colored Troops at Petersburg," 563, 565n.

22. Thomas testimony, September 1, 1864, report of court of inquiry: Thomas to Hicks, August 2, 1864, *OR,* vol. 40, pt. 1, 598; Thomas, "Colored Troops at Petersburg," 565.

23. Bowley, "Petersburg Mine," 34–35; Bates statement, January, 1891, Bernard, *War Talks,* 183–84; Proctor, "Massacre in the Crater," *National Tribune,* October 17, 1907; Bowley, "The Crater," *National Tribune,* November 6, 1884; McMaster, "Battle of the Crater," 121–22; John Floyd, "First Fighting at the Crater," *Confederate Veteran* Papers, SCL-DU; McMaster, "Elliott's Brigade," 22; Cavanaugh and Marvel, *Battle of the Crater,* 58. Despite his horrible head wound, Bates returned to duty within eight weeks and led a brigade for the rest of the war.

24. Bowley, "The Crater," *National Tribune,* November 6, 1884; Thomas, "Colored Troops at Petersburg," 565; Forstchen, "28th United States Colored Troops," 129–31; Russell testimony, September 1, 1864: Barnes testimony, September 3, 1864, report of court of inquiry, *OR,* vol. 40, pt. 1, 106–7, 112; H. S. Hall, "Mine Run to Petersburg," 229; Cavanaugh and Marvel, *Battle of the Crater,* 85.

25. Stevens, *As If It Were Glory,* 183–84.

26. Ibid., 184.

27. Forstchen, "28th United States Colored Troops," 134.

28. *Memorial of Colonel John A. Bross,* 17–18, 34–35. Five men had carried the flag of the 29th USCT before Bross took it; three had been killed and two wounded.

29. Bowley, "Petersburg Mine," 35.

30. N. M. Blake, *William Mahone,* 6–7, 10–12, 14, 19, 21–22, 26, 31–32, 41–45, 47–50; summary of war service, Mahone Family Papers, LOV; Longstreet to Cooper, July 14, 1864, *OR,* vol. 40, pt. 3, 775; Trudeau, *Last Citadel,* 68–80.

31. Mahone, *Battle of the Crater,* 4; Mahone, "The Crater, Petersburg, Va.," 675; Mahone letter, August 20, 1892: Hinton statement, September 5, 1892, Bernard, *War Talks,* 213, 223; Harrison, "Route of Mahone's Troops to the Crater Battlefield," unpaginated, PNB; *Reply to a Communication Published by Gen. C. M. Wilcox, in the New Orleans Times, of January 1st, 1872,* 11: Charles S. Venable statement, April 10, 1872:

Walter H. Taylor to Mahone, June 3, 1872, Mahone Family Papers, LOV; entry of July 30, 1864, Sale diary, John F. Sale Papers, LOV; James Paul Verdery to sister, July 31, 1864, Eugene and James Paul Verdery Papers, SCL-DU; Evans, *16th Mississippi,* 279; James E. Phillips statement, October 1, 1903, in Stewart, comp., "Charge of the Crater," 96, MOC.

32. Julius H. Tyler statement, July 7, 1903: William T. Dewberry statement, July 7, 1903: Robert E. Norfleet statement, September 15, 1903: Josiah Joyner statement, September 15, 1903, in Stewart, comp., "Charge of the Crater," 17, 20, 65, 67, MOC; James E. Phillips to William H. Stewart, sometime after 1900, James Eldred Phillips Papers, VHS.

33. Stewart, *Battle of the Crater,* 5–6; Stewart, "Charge of the Crater," 78; Crow letter, October 7, 1892, in Bernard, *War Talks,* 223, 314; John T. Woodhouse statement, August 8, 1903: Jesse A. Hamilton statement, August 12, 1903, in Stewart, comp., "Charge of the Crater," 46, 48, MOC.

34. Weisiger to B. Perry, April 20, 1896, David Addison Weisiger Papers, VHS; Richard Watson Jones statement, ca. October 1903, in Stewart, comp., "Charge of the Crater," 104, MOC; James E. Phillips to William H. Stewart, sometime after 1900, James Eldred Phillips Papers, VHS; entry of July 30, 1864, Sale diary, John F. Sale Papers, LOV; Dorsey N. Binion to sister, August 1, 1864, Confederate Miscellany Collection I, SC-EU; Hinton statement, September 5, 1892, in Bernard, *War Talks,* 223.

35. Joshua Denby statement, July 6, 1903: John E. Laughton statement, September 19, 1903: R. O. Whitehurst to William H. Stewart, September 27, 1903, in Stewart, comp., "Charge of the Crater," 16, 70, 81, MOC; Stewart, "Charge of the Crater," 78; Stewart, *Spirit of the South,* 133; Etheredge, "Another Story of the Crater Battle" (*SHSP*), 204; McCabe, "Defence of Petersburg," 289, 293; W. R. S., "Sharpshooters of Mahone's Old Brigade" 307–8; Laughton, "Sharpshooters of Mahone's Brigade," 104; Featherston, "Battle of the 'Crater' as I Saw It," 23; Cavanaugh and Marvel, *Battle of the Crater,* 55.

36. Stewart, *Spirit of the South,* 133; James E. Phillips statement, October 1, 1903, 96: William H. Stewart, "History of the Crater," *Norfolk Dispatch,* October 24, 1905, in Stewart, comp., "Charge of the Crater," unpaginated, MOC; James E. Phillips to William H. Stewart, sometime after 1900, James Eldred Phillips Papers, VHS; Bernard letter, June 28, 1892, in Bernard, *War Talks,* 189; Bernard, "Battle of the Crater," 5.

37. Harrison, "Route of Mahone's Troops to the Crater Battlefield," unpaginated, PNB; Charles S. Venable statement, April 10, 1872, in *Reply to a Communication Published by Gen. C. M. Wilcox, in the New Orleans Times, of January 1st, 1872,* 22, Mahone Family Papers, LOV; Ivey statement, December, n.d., 1890, in Bernard, *War Talks,* 151n; McCabe, "Defence of Petersburg," 290; Bernard, "Battle of the Crater," 5; James E. Phillips to William H. Stewart, sometime after 1900, James Eldred Phillips Papers, VHS; Stewart, "Charge of the Crater," 79; Stewart, *Spirit of the South,* 134.

38. Bernard, "Battle of the Crater," 5–7; Harrison, "Route of Mahone's Troops to the Crater Battlefield," unpaginated, PNB; James E. Phillips to William H. Stewart, sometime after 1900, James Eldred Phillips Papers, VHS; Stewart, "Charge of the Crater," 79; Stewart, *Spirit of the South,* 134.

39. Charles S. Venable statement, April 10, 1872, in *Reply to a Communication Published by Gen. C. M. Wilcox, in the New Orleans Times, of January 1st, 1872,* 22, Mahone Family Papers, LOV.

40. Stewart, *Pair of Blankets*, 155; Cummings, *Yankee Quaker*, 297; Mahone letter, August 20, 1892, in Bernard, *War Talks*, 213; Mahone, *Battle of the Crater*, 5–6; McCabe, "Defence of Petersburg," 290.

41. McMaster, "Battle of the Crater," 122; McMaster, "Elliott's Brigade," 21; McMaster to Bernard, August 3, 1892, in Bernard, *War Talks*, 199; McMaster to Beauregard, February 14, 1872, in Roman, *Military Operations of General Beauregard*, 589; McCabe, "Defence of Petersburg," 290n.

42. Mahone letter, August 20, 1892, in Bernard, *War Talks*, 214; "Famous Fight at the Crater," *New York Times*, July 30, 1895; James H. Blakemore to committee of Mahone's Brigade, July 28, 1880, in undated clipping from *Richmond Whig*, Mahone Family Papers, LOV.

43. Stewart, "Charge of the Crater," 79–80; Stewart, *Battle of the Crater*, 8.

44. Harrison, "Route of Mahone's Troops to the Crater Battlefield," PNB; Bernard, "Battle of the Crater," 6–7; McCabe, "Defence of Petersburg," 290; Barnwell, "A View on the Crater Battle," 177.

45. Young, "Account of the Battle of the Crater," in Fortin, "Colonel Hilary A. Herbert's History of the Eighth Alabama," 197; Govan and Livingood, *Haskell Memoirs*, 74–76.

46. James E. Phillips statement, October 1, 1903: Richard Watson Jones statement, ca. October 1903, in Stewart, comp., "Charge of the Crater," 96–97, 104, MOC; Bernard, "Battle of the Crater," 7; William W. Coldwell letter, June 30, 1880, quoted in Mahone to committee of Mahone's Brigade, in undated clipping from *Richmond Whig*, Mahone Family Papers, LOV; Cavanaugh and Marvel, *Battle of the Crater*, 55.

47. Taylor letter, July 16, 1880, in Bernard, "Battle of the Crater," 7n; Josephus Scott statement, August 3, 1903: John T. Woodhouse statement, August 8, 1903, in Stewart, comp., "Charge of the Crater," 42, 46–47, MOC; Bernard letter, June 28, 1892, in Bernard, *War Talks*, 190.

48. Etheredge, "Another Story of the Crater Battle" (*SHSP*), 204; McCabe, "Defence of Petersburg," 290; Bernard, "Battle of the Crater," 7; R. O. Whitehurst to Stewart, September 27, 1903: James E. Phillips statement, October 1, 1903, in Stewart, comp., "Charge of the Crater," 83, 97, MOC; Whitehorne statement, July, 1890, in Bernard, *War Talks*, 180; John E. Laughton, Jr., letter, December 11, 1876, in Mahone to Committee of Mahone's Brigade, in undated clipping from *Richmond Whig*, Mahone Family Papers, LOV.

49. Warner, *Generals in Gray*, 330; Thomas P. Pollard letter, June 30, 1880, quoted in Mahone to Committee of Mahone's Brigade, in undated clipping from *Richmond Whig*, Mahone Family Papers, LOV.

50. McMaster, "Elliott's Brigade," 21; McMaster, "Battle of the Crater," 122–23; McMaster to Bernard, August 3, 1892, in Bernard, *War Talks*, 199; Thrash, "Vivid Reminiscence of the Crater," 509; Matthew Norris Love to mother, August 6, 1864, PNB; Bernard, "Battle of the Crater," 7.

51. Bernard letter, June 28, 1892, in Bernard, *War Talks*, 190; Weisiger to B. Perry, April 20, 1896, David Addison Weisiger Papers, VHS; Stewart, *Battle of the Crater*, 9; Stewart, *Spirit of the South*, 134; H. V. L. Bird to Sir, June 30, 1880, Bird Family Papers, VHS; John Edgar Foreman statement, July 3, 1903: John T. West statement, September 8, 1903, in Stewart, comp., "Charge of the Crater," 9, 59, MOC.

52. Whitehead, "Retaking of the Lines," 469–70; Hinton statement, September 5, 1892, in Bernard, *War Talks,* 224; Weisiger to B. Perry, April 20, 1896, David Addison Weisiger Papers, VHS.

53. Etheredge, "Another Story of the Crater Battle" (*SHSP*), 204; Weisiger to B. Perry, April 20, 1896, David Addison Weisiger Papers, VHS; Bernard, "Battle of the Crater," 37; George T. Rogers letter, July 22, 1880, and William H. Stewart letter, July 24, 1880, in Mahone to Committee of Mahone Brigade, undated clipping from *Richmond Whig,* Mahone Family Papers, LOV; Stewart statement, July 21, 1880, from *Richmond Whig,* August, 1880, in Bernard, *War Talks,* 219; Stewart, *Battle of the Crater,* 9; William J. Murphy statement, August 14, 1903: Edmund Curling statement, August 28, 1903, in Stewart, comp., "Charge of the Crater," 51, 55, MOC.

54. W. D. Barnard statement, August 3, 1903: Robert E. Norfleet statement, September 15, 1903: Samuel M. Gregory statement, October 16, 1903, in Stewart, comp., "Charge of the Crater," 44, 65, 95, MOC; H. V. L. Bird letter to committee, n.d., in Mahone to Committee of Mahone's Brigade, undated clipping from *Richmond Whig,* Mahone Family Papers, LOV.

55. Weisiger to B. Perry, April 20, 1896, David Addison Weisiger Papers, VHS; A. W. Grandy statement, July 2, 1903: James L. Welton statement, July 14, 1903: Jethro Raiford statement, September 23, 1903: R. O. Whitehurst to Stewart, September 27, 1903: Richard W. Jones statement, ca. October 1903, in Stewart, comp., "Charge of the Crater," 6, 28, 73, 83, 105, MOC; Stewart, *Spirit of the South,* 134; Bernard, "Battle of the Crater," 8–9.

56. Whitehorne statement, July 1890: Stith statement, November, 1891: Hinton statement, September 5, 1892, in Bernard, *War Talks,* 180, 188, 224; Henry E. Chase statement, August 17, 1903: John T. West statement, September 8, 1903, in Stewart, comp., "Charge of the Crater," 54, 59, MOC.

57. Mahone, *Battle of the Crater,* 7–8; biographical information and Lee's assessment of Girardey found in Warner, *Generals in Gray,* 105–6, and Crist, *Papers of Jefferson Davis,* 10:581–82n; Mahone letter, August 20, 1892: Blakemore statement, July 28, 1880, in Bernard, *War Talks,* 214, 219–20; James H. Blakemore to committee, July 28, 1880, in Mahone to Committee of Mahone's Brigade, undated clipping from *Richmond Whig,* Mahone Family Papers, LOV. Mahone apparently was standing some eighty feet from the left flank of Weisiger's brigade, and behind its line, to oversee the deployment of Hall's brigade when it became apparent that the Virginians needed to attack immediately. According to Henry C. Reynolds, he was just behind Company D, 61st Virginia. Girardey was in front of Weisiger's line and closer to its left flank than Mahone. Henry C. Reynolds statement, July 8, 1903, in Stewart, comp., "Charge of the Crater," 22, MOC.

58. Weisiger to B. Perry, April 20, 1896, David Addison Weisiger Papers, VHS; Weisiger letter in *Richmond State,* September 1880: Weisiger to Mahone, April 25, 1872: Coldwell statement, June 30, 1880: Hinton statement, September 5, 1892, in Bernard, *War Talks,* 217, 221–22, 224; Charles Ridgeley Goodwin letter, January 4, 1876: Thomas E. Richardson letter, December, 1876: Putnam Stith letter, December 23, 1876; John E. Laughton, Jr., letter, December 11, 1876: William W. Coldwell letter, June 30, 1880: H. V. L. Bird to committee, n.d.: William H. Etheredge letter, July 16, 1880: W. A. S. Taylor letter, July 16, 1880, in Mahone to Committee of Mahone's Brigade, undated clipping from *Richmond Whig,* Mahone Family Papers, LOV; H. V. L. Bird to Sir, June 30,

1880, Bird Family Papers, VHS; W. R. S., "Sharpshooters of Mahone's Old Brigade," 308; Etheredge, "Another Story of the Crater Battle" (*SHSP*), 204; William J. Pate statement, July 3, 1903: John T. Woodhouse statement, August 8, 1903: Edmund Curling statement, August 28, 1903, in Stewart, comp., "Charge of the Crater," 7, 47, 55, MOC.

59. Henry C. Reynolds statement, July 8, 1903: Edmund Curling statement, August 28, 1903, in Stewart, comp., "Charge of the Crater," 22, 55, MOC.

12. Weisiger Attacks

1. Bernard, "Battle of the Crater," 15, 27; Jones letter, June 22, 1892: Powell letter, July 25, 1892, in Bernard, *War Talks*, 201–2; Suderow, "Confederate Casualties at the Crater, 26; Stewart, *Battle of the Crater*, 7; Weisiger to B. Perry, April 20, 1896, David Addison Weisiger Papers, VHS; Stewart, *Spirit of the South*, 197; Stewart, "Charge of the Crater," 79; field visit to Crater battlefield, October 14, 1999; Thomas F. Rives map of Crater battlefield, 1892, in Bernard, *War Talks*, 229. Some sources indicate that Weisiger's attack began at 9:15 A.M. (Mahone, *Battle of the Crater*, 8), or at 8:45 A.M. (Stewart, "Charge of the Crater," 81). Stewart, in *Spirit of the South*, 132, and in "Field of Blood Was the Crater," 355, claimed the distance charged amounted to two hundred yards.

2. Beaty, "Battle of the Crater," in Hudson, *Sketches and Reminiscences*, 55–56; McMaster, "Elliott's Brigade," 22; Crowder to McMaster, August 10, 1892, in Bernard, *War Talks*, 200n; Smith Lipscomb to Daniel, November 30, 1905, John Warwick Daniel Papers, UVA.

3. Day, "Breastworks at Petersburg," 175; Pearce, *Diary of Captain Henry A. Chambers*, 210; Dixon, "Additional Sketch Forty-ninth Regiment," 157; Johnson statement, in Roman, *Military Operations of General Beauregard*, 586; Johnson to Brent, August 20, 1864, *OR*, vol. 40, pt. 1, 791; Matthew Norris Love to mother, August 6, 1864, PNB; Ferguson, "Twenty-fifth Regiment," 299; J. W. Love to sister, August 2, 1864, Matthew N. Love Papers, SCL-DU; James Paul Verdery to sister, July 31, 1864, Eugene and James Paul Verdery Papers, SCL-DU; Odom to wife, August 2, 1864, Laban Odom Letters, Microfilm Library, GA; Dorsey N. Binion to sister, August 1, 1864, Confederate Miscellany Collection I, EU; Zwemer, *For Home and the Southland*, 50; Cavanaugh and Marvel, *Battle of the Crater*, 88; Bernard letter, June 28, 1892: Smith letter, September 8, 1890, in Bernard, *War Talks*, 190, 200n; Bernard, "Battle of the Crater," 36.

4. Stewart, *Spirit of the South*, 134; Zwemer, *For Home and the Southland*, 50; Matthew R. Hall to editor of *Petersburg Express*, August 2, 1864, *Supplement to the Official Records*, pt. 1, vol. 7, 309–10; Laughton letter, October 15, 1892, in Bernard, *War Talks*, 320.

5. Whitehorne statement, July 1890, Bernard, *War Talks*, 180; McCabe, "Defence of Petersburg," 291; Virginius S. Kilby statement, September 15, 1903, in Stewart, comp., "Charge of the Crater," 64, MOC.

6. Stewart, *Battle of the Crater*, 10; Bernard, "Battle of the Crater," 9–10; Henry E. Chase statement, August 17, 1903: Raynor Speight statement, August 23, 1903, in Stewart, comp., "Charge of the Crater," 54, 57, MOC; Whitehorne statement, July 1890, in Bernard, *War Talks*, 180; H. V. L. Bird to Sir, June 30, 1880, Bird Family Papers, VHS.

7. Laughton statement, September 1890, in Bernard, *War Talks*, 185–86; McMaster, "Elliott's Brigade," 23; Henry E. Chase statement, August 17, 1903, in Stewart, comp., "Charge of the Crater," 54, MOC.

8. William H. Etheredge statement, July 27, 1903, in Stewart, comp., "Charge of the Crater," 38, MOC; Stewart, *Battle of the Crater,* 12; Stewart, *Spirit of the South,* 134–35.

9. McCabe letter, n.d., in Bernard, "Battle of the Crater," 36n; "Notes of Genl. Beauregard on W. J. Marrin's acct. of the explosion of the Federal Mine at Petersburg Va. July 30th 1864," July 17, 1876, Pierre G. T. Beauregard Papers, ALPL; McCabe to Mahone, July 17, 1872, in *Reply to a Communication Published by Gen. C. M. Wilcox, in the New Orleans Times, of January 1st, 1872,* 18, Mahone Family Papers, LOV; Robinson, "Artillery in Battle of the Crater," 165.

10. Howard Aston, "Crater Fight Reminiscences," in Aston, *History and Roster,* 102; Hartranft to Hutchins, August 5, 1864, *OR,* vol. 40, pt. 1, 579; Hartranft to father, August 16, 1864, John F. Hartranft Papers, Helen L. Shireman; Powell, "Battle of the Petersburg Crater," 557.

11. William H. Pate statement, July 3, 1903: Williamson Smith statement, July 6, 1903: William T. Dewberry statement, July 7, 1903: Robert E. Norfleet statement, September 15, 1903, in Stewart, comp., "Charge of the Crater," 7, 16, 20, 65–66, MOC;

12. Weisiger to B. Perry, April 20, 1896, David Addison Weisiger Papers, VHS; McCabe, "Defence of Petersburg," 291n; John Edgar Foreman statement, July 3, 1903: Calvin L. Peek statement, August 15, 1903: Amnon Peek statement, September 15, 1903, in Stewart, comp., "Charge of the Crater," 9, 53, 62, MOC.

13. Stevens, *As If It Were Glory,* 184–85; Weld, "Petersburg Mine," 210–11.

14. Davis statement, January 1891, in Bernard, *War Talks,* 187; Etheredge, "Another Story of the Crater Battle" *(SHSP),* 205.

15. Phillips to William H. Stewart, sometime after 1900, James Eldred Phillips Papers, VHS; James E. Phillips statement, October 1, 1903: Richard Watson Jones statement, ca. October, 1903, in Stewart, comp., "Charge of the Crater," 97, 106, MOC.

16. John T. West statement, September 8, 1903, in Stewart, comp., "Charge of the Crater," 60, MOC.

17. Phillips to William H. Stewart, sometime after 1900, James Eldred Phillips Papers, VHS; Edmund Curling statement, August 28, 1903: James E. Phillips statement, October 1, 1903, in Stewart, comp., "Charge of the Crater," 55–56, 97, MOC.

18. Henry E. Chase statement, August 17, 1903: John E. Laughton statement, September 19, 1903: R. O. Whitehurst to Stewart, September 27, 1903, in Stewart, comp., "Charge of the Crater," 54, 71, 84–85, MOC.

19. Cutchin, "Reminiscence of the Charge of the Crater," PNB; William Emmerson statement, July 16, 1903: Josiah Frank Cutchin statement, August 3, 1903, in Stewart, comp., "Charge of the Crater," 31, 43, MOC.

20. Weisiger to B. Perry, April 20, 1896, David Addison Weisiger Papers, VHS; Welsh, *Medical Histories of Confederate Generals,* 231; Rogers statement, July 22, 1880, in Bernard, *War Talks,* 219; Stewart, *Spirit of the South,* 137.

21. W. F. Baugh to Stewart, December 4, 1905, in Stewart, comp., "Charge of the Crater," 120, MOC; Scott, *Forgotten Valor,* 558–59.

22. Coit to All, August 3, 1864, Charles M. Coit Papers, YU; entry of July 30, 1864, Albert Rogall Diary, OHS; Forstchen, "28th United States Colored Troops," 133.

23. John W. Morrison to H. Warren, August 3, 1864, in John W. Morrison, "Mine Explosion, Petersburg, Va., July 30th 1864," CWURM; Taylor to Jane, July 31, 1864,

William Taylor Letters, CWM; *History of the Thirty-fifth Regiment Massachusetts,* 271–72; Cavanaugh and Marvel, *Battle of the Crater,* 89.

24. Newell Dutton account: Clement account, in Lord, *History of the Ninth Regiment New Hampshire,* 498, 502; Dutton to Elmer Bragg, ca. August 29, 1864, in "Letters and Diary of Corporal Elmer Bragg, 1862–1864," 77, DC; Cavanaugh and Marvel, *Battle of the Crater,* 88–89.

25. Thomas W. Clarke account, 1865, in Anderson, *Fifty-seventh Regiment of Massachusetts,* 211; Kenfield, "Captured by Rebels," 233.

26. Livermore, *Days and Events,* 385–86.

27. Carr testimony, September 3, 1864, report of court of inquiry, OR, vol. 40, pt. 1, 120–21.

28. Proctor, "Massacre in the Crater," *National Tribune,* October 17, 1907; Bell to Sealy, August 3, 1864, OR, vol. 40, pt. 1, 704; J. H. Clark, *Iron Hearted Regiment,* 151–52; Louis H. Bell to George, August 12, 1864, Bell Family Papers, NHHS; Bouton, *Memoir of General Louis Bell,* 22–23; Bryant, *Diary of Elias A. Bryant,* 178–79; Cavanaugh and Marvel, *Battle of the Crater,* 89.

29. Farquhar testimony, September 5, 1864, report of court of inquiry, OR, vol. 40, pt. 1, 122; Cavanaugh and Marvel, *Battle of the Crater,* 90.

30. Coan to Sealy, August 3, 1864, OR, vol. 40, pt. 1, 702; Price, *History of the Ninety-seventh Regiment, Pennsylvania,* 310–11.

31. Curtis to Sealy, August 3, 1864, OR, vol. 40, pt. 1, 701; Rockwell, *Dear Frank,* 539; Rowland, "Petersburg Mine," *National Tribune,* July 18, 1907; Hyde, *History of the One Hundred and Twelfth Regiment N.Y.,* 94–95; Cavanaugh and Marvel, *Battle of the Crater,* 89.

32. Loving, *Civil War Letters,* 128.

33. Proctor, "Massacre in the Crater," *National Tribune,* October 17, 1907; Burnham to Russell, July 31, 1864: Johnson to Brent, August 20, 1864, OR, vol. 40, pt. 1, 709, 791; Coit, "Battle of the Crater," 130; Ludlow to Butler, July 30, 1864, OR, vol. 40, pt. 3, 676–77; Smith testimony, September 3, 1864: Chubb testimony, September 1, 1864, report of court of inquiry, OR, vol. 40, pt. 1, 103, 118–19.

34. Thomas to Hicks, August 2, 1864, OR, vol. 40, pt. 1, 599; Thomas, "Colored Troops at Petersburg," 567.

35. Etheredge, "Another Story of the Crater Battle," 205.

36. James L. Welton statement, July 14, 1903, in Stewart, comp., "Charge of the Crater," 28, MOC; Smith letter, September 8, 1890, in Bernard, *War Talks,* 184.

37. Stith statement, November 1891: Bernard letter, June 28, 1892, in Bernard, *War Talks,* 188, 191.

38. Bernard, "Battle of the Crater," 10–11.

39. Ibid., 11–14.

40. Crow letter, October 7, 1892, in Bernard, *War Talks,* 316–17.

41. Phillips to William H. Stewart, sometime after 1900, James Eldred Phillips Papers, VHS; Bernard, "Battle of the Crater," 15.

42. William H. Stewart statement, July 3, 1903: Josephus Scott statement, August 3, 1903: William J. Murphy statement, August 14, 1903, in Stewart, comp., "Charge of the Crater," 12, 42, 51, MOC; William Fielding Baugh to Stewart, December 4, 1905, LOV.

43. William J. Pate statement, July 3, 1903: A. W. Grandy statement, July 2, 1903, in Stewart, comp., "Charge of the Crater," 5, 6, MOC.

44. Amnon Peek statement, September 15, 1903, in Stewart, comp., "Charge of the Crater," 62, MOC.

45. Antonio M. Cooke statement, July 10, 1903: William Wright statement, August 4, 1903: Raynor Speight statement, August 23, 1903: John W. Robertson statement, September 23, 1903, in Stewart, comp., "Charge of the Crater," 27, 45, 57, 74, MOC.

46. Stewart, *Battle of the Crater,* 12; Le Roy McC. West statement, June 30, 1903: J. J. Bilisoly statement, July 4, 1903: John T. West statement, September 8, 1903, in Stewart, comp., "Charge of the Crater," 4, 13, 61, MOC.

47. Etheredge, "Another Story of the Crater Battle," 206–7; William H. Etheredge to George J. Rogers, March 23, 1892 (unpaginated): John W. Beaton statement, July 6, 1903: Virgil B. Dunford statement, July 17, 1903: J. Thomas Dunn statement, July 22, 1903: William H. Etheredge statement, July 27, 1903, in Stewart, comp., "Charge of the Crater," 14, 34, 35, 39, MOC; Stewart, *Battle of the Crater,* 13.

48. J. H. Parker statement, August 12, 1903: Robert E. Norfleet statement, September 15, 1903: John M. Sheperd statement, September 15, 1903, in Stewart, comp., "Charge of the Crater," 49–50, 66, 69, MOC.

49. Matthew Norris Love to mother, August 6, 1864, PNB; James Paul Verdery to sister, July 31, 1864, Eugene and James Paul Verdery Papers, SCL-DU; Odom to wife, August 2, 1864, Laban Odom Letters, Microfilm Library, GA; Dorsey N. Binion to sister, August 1, 1864, Confederate Miscellany Collection I, EU; Zwemer, *For Home and the Southland,* 50.

50. H. V. L. Bird to Darling, August 5, 1864, Bird Family Papers, VHS; Case, "Battle of the Mine," 28–29; H. S. Hall, "Mine Run to Petersburg," 232, 234, 239.

51. Delevan Bates to editor of *Otsego (N.Y.) Republican,* October 1, 1895, in Saint, "Civil War Letters of Delevan Bates," Nebraska Genealogical Project, http://files.usgw archives.org/ne/state/military/cwletter.txt.

52. Bowley, "Petersburg Mine," 35–36; Seagrave, *Boy Lieutenant,* 83–85; Proctor, "Massacre in the Crater," *National Tribune,* October 17, 1907; Bowley, "The Crater," *National Tribune,* November 6, 1884.

53. Griffin to Wright, July 31, 1864, *OR,* vol. 40, pt. 1, 567; Marvel, *Race of the Soil,* 271.

54. Lathe account, in Lord, *History of the Ninth Regiment New Hampshire,* 505–7; Marvel, *Race of the Soil,* 271.

55. Gregg to Bliss, August 9, 1864, *OR,* vol. 40, pt. 1, 554; Richards," Forty-fifth in the Battle of the Crater," 51; Richards, "Blunder at the Petersburg Mine," *National Tribune,* June 18, 1925.

56. Kenfield, "Captured by Rebels," 233; R. O. Whitehurst to Stewart, September 27, 1903, in Stewart, comp., "Charge of the Crater," 84, MOC.

57. Bernard, "Battle of the Crater," 14–15.

58. William J. Pate statement, July 3, 1903: George D. White statement, July 3, 1903: Joshua Denby statement, July 6, 1903: Griffin F. Edwards statement, July 15, 1903, in Stewart, comp., "Charge of the Crater," 7, 8, 16, 30, MOC; H. V. L. Bird to Darling, August 5, 1864, Bird Family Papers, VHS.

59. Cross, "Battle of the Crater," *National Tribune,* February 25, 1882; Etheredge, "Another Story of the Crater Battle," 205; "Notes of Genl. Beauregard on W. J. Marrin's acct. of the explosion of the Federal Mine at Petersburg Va. July 30th 1864," July 17,

1876, Pierre G. T. Beauregard Papers, ALPL; Stewart, "Charge of the Crater," 82; R. O. Whitehurst statement, n.d., in Stewart, comp., "Charge of the Crater," 85, MOC; Mahone, *Battle of the Crater,* 8–9; Weisiger to B. Perry, April 20, 1896, David Addison Weisiger Papers, VHS.

60. Aston, "Crater Fight Reminiscences," in Aston, *History and Roster,* 102; Seagrave, *Boy Lieutenant,* 85; Cutcheon autobiography, 289, 313, 316, 325, Byron Cutcheon Papers, BHL-UM; Cutcheon, "Twentieth Michigan Regiment in the Assault on Petersburg," 136; Cutcheon to Mathews, August 3, 1864: Thomas to Hicks, August 2, 1864, *OR,* vol. 40, pt. 1, 590, 599; Cavanaugh and Marvel, *Battle of the Crater,* 91–93.

61. Bowley, "Petersburg Mine," 36–37.

62. Bernard, "Battle of the Crater," 28; Gallagher, *Fighting for the Confederacy,* 465.

63. Etheredge, "Another Story of the Crater Battle," 205; Williamson Smith statement, July 6, 1903: Antonio M. Cooke statement, July 10, 1903: William H. Etheredge statement, July 27, 1903: E. S. Godwin statement, August 3, 1903: William J. Murphy statement, August 14, 1904: James E. Phillips statement, October 1, 1903, in Stewart, comp., "Charge of the Crater," 15, 27, 39–40, 44, 52, 98, MOC; Stewart, *Battle of the Crater,* 14; Stewart, *Spirit of the South,* 135.

64. Whitehead, "Retaking of the Lines," 471; Henry E. Chase statement, August 17, 1903, in Stewart, comp., "Charge of the Crater," 54, MOC; George J. Rogers letter, September 27, 1890, in Bernard, *War Talks,* 179n; W. R. S., "Sharpshooters of Mahone's Old Brigade at the Crater," 308; Stewart, *Battle of the Crater,* 13.

65. George T. Rogers letter, July 22, 1880, quoted in undated clipping of *Richmond Whig,* Mahone Family Papers, LOV; Mahone letter, August 20, 1892: Weisiger letter, September, 1880: Coldwell statement, June 30, 1880, in Bernard, *War Talks,* 215, 222; Mahone, *Battle of the Crater,* 8; Griffin F. Edwards statement, July 15, 1903, in Stewart, comp., "Charge of the Crater," 30, MOC.

66. Taylor statement, July 16, 1880, in Bernard, *War Talks,* 218; Stewart, *Spirit of the South,* 138.

67. John Edgar Foreman statement, July 3, 1903: Julius H. Tyler statement, July 7, 1903: Antonio M. Cooke statement, July 10, 1903: Calvin L. Peek statement, August 15, 1903: Edmund Curling statement, August 28, 1903, in Stewart, comp., "Charge of the Crater," 9, 18, 27, 53, 56, MOC.

68. Kenfield, "Captured by Rebels," 233; Weld, *War Diary and Letters,* 356–57; Weld, "Petersburg Mine," 211; Cavanaugh and Marvel, *Battle of the Crater,* 90.

69. Francis M. Whitehurst statement, July 9, 1903: R. H. Holland statement, August 12, 1903, in Stewart, comp., "Charge of the Crater," 23–25, 50, MOC.

70. Bernard, "Battle of the Crater," 37; Smith letter, September 8, 1890, in Bernard, *War Talks,* 184–85; Le Roy McC. West statement, June 30, 1903, in Stewart, comp., "Charge of the Crater," 5, MOC.

71. John Edgar Foreman statement, July 3, 1903: J. Thomas Dunn statement, July 22, 1903, in Stewart, comp., "Charge of the Crater," 10, 35, MOC.

72. Weisiger to McCabe, November 17, 1876; Hinton statement, September 5, 1892, in Bernard, *War Talks,* 222–23, 225.

13. Hall Attacks

1. Warren to Humphreys, July 30, 1864: Meade to Warren, July 30, 1864, *OR,* vol. 40, pt. 1, 452; Humphreys to Burnside, July 30, 1864, 9:30 A.M. and 9:45 A.M.: Meade to

Burnside, July 30, 1864, *OR,* vol. 40, pt. 3, 662; Meade testimony, August 10, 1864, report of court of inquiry, *OR,* vol. 40, pt. 1, 57; Cavanaugh and Marvel, *Battle of the Crater,* 92; Marvel, *Burnside,* 405–6.

2. Meade to Hancock, July 30, 1864: Hancock to Humphreys, July 30, 1864: Humphreys to Ord, July 30, 1864, *OR,* vol. 40, pt. 3, 646, 685; Hancock to Williams, August 3, 1864: Circular, Headquarters, Second Corps, July 30, 1864: Carr to Russell, August 3, 1864, *OR,* vol. 40, pt. 1, 312–13, 649, 724.

3. H. Porter, *Campaigning with Grant,* 269; Grant to Halleck, July 30, 1864, *OR,* vol. 40, pt. 3, 636.

4. Grant to Lincoln, July 30, 1864: Grant to Meade, July 30, 1864: Meade to Grant, July 30, 1864, 2:15 P.M., 2:20 P.M., 4 P.M.: Ord to Meade, July 30, 1864: Meade to Hancock, July 30, 1864, *OR,* vol. 40, pt. 3, 636–39, 649; Sheridan to Rawlins, May 13, 1866, *OR,* vol. 36, pt. 1, 801; Grant, *Personal Memoirs,* 2:613–14; entry of July 30, 1864, Willoughby diary, William A. Willoughby Papers, AAS.

5. Grant to Lincoln, July 30, 1864, *OR,* vol. 40, pt. 3, 636; Grant, *Personal Memoirs,* 2:613–14.

6. Hartranft to Willcox, July 30, 1864, *OR,* vol. 40, pt. 3, 668; Potter testimony, December 20, 1864, *RCCW,* 101; Powell, "Battle of the Petersburg Crater," 557–58.

7. Meade testimony, August 8, 1864: Burnside testimony, August 10, 1864: Ord testimony, August 30, 1864, report of court of inquiry, *OR,* vol. 40, pt. 1, 49, 64–65, 86.

8. Agassiz, *Meade's Headquarters,* 200–201; Marvel, *Burnside,* 406–7; Cavanaugh and Marvel, *Battle of the Crater,* 92–93.

9. Burnside testimony, August 10, 1864: Potter testimony, August 30, 1864, report of court of inquiry, *OR,* vol. 40, pt. 1, 65, 90; White to Burnside, July 30, 1864: Burnside to White, July 30, 1864, and White's endorsement, Ambrose E. Burnside Papers, RG94, NARA.

10. Lowe, *Meade's Army,* 243; Sumner, *Diary of Cyrus B. Comstock,* 284–85; Marvel, *Burnside,* 407.

11. Mahone letter, August 20, 1892, in Bernard, *War Talks,* 215; Mahone, *Battle of the Crater,* 9; Henderson, *Roster of the Confederate Soldiers of Georgia,* 5:111; Suderow, "Confederate Casualties at the Crater," 26; Charles S. Venable statement, April 10, 1872, *Reply to a Communication Published by Gen. C. M. Wilcox, in the New Orleans Times, of January 1st, 1872,* p. 23, Mahone Family Papers, LOV; Aston, "Crater Fight Reminiscences," in Aston, *History and Roster,* 102; Bernard, "Battle of the Crater," 15. Some observers thought Hall attacked at 10:30 A.M. (McCabe, "Defence of Petersburg," 292; Saussy, "Story of the Crater," 116) or at 11 A.M. (Bernard, "Battle of the Crater," 16; Stewart, "Charge of the Crater," 82; Stevenson, *Account of the Battle of the Mine,* 13; Bowley, "Petersburg Mine," 37), but the weight of evidence supports the 10 A.M. timing.

12. Bernard, "Battle of the Crater," 15; Phillips to William H. Stewart, sometime after 1900, James Eldred Phillips Papers, VHS; Hartranft to Hutchins, August 5, 1864, *OR,* vol. 40, pt. 1, 579; Hartranft to wife, July 31, 1864, and to father, August 16, 1864, John F. Hartranft Papers, Helen L. Shireman; Bowley, "Petersburg Mine," 37.

13. William J. Murphy statement, August 14, 1903, in Stewart, comp., "Charge of the Crater," 51, MOC; George T. Rogers letter, July 22, 1880, quoted in Mahone to Committee of Mahone's Brigade, July 1880, in clipping from *Richmond Whig,* Mahone Family Papers, LOV; Mahone letter, August 20, 1892, in Bernard, *War Talks,* 215; Lee to Davis,

August 1, 1864, in Crist, *Papers of Jefferson Davis,* 10:577; Howard Aston to Cabaniss and Company, August 20, 1890, in Bernard, *War Talks,* 181; Cavanaugh and Marvel, *Battle of the Crater,* 93. There is some evidence that a few of Hall's men sought shelter in the Confederate main line south of the Crater as well. Andrews, *Sketch of Company K,* 22.

14. McMaster, "Elliott's Brigade," 23; George T. Rogers letter, July 22, 1880, quoted in Mahone to Committee of Mahone's Brigade, July 1880, in clipping from *Richmond Whig,* Mahone Family Papers, LOV.

15. Matthew R. Hall to editor of *Petersburg Express,* August 2, 1864, *Supplement to the Official Records,* pt. 1, vol. 7, 310; article by correspondent of *Richmond Dispatch,* July 30, 1864, reprinted in *Charleston Mercury,* August 4, 1864. Many observers referred to two attacks by Hall's brigade, but they were confused by the fact that a small portion of Hall's command advanced with Weisiger at 9 A.M. and the rest at 10 A.M. See Stewart, *Battle of the Crater,* 10; William H. Etheredge to George J. Rogers, March 23, 1892, in Stewart, comp., "Charge of the Crater," unpaginated, MOC.

16. K. Wiley, *Norfolk Blues,* 134; Crute, *Units of the Confederate States Army,* 116; William H. Etheredge statement, July 17, 1903: George W. Clark to William H. Stewart, November 13, 1905, in Stewart, comp., "Charge of the Crater," 40, 116, MOC; Bernard to editor, undated clipping from *Richmond Times,* May 28, 1899, George S. Bernard Papers, SCL-DU; Wiggins, *My Dear Friend,* 137; "Notes of Genl. Beauregard on W. J. Marrin's acct. of the explosion of the Federal Mine at Petersburg Va. July 30th 1864," July 17, 1876, Pierre G. T. Beauregard Papers, ALPL.

17. Wiatt, *26th Virginia Infantry,* 28; Cutchins, *A Famous Command,* 155; Cavanaugh and Marvel, *Battle of the Crater,* 148.

18. John E. Crow letter, October 7, 1892, in Bernard, *War Talks,* 316–17; Bernard, "Battle of the Crater," 16.

19. Day, "Breastworks at Petersburg," 175; Day, *A True History,* 82; Day, "Battle of the Crater," 356.

20. William R. J. Pegram to Jenny, August 1, 1864, Pegram-Johnson-McIntosh Family Papers, VHS.

21. Richards, "Forty-fifth in the Battle of the Crater," in Albert, *History of the Forty-fifth Regiment Pennsylvania,* 154–56.

22. Bowley, "The Crater," *National Tribune,* November 6, 1884; William H. Randall Reminiscences, BHL-UM; Hauptman, *Between Two Fires,* 101, 126–27, 155.

23. Rickard, *Services with Colored Troops,* 28.

24. Bowley, "The Crater," *National Tribune,* November 6, 1884.

25. Serg. Hilling letter to newspaper, August 1, 1864, in Houston, *Thirty-second Maine,* 364–65.

26. Bowley, "The Crater," *National Tribune,* November 6, 1884; Bowley, "Petersburg Mine," 36–37; Aston, "Crater Fight Reminiscences," in Aston, *History and Roster,* 104.

27. Bowley, "The Crater," *National Tribune,* November 6, 1884; Aston, "Crater Fight Reminiscences," in Aston, *History and Roster,* 105.

28. Aston, "Crater Fight Reminiscences," in Aston, *History and Roster,* 104.

29. Ibid., 105–6.

30. Mahone, *Battle of the Crater,* 10; Govan and Livingood, *Haskell Memoirs,* 74–77; McCabe, "Defence of Petersburg," 292; Jethro Raiford statement, September 23, 1903:

Isaac S. Harrell statement, September 23, 1903: R. O. Whitehurst to Stewart, September 27, 1903, in Stewart, comp., "Charge of the Crater," 73, 76, 85, MOC; Pendleton to Taylor, February 28, 1865, *OR,* vol. 40, pt. 1, 759–60; Cavanaugh and Marvel, *Battle of the Crater,* 91, 148. There is a photograph of a Coehorn mortar in Calkins, *From Petersburg to Appomattox,* 23, one of four such pieces belonging to Lamkin's battery that was captured near Flat Creek on April 5 during the retreat to Appomattox. It is mounted on the lawn of Amelia Court House.

31. Cutcheon autobiography, 324, Byron Cutcheon Papers, BHL-UM; Freeman S. Bowley, "The Crater," *National Tribune,* November 6, 1884; Simon Griffin quoted in Jackman, *History of the Sixth New Hampshire,* 317–18; Bowley, "Petersburg Mine," 37.

32. William H. Randall Reminiscences, BHL-UM; Hartranft to wife, July 31, 1864, John F. Hartranft Papers, Helen L. Shireman; Cutcheon autobiography, 324, Byron Cutcheon Papers, BHL-UM; Rickard, *Services with Colored Troops,* 28–29.

33. S. L. Montgomery to R. Craven, July 31, 1864, Michael A. Cavanaugh Collection, HSSC; Bowley, "The Crater," *National Tribune,* November 6, 1884; Aston, "Crater Fight Reminiscences," in Aston, *History and Roster,* 103; entry of July 30, 1864, Giles Buckner Cooke diary, VHS; Roemer, *Reminiscences,* 249; Cutcheon autobiography, 324–25, Byron Cutcheon Papers, BHL-UM; Wakefield account, in Lord, *History of the Ninth Regiment New Hampshire,* 501; Codman to sister, July 31, 1864, George Benton Codman Letters, DC.

34. B. A. Spear, "In Front of Petersburg," *National Tribune,* June 20, 1889; Palfrey, *Memoir of William Francis Bartlett,* 119; Powell, "Battle of the Petersburg Crater," 558–59n.

35. Powell, "Battle of the Petersburg Crater," 557; Burnside to Williams, August 13, 1864: Willcox to Richmond, August 6, 1864, *OR,* vol. 40, pt. 1, 529, 575; Thomas W. Clarke account, 1865, in Anderson, *Fifty-seventh Regiment of Massachusetts,* 211; *History of the Thirty-fifth Regiment Massachusetts,* 272.

36. Cutcheon autobiography, 289–90, Byron Cutcheon Papers, BHL-UM; Bowley, "Petersburg Mine," 38; Aston, "Crater Fight Reminiscences," in Aston, *History and Roster,* 104.

37. Allen, *Forty-six Months with the Fourth R.I.,* 290–91; Marvel, *Race of the Soil,* 274–75; Sholes, "Crater Fight Vividly Portrayed," *National Tribune,* January 12, 1928.

38. Farquhar testimony, September 5, 1864, report of court of inquiry, *OR,* vol. 40, pt. 1, 122; Lathe account, in Lord, *History of the Ninth Regiment New Hampshire,* 511; Aston, "Crater Fight Reminiscences," in Aston, *History and Roster,* 103, 106.

39. Van Den Bossche, "War and Other Reminiscences," 141–42.

40. Burnham diary and Clement account, in Lord, *History of the Ninth Regiment New Hampshire,* 491–93.

41. Willcox to Richmond, August 6, 1864: Hartranft to Hutchins, August 5, 1864, *OR,* vol. 40, pt. 1, 575, 579; Sauers, *Civil War Journal of Colonel William J. Bolton,* 225; *History of the Thirty-fifth Regiment Massachusetts,* 272; Aston, "Crater Fight Reminiscences," in Aston, *History and Roster,* 103; Bowley, "Petersburg Mine," 37; Bowley, "The Crater," *National Tribune,* November 6, 1884; Cavanaugh and Marvel, *Battle of the Crater,* 94.

42. Griffin, quoted in Case, "Battle of the Mine," 30–31; Aston, "Crater Fight Reminiscences," in Aston, *History and Roster,* 103.

43. Burnside to White, July 30, 1864, and White's endorsement, John F. Hartranft Papers, Helen L. Shireman; Cutcheon autobiography, 290, 315, Byron Cutcheon Papers, BHL-UM; Cutcheon, "Twentieth Michigan," 136; Hartranft testimony, September 1, 1864, report of court of inquiry: Burnside to Williams, August 13, 1864: Robinson to Mills, August 3, 1864: Hartranft to Hutchins, August 5, 1864, *OR,* vol. 40, pt. 1, 102, 529, 542, 579; A. A. Humphreys, *Virginia Campaign,* 262.

44. Hartranft to Hutchins, August 5, 1864: Cutcheon to Mathews, August 3, 1864, *OR,* vol. 40, pt. 1, 579, 591; copy of Burnside's order to retire, Hartranft, Griffin, and Bartlett endorsements, John F. Hartranft Papers, Helen L. Shireman. Additional copies of this document and its endorsements can be found in Ambrose E. Burnside Papers, RG94, NARA, and *OR,* vol. 40, pt. 3, 663. Cutcheon, "Twentieth Michigan," 136–37; Cutcheon autobiography, 290–91, Byron Cutcheon Papers, BHL-UM.

45. Entry of July 30, 1864, William Stowell Tilton Diary, Mass-HS; Charles Knickerbocker Winne Journal, July 30, 1864, Josiah Trent Collection, MCL-DU; Powell, "Battle of the Petersburg Crater," 558. Potter estimated that about two hundred men of his division were "entirely prostrated by the heat and exertion," apparently within the captured Confederate works. Potter to Richmond, August 1, 1864, *OR,* vol. 40, pt. 1, 548.

46. C. H. Houghton, "In the Crater," 562; Gregg to Bliss, August 9, 1864, *OR,* vol. 40, pt. 1, 555; Cutcheon autobiography, 315–16, 321, Byron Cutcheon Papers, BHL-UM.

47. Bowley, "Petersburg Mine," 38; Bowley, "The Crater," *National Tribune,* November 6, 1884.

14. Sanders Attacks

1. William H. Etheredge statement, July 27, 1903, in Stewart, comp., "Charge of the Crater," 40, MOC.

2. Mahone letter, August 20, 1892, in Bernard, *War Talks,* 215; Mahone, *Battle of the Crater,* 10; Cummings, *Yankee Quaker,* 299; Cavanaugh and Marvel, *Battle of the Crater,* 94; McMaster to Beauregard, February 14, 1872, in Roman, *Military Operations of General Beauregard,* 589; LaMotte, "Battle of the Crater," *Charleston News and Courier,* May 14, 1899.

3. Thomson, "John C. C. Sanders," 83, 85–91, 93, 96–97, 99–100; Trimmier to wife, July 6, 15, 1864, Theodore G. Trimmier Papers, TSLA; Featherston, *Battle of the Crater,* 20; Cavanaugh and Marvel, *Battle of the Crater,* 97; Suderow, "Confederate Casualties at the Crater," 26.

4. G. Clark, "Alabamians in the Crater Battle," 68; Alfred Lewis Scott Memoir, 24–25, VHS; Featherston, "Graphic Account of Battle of Crater," 360; Featherston, "Battle of the 'Crater' as I Saw It," 23; Davis to Mrs. G. A. Davis, August 3, 1864, Elias Davis Papers, UNC; Cavanaugh and Marvel, *Battle of the Crater,* 92.

5. Paine to Burnside, July 30, 1864, *OR,* vol. 40, pt. 3, 661; Cavanaugh and Marvel, *Battle of the Crater,* 90.

6. Featherston, "Graphic Account of Battle of Crater," 360, 362, 372; Alfred Lewis Scott Memoir, 25–26, VHS; Featherston, "Battle of the Crater," 297; Featherston, "Battle of the 'Crater' as I Saw It," 23; G. Clark, "Alabamians in the Crater Battle," 68.

7. Featherston, "Battle of the Crater," 297; Young, "Account of the Battle of the Crater," in Fortin, "Colonel Hilary A. Herbert's History of the Eighth Alabama," 198; Featherston, *Battle of the Crater,* 19; Fagan, "Petersburg Crater," in Fortin, "Colonel

Hilary A. Herbert's History of the Eighth Alabama," 149; Draper, "Who Fought in the Battle of the Crater?" 502; Featherston, "Battle of the 'Crater' as I Saw It," 24; G. Clark, "Alabamians in the Crater Battle," 68; Featherston, "Graphic Account of Battle of Crater," 358–59; Alfred Lewis Scott Memoir, 25, VHS.

8. LaMotte, "Battle of the Crater," *Charleston News and Courier,* May 14, 1899; Johnson statement, in Roman, *Military Operations of General Beauregard,* 586; Draper, "Who Fought in the Battle of the Crater?" 502; Featherston, "Graphic Account of Battle of Crater," 361–62.

9. Edward Mallet letter, *Raleigh Daily Confederate,* August 6, 1864; Lewis to S. C. Lewis, August 4, 1864, John Manly Lewis Confederate Pension Application File, NCDAH.

10. Sanders to Pa, August 3, 1864, John C. C. Sanders Collection, UA; Saussy, "Story of the Crater," 116; McCabe, "Defence of Petersburg," 293; Alfred Lewis Scott Memoir, 27, VHS; William H. Stewart statement, July 3, 1903, in Stewart, comp., "Charge of the Crater," 12, MOC; Featherston, "Graphic Account of Battle of Crater," 358–59.

11. Bernard, "Battle of the Crater," 18; entry of July 30, 1864, John Bell Vincent Diary, VHS; Young, "Account of the Battle of the Crater," in Fortin, "Colonel Hilary A. Herbert's History of the Eighth Alabama," 198; William H. Etheredge to George J. Rogers, March 23, 1892: statement of James E. Phillips, October 1, 1903, in Stewart, comp., "Charge of the Crater," unpaginated and 98, MOC; Featherston, "Battle of the Crater," 297; George T. Rogers letter, July 22, 1880, quoted in Mahone to Committee of Mahone's Brigade, July 1880, *Richmond Whig* clipping, Mahone Family Papers, LOV; Powell, "Battle of the Petersburg Crater," 558; Monks to sister, August 2, 1864, Zerah Coston Monks Papers, WRHS; Hartranft to father, August 16, 1864, John F. Hartranft Papers, Helen L. Shireman.

12. William H. Randall Reminiscences, BHL-UM; Powell, "Battle of the Petersburg Crater," 558; Aston to Cabaniss and Co., August 20, 1890, in Bernard, *War Talks,* 181; Ord testimony, December 20, 1864, *RCCW,* 117.

13. Hartranft testimony, September 1, 1864, report of court of inquiry, *OR,* vol. 40, pt. 1, 102; Hartranft to Sallie, August 1, 1864, John F. Hartranft Papers, Helen L. Shireman; C. H. Houghton, "In the Crater," 562; Case, "Battle of the Mine," 32; Young, "Account of the Battle of the Crater," in Fortin, "Colonel Hilary A. Herbert's History of the Eighth Alabama," 198; Jackman, *History of the Sixth New Hampshire,* 322; Lord, *History of the Ninth Regiment New Hampshire,* 511–12.

14. McMaster, "Elliott's Brigade," 23–24; Mahone letter, August 20, 1892, in Bernard, *War Talks,* 216; Thomas J. LaMotte, "Battle of the Crater," *Charleston News and Courier,* May 14, 1899; James Paul Verdery to sister, July 31, 1864, Eugene and James Paul Verdery Papers, SCL-DU; Featherston, "Battle of the Crater," 297.

15. Bowley, "Petersburg Crater," 38; Bowley, "The Crater," *National Tribune,* November 6, 1884.

16. Bowley, "Petersburg Crater," 38; Bowley, "The Crater," *National Tribune,* November 6, 1884; McCabe, "Defence of Petersburg," 292; Featherston, "Graphic Account of Battle of Crater," 364; William F. Bartlett letter, n.d., in Anderson, *Fifty-seventh Regiment of Massachusetts,* 188. After the war, efforts were made to give Sanders credit for thinking of gathering bayoneted muskets and tossing them over the rim of the

crater. C. W. Sanders to editor, n.d., *Petersburg Daily Index-Appeal,* January 3, 1896, John C. C. Sanders Collection, UA.

17. B. A. Spear, "In Front of Petersburg," *National Tribune,* June 20, 1889.

18. E. B. Williams, *Rebel Brothers,* 116; G. I. Turnley reminiscence in *Houston Daily Post,* April 22, 1906, John C. C. Sanders Collection, UA; Gregg to Bliss, August 9, 1864, *OR,* vol. 40, pt. 1, 555.

19. Young, "Account of the Battle of the Crater," in Fortin, "Colonel Hilary A. Herbert's History of the Eighth Alabama," 198–99.

20. Young, "Account of the Battle of the Crater," in Fortin, "Colonel Hilary A. Herbert's History of the Eighth Alabama," 199.

21. Mahone letter, August 20, 1892, in Bernard, *War Talks,* 216; Mahone, *Battle of the Crater,* 11.

22. Featherston, "Battle of the Crater," 297; Featherston, "Battle of the 'Crater' as I Saw It," 24; Featherston, *Battle of the Crater,* 21; Featherston, "Graphic Account of Battle of Crater," 365–66; Bowley, "Petersburg Mine," 38; Bowley, "The Crater," *National Tribune,* November 6, 1884.

23. Bowley, "The Crater," *National Tribune,* November 6, 1884; Aston, "Crater Fight Reminiscences," in Aston, *History and Roster,* 106–7.

24. Vance, "Incidents of the Crater Battle," 178; John G. Alexander Reminiscences, Lowry Shuford Collection, NCDAH; G. Clark, "Alabamians in the Crater Battle," 69; W. R. Houghton and M. B. Houghton, *Two Brothers in the Civil War,* 133; Lewis to S. C. Lewis, August 4, 1864, John Manly Lewis Confederate Pension Application File, NCDAH.

25. G. Clark, "Alabamians in the Crater Battle," 69; Featherston, "Graphic Account of Battle of Crater," 372–73; Edward Mallet letter, *Raleigh Daily Confederate,* August 6, 1864; Featherston, *Battle of the Crater,* 21–22; Featherston, "Battle of the Crater," 297.

26. James Paul Verdery to sister, July 31, 1864, Eugene and James Paul Verdery Papers, SCL-DU; Kenfield, "Captured by Rebels," 233.

27. Kilmer, "Dash into the Crater," 776; Govan and Livingood, *Haskell Memoirs,* 77–78.

28. Bowley, "The Crater," *National Tribune,* November 6, 1884; Bowley, "Petersburg Mine," 38–39; B. A. Spear, "In Front of Petersburg," *National Tribune,* June 20, 1889; Carter, *Welcome the Hour of Conflict,* 264.

29. Alfred Lewis Scott Memoir, 26, VHS.

30. Johnson to Brent, August 20, 1864, *OR,* vol. 40, pt. 1, 792; Andrews, *Sketch of Company K,* 23–24; entry of July 30, 1864, Robert W. Hicks Diary, MOC; Walker to Bernard, August 2, 1892, in Bernard, *War Talks,* 206; Featherston, "Graphic Account of Battle of Crater," 362; Julian to Lottie, August 14–15, 1864, George Naylor Julian Papers, UNH.

15. Afternoon and Evening, July 30

1. William R. J. Pegram to Jenny, August 1, 1864, Pegram-Johnson-McIntosh Family Papers, VHS; Fred Harris to uncle, July 31, 1864, David B. Harris Papers, SCL-DU; Beaty, "Battle of the Crater," in Hudson, *Sketches and Reminiscences,* 60; Fagan, "Petersburg

Crater," in Fortin, "Colonel Hilary A. Herbert's History of the Eighth Alabama," 150; Matthew Norris Love to mother, August 6, 1864, PNB.

2. Edwin N. Wise to Daniel, November 14, 1905, John Warwick Daniel Papers, UVA; Freeman Bowley letter, November 9, 1890, in Bernard, *War Talks,* 182; Featherston, "Battle of the Crater," 298; Andrews, *Sketch of Company K,* 24; E. B. Williams, *Rebel Brothers,* 115; Daniel Boyd to father, August 10, 1864, Robert A. Boyd Papers, SCL-DU.

3. Cockrell and Ballard, *Mississippi Rebel,* 288; G. I. Turnley reminiscence in *Houston Daily Post,* April 22, 1906, John C. C. Sanders Collection, UA; Stewart, *Spirit of the South,* 140; Dorsey N. Binion to sister, August 1, 1864, Confederate Miscellany Collection I, SC-EU; James Paul Verdery to sister, July 31, 1864, Eugene and James Paul Verdery Papers, SCL-DU; Fred Harris to uncle, July 31, 1864, David B. Harris Papers, SCL-DU; Hugh T. Douglas, "Confederate Countermining in Front of Petersburg," Petersburg Crater Collection, SC-UVA; Alfred Lewis Scott Memoir, 28, VHS.

4. Charles Knickerbocker Winne Journal, July 30, 1864, Josiah Trent Collection, MCL-DU; Matthews, *149th Pennsylvania,* 189.

5. Aston, "Crater Fight Reminiscences," in Aston, *History and Roster,* 107–8.

6. Lee to Seddon, July 30, 1864, OR, vol. 40, pt. 1, 753; Bowley, "The Crater," *National Tribune,* November 6, 1884; Bowley, "Petersburg Mine," 39; Seagrave, *Boy Lieutenant,* 85; Shearman, "Battle of the Crater," 15; William H. Randall Reminiscences, BHL-UM; William Baird Memoirs, 20, BHL-UM; Kenfield, "Captured by Rebels," 233. A Federal officer placed the number of captives at 917 enlisted men and 77 officers; Mahone fixed it at 1,100 men. Bowley related that only about 400 blacks were accounted for as prisoners of war, although 801 men of Fererro's division were listed as missing. He assumed the other 400 were killed or had been wounded and were allowed to die by the Rebels. See Beller, "Mine Explosion," *National Tribune,* June 20, 1889; Mahone, *Battle of the Crater,* 11; Bowley, "The Crater," *National Tribune,* November 6, 1884.

7. Gallagher, *Fighting for the Confederacy,* 460.

8. Hugh L. Kerrick to sister, August 30, 1864, PNB; K. Wiley, *Norfolk Blues,* 138; Seagrave, *Boy Lieutenant,* 85; Bowley, "The Crater," *National Tribune,* November 6, 1884; Rickard, *Services with Colored Troops,* 29; Hill to Cooper, August 4, 1864, OR, ser. 2, vol. 7, 539–40.

9. E. B. Williams, *Rebel Brothers,* 115–16; Stewart, *Battle of the Crater,* 14; Stewart, "Carnage at 'The Crater,'" 42; Rogers, "Crater Battle," 14; K. Wiley, *Norfolk Blues,* 138; Josiah Joyner statement, September 15, 1903, in Stewart, comp., "Charge of the Crater," 67–68, MOC; Alfred Lewis Scott Memoir, 27, VHS.

10. William R. J. Pegram to Jenny, August 1, 1864, Pegram-Johnson-McIntosh Family Papers, VHS; Isaac Gaskins, quoted in E. A. Miller, *Black Civil War Soldiers of Illinois,* 77; Govan and Livingood, *Haskell Memoirs,* 78–79.

11. R. O. Whitehurst to Stewart, September 27 and October 23, 1903, in Stewart, comp., "Charge of the Crater," 86–89, and unpaginated, MOC; Alfred Lewis Scott Memoir, 27, VHS.

12. Stewart, "History of the Crater," in *Norfolk Dispatch,* October 24, 1905, and E. N. Wise letter to editor, November 1905, both clippings pasted in Stewart, comp., "Charge of the Crater," unpaginated, MOC; Matthew Norris Love to mother, August 6, 1864, PNB; entry of July 30, 1864, Robert W. Hicks Diary, MOC; Featherston, *Battle of the*

Crater, 22; R. O. Whitehurst to Stewart, September 27, 1903, in Stewart, comp., "Charge of the Crater," 88, MOC.

13. *History of the Thirty-sixth Regiment Massachusetts,* 239–40.

14. Williams to Hancock, Warren, Burnside, Ord, July 30, 1864: Potter to Richmond, July 30, 1864, *OR,* vol. 40, pt. 3, 647, 666–68.

15. Lubey to Weitzel, July 30, 1864: Ord to Meade, July 30, 1864: Burnside to Ord, n.d.: Weitzel to Ord, July 30, 1864, 11 P.M., *OR,* vol. 40, pt. 3, 677, 686–87; Potter to Richmond, n.d., 12:30 A.M., Ambrose E. Burnside Papers, RG94, NARA; Hancock to Williams, August 3, 1864: Second Corps journal, July 30, 1864: Ord to Humphreys, August 3, 1864: Carr to Russell, August 3, 1864, *OR,* vol. 40, pt. 1, 312–13, 324, 708–9, 724.

16. Meade to Grant, July 30, 1864, 5 P.M.: Meade to Warren, July 30, 1864, 5 P.M. and 6 P.M.: Butler to Grant, July 30, 1864, 12:30 P.M., and 3:50 P.M.: Hunt to Wainwright, July 30, 1864: Hunt to Abbot, July 30, 1864, 10:45 and 11:45 P.M.: Hunt to Ord, July 30, 1864, *OR,* vol. 40, pt. 3, 640, 654–55, 674–75, 680–81, 687; Meade to Warren and Burnside, July 30, 1864, report of court of inquiry: Hunt to Williams, October 31, 1864: Abbot to Davis, December 5, 1864, *OR,* vol. 40, pt. 1, 152, 281, 659–60; Nevins, *Diary of Battle,* 447.

17. Meade to Warren, July 30, 1864, *OR,* vol. 40, pt. 3, 655; Burnside testimony, December 17, 1864, *RCCW,* 24–25; Agassiz, *Meade's Headquarters,* 201; Meade testimony, August 8, 1864, report of court of inquiry, *OR,* vol. 40, pt. 1, 49; Humphreys to Burnside, July 30, 1864, 7:40 P.M. and 10:35. P.M., *OR,* vol. 40, pt. 3, 664.

18. Lowe, *Meade's Army,* 243.

19. Grant to Meade, July 30, 1864: Bowers to Meade, July 30, 1864, 11:15 P.M., and 11:30 P.M.: Grant to Butler, July 30, 1864, *OR,* vol. 40, pt. 3, 640–42, 675.

20. Grant to Meade, July 30, 1864, *OR,* vol. 40, pt. 3, 638–39.

21. Grant to Butler, July 30, 1864: Sarah to Butler, July 31, 1864, *Private and Official Correspondence of Gen. Benjamin F. Butler,* 4:564–66; Robinson to sister, August 5, 1864, Oscar D. Robinson Papers, DC; Wert, *From Winchester to Cedar Creek,* 10–12.

22. George Harrington to William Pitt Fessenden, August 1, 1864, Abraham Lincoln Collection, YU.

23. "Notes of Gen. Beauregard on W. J. Marrin's Acct. of the explosion of the Federal Mine at Petersburg Va. July 30th 1864," July 17, 1876, Pierre G. T. Beauregard Papers, ALPL; Lee to Seddon, July 30, 1864, 3:25 P.M. and 6:30 P.M., *OR,* vol. 40, pt. 3, 818; Lee to Davis, August 1, 1864, in Crist, *Papers of Jefferson Davis,* 10:576.

24. John Thomas Goode to George S. Bernard, February 7, 1911, PNB.

25. Chambers, "Bloody Crater," 177; Pearce, *Diary of Captain Henry A. Chambers,* 210; Roulhac, "Forty-ninth N.C.," 73; entry of July 30, 1864, J. M. Cutchin diary, Cutchin Family Papers, ECU.

26. McMaster, "Elliott's Brigade," 24, 26; McMaster to Beauregard, February 14, 1872, in Roman, *Military Operations of General Beauregard,* 589–90.

27. Hugh T. Douglas, "Petersburg Crater," and "Confederate Countermining in Front of Petersburg," Petersburg Crater Collection, SC-UVA; E. N. Wise to editor, November, 1905, in Stewart, comp., "Charge of the Crater," unpaginated, MOC; Douglas to Stevens, July 30, 1864, *OR,* vol. 40, pt. 3, 819–20. Armistead L. Long of Lee's staff measured the crater at 135 feet long, 90 feet wide, and 30 feet deep. R. O. Whitehurst to Stewart,

September 27, 1903, in Stewart, comp., "Charge of the Crater," 86–87, MOC.

28. Featherston, *Battle of the Crater,* 23; Featherston, "Battle of the Crater," 298; Young, "Account of the Battle of the Crater," in Fortin, "Colonel Hilary A. Herbert's History of the Eighth Alabama," 199–200; Stewart, *Spirit of the South,* 140.

29. Bernard, "Battle of the Crater," 19; Whitehead, "Retaking of the Lines," 470; Caleb Hodges statement, September 15, 1903: R. O. Whitehurst to Stewart, September 27, 1903, in Stewart, comp., "Charge of the Crater," 68, 87–88, MOC; Featherston, "Graphic Account of Battle of Crater," 366. Other estimates of the number of bodies buried inside the crater include 128 (Williamson Smith statement, July 6, 1903, in Stewart, comp., "Charge of the Crater," 16, MOC), 142 (Cross, "Battle of the Crater," *National Tribune,* February 25, 1882), and 233 (Stewart, "Charge of the Crater," 86).

30. D. M. Bernard letter, June 28, 1892, in Bernard, *War Talks,* 192; Rogers, "Crater Battle," 13–14.

31. William Emmerson statement, July 16, 1903: Josiah Frank Cutchin statement, August 3, 1903, in Stewart, comp., "Charge of the Crater," 32, 43, MOC; Stewart, *Battle of the Crater,* 15; Stewart, "Charge of the Crater," 86.

32. Grant to Meade, July 30, 1864: Willcox to Richmond, July 30, 1864: Meade to Ord, July 30, 1864, *OR,* vol. 40, pt. 3, 640, 667, 686; "Notes of Genl. Beauregard on W. J. Marrin's Acct. of the explosion of the Federal Mine at Petersburg Va. July 30th 1864," July 17, 1876, Pierre G. T. Beauregard Papers, ALPL; Reid-Green, *Letters Home,* 90; Aston, "Crater Fight Reminiscences," Aston, *History and Roster,* 108.

33. Weld, *War Diary and Letters,* 354; Shearman, "Battle of the Crater," 16; B. A. Spear, "In Front of Petersburg," *National Tribune,* June 20, 1889.

34. Stewart, *Battle of the Crater,* 15.

16. July 31 and August 1

1. Cavanaugh and Marvel, *Battle of the Crater,* 108, 128.

2. Burnside to Williams, August 13, 1864: Potter to Richmond, August 1, 1864, *OR,* vol. 40, pt. 1, 529, 548; Marvel, *Race of the Soil,* 278, 283; Ord to Meade, July 31, 1864, *OR,* vol. 40, pt. 3, 725; Cavanaugh and Marvel, *Battle of the Crater,* 128; Powell, "Battle of the Petersburg Crater," 56; Robert Whitcomb to parents, April 25, 1865, Robert and George Whitcomb Papers, James M. Schoff Civil War Collections, WLC-UM.

3. Suderow, "Battle of the Crater," 222–24; Stevens, *As If It Were Glory,* 186; Richard Watson Jones statement, ca. October 1903, in Stewart, comp., "Charge of the Crater," 106, MOC.

4. Cavanaugh and Marvel, *Battle of the Crater,* 108, 129; Suderow, "Confederate Casualties," 26–28; Mahone, *Battle of the Crater,* 12; Weisiger to B. Perry, April 20, 1896, David Addison Weisiger Papers, VHS; Stewart, "Charge of the Crater," 83; McMaster, "Battle of the Crater," 123; McMaster to Beauregard, February 14, 1872, in Roman, *Military Operations of General Beauregard,* 590; McMaster, "Elliott's Brigade," 27; Wiatt, *26th Virginia Infantry,* 30; Edward Mallett letter, August 4, 1864, *Raleigh Daily Confederate,* August 6, 1864. In 1871 Beauregard estimated Confederate losses at 1,500. See Beauregard marginal note on Brent to Beauregard, November 28, 1871, George W. Brent Letter, LSU.

5. Ord to Mead, July 30, 1864: list of wounded admitted to 9th Corps field hospitals, July 30–31, *OR,* vol. 40, pt. 3, 686–87, 707; J. M. Stone, *Personal Recollections,* 182; entries of July 30–August 1, 1864, Conrad Noll Diaries, BHL-UM.

6. S. S. W. Blake, *Diaries and Letters of Francis Minot Weld,* 165–66.

7. Ibid., 166.

8. Lathe account, in Lord, *History of the Ninth Regiment New Hampshire,* 508–9.

9. Sauers, *Civil War Journal of Colonel William J. Bolton,* 225–27, 232–33.

10. Chase, *Charge at Day-Break,* 26–31.

11. Stewart, *Battle of the Crater,* 16; Cutcheon autobiography, 326–27, Byron Cutcheon Papers, BHL-UM; Willcox to White, July 31, 1864, *OR,* vol. 40, pt. 3, 708; Bliss reminiscences, 146, Zenas R. Bliss Papers, USAMHI; Boston to Aunt Rosa, August 1, 1864, in William Boston Diary, WLC-UM.

12. Entry of July 31, 1864, Jones diary, Josiah N. Jones Papers, NHHS; Owen, "Explosion of Mine at Petersburg," *National Tribune,* November 1, 1934; Richard Watson Jones statement, ca. October 1903, in Stewart, comp., "Charge of the Crater," 106, MOC; Stewart, *Battle of the Crater,* 16.

13. Claiborne, *Seventy-five Years in Old Virginia,* 207–10; Greene, *Civil War Petersburg,* 210; Govan and Livingood, *Haskell Memoirs,* 79–80.

14. D'Avignon to Butler, October 13, 1864, in Simon, *Papers of Ulysses S. Grant,* 12:326–27.

15. List of colors captured by Mahone's division, July 30, 1864, *OR,* vol. 40, pt. 1, 754; Ferrero to not stated, November 7, 1864, *Supplement to the Official Records,* pt. 1, vol. 7, 233; Proctor, "Massacre in the Crater," *National Tribune,* October 17, 1907; E. A. Miller, *Black Civil War Soldiers of Illinois,* 71.

16. Julius H. Tyler statement, July 7, 1903: David Barnes statement, December 24, 1903, in Stewart, comp., "Charge of the Crater," 18, 110, MOC; McMaster, "Battle of the Crater," 123; McMaster, "Elliott's Brigade," 24–25; Beauregard to Taylor, August 1, 1864, *OR,* vol. 40, pt. 1, 755; Ferrero to not stated, November 7, 1864, *Supplement to the Official Records,* pt. 1, vol. 7, 233.

17. Harris to Emily, August 3, 1864, Leander Harris Letters, UNH.

18. Correspondent of *Richmond Dispatch,* July 30, 1864, in *Charleston Mercury,* August 4, 1864; W. R. S., "Sharpshooters of Mahone's Old Brigade at the Crater," 308; James Paul Verdery to sister, July 31, 1864, Eugene and James Paul Verdery Papers, SCL-DU; Dorsey N. Binion to sister, August 1, 1864, Confederate Miscellany Collection I, SC-EU; Reuben Lovett Whitehurst Commonplace Book, July 28–30, 1864, VHS.

19. W. G. Robertson, "From the Crater to New Market Heights," 187; Cavanaugh and Marvel, *Battle of the Crater,* 130–33; medals of honor awarded for actions on July 30, 1864, *OR,* vol. 40, pt. 1, 748; Schmutz, *Battle of the Crater,* 357–59; Clemmer, *Valor in Gray,* 476.

20. Kenfield, "Captured by Rebels," 234; Bowley, "The Crater," *National Tribune,* November 6, 1884; Bowley, "Petersburg Mine," 40; Mahone, *Battle of the Crater,* 12; H. S. Hall, "Mine Run to Petersburg," 231; Greene, *Civil War Petersburg,* 209.

21. Shearman, "Battle of the Crater," 16–18; Benedict, *Vermont in the Civil War,* 2:519–20.

22. Greene, *Civil War Petersburg,* 210; Shearman, "Battle of the Crater," 18; entry of July 31, 1864, Grierson diary, John Grierson Papers, KC; William Baird Memoirs, BHL-UM; E. N. Wise to Daniel, November 14, 1905, John Warwick Daniel Papers, SC-UVA.

23. J. S. Wise, *End of an Era,* 368; record of events, Company K, 19th USCT, May–June, 1865, *Supplement to the Official Records,* pt. 2, vol. 77, 539; Welch, *Confederate Surgeon's Letters,* 104.

24. Orders, Headquarters, Army of the Potomac, July 31, 1864: Potter to Richmond, July 31, 1864: Ord to Weitzel, July 31, 1864: Ord to Meade, July 31, 1864 (four documents): Meade to Ord, July 31, 1864 (two documents), *OR*, vol. 40, pt. 3, 695, 708, 723–25.

25. John W. Turner to commanding officers of 1st, 2nd, and 3rd Brigades, July 31, 1864, Louis Bell Papers, UNH; Mowris, *History of the One Hundred and Seventeenth Regiment, N.Y.*, 126–28; Foote to Mary, August 5, 1864, John B. Foote Papers, SCL-DU; J. H. Clark, *Iron Hearted Regiment*, 156; Turner to Smith, July 31, 1864, *OR*, vol. 40, pt. 3, 723; Longacre, *Army of Amateurs*, 191–92.

26. Meade to Warren, July 31, 1864: Burnside to Meade, July 31, 1864: Humphreys to Burnside, July 31, 1864: Willcox to White, July 31, 1864: Richmond to Ferrero, July 31, 1864, *OR*, vol. 40, pt. 3, 695–97, 699, 704, 708–9.

27. Humphreys to Burnside, July 31, 1864, 8:40 A.M., 7:20 P.M., and 9:30 P.M.: Burnside to Humphreys, July 31, 1864, 9 A.M., 6:40 P.M., and received 9:10 P.M.: Burnside to Williams, July 31, 1864: Williams to Burnside, July 31, 1864, *OR*, vol. 40, pt. 3, 701, 705–7; Marvel, *Burnside*, 409.

28. Entry of July 31, 1864, John Bell Vincent Diary, VHS; Pearce, *Diary of Captain Henry A. Chambers*, 211; Fred Harris to uncle, July 31, 1864, David B. Harris Papers, SCL-DU; K. Wiley, *Norfolk Blues*, 140.

29. Lee, *Memoirs of William Nelson Pendleton*, 359; Stewart, *Spirit of the South*, 141; Rickard, *Services with Colored Troops*, 30; Aston diary, entry of July 31, 1864, in Aston, *History and Roster*, 20; Comstock to Meade, July 31, 1864: Meade to Comstock, July 31, 1864: Meade to Lee, July 31, 1864: Warren to Humphreys, July 31, 1864: Humphreys to Warren, July 31, 1864: Burnside to Meade, July 31, 1864: Williams to Burnside, July 31, 1864: Burnside to Humphreys, July 31, 1864; Williams to Burnside, July 31, 1864, 11:30 A.M., *OR*, vol. 40, pt. 3, 691, 699, 702–3; John Irwin to sister, August 3, 1864, James and Sybil Irwin Family Papers, BHL-UM.

30. Featherston, "Battle of the Crater," 298; Featherston, "Graphic Account of Battle of Crater," 366–67, 373; Burnside to Humphreys, July 31, 1864, *OR*, vol. 40, pt. 3, 705; Cutcheon autobiography, 327–28, Byron Cutcheon Papers, BHL-UM; K. Wiley, *Norfolk Blues*, 140; Crawford, "Civil War Letters," 108.

31. Cutcheon autobiography, 329, Byron Cutcheon Papers, BHL-UM; Featherston, "Graphic Account of Battle of Crater," 366–67; Aston, "Crater Fight Reminiscences," Aston, *History and Roster*, 109; Crawford, "Civil War Letters," 108.

32. Burnside to Williams, July 31, 1864, 6 P.M., 9 P.M.: Burnside to Humphreys, July 31, 1864, 6:38 P.M.: Williams to Burnside, July 31, 1864, 7 P. M.: Beauregard to Meade, July 31, 1864, *OR*, vol. 40, pt. 3, 704, 821; Aston, "Crater Fight Reminiscences," in Aston, *History and Roster*, 109; Cavanaugh and Marvel, *Battle of the Crater*, 104–5.

33. Agassiz, *Meade's Headquarters*, 201; entry of August 1, 1864, John Bell Vincent Diary, VHS; Julian to Lottie, August 14–15, 1864, George Naylor Julian Papers, UNH; Young, "Account of the Battle of the Crater," in Fortin, "Colonel Hilary A. Herbert's History of the Eighth Alabama," 200; Featherston, "Graphic Account of Battle of Crater," 373; Bernard, "Battle of the Crater," 21.

34. Featherston, "Battle of the Crater," 298; J. A. Hobbs diary, in Houston, *Thirty-second Maine*, 371; K. Wiley, *Norfolk Blues*, 140; *History of the Thirty-fifth Regiment Massachusetts*, 280; Sargent to wife, August 1, 1864, Ransom Sargent Papers, DC; Pippitt

to mother, August 7, 1864, Henry Pippitt Papers, James M. Schoff Civil War Collections, WLC-UM; Rickard, *Services with Colored Troops,* 30; Owen, "Explosion of Mine at Petersburg," *National Tribune,* November 1, 1934; Allen, *Forty-six Months with the Fourth R.I.,* 293.

35. Don E. Scott to mother, August 2, 1864, Scott Family Papers, UNC; Case, "Battle of the Mine," 36; Cavanaugh and Marvel, *Battle of the Crater,* 105; *History of the Thirty-fifth Regiment Massachusetts,* 280; Newell Dutton to Elmer Bragg, ca. August 29, 1864, "Letters and Diary of Corporal Elmer Bragg, 1862–1864," 75, DC.

36. Allen, *Forty-six Months with the Fourth R.I.,* 293; Day, "Breastworks at Petersburg," 175; entry of August 1, 1864, Hamilton R. Dunlap diary, Gyla McDowell Collection, HCLA-PSU; H. S. Hall, "Mine Run to Petersburg," 240–41; Aston diary, entry of August 1, 1864, in Aston, *History and Roster,* 20; William H. Etheredge statement, July 27, 1903, in Stewart, comp., "Charge of the Crater," 40, MOC; Stewart, *Battle of the Crater,* 16; Rickard, *Services with Colored Troops,* 30; Featherston, "Graphic Account of Battle of Crater," 366–67; Featherston, *Battle of the Crater,* 25; *History of the Thirty-fifth Regiment Massachusetts,* 280; Pendleton to wife, August 2, 1864, in Lee, *Memoirs of William Nelson Pendleton,* 359. One Federal observer reported that the blacks were interred in one end of the burial trenches and whites in the other end. See Cutcheon autobiography, 331, Byron Cutcheon Papers, BHL-UM.

37. Thomas, "Twenty-two Hours," 30; R. O. Whitehurst to Stewart, September 27, 1903, in Stewart, comp., "Charge of the Crater," 89–90, MOC.

38. Day, "Battle of the Crater," 356; Agassiz, *Meade's Headquarters,* 203; entry of August 1, 1864, Albright diary, James W. Albright Papers, UNC; Lee, *Memoirs of William Nelson Pendleton,* 359; entry of August 1, 1864, Howard M. Hanson Diary, SC-UNH; Adam Henry to brother, August 3, 1864, Henry Family Letters, Ronald D. Boyer Collection, USAMHI.

39. Day, "Breastworks at Petersburg," 175; Powell, "Battle of the Petersburg Crater," 555.

40. Cutcheon autobiography, 330, Byron Cutcheon Papers, BHL-UM; Featherston, "Battle of the Crater," 298.

41. Featherston, "Graphic Account of Battle of Crater," 373; Olin to unknown, August 2, 1864, William Milo Olin Papers, Mass-HS; entry of August 1, 1864, Lyman Jackman Diary, NHHS; entry of August 1, 1864, Jones diary, Josiah N. Jones Papers, NHHS; Tower, *Lee's Adjutant,* 179.

42. Thomas, "Colored Troops at Petersburg," 565; R. O. Whitehurst to Stewart, September 27, 1903, in Stewart, comp., "Charge of the Crater," 90, MOC; Thomas, "Twenty-two Hours," 31–33.

43. Thomas, "Twenty-two Hours," 34–48; R. O. Whitehurst to Stewart, September 27, 1903, in Stewart, comp., "Charge of the Crater," 90–93, MOC; Whitehead, "Retaking of the Lines," 472; entry of August 1, 1864, John Bell Vincent Diary, VHS. In his 1903 letter to Stewart, Whitehurst (his name, for some reason, was misspelled when his article "Retaking of the Lines" was published) recalled meeting Thomas on a steamer plying the James River soon after the surrender at Appomattox. Thomas generously offered to let Whitehurst live on his farm near Portland, Maine, until the Confederate regained his health, but Whitehurst was on his way to family members at Suffolk. The two met again sometime after the war in San Francisco.

44. Entry of August 1, 1864, Grant diary, Claudius Buchanan Grant Papers, BHL-UM; *History of the Thirty-fifth Regiment Massachusetts,* 280; Codman to parents, August 4, 1864, George Benton Codman Letters, DC; Beaty, "Battle of the Crater," in Hudson, *Sketches and Reminiscences,* 57; Cavanaugh and Marvel, *Battle of the Crater,* 105; Stewart, "Charge of the Crater," 90. Several Confederate accounts cite much higher figures for the number of dead buried on August 1, perhaps taking their cue from Lee, who reported that 700 were interred. See Lee to Seddon, August 1, 1864, *OR,* vol. 40, pt. 1, 753, and Featherston, *Battle of the Crater,* 25.

45. Entry of August 1, 1864, John Alfred Feister Coleman Diary, Confederate Miscellany Collection I, SC-EU; unsigned recollection of Crater battle, Bird Family Papers, VHS; Rickard, *Services with Colored Troops,* 30; Trudeau, *Like Men of War,* 249.

46. Harman Bower to Maggie B. Monks, August 2, 1864, Zerah Coston Monks Papers, WRHS.

47. John A. Bodamer Journal, August 2, 1864, James M. Schoff Civil War Collections, WLC-UM.

48. Bernard, "Battle of the Crater," 21; Stewart, *Spirit of the South,* 141.

17. Aftermath

1. Lowe, *Meade's Army,* 245; Grant to Halleck, August 1, 1864: Grant to Meade, August 1, 1864, report of court of inquiry, *OR,* vol. 40, pt. 1, 17, 134; Bowers to Wilson, August 1, 1864, in Simon, *Papers of Ulysses S. Grant,* 11:363n; Grant to Ammen, August 18, 1864, in Simon, *Papers of Ulysses S. Grant,* 12:35; Meade to wife, July 31, 1864, in Meade, *Life and Letters,* 2:218; Kautz journal, July 30, 1864, *Supplement to the Official Records,* 7:246.

2. Nevins, *Diary of Battle,* 443; Miers, ed., *Wash Roebling's War,* 28–29; Washington Roebling to "My own love," July 30, 1864, Roebling Family Papers, RU.

3. Cutcheon autobiography, 292, 318, Byron Cutcheon Papers, BHL-UM; Charles J. Mills to mother, July 31, 1864, "Civil War Letters of Major Charles J. Mills," 140, Gregory A. Coco Collection, USAMHI; Taylor to Jane, July 31, 1864, William Taylor Letters, CWM; Bliss reminiscences, 141, Zenas R. Bliss Papers, USAMHI.

4. Heisler to sister, July 31, 1864, Henry C. Heisler Papers, LC; Bosbyshell, "Petersburg Mine," 219.

5. Livermore, *Days and Events,* 387; Ord to Molly, July 31 and August 8, 1864, Edward Otho Cresap Ord Papers, SU; Louis H. Bell to George, August 12, 1864, Bell Family Papers, NHHS; Cunningham, *Three Years with the Adirondack Regiment,* 140.

6. Welles, *Diary of Gideon Welles,* 2:89–92.

7. *Memorial of Colonel John A. Bross,* 15.

8. Nevins, *Diary of the Civil War,* 471–74.

9. Power, *Lee's Miserables,* 136, 139–40; General Orders No., not stated, Headquarters, Anderson's Division, August 6, 1864, *Supplement to the Official Records,* pt. 3, vol. 3, 599; Lee, *Memoirs of William Nelson Pendleton,* 358–59; R. W. Jones letter, January 3, 1877, quoted in Mahone to Committee of Mahone's Brigade Organization, July 1880, found in clipping from *Richmond Whig,* Mahone Family Papers, LOV; William R. J. Pegram to Jenny, August 1, 1864, Pegram-Johnson-McIntosh Family Papers, VHS.

10. Cutchins, *A Famous Command,* 154; Watson to Harriet Louis, August 20, 1864, Samuel S. Watson Letters, PNB; Fred Harris to uncle, July 31, 1864, David B. Harris Papers, SCL-DU.

11. Chamberlayne, *Ham Chamberlayne,* 249–51; McFall to mother and sister, September 4, 1864, William McFall Papers, EU; Alexander to wife, August 28, September 5, 15, 1864, Edward Porter Alexander Papers, UNC; Davis to Speed, September 8, 1864, in Crist, *Papers of Jefferson Davis,* 11:19.

12. Cutcheon autobiography, 331, Byron Cutcheon Papers, BHL-UM; *History of the Thirty-fifth Regiment Massachusetts,* 281; entries of July 30, 31, August 1, 14, 1864, John B. Bailey Diary, NHHS; Marshall, *A War of the People,* 250–51; Derby letter, July 31, 1864, in Benedict, *Vermont in the Civil War,* 2:520; Newell Dutton to Elmer Bragg, ca. August 29, 1864, "Letters and Diary of Corporal Elmer Bragg, 1862–1864," 76, DC; Lord, *History of the Ninth Regiment New Hampshire,* 493–94; Aston diary, entries of August 6–7, 1864, in Aston, *History and Roster,* 21.

13. Scott, *Forgotten Valor,* 559; entries of August 3–4, 1864, Wortley diary, Clark S. Wortley Papers, EU; Hartranft to wife, August 4, 1864, John F. Hartranft Papers, Helen L. Shireman; Special Orders No. 62, Second Brigade, First Division, Ninth Corps, August 1, 1864: William Humphrey to George A. Wells, August 28, 1864, Special Orders and Circulars, June–September, 1864 (2nd Brig., 1st Div., 9th Corps), vol. 51/155, RG393, NARA; Seth Williams to Burnside, July 31, 1864, Ambrose E. Burnside Papers, RG94, NARA.

14. Grant, *Personal Memoirs,* 2:613; transcript of Barnard's evaluation of mine attack, August 6, 1864, John Gross Barnard Papers, SCL-DU; Monks to sister, August 2, 1864, Zerah Coston Monks Papers, WRHS; Butler to Sarah, August 1, 1864, *Private and Official Correspondence of Gen. Benjamin F. Butler,* 4:575.

15. James H. Wilson to Smith, August 4, 1864, William F. Smith Papers, Ver-HS; Lyman to Dearest, July 31, 1864, Theodore Lyman Letters and Diary, Mass-HS; William Hamilton Harris Journal, July 30, 1864, VHS; Ford, *Cycle of Adams Letters,* 2:173.

16. Cutcheon autobiography, 322, Byron Cutcheon Papers, BHL-UM; entry of July 30, 1864, Henry White Diary, AAS; Warren to Emmie, July 31, 1864, Gouverneur Kemble Warren Papers, NYSL; entry of August 1, 1864, William Stowell Tilton Diary, Mass-HS; Lowe, *Meade's Army,* 241; Nevins, *Diary of Battle,* 449; D. M. Jordan, *"Happiness Is Not My Companion,"* 179; Second Corps journal, *OR,* vol. 40, pt. 1, 324; Livermore, *Days and Events,* 384; Ford, *Cycle of Adams Letters,* 2:173; Ord to Molly, August 8, 1864, Edward Otho Cresap Ord Papers, SU; Robert Dawson to sister, August 8, 1864, http://www.100thpenn.com/rdawsonletters.htm (accessed November 23, 2009); Campbell, *A Grand Terrible Dramma,"* 253–54.

17. Lowe, *Meade's Army,* 292; Simon Goodell Griffin, "Civil War Recollections," 23, DC; entry of July 30, 1864, Henderson George Diary, http://www.100thpenn.com/hendersongeorgediary.htm (accessed November 23, 2009).

18. Scott, *Forgotten Valor,* 556; Hartranft to wife, July 31, 1864, John F. Hartranft Papers, Helen L. Shireman; Cutcheon autobiography, 321, Byron Cutcheon Papers, BHL-UM; Robert Dawson to sister, August 8, 1864, http://www.100thpenn.com/rdawsonletters.htm (accessed November 23, 2009); C. H. Porter, "Petersburg Mine," 232–33.

19. Foote to Mary, August 5, 1864, John B. Foote Papers, SCL-DU; Cross to wife, August 7, 1864, Joseph Cross Civil War Letters, AAS; Alfred Milnes to father, August 3,

1864, BHL-UM; Adam Henry to brother, August 3, 1864, Henry Family Letters, Ronald D. Boyer Collection, USAMHI; Austin Kendall to friends, August 7, 1864, David Walbridge Kendall Papers, BHL-UM; entry of July 30, 1864, John E. Bassett Diary, Mass-HS; Rich to father, July 31, 1864, Alonzo G. Rich Letters, Mass-HS.

20. Mills to father, July 31, August 3, 1864, and Mills to mother, September 26, 1864, "Civil War Letters of Major Charles J. Mills," Gregory A. Coco Collection, USAMHI; Coco, *Through Blood and Fire,* 142; Cain to mother, August 4, 1864, Avery B. Cain Letters, Ver-HS; William A. Childs to William P. Spalding, July 27 and August 1, 1864, Spalding Family Papers, BHL-UM; John A. Bodamer Journal, July 30, 1864, James M. Schoff Civil War Collections, WLC-UM; Rich to father, July 31, 1864, Alonzo G. Rich Letters, Mass-HS; *Civil War Letters of Hugh McInnes,* 12; Tapert, *Brothers' War,* 210; entry of July 30, 1864, William Stowell Tilton Diary, Mass-HS; Edward L. Cook to Laura, August 4, 1864, UCSB; entry of July 31, 1864, Wortley diary, Clark S. Wortley Papers, EU; Mushkat, *Citizen-Soldier's Civil War,* 205–6; entries of July 30–31, 1864, Henry White Diary, AAS; Young to Delia, August 4, 1864, Henry F. Young Papers, WHS; *Louisville Daily Journal,* August 3, 1864.

21. Rockwell, *Dear Frank,* 539; Taylor to Jane, July 31, 1864, William Taylor Letters, CWM; Herdegen and Murphy, *Four Years with the Iron Brigade,* 299; Bates, "A Day with the Colored Troops," *National Tribune,* January 30, 1908; Rickard to sister, July 31, 1864, James Helme Rickard Letters, AAS; New York *Evening Post,* quoted in J. T. Wilson, *Black Phalanx,* 426–27; E. A. Miller, *Black Civil War Soldiers of Illinois,* 105; White letter to *Christian Recorder,* August 20, 1864, in Redkey, *Grand Army of Black Men,* 112.

22. Monks to sister, August 9, 1864, Zerah Coston Monks Papers, WRHS. The black troops actually were told to load their weapons and fix their bayonets, but not to cap their guns. H. S. Hall, "Mine Run to Petersburg," 222.

23. James Paul Verdery to sister, July 31, 1864, Eugene and James Paul Verdery Papers, SCL-DU; correspondence in *Richmond Dispatch,* reprinted in *Charleston Mercury,* August 4, 1864; Perkins to Newton Perkins, August 2, 1864, Andrew J. Perkins Papers, GA; Barfield to wife, August 2, 1864, "Confederate Letters Written by Mr. Lee Barfield of Dooly County, Georgia, 1861–1865," GA; Edmund Lockett Womack to Sallie, July 31, 1864, and A. T. Fleming to Mrs. N. J. R. Fleming, August 3, 1864, Michael A. Cavanaugh Collection, HSSC; W. C. McClelland to Robert McClellan, August 15, 1864, quoted in B. I. Wiley, *Life of Johnny Reb,* 314–15; Wiggins, *My Dear Friend,* 138; Power, *Lee's Miserables,* 139.

24. Jimerson, *Private Civil War,* 115; Wyatt-Brown, *Southern Honor,* 369–80; Gallagher, *Fighting for the Confederacy,* 462.

25. Calton to brother and sister, March 27, 1864, John Washington Calton Letters, NCDAH; Day, "Battle of the Crater," 356.

26. Cockrell and Ballard, *Mississippi Rebel,* 289; John C. C. Sanders to Pa, August 3, 1864, John C. C. Sanders Collection, UA; Peterson to sister, August 1, 1864, J. Edward Peterson Papers, MMF; William R. J. Pegram to Jenny, August 1, 1864, Pegram-Johnson-McIntosh Family Papers, VHS; K. Wiley, *Norfolk Blues,* 138.

27. Hunt to Williams, October 31, 1864: Monroe to Craig, August 5, 1864: Abbot to Davis, December 5, 1864: Piper to Hunt, August 6, 1864, *OR,* vol. 40, pt. 1, 280–81, 599–600, 659, 726–27; Taintor to mother, August 4, 1864, Henry E. Taintor Papers, SCL-DU; Roemer, *Reminiscences,* 249.

28. Cavanaugh and Marvel, *Battle of the Crater,* 146–48; Coit, "Battle of the Crater," 127; Gallagher, *Fighting for the Confederacy,* 467.

29. Meade testimony, August 8, 1864, report of court of inquiry, *OR,* vol. 40, pt. 1, 52.

30. Palfrey, *Memoir of William Francis Bartlett,* 120; Sheahan journal, August 2, 9, 1864, John Parris Sheahan Papers, Maine-HS.

31. Kenfield, "Captured by Rebels," 234–35; Shearman, "Battle of the Crater," 19–21, 23, 25–27, 30–31; William Baird Memoirs, 21–22, BHL-UM.

32. Hill to Cooper, August 4, 1864, *OR,* ser. 2, vol. 7, 539–40; E. A. Miller, *Black Civil War Soldiers of Illinois,* 91.

33. Turner to Hatch, October 14, 1864: Seddon to Lee, October 15, 1864: Lee to Grant, October 19, 1864, *OR,* ser. 2, vol. 7, 987, 991, 1010.

34. Hitchcock to Butler, November 25, 1864: General Orders No. 299, War Department, Adjutant General's Office, December 7, 1864, *OR,* ser. 2, vol. 7, 1159, 1198; Lowe, *Meade's Army,* 313.

35. LoPiano, "Gallantry in the Crater," 43; Forstchen, "28th United States Colored Troops," 142; Benedict, *Vermont in the Civil War,* 2:519n; B. A. Spear, "In Front of Petersburg," *National Tribune,* June 20, 1889.

36. Braman to Libbie, August 8, 1864, Waters Whipple Braman Letters, NYSL; Fisher S. Cleaveland to Jennie, August 8, 1864, Michael A. Cavanaugh Collection, HSSC; Nevins, *Diary of Battle,* 448; Agassiz, *Meade's Headquarters,* 204; Sparks, *Inside Lincoln's Army,* 407; Scott, *Forgotten Valor,* 562.

37. Meade to wife, July 31, August 3, 10, 1864, in Meade, *Life and Letters,* 2:217–18, 221; Burnside testimony, August 1, 1864: Meade to Rawlins, August 3, 1864, and enclosed charges and specifications, report of court of inquiry: Meade to Burnside, August 3, 1864: Burnside to Stanton, August 6, 1864: Stanton to Burnside, August 8, 1864, *OR,* vol. 40, pt. 1, 67, 172–76, 531–32; Sparks, *Inside Lincoln's Army,* 410; Scott, *Forgotten Valor,* 562–63.

38. Grant to Halleck, August 2, 1864: Special Orders No. 258, War Department, Adjutant General's Office, August 3, 1864: Special Orders No. 205, Headquarters, Army of the Potomac, August 1, 1864: note by court members, August 2, 1864, report of court of inquiry, *OR,* vol. 40, pt. 1, 18, 42–43, 172–73; Marvel, *Burnside,* 409–10; Cavanaugh and Marvel, *Battle of the Crater,* 108–9.

39. Meade testimony, August 8, 1864, report of court of inquiry, *OR,* vol. 40, pt. 1, 43–44, 49–50, 52–54; Meade to wife, August 10, 1864, in Meade, *Life and Letters,* 2:221.

40. Sparks, *Inside Lincoln's Army,* 411; Burnside testimony, August 10–11, 1864, report of court of inquiry, *OR,* vol. 40, pt. 1, 64, 70, 74–75.

41. Lowe, *Meade's Army,* 249; Scott, *Forgotten Valor,* 563–64; Hartranft to father, August 16, 1864, John F. Hartranft Papers, Helen L. Shireman; Sparks, *Inside Lincoln's Army,* 414; Agassiz, *Meade's Headquarters,* 213.

42. Duane testimony, August 29, 1864: Warren testimony, August 29, 1864: Ayres testimony, August 29, 1864: Grant testimony, August 30, 1864: Ord testimony, August 30, 1864: Potter testimony, August 30, 1864: Ferrero testimony, August 31, 1864: Willcox testimony, August 31, 1864: Ames testimony, September 2, 1864: Farquhar testimony, September 5, 1864, report of court of inquiry, *OR,* vol. 40, pt. 1, 75, 78, 82, 84–85, 88, 92–94, 108, 122.

43. Report of court of inquiry, *OR,* vol. 40, pt. 1, 42–129.

44. Bliss reminiscences, Zenas R. Bliss Papers, 142, USAMHI.

45. Burnside to Grant, August 25, 1864: Bowers to Burnside, September 1, 1864: Grant to Burnside, September 28, 1864, Simon, *Papers of Ulysses S. Grant,* 11:414–25nn; Grant to Burnside, October 17, 1864, in Simon, *Papers of Ulysses S. Grant,* 12:317; Scott, *Forgotten Valor,* 586; Marvel, *Burnside,* 412–13, 417.

46. Welsh, *Medical Histories of Union Generals,* 200–201; Coco, *Through Blood and Fire,* 145; Joseph White affidavit, August 24, November 15, 1864: Ledlie to Lorenzo Thomas, January 17, 1865: Annie Heideberger affidavit, November 30, 1888: Jefferson Scales affidavit, n.d., James H. Ledlie Pension File, RG94 NARA; Meade to Grant, December 8, 1864: Grant to Meade, December 8, 1864, *OR,* vol. 42, pt. 3, 867; *New York Times,* August 16, 1882; McWhiney and Jenkins, "Union's Worst General," 39.

47. Tap, *Over Lincoln's Shoulder,* 189–90; Meade to wife, December, n.d., 1864, in Meade, *Life and Letters,* 2:253.

48. Grant to Meade, December 19, 1864, in Simon, *Papers of Ulysses S. Grant,* 13:135–36; Burnside testimony, December 17, 1864: Meade testimony, December 20, 1864, *RCCW,* 23, 39–41; Meade to wife, December 20, 1864, in Meade, *Life and Letters,* 2:254.

49. Pleasants testimony, January 13, 1865, *RCCW,* 126–27, 130.

50. *RCCW,* 8.

51. Cutcheon, quoted in Herek, *These Men Have Seen Hard Service,* 231; Sparks, *Inside Lincoln's Army,* 469; Meade to Stanton, February 13, 1865, *OR,* vol. 46, pt. 2, 548; Grant to Meade, February 9, 1865, in Simon, *Papers of Ulysses S. Grant,* 13:399; Meade to wife, March 4, 13, 1865, in Meade, *Life and Letters,* 2:266–67.

52. Meade to wife, February 9, 1865, in Meade, *Life and Letters,* 2:261–62; Grant testimony, December 20, 1864, *RCCW,* 124; Scott, *Forgotten Valor,* 609–10.

53. Clipping from *New York Herald,* July 24, 1878, in Warren court of inquiry, *Supplement to the Official Records,* pt. 1, vol. 8, 17; D. M. Jordan, *"Happiness Is Not My Companion,"* 179–80; Grant, *Personal Memoirs,* 2:607–13.

54. Tap, *Over Lincoln's Shoulder,* 191–92; Scott, *Forgotten Valor,* 563–64.

Conclusion

1. Featherston, *Battle of the Crater,* 26; Edwards, *Condensed History,* 47; Pegram letter, August 26, 1892, in Bernard, *War Talks,* 209; Coit, "Battle of the Crater," 128–29n.

2. Andrews, *Sketch of Company K,* 24–25; Fleet and Fuller, *Green Mount,* 337; J. Warren Pursley to sister, August 10, 1864, Mary Frances Jane Pursley Papers, SCL-DU.

3. Stewart, *Spirit of the South,* 141; Graham, "Fifty-sixth Regiment," 375; Fagan, "Petersburg Crater," in Fortin, "Colonel Hilary A. Herbert's History of the Eighth Alabama," 151; field visit to Petersburg crater, October 14, 1999; Bernard, *War Talks,* 334; entries of August 4, 8, 10, 17, 1864, John Alfred Feister Coleman Diary, Confederate Miscellany Collection I, EU.

4. Bernard, *War Talks,* 334; Douglas, "Confederate Countermining in Front of Petersburg," Petersburg Crater Collection, UVA; Johnson to Brent, September 15, 1864, *OR,* vol. 42, pt. 1, 891–92; Whitney, "Petersburg: Anatomy of an Earthwork," photocopy at PNB; Orr, "Archaeology of Trauma," 24–25; Allen, *Forty-six Months with the Fourth R.I.,* 293.

5. Whitner to Johnson, August 31, 1864, *OR,* vol. 40, pt. 1, 795; Coit, "Battle of the Crater," 128n.

6. Mackintosh, *"Dear Martha . . . ,"* 149; Featherstonhaugh, "Notes on the Defences of Petersburg," 192–93; William Alexander Gordon Memoirs, 152, WLU.

7. Wise to Douglas, August 2, 1864, *OR,* vol. 42, pt. 2, 1160; Douglas, "Petersburg Crater," Petersburg Crater Collection, UVA.

8. Blackford, *War Years with Jeb Stuart,* 265–67.

9. Ibid., 267; Johnson to Brent, September 26, 27, 1864, *OR,* vol. 42, pt. 1, 896–97; J. F. Gilmer to W. H. Stevens, August 2, 1864, and J. H. Alexander to Stevens, August 6, 1864, Letters and Telegrams Sent by the Engineer Bureau of the Confederate War Department, M628, RG109, NARA.

10. Potter report, August 5, 1864, Ambrose E. Burnside Papers, RG94, NARA; Burnside to Williams, August 5, 1864, *OR,* vol. 42, pt. 2, 58.

11. Binion to sister, August 1, 1864, Dorsey N. Binion Letters, Confederate Miscellany Collection I, EU; Longest to brother, August 4, 1864, Younger Longest Letters, VHS; Stuart to mother, August 10, 1864, John Lane Stuart Papers, SCL-DU; Power, *Lee's Miserables,* 179–80; Johnson to Brent, August 3, 8, 11, 1864: Gracie to Brent, August 17, 1864, *OR,* vol. 42, pt. 1, 884, 886–87, 925; Johnson journal, August 6, 1864, *Supplement to the Official Records,* 7:460; entry of August 6, 1864, John Alfred Feister Coleman Diary, Confederate Miscellany Collection I, EU.

12. Douglas to Stevens, August 1, 1864, *OR,* vol. 42, pt. 2, 1155; Hugh T. Douglas, "Confederate Countermining in Front of Petersburg," Petersburg Crater Collection, UVA.

13. Hugh T. Douglas, "Confederate Countermining in Front of Petersburg," Petersburg Crater Collection, UVA; Douglas to Talcott, August 2, 5, 1864, *OR,* vol. 42, pt. 2, 1158, 1162–63; Meade to Butler, August 5, 1864: Meade to Ord, August 5, 1864: Ord to Humphreys, August 5, 1864: Ord to Shaffer, August 6, 1864: Johnson to Brent, August 6, 1864, *OR,* vol. 42, pt. 1, 52–53, 64, 792–93, 885; Johnson journal, August 5, 1864, *Supplement to the Official Records,* 7:460.

14. Charges and specifications: Douglas to Thomas M. R. Talcott, August 9, 1864: Douglas to James A. Seddon, August 10, 1864: Talcott to McHenry Howard, September 4, 1864, Hugh Thomas Douglas service record, M258, Roll 93, RG109, NARA.

15. Brightman, "Glory Enough," 141–42, 144–47, 149–50, 152–53; Muffly, *Story of Our Regiment,* 50–52; Johnson to McWillie, October 28, 1864, *OR,* vol. 42, pt. 1, 906.

16. Anderson to not stated, June 15, 1866, *Supplement to the Official Records,* pt. 1, vol. 7, 818–19; Johnson to McWillie, November 6, 1864: Wallace to Foote, November 6, 1864, *OR,* vol. 42, pt. 1, 909, 933–934.

17. Scott, *Forgotten Valor,* 603–4.

18. Coit, "Battle of the Crater," 128–29n.

19. Lowe, *Meade's Army,* 359.

20. Muster roll, Jacob Douty service record, 48th Pennsylvania, RG94, NARA; examining surgeon's certificate, May 31, 1882: file cards, Jacob Douty Pension File, NARA.

21. Henry Reese to P. M. Lydig, November 26, 1864: Special Order No. 216, Headquarters, 9th Corps, October 31, 1864: notation by Adjutant General's Office, February 9, 1887, Henry Reese service record, 48th Pennsylvania, RG94, NARA; Pension Office to Surgeon General, October 20, 1881: Declaration for Original Invalid Pension, June 2, 1879: Henry Reese Pension File, NARA.

22. Declaration for Original Invalid Pension, June 2, 1879: examining surgeon's certificate, December 9, 1880, August 23, 1882, and January 7, 1891: General Affidavit, April

1, 1891: Appeal to Secretary of the Interior, August 21, 1891: death certificate, Henry Reese Pension File, NARA; Haas, "Famous 48th," 61.

23. Reese account, in Guthrie, *Camp-Fires of the Afro-American,* 529.

24. Draft of charges and specifications: muster cards, Henry Pleasants service record, 48th Pennsylvania, RG94, NARA; Bosbyshell, *48th in the War,* 177, 179; Parke to Williams, November 19, 1864, *OR,* vol. 51, pt. 1, 1189–90.

25. Pleasants, *Tragedy of the Crater,* 108.

26. *Pottsville Weekly Miners' Journal,* April 2, 1880, clipping in Michael A. Cavanaugh Collection, HSSC.

27. Cavanaugh and Marvel, *Battle of the Crater,* 117–18; Marvel, *Burnside,* 411–12.

28. Charles S. Venable statement, April 10, 1872, *Reply to a Communication Published by Gen. C. M. Wilcox, in the New Orleans Times, of January 1st, 1872,* 24, Mahone Family Papers, LOV.

29. Willcox testimony, December 20, 1864, *RCCW,* 91; Scott, *Forgotten Valor,* 555.

30. LaMotte, "Battle of the Crater," *Charleston News and Courier,* May 14, 1899; McMaster, "Elliott's Brigade," 26; Gallagher, ed., *Fighting for the Confederacy,* 465; Charles S. Venable statement, April 10, 1872, *Reply to a Communication Published by Gen. C. M. Wilcox, in the New Orleans Times, of January 1st, 1872,* 24, Mahone Family Papers, LOV.

31. Hess, *In the Trenches at Petersburg,* 285.

Appendix 1—After the War

1. Trowbridge, *Desolate South,* 115; *Guide to the Fortifications and Battlefields,* 14; "W" Letter, May 11, 1870, VHS; R. O. Whitehurst to Stewart, October 23, 1903, in Stewart, comp., "Charge of the Crater," unpaginated, MOC.

2. Trowbridge, *Desolate South,* 115; Davis and Wiley, *Photographic History of the Civil War,* 2:1116, 1118, 1321; Cavanaugh and Marvel, *Battle of the Crater,* 82, 112–13; Joseph P. Cullen, "Report on the Physical History of the Crater," 6, PNB.

3. Cavanaugh and Marvel, *Battle of the Crater,* 112; Calkins, "History of the Crater Battlefield," 156–57; Powell, "Battle of the Petersburg Crater," 559–60.

4. Calkins, "History of the Crater Battlefield," 157; Griffith statement, September 13, 1892, in Bernard, *War Talks,* 224n-225n; W. R. Houghton and M. B. Houghton, *Two Brothers in the Civil War,* 134; Owen, "Explosion of Mine at Petersburg," *National Tribune,* November 1, 1934; William Alexander Gordon Memoirs, 152, WLU.

5. Bowley, "Petersburg Mine," 41; Guthrie, *Camp-Fires of the Afro-American,* 518; Cunningham, *Three Years with the Adirondack Regiment,* 140n; Lathe account, in Lord, *History of the Ninth Regiment New Hampshire,* 509–10.

6. Reid, "Petersburg Crater," *National Tribune,* January 5, 1905; Day, "Breastworks at Petersburg," 175; Bradwell, "On Picket Duty in Front of Fort Stedman," 307; W. R. Houghton and M. B. Houghton, *Two Brothers in the Civil War,* 134.

7. Calkins, "History of the Crater Battlefield," 157; Cavanaugh and Marvel, *Battle of the Crater,* 113; "Crater Yields 25 Skeletons," *National Tribune,* April 9, 1931; "Military Honors for Crater Dead," *National Tribune,* April 16, 1931; Charles I. Wilson, "Archeological Investigations and Excavations, Crater Area," 5–6, PNB.

8. Calkins, "History of the Crater Battlefield," 157–58.

9. Charles I. Wilson, "Archeological Investigations and Excavations, Crater Area," 8–9, 11–14, PNB; Vernon Earle, "Battle of the Crater, Petersburg, Va.," 47–48, PNB; John Griffin and Rex Wilson, "Crater Tunnel Excavation," 4, PNB;

10. Field visit to Petersburg Crater, October 14, 1999; Stewart, "Field of Blood Was the Crater," 351–52; K. P. Wilson, *Campfires of Freedom,* 210. For good modern photographs of the crater, see Cannan, *The Crater,* 96–97, 156–57.

11. N. M. Blake, *William Mahone,* 73, 105–6, 118, 151, 179, 220, 224, 244, 260–63; Levin, "William Mahone," 380, 382; Levin, "'On That Day,'" 28–30.

12. Mahone to Committee of Mahone's Brigade, n.d., in clipping of *Richmond Whig,* no date, Mahone Family Papers, LOV; Bernard, ed., *War Talks,* 217–22; Levin, "William Mahone," 403; Levin, "Is Not the Glory Enough," 168, 172–77; Levin, "'On That Day,'" 30; N. M. Blake, *William Mahone,* 57n-58n.

13. J. T. Wilson, *Black Phalanx,* 420–21.

14. Simms, "John A. Elder," 29–31; Elder to Carter Harmon, February 2, 1880, John Adams Elder Papers, SCL-DU; Coons, "Portrait of His Times," 17, 19, 22; Levin, "William Mahone," 383; John W. Morrison, "Mine Explosion, Petersburg, Va., July 30th 1864," 12, CWURM.

15. DeLeon, *Four Years in Rebel Capitals,* 300; J. D., "Battle of the Crater," 98–99, 101–3; Young, "Campaign with Sharpshooters," *Philadelphia Weekly Times,* January 26, 1878; Carter R. Bishop to Laura Lee Richardson, February 13, 1932, PNB; Davis, *Death in the Trenches,* 84–85.

16. N. M. Blake, *William Mahone,* 151; Cavanaugh and Marvel, *Battle of the Crater,* 84; Levin, "'On That Day . . . ,'" 25–27.

17. N. M. Blake, *William Mahone,* 254; Stewart, "Field of Blood Was the Crater," 355; Stewart, *Spirit of the South,* 195, 198–200; clipping, *Richmond Dispatch,* 1903, and clipping, unidentified newspaper, 1905, in Stewart, comp., "Charge of the Crater," unpaginated, MOC; clipping, *Petersburg Index-Appeal,* July 9, 1905, George S. Bernard Papers, SCL-DU; Levin, "'On That Day,'" 18–19.

18. N. M. Blake, *William Mahone,* 254; Levin, "'On That Day . . . ,'" 31; Carter R. Bishop to Laura Lee Richardson, February 13, 1932, PNB; Calkins, "History of the Crater Battlefield," 157.

BIBLIOGRAPHY

Archival Sources

Abraham Lincoln Presidential Library, Springfield, Illinois
    Pierre G. T. Beauregard Papers
American Antiquarian Society, Worcester, Massachusetts
    Joseph Cross Civil War Letters
    James Helme Rickard Letters
    Henry White Diaries
    William A. Willoughby Papers
Boston Public Library, Boston, Massachusetts
    20th Massachusetts Regimental Collection
Civil War and Underground Railroad Museum, Philadelphia, Pennsylvania
    William H. Bolton Journal
    John W. Morrison. "The Mine Explosion, Petersburg, Va., July 30th 1864"
College of William and Mary, Williamsburg, Virginia
    William Taylor Letters
Dartmouth College, Rauner Special Collections Library, Hanover, New Hampshire
    George Benton Codman Letters
    Simon Goodell Griffin. "Civil War Recollections"
    "Letters and Diary of Corporal Elmer Bragg, 1862–1864"
    Oscar D. Robinson Papers
    Ransom Sargent Papers
Duke University, Medical Center Library, Durham, North Carolina
    Charles Knickerbocker Winne Journal. Josiah Trent Collection
Duke University, Special Collections Library, Durham, North Carolina
    John Gross Barnard Papers
    George S. Bernard Papers
    Robert A. Boyd Papers
    Confederate Veteran Papers
    John Adams Elder Papers
    John B. Foote Papers
    John Mead Gould Papers
    David B. Harris Papers
    Mathew N. Love Papers
    Marshall McDonald Papers
    Mary Frances Jane Pursley Papers
    William Russell Papers

John Lane Stuart Papers
Henry E. Taintor Papers
Eugene and James Paul Verdery Papers
East Carolina University, East Carolina Manuscript Collection,
    Greenville, North Carolina
    Cutchin Family Papers
    Francis W. Knowles Papers
Emory University, Special Collections, Atlanta, Georgia
    Dorsey N. Binion Letters. Confederate Miscellany Collection I
    John Alfred Feister Coleman Diary. Confederate Miscellany Collection I
    William McFall Papers
    Augustin E. Shore Papers
    Clark S. Wortley Papers
Georgia Archives, Morrow
    Lee Barfield. "Confederate Letters Written by Mr. Lee Barfield of Dooly County,
        Georgia, 1861–1865." Reading Room Stacks
    Laban Odom Letters. Microfilm Library
    Andrew J. Perkins Papers
Historical Society of Schuylkill County, Pottsville, Pennsylvania
    Michael A. Cavanaugh Collection
        Fisher S. Cleaveland Letter
        Elbert Corbin Diary
        S. H. Dearborn Letters
        A. T. Fleming Letter
        Warren H. Hurd Diary
        S. L. Montgomery Letter
        Pottsville, Pennsylvania, *Weekly Miners' Journal,* Clippings
        Edmund Lockett Womack Letter
Knox College, Archives, Galesburg, Illinois
    John Grierson Papers
Library of Congress, Manuscript Division, Washington, D.C.
    Henry C. Heisler Papers
    Henry Jackson Hunt Papers
Library of Virginia, Richmond
    William Fielding Baugh Letter
    Dewese Family Letters
    J. C. Duane Papers
    Mahone Family Papers
    John F. Sale Papers
Louisiana State University, Special Collections, Louisiana and Lower Mississippi Valley
    Collections, Baton Rouge
    George W. Brent Letter
Maine Historical Society, Portland
    Lunt Family Collection
    John Parris Sheahan Papers

Massachusetts Historical Society, Boston
    John E. Bassett Diary
    Caleb Hadley Beal Papers
    George Edward Fowle Correspondence
    Theodore Lyman Letters and Diary
    William Milo Olin Papers
    Alonzo G. Rich Letters
    Andrew Robeson Letters
    William Stowell Tilton Diary
Moravian Music Foundation, Winston-Salem, North Carolina
    J. Edward Peterson Papers
Museum of the Confederacy, Richmond
    Robert W. Hicks Diary
    William H. Stewart. Compiler. "The Charge of the Crater: Personal Recollections of
        Participants in the Charge of the Crater at Petersburg, Va, July 30th, 1864"
National Archives and Records Administration, Washington, D.C.
    RG77 Records of the Office of the Chief of Engineers
        "Sketch of Mine in front of 2d Div., 9 Corps, near Petersburg, Va." Dr. 150–58
    RG94 Records of the Adjutant General's Office
        Ambrose E. Burnside Papers
        Jacob Douty Pension File
        James H. Ledlie Pension File
        Henry Reese Pension File
        Albert D. Wright Congressional Medal of Honor File
        Compiled Service Records of Volunteer Union Soldiers Who Served in
            Organizations from the State of Pennsylvania
    RG109 War Department Collection of Confederate Records
        M258 Compiled Service Records of Confederate Soldiers Who Served in
            Organizations Raised Directly by the Confederate Government
        M628 Letters and Telegrams Sent by the Engineer Bureau of the Confederate
            War Department, 1861–1864
    RG393 Records of United States Army Continental Commands, 1821–1890
        Special Orders and Circulars, June–September, 1864 (2nd Brig., 1st Div.,
            9th Corps), Vol. 51/155
New Hampshire Historical Society, Concord
    John B. Bailey Diary
    Bell Family Papers
    George Henry Chandler Papers
    Lyman Jackman Diary
    Josiah N. Jones Papers
New York Public Library, New York
    William Hamilton Harris Papers
New York State Library, Manuscripts and Special Collections, Albany
    Waters Whipple Braman Letters
    Gouverneur Kemble Warren Papers

North Carolina Division of Archives and History, Raleigh
  John G. Alexander Reminiscences. Lowry Shuford Collection
  John Washington Calton Letters
  Robert F. Hoke Papers
  John Manly Lewis Confederate Pension Application File
  J. Ward. "Personal Experience." Lowry Shuford Collection
Ohio Historical Society, Columbus
  Albert Rogall Diary
Pennsylvania State University, Historical Collections and Labor Archives,
  University Park
  Gyla McDowell Collection
Petersburg National Battlefield, Petersburg, Virginia
  Carter R. Bishop Letter
  Cameron Scrapbook
  Joseph P. Cullen. "A Report on the Physical History of the Crater." 1975
  J. Frank Cutchin. "Reminiscence of the Charge of the Crater"
  Robert D. Dawson Letter
  Vernon Earle. "The Battle of the Crater, Petersburg, Va." 1956
  John Thomas Goode Letter
  John Griffin and Rex Wilson. "Crater Tunnel Excavation." 1962
  George W. Guy. Transcriber. "Those Blown Up at Crater"
  Thomas Harrison. "Route of Mahone's Troops to the Crater Battlefield"
  C. R. Jackson. "Report on Artillery Operations in the Battle of the Crater." 1934
  Hugh L. Kerrick Letter
  Matthew Norris Love Letter
  Photograph Collection
  William Russell Diary
  Lee A. Wallace, Jr., and Herbert Olsen. "Study of the Taylor House Remains." 1954
  Samuel S. Watson Letters
  J. Ellis Whitney. "Petersburg: Anatomy of an Earthwork." *Military Explorations.*
    Copy of 1985 article
  Charles I. Wilson. "Archeological Investigations and Excavations, Crater Area,
    Petersburg National Battlefield, Petersburg, Virginia." Historic Conservation
    and Interpretation, Inc. 1976
Rhode Island Historical Society, Manuscripts Division, Providence
  Ambrose Everts Burnside Collection
Rutgers University, Special Collections and University Archives, New Brunswick,
  New Jersey
  Roebling Family Papers
Helen L. Shireman, Private Collection
  John F. Hartranft Papers
South Carolina Historical Society, Charleston
  Theodore Dehon Jervey Papers
Stanford University, Department of Special Collections, Stanford, California
  Edward Otho Cresap Ord Papers

State Historical Society of Nebraska, Lincoln
  Charles Hadsall Diaries
Tennessee State Library and Archives, Nashville
  Theodore G. Trimmier Papers
University of Alabama, Special Collections, Tuscaloosa
  John C. C. Sanders Collection
University of California, Bancroft Library, Berkeley
  E. O. C. Ord Papers
University of California, Santa Barbara, Special Collections
  Edward L. Cook Letter
University of Michigan, Bentley Historical Library, Ann Arbor
  William Baird Memoirs
  Byron Cutcheon Papers
  Charles W. Ford Diary
  Claudius Buchanan Grant Papers
  Charles Horace Hodskin Papers
  James and Sybil Irwin Family Papers
  David Walbridge Kendall Papers
  Alfred Milnes Letter
  Conrad Noll Diaries
  William H. Randall Reminiscences
  Spalding Family Papers
University of Michigan, William L. Clements Library, Ann Arbor
  John A. Bodamer Journal. James M. Schoff Civil War Collections
  William Boston Diary. James M. Schoff Civil War Collections
  Hiram W. Coppernall Collection
  Hilon A. Parker Papers. James M. Schoff Civil War Collections
  Henry Pippitt Papers. James M. Schoff Civil War Collections
  Robert and George Whitcomb Papers. James M. Schoff Civil War Collections
University of New Hampshire, Special Collections, Durham
  Louis Bell Papers
  Howard M. Hanson Diary
  Leander Harris Letters
  George Naylor Julian Papers
University of North Carolina, Southern Historical Collection, Chapel Hill
  James W. Albright Papers
  Edward Porter Alexander Papers
  Henry A. Chambers Papers
  Elias Davis Papers
  Scott Family Papers
University of South Carolina, South Caroliniana Library, Columbia
  Elliott Family Papers
University of Virginia, Special Collections, Charlottesville
  Anne A. Banister. "Incidents in the Life of a Civil War Child"
  John Warwick Daniel Papers

Hugh T. Douglas. "The Petersburg Crater" and "Confederate Countermining in Front of Petersburg: Experiences and Recollections." Petersburg Crater Collection

J. C. Duane Letter Book

U.S. Army Military History Institute, Carlisle, Pennsylvania
Samuel A. Beddall Diary. Civil War Miscellaneous Collection
Zenas R. Bliss Papers
John C. Hackhiser Letters. Earl J. Hess Collection
Henry Family Letters. Ronald D. Boyer Collection
Charles J. Mills. "The Civil War Letters of Major Charles J. Mills." Gregory A. Coco Collection

Vermont Historical Society, Barre
Avery B. Cain Letters
Charles Cummings Papers
William F. Smith Papers

Virginia Historical Society, Richmond
Bird Family Papers
Chamberlayne Family Papers
Giles Buckner Cooke Diary
Joseph William Eggleston Autobiography
William Hamilton Harris Journal
William Henry Lewin Papers
Younger Longest Letters
William Goodridge Morton Papers
Pegram-Johnson-McIntosh Family Papers
James Eldred Phillips Papers
Alfred Lewis Scott Memoir
John Bell Vincent Diary
"W." Letter
David Addison Weisiger Papers
Reuben Lovett Whitehurst Commonplace Book

Washington and Lee University, Special Collections, Lexington, Virginia
William Alexander Gordon Memoirs

Western Reserve Historical Society, Cleveland, Ohio
Darling Family Papers
Zerah Coston Monks Papers

Wisconsin Historical Society, Madison
Henry F. Young Papers

Yale University, Special Collections, New Haven, Connecticut
Charles M. Coit Papers
Abraham Lincoln Collection

Newspapers

Ashland (Va.) Herald-Progress
Charleston (S.C.) Mercury
Christian Recorder

Houston Daily Post
Indianapolis Daily Journal
Louisville Daily Journal
National Tribune
New York Daily Tribune
New York Evening Post
New York Herald
New York Times
Norfolk Dispatch
Petersburg Daily Index-Appeal
Petersburg Express
Philadelphia Times
Philadelphia Weekly Times
Pottsville Weekly Miners' Journal
Otsego (N.Y.) Republican
Raleigh Daily Confederate
Richmond Dispatch
Richmond State
Richmond Times
Richmond Whig
Vicksburg Daily Herald

Web Sites

The 100th Regiment, Pennsylvania Veteran Volunteer Infantry Web site, "The Civil War History and Letters of Then Private Robert Doyne Dawson, Company D to His Sister, Rebecca Dawson," http://www.100thpenn.com/rdawsonletters.htm (accessed November 23, 2009).

The 100th Regiment, Pennsylvania Veteran Volunteer Infantry Web site, "Pvt. Henderson George Diary and Memoirs, Company G," http://www.100thpenn.com/hendersongeorgediary.htm (accessed November 23, 2009).

The 100th Regiment, Pennsylvania Veteran Volunteer Infantry Web site, "Letter by Pvt. Ethan S. Morehead, Co. K to His Brother Capt. Joseph Morehead, While Capt. Morehead Was Located in Vicksburg, MS," http://www.100thpenn.com/esmoreheadlet.htm (accessed November 23, 2009).

Saint, William S., Jr., ed. "Civil War Letters of General Delevan Bates: May 1862 to June 1867." http://files.usgwarchives.org/ne/state/military/cwletter.txt (accessed December 10, 2009).

Books, Articles, Dissertations, Theses, Archaeological Reports, and Tour Guides

Adams, J. C. "Battle of the Crater." *National Tribune*, June 25, 1903.

Agassiz, George R., ed. *Meade's Headquarters, 1863–1865: Letters of Colonel Theodore Lyman from the Wilderness to Appomattox*. Boston: Atlantic Monthly Press, 1922.

Albert, Allen D., ed. *History of the Forty-fifth Regiment Pennsylvania Veteran Volunteer Infantry, 1861–1865*. Williamsport, Pa.: Grit Publishing, 1912.

Allen, George H. *Forty-six Months with the Fourth R.I. Volunteers*. Providence, R.I.: J. A. & R. A. Reid, 1887.

Anderson, John. *The Fifty-seventh Regiment of Massachusetts Volunteers in the War of the Rebellion.* Boston: E. B. Stillings, 1896.

Andrews, W. J. *Sketch of Company K., 23rd South Carolina Volunteers, in the Civil War, from 1862–1865.* Richmond, Va.: Whittet and Shepperson, n.d.

Aston, Howard. *History and Roster of the Fourth and Fifth Independent Battalions and Thirteenth Regiment Ohio Cavalry Volunteers.* Columbus, Ohio: Fred. J. Heer, 1902.

Axelrod, Alan. *The Horrid Pit: The Battle of the Crater, the Civil War's Cruelest Mission.* New York: Carroll and Graf, 2007.

Bacon, James T. "Capt. George B. Lake." *Confederate Veteran* 2 (1894): 153.

Ballou, Daniel R. "The Petersburg Mine." *National Tribune,* June 5, 1913.

Barefoot, Daniel W. *General Robert F. Hoke: Lee's Modest Warrior.* Winston-Salem, N.C.: John F. Blair, 1996.

Barnwell, Robert W. "A View on the Crater Battle." *Confederate Veteran* 33 (1925): 176–78.

Bates, Delevan. "A Day with the Colored Troops." *National Tribune,* January 30, 1908.

"The Battle of the Crater." *Confederate Veteran* 34 (1926): 296–98.

Bausum, Daniel F. "Personal Reminiscences of Sergeant Daniel F. Bausum, Co. K, 48th Regt., Penna. Vol. Inf., 1861–1865." *Publications of the Historical Society of Schuylkill County* 4, no. 3 (1914): 240–49.

Beller, James W. "The Mine Explosion." *National Tribune,* June 20, 1889.

Benedict, G. G. *Vermont in the Civil War.* 2 vols. Burlington, Vt.: Free Press, 1888.

Bernard, George S. "The Battle of the Crater." *Southern Historical Society Papers* 18 (1890): 3–38.

———. *The Battle of the Crater in Front of Petersburg, July 30, 1864.* Petersburg, Va.: Index-Appeal, n.d.

———, ed. *War Talks of Confederate Veterans.* Petersburg, Va.: Fenn and Owen, 1892.

Beyer, W. F., and O. F. Keydel, eds. *Deeds of Valor from Records in the Archives of the United States Government.* 2 vols. Detroit: Perrien-Keydel, 1907.

Billings, John D. *The History of the Tenth Massachusetts Battery of Light Artillery in the War of the Rebellion, 1862–1865.* Boston: Hall and Whiting, 1881.

Blackford, W. W. *War Years with Jeb Stuart.* New York: Charles Scribner's Sons, 1945.

Blake, Nelson Morehouse. *William Mahone of Virginia: Soldier and Political Insurgent.* Richmond, Va.: Garret and Massie, 1935.

Blake, Sarah Swan Weld. *Diaries and Letters of Francis Minot Weld, M.D.* Boston: privately printed, 1925.

Bosbyshell, Oliver Christian. *The 48th in the War: Being a Narrative of the Campaigns of the 48th Regiment, Infantry, Pennsylvania Veteran Volunteers, during the War of the Rebellion.* Philadelphia: Avil Printing, 1895.

———. "The Petersburg Mine." *Maine Bugle,* campaign 3, call 3 (July 1896): 211–23.

Bouton, John Bell. *A Memoir of General Louis Bell.* New York: privately printed, 1865.

Bowen, George A., ed. "The Diary of Captain George D. Bowen, 12th Regiment New Jersey Volunteers." *Valley Forge Journal* 2 (June 1985): 176–231.

Bowley, Freeman S. "The Crater." *National Tribune,* November 6, 1884.

———. "The Petersburg Mine." In *Civil War Papers of the California Commandery and the Oregon Commandery of the Military Order of the Loyal Legion of the United States,* 27–41. Wilmington, N.C.: Broadfoot, 1995.

Bradwell, I. G. "On Picket Duty in Front of Fort Steadman." *Confederate Veteran* 38 (1930): 302–7.

Branson, D. F. "The Petersburg Mine." *National Tribune,* September 13, 1911.

Brightman, Austin C., Jr. "Glory Enough: The 148th Pennsylvania Volunteers at Fort Crater." *Civil War Regiments* 2, no. 2 (1992): 141–55.

Bryant, Elias A. *The Diary of Elias A. Bryant of Francestown, N.H.* Concord, N.H.: Rumford Press, n.d.

Burbank, Horace H. "The Battle of 'The Crater.'" In *War Papers Read before the Commandery of the State of Maine, Military Order of the Loyal Legion of the United States,* 1:283–94. Portland, Maine: Thurston, 1898.

Burgwyn, William H. S. "Clingman's Brigade." In *Histories of the Several Regiments and Battalions from North Carolina in the Great War, 1861–'65,* edited by Walter Clark, 4:481–500. Goldsboro, N.C.: Nash Brothers, 1901.

———. "Thirty-fifth Regiment." In *Histories of the Several Regiments and Battalions from North Carolina in the Great War, 1861–'65,* edited by Walter Clark, 2:591–628. Goldsboro, N.C.: Nash Brothers, 1901.

Caldwell, J. F. J. *The History of a Brigade of South Carolinians, Known First as "Gregg's" and Subsequently as "McGowan's Brigade."* Philadelphia: King and Baird, 1866.

Calkins, Christopher M. *From Petersburg to Appomattox: A Tour Guide to the Routes of Lee's Withdrawal and Grant's Pursuit, April 2–9, 1865.* Farmville, Va.: Farmville Herald, 1983.

———. "A History of the Crater Battlefield, 1865–1992." *Civil War Regiments* 2, no. 2 (1992): 156–58.

Campbell, Eric A., ed. *"A Grand Terrible Dramma:" From Gettysburg to Petersburg; The Civil War Letters of Charles Wellington Reed.* New York: Fordham University Press, 2000.

Cannan, John. *The Crater: Burnside's Assault on the Confederate Trenches, July 30, 1864.* Cambridge, Mass.: DaCapo Press, 2002.

Carter, John C., ed. *Welcome the Hour of Conflict: William Cowan McClellan and the 9th Alabama.* Tuscaloosa: University of Alabama Press, 2007.

Case, Ervin T. "The Battle of the Mine." *Personal Narratives of the Battles of the Rebellion, Being Papers Read before the Rhode Island Soldiers and Sailors Historical Society,* 1st ser., no. 1 (1879): 5–37.

Cavanaugh, Michael A., and William Marvel. *The Battle of the Crater: "The Horrid Pit,"* June 25–August 6, 1864. Lynchburg, Va.: H. E. Howard, 1989.

Chamberlayne, C. G. *Ham Chamberlayne-Virginian: Letters and Papers of an Artillery Officer in the War for Southern Independence, 1861–1865.* Richmond, Va.: Dietz, 1932.

Chambers, H. A. "The Bloody Crater." *Confederate Veteran* 31 (1923): 174–77.

Chase, J. J. *The Charge at Day-Break: Scenes and Incidents at the Battle of the Mine Explosion.* Lewiston, Maine: Journal, 1875.

Cheney, Newel. *History of the Ninth Regiment, New York Volunteer Cavalry.* Jamestown, N.Y.: M. Merz, 1901.

Civil War Letters of Hugh McInnes. Parsons, W.V.: McClain Printing, 1981.

Claiborne, John Herbert. *Seventy-five Years in Old Virginia.* New York: Neale, 1904.

Clark, George. "Alabamians in the Crater Battle." *Confederate Veteran* 3 (1895): 68–70.

Clark, James H. *The Iron Hearted Regiment: Being an Account of the Battles, Marches and Gallant Deeds Performed by the 115th Regiment N.Y. Vols.* Albany, N.Y.: J. Munsell, 1865.

Clark, Walter. *Histories of the Several Regiments and Battalions from North Carolina in the Great War, 1861–'65.* 5 vols. Goldsboro, N.C.: Nash Brothers, 1901.

Clemmer, Gregg S. *Valor in Gray: The Recipients of the Confederate Medal of Honor.* Staunton, Va.: Hearthside Publishing, 1996.

Cockrell, Thomas D., and Michael D. Ballard, eds. *A Mississippi Rebel in the Army of Northern Virginia: The Civil War Memoirs of Private David Holt.* Baton Rouge: Louisiana State University Press, 1995.

Coco, Gregory A., ed. *Through Blood and Fire: The Civil War Letters of Major Charles J. Mills, 1862–1865.* Gettysburg, Pa.: Author, 1982.

Cogswell, Leander W. *A History of the Eleventh New Hampshire Regiment Volunteer Infantry in the Rebellion War, 1861–1865.* Concord, N.H.: Republican Press, 1891.

Coit, J. C. "The Battle of the Crater, July 30, 1864: Letter from Major J. C. Coit." *Southern Historical Society Papers* 10 (1882): 123–30.

Conrad, James L. "From Glory to Contention: The Sad History of 'Shanks' Evans." *Civil War Times Illustrated.* Vol. 22 (1983): 32–38.

Coons, Margaret. "A Portrait of His Times: John Elder's Paintings Reflect People and Events during a Critical Period in Virginia History." *Virginia Cavalcade* 16, no. 4 (1967): 15–31.

Corrigan, Jim. *The 48th Pennsylvania in the Battle of the Crater: A Regiment of Coal Miners Who Tunnelled under the Enemy.* Jefferson, N.C.: McFarland, 2006.

Crater, Lewis. *History of the Fiftieth Regiment, Penna. Vet. Vols., 1861–65.* Reading, Pa: Coleman, 1884.

"Crater Yields 25 Skeletons." *National Tribune,* April 9, 1931.

Crawford, Robert. "The Civil War Letters of S. Rodman and Linton Smith." *Delaware History* 21 (Fall–Winter 1984): 86–116.

Crist, Lynda Lasswell, ed. *The Papers of Jefferson Davis.* 12 vols. Baton Rouge: Louisiana State University Press, 1971–2008.

Cross, Thomas H. "Battle of the Crater." *National Tribune,* February 25, 1882.

Crute, Joseph H., Jr. *Units of the Confederate States Army.* Midlothian, Va.: Derwent Books, 1987.

Culver, J. B. "The Petersburg Mine." *National Tribune,* September 4, 1919.

Cummings, Charles M. *Yankee Quaker, Confederate General: The Curious Career of Bushrod Rust Johnson.* Rutherford, N.J.: Fairleigh Dickinson University Press, 1971.

Cunningham, John L. *Three Years with the Adirondack Regiment: 118th New York Volunteers Infantry.* N.p.: privately published, 1920.

Cushman, Frederick E. *History of the 58th Regt. Massachusetts Vols.* Washington, D.C.: Gibson Brothers, 1865.

Cutcheon, Byron M. "The Twentieth Michigan Regiment in the Assault on Petersburg, July, 1864." *Historical Collections, Michigan Pioneer and Historical Society* 30 (1905): 127–39.

Cutchins, John A. *A Famous Command: The Richmond Light Infantry Blues.* Richmond, Va.: Garrett and Massie, 1934.

Cutrer, Thomas W. "Bliss, Zenas Randall." In *The New Handbook of Texas,* edited by Ron Tyler et al., 1:594. Austin: Texas State Historical Association, 1996.

Davies, A. M. "Petersburg—the Battle of the Crater." *Blue and Gray* 3 (May 1894): 249–52.

Davis, William C. *Death in the Trenches: Grant at Petersburg.* Alexandria, Va.: Time-Life, 1986.

Davis, William C., and Bell I. Wiley, eds. *Photographic History of the Civil War.* 2 vols. New York: Black Dog and Leventhal, 1994.

Day, W. A. "Battle of the Crater." *Confederate Veteran* 11 (1903): 355–56.

———. "The Breastworks at Petersburg." *Confederate Veteran* 29 (1921): 173–75.

———. *A True History of Company I, 49th Regiment, North Carolina Troops.* Newton, N.C.: Enterprise, 1893.

DeLeon, Thomas Cooper. *Four Years in Rebel Capitals: An Inside View of Life in the Southern Confederacy, from Birth to Death.* Mobile, Ala.: Gossip Printing, 1890.

Dixon, B. F. "Additional Sketch Forty-ninth Regiment." In *Histories of the Several Regiments and Battalions from North Carolina in the Great War, 1861–'65,* edited by Walter Clark, 3:151–60. Goldsboro, N.C.: Nash Brothers, 1901.

Dowdey, Clifford, and Louis H. Manarin, eds. *The Wartime Papers of R. E. Lee.* Boston: Little, Brown, 1961.

Draper, Joseph. "Who Fought in the Battle of the Crater?" *Confederate Veteran* 8 (1900): 502.

Duane, J. C. *Manual for Engineer Troops.* New York: D. Van Nostrand, 1862.

Dunlop, W. S. *Lee's Sharpshooters: Or, The Forefront of Battle.* Dayton, Ohio: Morningside Bookshop, 1982.

Eden, R. C. *The Sword and the Gun: A History of the 37th Wis. Volunteer Infantry.* Madison, Wis.: Atwood and Rublee, 1865.

Edwards, W. H. *A Condensed History of Seventeenth Regiment S.C.V. from Its Organization to the Close of the War.* Columbia, S.C.: R. L. Bryan, 1908.

Elliott, Charles Pinckney. *Elliott's Brigade: How It Held the Crater and Saved Petersburg.* Savannah, Ga.: Review Printing Company, n.d.

Etheredge, William H. "Another Story of the Crater Battle." *Confederate Veteran* 15 (1907): 167.

———. "Another Story of the Crater Battle." *Southern Historical Society Papers* 37 (1909): 203–7.

Evans, Robert G., ed. *The 16th Mississippi Infantry: Civil War Letters and Reminiscences.* Jackson: University Press of Mississippi, 2002.

Fagan, W. L. "The Petersburg Crater." *Philadelphia Times,* July 6, 1882.

"Famous Fight at the Crater." *New York Times,* July 30, 1895.

Featherston, John C. "The Battle of the Crater." *Confederate Veteran* 34 (1926): 296–98.

———. "The Battle of the 'Crater' as I Saw It." *Confederate Veteran* 14 (1906): 23–26.

———. *Battle of the Crater: The Work of the 48th Regiment, Pennsylvania V.V.I., at Petersburg Mine.* N.p: [1906].

———. "Graphic Account of Battle of Crater." *Southern Historical Society Papers* 33 (1905): 358–74.

———. "Incidents of the Battle of the Crater." *Confederate Veteran* 14 (1906): 107–8.

Featherstonhaugh, A. "Notes on the Defences of Petersburg." *Papers on Subjects Connected with the Duties of the Royal Engineers,* n. s., 14 (1865): 190–94.

Feis, William B. *Grant's Secret Service: The Intelligence War from Belmont to Appomattox.* Lincoln: University of Nebraska Press, 2002.

Ferguson, Garland S. "Twenty-fifth Regiment." In *Histories of the Several Regiments and Battalions from North Carolina in the Great War, 1861–'65,* edited by Walter Clark, 2:291–01. Goldsboro, N.C.: Nash Brothers, 1901.

Ferrero, Edward. *The Art of Dancing, Historically Illustrated: To Which Is Added a Few Hints on Etiquette.* New York: W. H. Timson, 1859.

Flanner, Henry G. "Flanner's Battery at the Crater, 30 July, 1864." In *Histories of the Several Regiments and Battalions from North Carolina in the Great War, 1861–'65,* edited by Walter Clark, 5:617–1. Goldsboro, N.C.: Nash Brothers, 1901.

———. "Flanner's North Carolina Battery at the Battle of the Crater." *Southern Historical Society Papers* 5 (1878): 247–48.

Fleet, Betsy, and John D. P. Fuller, eds. *Green Mount: A Virginia Plantation Family during the Civil War: Being the Journal of Benjamin Robert Fleet and Letters of His Family.* Lexington: University of Kentucky Press, 1962.

Floyd, Fred C. *History of the Fortieth (Mozart) Regiment New York Volunteers.* Boston: F. H. Gilson, 1909.

Floyd, N. J. "Concerning Battle of the Crater." *Confederate Veteran* 16 (1908): 159.

Folk, Humphrey Bate. *The Petersburg Mine, and Other Letters.* Boston: R. C. Badger, 1928.

Ford, Worthington Chauncey, ed. *A Cycle of Adams Letters, 1861–1865.* 2 vols. Boston: Houghton Mifflin, 1920.

Forstchen, William Robert. "The 28th United States Colored Troops: Indiana's African Americans Go to War, 1863–1865." Ph.D. diss., Purdue University, 1994.

Fortin, Maurice S., ed. "Colonel Hilary A. Herbert's History of the Eighth Alabama Volunteer Regiment, C.S.A." *Alabama Historical Quarterly* 39, nos. 1-4 (1977): 5–321.

Frassanito, William A. *Grant and Lee: The Virginia Campaigns, 1864–1865.* New York: Charles Scribner's Sons, 1983.

Gallagher, Gary W., ed. *Fighting for the Confederacy: The Personal Recollections of General Edward Porter Alexander.* Chapel Hill: University of North Carolina Press, 1989.

"Gen. David A. Weisiger, of Virginia." *Confederate Veteran* 7 (1899): 362–64.

George, Larry. "Battle of the Crater: A Combat Engineer Case Study." *Military Review* 44 (February 1984): 35–47.

Gibbon, John. *Personal Recollections of the Civil War.* New York: G. P. Putnam's Sons, 1928.

Gould, Joseph. *The Story of the Forty-eighth: A Record of the Campaigns of the Forty-eighth Regiment Pennsylvania Veteran Volunteer Infantry.* Philadelphia: Regimental Association, 1908.

Govan, Gilbert E., and James W. Livingood, eds. *The Haskell Memoirs.* New York: G. P. Putnam's Sons, 1960.

Graham, Robert D. "Fifty-sixth Regiment." In *Histories of the Several Regiments and Battalions from North Carolina in the Great War, 1861–'65,* edited by Walter Clark, 3:313–404. Goldsboro, N.C.: Nash Brothers, 1901.

Grant, Ulysses S. *Personal Memoirs of U. S. Grant.* 2 vols. New York: Viking, 1990.

Greene, A. Wilson. *Civil War Petersburg: Confederate City in the Crucible of War.* Charlottesville: University of Virginia Press, 2006.

A Guide to the Fortifications and Battlefields around Petersburg. Petersburg, Va.: Daily Index Job Print, 1866.

Guthrie, James M. *Camp-Fires of the Afro-American: Or, The Colored Man as a Patriot.* New York: Johnson Reprint, 1970.

Haas, James F. "The Famous 48th." *Schuylkill County in the Civil War* 7 (1961): 52–62.

Hall, H. Seymour. "Mine Run to Petersburg." In *War Talks in Kansas: A Series of Papers Read before the Kansas Commandery of the Military Order of the Loyal Legion of the United States,* 220–49. Kansas City: Franklin Hudson, 1906.

Hall, Hillman A., William B. Besley, and Gilbert Guion Wood. *History of the Sixth New York Cavalry.* Worcester, Mass.: Blanchard Press, 1908.

Harrill, Lawson. *Reminiscences, 1861–1865.* Statesville, N.C.: Brady, 1910.

Harris, J. S. *Historical Sketches of the Seventh Regiment North Carolina Troops, 1861–'65.* Mooresville, N.C.: Mooresville Printing Company, [1893].

Hauptman, Lawrence M. *Between Two Fires: American Indians in the Civil War.* New York: Free Press, 1995.

Henderson, Lillian. *Roster of the Confederate Soldiers of Georgia, 1861–1865.* 6 vols. Hapeville, Ga.: Longino and Porter, 1959–1964.

Herdegen, Lance, and Sherry Murphy, eds. *Four Years with the Iron Brigade: The Civil War Journals of William R. Ray, Co. F., Seventh Wisconsin Infantry.* Cambridge, Mass.: DaCapo Press, 2002.

Herek, Raymond J. *These Men Have Seen Hard Service: The First Michigan Sharpshooters in the Civil War.* Detroit: Wayne State University Press, 1998.

Hess, Earl J. *In the Trenches at Petersburg—Field Fortifications and Confederate Defeat.* Chapel Hill: University of North Carolina Press, 2009.

Hickenlooper, Andrew. "The Vicksburg Mine." In *Battles and Leaders of the Civil War,* edited by Robert Underwood Johnson and Clarence Clough Buel, 3:539–42. New York: Thomas Yoseloff, 1956.

History of the Darlington Rifles, Co. "I," 18th S. C. V., late C. S. A. Darlington, S.C.: County Messenger Job Print, n.d.

History of the Thirty-fifth Regiment Massachusetts Volunteers, 1862–1865. Boston: Mills, Knight, 1884.

History of the Thirty-sixth Regiment Massachusetts Volunteers, 1862–1865. Boston: Rockwell and Churchill, 1884.

Holsinger, Frank. "The Colored Troops at the Mine." *National Tribune,* October 19, 1905.

Hopkins, William P. *The Seventh Regiment Rhode Island Volunteers in the Civil War, 1862–1865.* Providence, R.I.: Snow and Farnham, 1903.

Horn, John. *The Destruction of the Weldon Railroad: Deep Bottom, Globe Tavern, and Reams Station, August 14–25, 1864.* Lynchburg, Va.: H. E. Howard, 1991.

Houghton, Charles H. "In the Crater." In *Battles and Leaders of the Civil War,* edited by Robert Underwood Johnson and Clarence Clough Buel, 4:561–62. New York: Thomas Yoseloff, 1956.

Houghton, W. R., and M. B. Houghton. *Two Brothers in the Civil War and After.* Montgomery, Ala.: Paragon Press, 1912.

Houston, Henry C. *The Thirty-second Maine Regiment of Infantry Volunteers*. Portland, Maine: Southworth Brothers, 1903.

Howe, Mark DeWolfe, ed. *Touched with Fire: Civil War Letters and Diary of Oliver Wendell Holmes, Jr., 1861–1864*. Cambridge, Mass.: Harvard University Press, 1946.

Howe, Thomas J. *Wasted Valor: June 15–18, 1864*. 2nd ed. Lynchburg, Va.: H. E. Howard, 1988.

Howland, Henry R. "An Anecdote of the Petersburg Crater." *Century Magazine* 35 (December 1887): 323.

Hudson, Joshua Hilary. *Sketches and Reminiscences*. Columbia, S.C.: The State Company, 1903.

Humphreys, Andrew A. *The Virginia Campaign of '64 and '65*. New York: Charles Scribner's Sons, 1883.

Humphreys, Henry H. *Andrew Atkinson Humphreys: A Biography*. Philadelphia: John C. Winston, 1924.

Hyde, William L. *History of the One Hundred and Twelfth Regiment N.Y. Volunteers*. Fredonia, N.Y.: W. McKinstry, 1866.

Inners, John D. "Colonel Henry Pleasants and the Military Geology of the Petersburg Mine—June–July, 1864." *Pennsylvania Geology* 20 (October 1989): 3–10.

J. D. "The Battle of the Crater." *Seminary Magazine* 2 (November 1869): 98–103.

Jackman, Lyman. *History of the Sixth New Hampshire Regiment in the War for the Union*. Concord, N.H.: Republican Press, 1891.

Jackson, Harry F., and Thomas F. O'Donnell. *Back Home in Oneida: Hermon Clarke and His Letters*. Syracuse, N.Y.: Syracuse University Press, 1965.

Jackson, Harry L. *First Regiment Engineer Troops, P.A.C.S.: Robert E. Lee's Combat Engineers*. Louisa, Va.: R.A.E. Design and Publishing, 1998.

James, Alfred P. "The Battle of the Crater." In *Military Analysis of the Civil War: An Anthology by the Editors of "Military Affairs,"* 349–66. Millwood, N.Y.: KTO Press, 1977.

Jimerson, Randall C. *The Private Civil War: Popular Thought during the Sectional Conflict*. Baton Rouge: Louisiana State University Press, 1988.

Johnson, Robert Underwood, and Clarence Clough Buel, eds. *Battles and Leaders of the Civil War*. 4 vols. New York: Century Company, 1887–88; New York: Thomas Yoseloff, 1956.

Jordan, David M. *"Happiness Is Not My Companion": The Life of General G. K. Warren*. Bloomington: Indiana University Press, 2001.

Jordan, Weymouth T., Jr., comp. *North Carolina Troops, 1861–1865: A Roster*. 14 vols. Raleigh, N.C.: Division of Archives and History, 1966–1998.

Kenfield, Frank. "Captured by Rebels: A Vermonter at Petersburg, 1864." *Vermont History* 36 (Autumn 1968): 230–35.

Kilmer, George L. "The Dash into the Crater." *Century Magazine* 34 (September 1887): 774–76.

LaMotte, Thomas J. "The Battle of the Crater." *Charleston News and Courier*, May 14, 1899.

Landrum, J. B .O. *History of Spartanburg County*. Atlanta: Franklin, 1900.

Lapham, William B. *My Recollections of the War of the Rebellion*. Augusta, Maine: Burleigh and Flynt, 1892.

Laughton, John E., Jr. "The Sharpshooters of Mahone's Brigade." *Southern Historical Society Papers* 22 (1894): 98–105.

Lee, Susan P. *Memoirs of William Nelson Pendleton, D.D.* Philadelphia: J. B. Lippincott, 1893.

Levin, Kevin M. "'Is Not the Glory Enough to Give Us All a Share?' An Analysis of Competing Memories of the Battle of the Crater." In *The View from the Ground: Experiences of Civil War Soldiers,* edited by Aaron Sheehan-Dean, 227–48. Lexington: University Press of Kentucky, 2006.

———. "'On That Day You Consummated the Full Measure of Your Fame:' Remembering the Battle of the Crater, 1864–1903." *Southern Historian* 25 (Spring 2004): 18–39.

———. "William Mahone, the Lost Cause, and Civil War History." *Virginia Magazine of History and Biography* 113, no. 4 (2005): 379–412.

Livermore, Thomas L. *Days and Events, 1860–1866.* Boston: Houghton Mifflin, 1920.

Longacre, Edward G. *Army of Amateurs: General Benjamin F. Butler and the Army of the James, 1863–1865.* Mechanicsburg, Pa.: Stackpole Books, 1997.

———. *The Man behind the Guns: A Biography of General Henry Jackson Hunt, Chief of Artillery, Army of the Potomac.* New York: A. S. Barnes, 1977.

LoPiano, Tom. "Gallantry in the Crater." *Arms Gazette,* July 1979, 16–19, 43, 48.

Lord, Edward O., ed. *History of the Ninth Regiment New Hampshire Volunteers in the War of the Rebellion.* Concord, N.H.: Republican Press, 1895.

Loving, Jerome M., ed. *Civil War Letters of George Washington Whitman.* Durham, N.C.: Duke University Press, 1975.

Lowe, David W., ed. *Meade's Army: The Private Notebooks of Lt. Col. Theodore Lyman.* Kent, Ohio: Kent State University Press, 2007.

Mackintosh, Robert Harley, Jr., ed. *"Dear Martha . . . :" The Confederate War Letters of a South Carolina Soldier, Alexander Faulkner Fewell.* Columbia, S.C.: R. L. Bryan, 1976.

McCabe, W. Gordon. "Defence of Petersburg." *Southern Historical Society Papers* 2 (1876): 257–306.

McDaid, William Kelsey. "'Four Years of Arduous Service': The History of the Branch-Lane Brigade in the Civil War." Ph.D. diss., Michigan State University, 1987.

McMaster, F. W. "The Battle of the Crater, July 30, 1864: Letter from Colonel McMaster." *Southern Historical Society Papers.* Vol. 10 (1882): 119–23.

———. "Elliott's Brigade." In *Elliott's Brigade: How It Held the Crater and Saved Petersburg,* by Charles Pinckney Elliott, 9–27. Savannah, Ga.: Review, n.d..

McWhiney, Grady, and Jack Jay Jenkins. "The Union's Worst General." *Civil War Times Illustrated* 14, no. 3 (1975): 30–39.

Mahone, William. *The Battle of the Crater.* Petersburg, Va.: Franklin Press, n.d..

———. "The Crater, Petersburg, Va., July 30, 1864." In *History of the Army of the Potomac,* by J. H. Stine, 674–81. Washington, D.C.: Gibson, 1893.

Marshall, Jeffrey D., ed. *A War of the People: Vermont Civil War Letters.* Hanover, N.H.: University Press of New England, 1999.

Marvel, William. "And Fire Shall Devour Them: The 9th New Hampshire in the Crater." *Civil War Regiments* 2, no. 2 (1992): 118–40.

————. *Burnside.* Chapel Hill: University of North Carolina Press, 1991.

————. *Race of the Soil: The Ninth New Hampshire Regiment in the Civil War.* Wilmington, N.C.: Broadfoot, 1988.

Mason, Kenneth. "The Battle of the Petersburg Crater." Master's thesis, Kent State University, 1982.

Matthews, Richard E. *The 149th Pennsylvania Volunteer Infantry Unit in the Civil War.* Jefferson, N.C.: McFarland, 1994.

Maxfield, Albert, and Robert Brady, Jr. *Roster and Statistical Record of Company D, of the Eleventh Regiment Maine Infantry Volunteers.* New York: T. Humphrey, 1890.

Meade, George. *The Life and Letters of George Gordon Meade.* 2 vols. New York: Charles Scribner's Sons, 1913.

Memorial of Colonel John A. Bross, Twenty-ninth U.S. Colored Troops, Who Fell in Leading the Assault on Petersburgh, July 30, 1864. Chicago: Tribune Book and Job Office, 1865.

Miers, Earl Schenck, ed. *Wash Roebling's War: Being a Selection from the Unpublished Civil War Letters of Washington Augustus Roebling.* Newark, Del.: Spiral Press, 1961.

"Military Honors for Crater Dead." *National Tribune,* April 16, 1931.

Miller, Edward A., Jr. *The Black Civil War Soldiers of Illinois: The Story of the Twenty-ninth U.S. Colored Infantry.* Columbia: University of South Carolina Press, 1998.

Miller, J. Michael. *The North Anna Campaign: "Even To Hell Itself," May 21–26, 1864.* Lynchburg, Va.: H. E. Howard, 1989.

Mowris, James A. *A History of the One Hundred and Seventeenth Regiment, N.Y. Volunteers.* Hartford, Conn.: Case, Lockwood, 1866.

Muffly, Joseph Wendel, ed. *The Story of Our Regiment: A History of the 148th Pennsylvania Vols.* Des Moines, Iowa: Kenyon Printing, 1904.

Mushkat, Jerome., ed. *A Citizen-Soldier's Civil War: The Letters of Brevet Major General Alvin C. Voris.* DeKalb: Northern Illinois University Press, 2002.

Nevins, Allan, ed. *A Diary of Battle: The Personal Journals of Colonel Charles S. Wainwright, 1861–1865.* New York: Harcourt, Brace, and World, 1962.

————, ed. *Diary of the Civil War, 1860–1865: George Templeton Strong.* New York: Macmillan, 1962.

Newberry, Walter C. "The Petersburg Mine." In *Military Essays and Recollections: Papers Read before the Commandery of the State of Illinois, Military Order of the Loyal Legion of the United States,* 3:111–24. Chicago: Dial, 1899.

Nichols, James M. *Perry's Saints: Or, The Fighting Parson's Regiment in the War of the Rebellion.* Boston: D. Lothrop, 1886.

Orr, David G. "The Archaeology of Trauma: An Introduction to the Historical Archaeology of the American Civil War." In *Look to the Earth: Historical Archaeology and the American Civil War,* edited by Clarence R. Geier, Jr., and Susan E. Winter, 21–35. Knoxville: University of Tennessee Press, 1994.

Osborne, William H. *The History of the Twenty-ninth Regiment of Massachusetts Volunteer Infantry, in the Late War of the Rebellion.* Boston: Albert J. Wright, 1877.

Owen, Charles W. "Explosion of Mine at Petersburg Described by Comrade C. W. Owen." *National Tribune,* November 1, 1934.

Palfrey, Francis Winthrop. *Memoir of William Francis Bartlett.* Boston: Houghton, Osgood, 1878.

Parker, Thomas H. *History of the 51st Regiment of P.V. and V.V.* Philadelphia: King and Baird, 1869.

Paul, Frank. "The Petersburg Mine." *Philadelphia Weekly Times,* April 24, 1880.

———. "Why It Was a Failure." *Philadelphia Weekly Times,* April 24, 1880.

Pearce, T. H., ed. *Diary of Captain Henry A. Chambers.* Wendell, N.C.: Broadfoot's Bookmark, 1983.

"The Petersburg Mine." *National Tribune,* January 17, 1884.

"Petersburg Mine." *Philadelphia Weekly Times,* April 24, 1880.

Pfanz, Donald C. *Richard S. Ewell: A Soldier's Life.* Chapel Hill: University of North Carolina Press, 1998.

Pleasants, Henry, Jr. *The Tragedy of the Crater.* [Petersburg, Va.?]: Eastern National Park and Monument Association, 1975.

Pleasants, Henry, Jr., and George H. Straley. *Inferno at Petersburg.* Philadelphia: Chilton, 1961.

Pollard, Henry R. "Edward Bagby, of Virginia." *Confederate Veteran* 27 (1919): 453–58.

Porter, Charles H. "The Petersburg Mine." In *Papers of the Military Historical Society of Massachusetts,* 5:223–39. Wilmington: Broadfoot Publishing, 1989.

Porter, Horace. *Campaigning with Grant.* New York: Century, 1897.

Post, Lydia Minturn, ed. *Soldiers' Letters from Camp, Battle-Field and Prison.* New York: Bunce and Huntington, 1865.

Potter, Henry C. "General Robert B. Potter and the Assault at the Petersburg Crater." *Century Magazine* 35 (January 1888): 481.

Powell, William H. "The Battle of the Petersburg Crater." In *Battles and Leaders of the Civil War,* edited by Robert Underwood Johnson and Clarence Clough Buel, 4:545–60. New York: Thomas Yoseloff, 1956.

Power, J. Tracy. *Lee's Miserables: Life in the Army of Northern Virginia from the Wilderness to Appomattox.* Chapel Hill: University of North Carolina Press, 1998.

Price, Isaiah. *History of the Ninety-seventh Regiment, Pennsylvania Volunteer Infantry, during the War of the Rebellion, 1861–1865.* Philadelphia: privately printed, 1875.

Private and Official Correspondence of Gen. Benjamin F. Butler during the Period of the Civil War. 5 vols. Norwood, Mass.: Plimpton Press, 1917.

Proctor, D. E. "The Massacre in the Crater." *National Tribune,* October 17, 1907.

Ray, Frederic. "Fiasco at Petersburg." *Civil War Times Illustrated* 2 (April 1960): 4–7.

A Record of the Dedication of the Statue of Major General William Francis Bartlett. Boston: Wright and Potter, 1905.

Redkey, Edwin S., ed. *A Grand Army of Black Men: Letters from African-American Soldiers in the Union Army, 1861–1865.* Cambridge: Cambridge University Press, 1992.

Reid, Robert A. "Petersburg Crater." *National Tribune,* January 5, 1905.

Reid-Green, Marcia., ed. *Letters Home: Henry Matrau of the Iron Brigade.* Lincoln: University of Nebraska Press, 1993.

Report of the Committee on the Conduct of the War on the Attack on Petersburg on the 30th Day of July, 1864. Washington, D.C.: Government Printing Office, 1865.

Richards, R. G. "The Blunder at the Petersburg Mine." *National Tribune,* June 18, 1925.

———. "The Forty-fifth in the Battle of the Crater." In *A True Story of a Civil War Veteran,* by Ephraim E. Myers. York, Pa.: n.p., 1910.

Rickard, James H. *Services with Colored Troops in Burnside's Corps.* Providence, R.I.: Rhode Island Soldiers and Sailors Historical Society, 1894.

Robertson, James I., Jr., ed. *The Civil War Letters of General Robert McAllister.* New Brunswick, N.J.: Rutgers University Press, 1965.

Robertson, William Glenn. "From the Crater to New Market Heights: A Tale of Two Divisions." In *Black Soldiers in Blue: African American Troops in the Civil War Era,* edited by John David Smith, 169–99. Chapel Hill: University of North Carolina Press, 2002.

Robinson, W. P. "Artillery in Battle of the Crater." *Confederate Veteran* 19 (1911): 164–66.

Rockwell, William L., ed. *Dear Frank: The War Years, 1862–1865.* N.p.: privately published, 2001.

Roemer, Jacob. *Reminiscences of the War of the Rebellion, 1861–1865.* New York: Flushing Journal, 1897.

Rogers, George T. "The Crater Battle, 30th July, 1864." *Confederate Veteran* 3 (1895): 12–14.

———. "Crater Battle—Reply to Mr. Clark." *Confederate Veteran* 3 (1895): 137.

Roman, Alfred. *The Military Operations of General Beauregard in the War Between the States, 1861 to 1865.* 2 vols. New York: Harper and Brothers, 1884.

Rose, W. N. "Twenty-fourth Regiment." In *Histories of the Several Regiments and Battalions from North Carolina in the Great War, 1861–'65,* edited by Walter Clark, 2:269–90. Goldsboro, N.C.: Nash Brothers, 1901.

Roulhac, Thomas R. "The Forty-ninth N.C. Infantry, C.S.A." *Southern Historical Society Papers* 23 (1895): 58–78.

———. "Forty-ninth Regiment." In *Histories of the Several Regiments and Battalions from North Carolina in the Great War, 1861–'65,* edited by Walter Clark, 3:126–49. Goldsboro, N.C.: Nash Brothers, 1901.

Rowland, J. C. "The Petersburg Mine." *National Tribune,* July 18, 1907.

Sandbrook, William J. "The Engineer Officer, Advisor or Leader: A Study of the Battle of Petersburg." *Engineer* 15 (Winter 1985/86): 22–25.

Sauers, Richard A., ed. *The Civil War Journal of Colonel William J. Bolton, 51st Pennsylvania, April 20, 1861–August 2, 1865.* Conshohocken, Pa.: Combined Publishing, 2000.

Saussy, G. N. "The Story of the Crater." *Addresses Delivered before the Confederate Veterans' Association of Savannah, GA.* Savannah, Ga.: Braid and Hutton, 1893.

Schmutz, John F. *The Battle of the Crater: A Complete History.* Jefferson, N.C.: McFarland, 2009.

Scott, Robert Garth, ed. *Forgotten Valor: The Memoirs, Journals, and Civil War Letters of Orlando B. Willcox.* Kent, Ohio: Kent State University Press, 1999.

Seagrave, Pia Seija, ed. *A Boy Lieutenant: Memoirs of Freeman S. Bowley, 30th United States Colored Troops Officer.* Fredericksburg, Va.: Sergeant Kirkland's Museum and Historical Society, 1997.

Shaver, Lewellyn A. *A History of the Sixtieth Alabama Regiment: Gracie's Alabama Brigade.* Montgomery, Ala.: Barrett and Brown, 1867.

Shearman, Sumner U. "Battle of the Crater and Experiences of Prison Life." *Personal Narratives of Events in the War of the Rebellion, Being Papers Read before the Rhode*

Island Soldiers and Sailors Historical Society, 5th ser.:5–38. Providence: Rhode Island Soldiers and Sailors Historical Society, 1898.

Sheridan, Philip H. *Personal Memoirs of P. H. Sheridan*. 2 vols. New York: Charles L. Webster, 1888.

Sholes, Albert E. "The Crater Fight Vividly Portrayed." *National Tribune*, January 12, 1928.

Sifakis, Stewart. *Who Was Who in the Civil War*. New York: Facts on File, 1988.

Simms, L. Moody, Jr. "John A. Elder: Memorial Artist of the Confederacy." *Lincoln Herald* 74 (Spring 1972): 29–33.

Simon, John Y., ed. *The Papers of Ulysses S. Grant*. 22 vols. Carbondale: Southern Illinois University Press, 1967–1998.

Simpson, Craig M. *A Good Southerner: The Life of Henry A. Wise of Virginia*. Chapel Hill: University of North Carolina Press, 1985.

"Sketch of Company I, 61st Virginia Infantry, Mahone's Brigade, C.S.A." *Southern Historical Society Papers* 24 (1896): 98–108.

Slotkin, Richard. *The Crater*. New York: Henry Holt, 1996.

Smith, Eric Ledell, ed. "The Civil War Letters of Quartermaster Sergeant John C. Brock, 43rd Regiment, United States Colored Troops." In *Making and Remaking Pennsylvania's Civil War*, edited by William Blair and William Pencak, 141–63. University Park: Pennsylvania State University Press, 2001.

Sommers, Richard J. *Richmond Redeemed: The Siege at Petersburg*. Garden City, N.Y.: Doubleday, 1981.

Sparks, David S., ed. *Inside Lincoln's Army: The Diary of Marsena Rudolph Patrick, Provost Marshal General, Army of the Potomac*. New York: Thomas Yoseloff, 1964.

Spear, Abbott, et al., eds. *The Civil War Recollections of General Ellis Spear*. Orono: University of Maine Press, 1997.

Spear, Benjamin A. "In Front of Petersburg." *National Tribune*, June 20, 1889.

Stevens, Michael E., ed. *As If It Were Glory: Robert Beecham's Civil War from the Iron Brigade to the Black Regiments*. Madison, Wis.: Madison House, 1998.

Stevenson, Silas. *Account of the Battle of the Mine, or Battle of the Crater in Front of Petersburg, VA., July 30th, 1864*. New Castle, Pa.: John A. Leathers, n.d.

Stewart, William H. *Battle of the Crater*. Norfolk, Va.: Landmark Book and Job Office, 1876.

———. "Carnage at 'The Crater,' Near Petersburg." *Confederate Veteran* 1 (1893): 41–42.

———. "The Charge of the Crater." *Southern Historical Society Papers* 25 (1897): 77–90.

———. "Crater Legion of Mahone's Brigade." *Confederate Veteran* 11 (1903): 557–58.

———. *Description of the Battle of the Crater: Recollections of the Recapture of the Lines*. Norfolk, Va.: Landmark Book and Job Service, 1876.

———. "Field of Blood Was the Crater." *Southern Historical Society Papers* 33 (1905): 351–57.

———. *A Pair of Blankets: War-Time History in Letters to the Young People of the South*. Wilmington, N.C.: Broadfoot Publishing, 1990.

———. *The Spirit of the South: Orations, Essays and Lectures*. New York: Neale, 1908.

Stone, DeWitt Boyd, Jr., ed. *Wandering to Glory: Confederate Veterans Remember Evans' Brigade*. Columbia: University of South Carolina Press, 2002.

Stone, James Madison. *Personal Recollections of the Civil War.* Boston: privately printed, 1918.

The Story of One Regiment: The Eleventh Maine Volunteers in the War of the Rebellion. New York: J. J. Little, 1896.

Suderow, Bryce A. "The Battle of the Crater: The Civil War's Worst Massacre." *Civil War History* 43 (September 1997): 219–24.

———. "Confederate Casualties at the Crater." *Kepi,* June–July 1985, 15–43.

———. "Glory Denied: The First Battle of Deep Bottom, July 27th–29th, 1864." *North and South* 3, no. 7 (2000): 17–32.

———. "War along the James." *North and South* 6, no. 3 (2003): 12–23.

Sumner, Merlin E., ed. *The Diary of Cyrus B. Comstock.* Dayton, Ohio: Morningside Bookshop, 1987.

Supplement to the Official Records of the Union and Confederate Armies. 100 vols. Wilmington, N.C.: Broadfoot Publishing, 1995–1999.

Synnestvedt, Sig., ed. "The Earth Shook and Quivered." *Civil War Times Illustrated* 11 (December 1972): 30–37.

Tap, Bruce. *Over Lincoln's Shoulder: The Committee on the Conduct of the War.* Lawrence: University Press of Kansas, 1998.

Tapert, Annette, ed. *The Brothers' War: Civil War Letters to Their Loved Ones from the Blue and Gray.* New York: Vintage Books, 1989.

Thomas, Henry Goddard. "The Colored Troops at Petersburg." In *Battles and Leaders of the Civil War,* edited by Robert Underwood Johnson and Clarence Clough Buel, 4:563–67. New York: Thomas Yoseloff, 1956.

———. "Twenty-two Hours Prisoner of War in Dixie." In *War Papers Read before the Commandery of the State of Maine, Military Order of the Loyal Legion of the United States,* 1: 29–48. Portland, Maine: Thurston, 1898.

Thomson, Bailey. "John C. C. Sanders: Lee's 'Boy Brigadier.'" *Alabama Review* 32, no. 2 (1979): 83–107.

Thrash, A. B. "Vivid Reminiscence of the Crater." *Confederate Veteran* 14 (1908): 508–9.

Tower, R. Lockwood, ed. *Lee's Adjutant: The Wartime Letters of Colonel Walter Herron Taylor, 1862–1865.* Columbia: University of South Carolina Press, 1995.

Tribou, Charles F. "At the Crater." *National Tribune,* June 29, 1911.

Trowbridge, John T. *The Desolate South, 1865–1866.* Freeport, N.Y.: Books for Libraries, 1970.

Trudeau, Noah Andre. *The Last Citadel: Petersburg, Virginia, June 1864–April 1865.* Baton Rouge: Louisiana State University Press, 1991.

———. *Like Men of War: Black Troops in the Civil War, 1862–1865.* Boston: Little, Brown, 1998.

Van Den Bossche, Kris, ed. "War and Other Reminiscences." *Rhode Island History* 47, no. 4 (1989): 115–47.

Vance, P. M. "Incidents of the Crater Battle." *Confederate Veteran* 14 (1906): 178–79.

W. R. S. "The Sharpshooters of Mahone's Old Brigade at the Crater." *Southern Historical Society Papers* 28 (1900): 307–8.

Walcott, Charles F. *History of the Twenty-first Regiment Massachusetts Volunteers in the War for the Preservation of the Union, 1861–1865.* Boston: Houghton, Mifflin, 1882.

Walker, Francis A. *History of the Second Army Corps in the Army of the Potomac.* New York: Charles Scribner's Sons, 1887.

The War of the Rebellion: A Compilation of the Official Records of the Union and Confederate Armies. 70 vols. in 128. Washington, D.C.: U.S. Government Printing Office, 1880–1901.

Ward, George Washington. *History of the Second Pennsylvania Veteran Heavy Artillery.* Philadelphia: G. W. Ward, 1904.

Warner, Ezra J. *Generals in Blue: Lives of the Union Commanders.* Baton Rouge: Louisiana State University Press, 1964.

———. *Generals in Gray: Lives of the Confederate Commanders.* Baton Rouge: Louisiana State University Press, 1959.

Washburn, George H. *A Complete Military History and Record of the 108th Regiment N.Y. Vols., from 1862 to 1864.* Rochester, N.Y.: E. R. Andrews, 1894.

Way, D. S. "The Battle of the Crater." *National Tribune,* June 3, 1904.

Welch, Spencer Glasgow. *A Confederate Surgeon's Letters to His Wife.* New York: Neale, 1911.

Weld, Stephen M. "The Petersburg Mine." In *Papers of the Military Historical Society of Massachusetts,* 5:207–19. Wilmington, N.C.: Broadfoot Publishing, 1989.

Weld, Stephen Minot. *War Diary and Letters of Stephen Minot Weld, 1861–1865.* Boston: Massachusetts Historical Society, 1979.

Welles, Gideon. *Diary of Gideon Welles: Secretary of the Navy under Lincoln and Johnson.* 2 vols. Boston: Houghton Mifflin, 1911.

Welsh, Jack D. *Medical Histories of Confederate Generals.* Kent, Ohio: Kent State University Press, 1995.

———. *Medical Histories of Union Generals.* Kent, Ohio: Kent State University Press, 1996.

Wert, Jeffery D. *From Winchester to Cedar Creek: The Shenandoah Campaign of 1864.* Mechanicsburg, Pa.: Stackpole Books, 1997.

Weymouth, J. H. "Otey Battery Organized." *Ashland(Va.) Herald-Progress,* August 27, 1925.

White, Daniel. "Charging the Crater." *National Tribune,* June 21, 1883.

Whitehead, Richard Owen. "The Retaking of the Lines." *The Story of American Heroism: Thrilling Narratives of Personal Adventures during the Great Civil War, as Told by the Medal Winners and Roll of Honor Men.* Springfield, Ohio: J. W. Jones, 1897.

Wiatt, Alex L. *26th Virginia Infantry.* Lynchburg, Va.: H. E. Howard, 1984.

Wiggins, Clyde G., III., ed. *My Dear Friend: The Civil War Letters of Alva Benjamin Spencer, 3rd Georgia Regiment, Company C.* Macon, Ga.: Mercer University Press, 2007.

Wiley, Bell Irvin. *The Life of Johnny Reb: The Common Soldier of the Confederacy.* Indianapolis: Bobbs-Merrill, 1943.

Wiley, Kenneth, ed. *Norfolk Blues: The Civil War Diary of the Norfolk Light Artillery Blues.* Shippensburg, Pa.: Burd Street Press, 1997.

Wilkinson, Warren. *Mother, May You Never See the Sights I Have Seen: The Fifty-seventh Massachusetts Veteran Volunteers in the Army of the Potomac, 1864–1865.* New York: Harper and Row, 1990.

Williams, Edward B., ed. *Rebel Brothers: The Civil War Letters of the Truehearts*. College Station: Texas A&M University Press, 1995.

Williams, George Washington. *A History of the Negro Troops in the War of the Rebellion, 1861–65*. New York: Bergman, 1968.

Wilson, Clarence. "The Petersburg Mine." *National Tribune*, July 3, 1919.

Wilson, Joseph T. *The Black Phalanx*. New York: Arno Press, 1968.

Wilson, Keith P. *Campfires of Freedom: The Camp Life of Black Soldiers during the Civil War*. Kent, Ohio: Kent State University Press, 2002.

Wise, Henry A. "The Career of Wise's Brigade, 1861–5." *Southern Historical Society Papers* 25 (1897): 1–22.

Wise, John S. *The End of an Era*. Boston: Houghton, Mifflin, 1902.

Woodbury, Augustus. *Major General Ambrose E. Burnside and the Ninth Army Corps*. Providence, R.I.: Sidney S. Rider, 1867.

Wyatt-Brown, Bertram. *Southern Honor: Ethics and Behavior in the Old South*. New York: Oxford University Press, 1982.

Young, John D. "A Campaign with Sharpshooters." *Philadelphia Weekly Times*, January 26, 1878.

Zwemer, John. *For Home and the Southland: A History of the 48th Georgia Infantry Regiment*. Baltimore, Md.: Butternut and Blue, 1999.

INDEX

183, 192, 194–97, 198, 207, 208, 211, 237, 279n46, 306n44
Lewin, William Henry, 87
Lewis, John M., 188
Lincoln, Abraham, 38, 47, 195, 214, 221, 223, 231
Lipscomb, Sgt. Smith, 104, 106, 152
Livermore, Thomas L., 78, 100, 123, 158
Loan, Rep. Benjamin F., 224
Longest, Younger, 83
Longstreet, James, 239
Loring, Col. Charles G., Jr., 58, 86, 98, 99, 125, 128, 281n23
Lotzy, John F., 164
Louisville Daily Journal, 217
Love, Lt. Col. Matthew Norris, 164
Lowry, Lt. Samuel C., 104
Ludlow, B. C., 160
Ludwick, Capt. Ephraim A., 160
Lydig, Maj., 207
Lyman, Theodore, 12, 51, 65, 83, 138, 172, 195, 209, 216, 222, 232
Lynch, J. D., 89, 90
Lynch, Col. James C., 39

Mahone, Brig. Gen. William, 83, 110, 114, 142, 144–51, 154, 155, 167–69, 173, 177, 182, 183, 187, 192, 193, 294, 205, 210, 212, 215, 242–46, 288n57, 300n6
Maine troops: 31st, 92, 165, 176, 204, 283n1; 32nd, 92, 176, 205, 283n1
Mallam, Capt. Charles E., 51
Marshall, Col. Elisha G., 58, 59, 61, 80, 88, 90, 91, 96, 128, 137, 180, 199
Maryland troops: 2nd, 92, 283n1; 3rd Battalion, 66, 90–92, 96, 283n1
Massachusetts troops: 21st, 66, 96, 165, 283n1; 29th, 66, 283n1; 35th, 58, 66, 88, 89, 91, 97, 136, 158, 178, 180, 208, 283n1; 36th, 67, 119; 56th, 66, 283n1; 57th, 66, 204, 245, 283n1; 58th, 118–20, 204; 59th, 66, 245, 283n1
McAfee, Col. Lee M., 10, 107, 159, 160
McAllister, Robert, 139

McCabe, Capt. W. Gordon, 110, 111, 115, 154
McDonald, Marshall, 18
McGlade, Sgt. John L., 179
McMaster, Lt. Col. Fitz William, 34, 103–5, 107–9, 116, 133, 146, 147, 148, 182, 197
McWilliams, Sgt. Andrew, 187
Meade, Maj. Gen. George G., 3, 22, 51, 62, 194, 195, 198, 199, 206–8, 213, 216, 217, 220–26, 229, 232, 234, 235, 265n33; and Deep Bottom, 37, 41–43, 46–48; and mine attack, 77–79, 99–101, 122, 125, 134, 137–39, 170, 171; and planning attack, 25, 26, 29, 32–34, 38, 55–57, 62, 64, 69–71
medals, 205, 232
Meyers, James, 212
Michigan troops: 1st Sharpshooters, 68, 75, 129, 130, 166, 175, 181, 283n1; 2nd, 68, 129, 130, 166, 204, 283n1; 8th, 283n1; 20th, 68, 129, 130, 166, 179, 204, 283n1; 27th 95, 96, 129, 283n1
Michler, Nathaniel, 28, 30, 69
Miles, Nelson A., 221
Mills, Maj. Charles J., 22–23, 216
Monroe, Col. J. A., 64
Moore, Pvt. Wilson Henry, 129
Morrison, Lt. John W., 91
Moss, Lt. J. R., 103
Mott, Brig. Gen. Gershom, 36, 39, 47, 48, 69, 101, 139
Murphy, William J. 149, 167

Native Americans, 175, 181
Nelson, Joseph, 273n14
New Hampshire troops: 4th, 204; 6th, 94, 185, 233; 9th, 92, 127, 158, 179, 185, 215, 283n1; 11th, 165, 204, 217, 283n1
New York troops: 1st Engineers, 69; 2nd Mounted Rifles (Dismounted), 118–21, 132, 160; 3rd, 159; 6th Cavalry, 45; 9th Cavalry, 45; 10th Cavalry, 44; 14th Heavy Artillery, 66, 88, 90, 95, 96, 176, 266n10, 283n1; 24th Cavalry